International Marketing

International Marketing

Dr Sunita Singh
Prof N.P. Singh
Prof Sangita

KALPAZ

First Published, 2019

Published by

Kalpaz Publications
C-30, Satyawati Nagar,
Delhi – 110052
Ph.: 011-47034999, 9811692060
www.kalpazpublications.com
E-mail: kalpaz@hotmail.com

Printed at: G. Print Process, Delhi

Cataloging in Publication Data—DK
Courtesy: D.K. Agencies (P) Ltd. <docinfo@dkagencies.com>

Singh, Sunita *(Associate professor of marketing management)*, **author.**
International marketing / Dr Sunita Singh, Prof N.P. Singh, Prof Sangita.
pages cm
ISBN 9789353240455

1. Export marketing. I. Singh, N. P. (Professor), author. II. Sangita (Professor), author. III. Title.

LCC HF1416.S56 2019 | DDC 658.84 23

Contents

Preface 7

Chapter - One : International Business 9

Chapter - Two : The Global environment 39

Chapter - Three : Entry of International Market 95

Chapter - Four : International Pricing and Financing 129

Chapter - Five : International Marketing and Technology 251

Chapter - Six : Building brands in International Markets 267

Chapter - Seven : International Marketing Research 299

Index 335

Preface

Today the corporate world cannot survive with restricting themselves within the domestic boundaries. As the consumers across countries become more universal in nature, the need to look at the whole world as a market is growing. The lure for international marketing is further encouraged by the rising demand for goods and services across national frontiers, achievement of higher degree of economic self-sufficiency, realization of more favorable terms of trade, and the university of similarity in human needs.

The aim of this unit is to introduce International Marketing, which explains how International Markets operate in an International Environment. An elementary approach is used in the module, which emphasizes the reasons for undertaking International Market analysis and their interpretation. Internationalization and globalization are concept is that are both current and important, so complex and likely to be approached in more and more diverse ways. Equally, international marketing and global marketing are invoked more often, along with "classic" marketing and competing with the latter, which tends to remain more and more in the area of theory. International marketing is present all around us, as is the case with global marketing, which can never be ignored. The globalization of markets has certainly accelerated through almost universal acceptance of the democratic free enterprise model and new communication technologies, including cell phones and the Internet.

This dynamic nature of the international marketplace is reflected in the number of substantially improved and expanded topics in this first edition, including the following Chapters, namely:—International Business; The Global environment; Entry of International Market; International Pricing and Financing; International Marketing and Technology; Building brands in International Markets; International Marketing Research.

To succeed in international marketing therefore, marketers have to identify, evaluate and plan to standardize or adapt its marketing mix where necessary, as to successfully exploit the international marketing barriers. Hence, the most outstanding firms international marketing will not give-in to the usual human tendency that people everywhere are the same.

Chapter - One

International Business

The marketing environment across the world has been becoming more global. It is true not only in the competitive and technological dimensions but also in the socio-cultural dimensions. Selling goods to international markets is not new to India and other Asian countries. The existence of international business is traceable to 3000 B.C. in India. During the last century, marketing activities around the world witnessed an unprecedented change. It was only during the latter half of 20th century when large US, European, Chinese, and Japanese companies expanded their markets as well as production facilities beyond national borders. The breakthroughs in information and communication technology and means of transport have contributed to the convergence in tastes and preferences of the consumers around the world. As a result of the liberalization and globalization, the marketing environment across the world has been becoming more global. Income growth have led to interdependency in international trade between nations.

International Marketing is simply the application of marketing principles to more than one country. However, there is a crossover between what is commonly expressed as international marketing and global marketing, which is a similar term. For the purposes of this lesson on international marketing and those that follow it, international marketing and global marketing are interchangeable. At its simplest level, international marketing involves the firm in making one or more marketing mix decisions across national boundaries. At its most complex level, it involves the firm in establishing manufacturing facilities overseas and coordinating marketing strategies across the globe." Doole and Lowe (2001). Doole and Lowe differentiate between international marketing (simple mix changes) and global marketing (more complex and extensive)."International Marketing is the performance of business activities that direct the flow of a company's goods and services to consumers or users in more than one nation for a profit." Cateora and Ghauri (1999) Cateora and Ghauri consider international marketing in the absence of global marketing."International marketing is the application of marketing orientation and marketing capabilities to international business. " Muhlbacher,

Helmuth, and Dahringer (2006) Muhlbacher et al consider international marketing in relation to marketing orientation and competences (see also Global Marketing). "The international market goes beyond the export marketer and becomes more involved in the marketing environment in the countries in which it is doing business." Keegan (2002)

The term international business refers to wide range of activities involved in conducting business transactions across national boundaries. Taking a comprehensive approach to operational of both large and small firms engaged in business overseas, The marketing environment across the world has been becoming more and more global. It is true not only in the competitive and technological dimension but also socio culture dimension. In other words, The Marketing environment is global firm to National To local, including many thing enterprises. International marketing as marketing internationally completive environment whiter the market is home foreign. Globalization, in fact, has implication not only for business but also for other organization and individual. The following two Anecdotes expose this, Peter ducker observe in the mgt challenge for the 21st century" No institution, whether a business, a university or hospital can hope to survive, let alone to succeed unless it measures unto the standard set by the leaders in its field and place in the world." Ramification of Globalization thus, is all pervasive. As a result of the globalization of even the domestic business environment the measure competition which many firms encounter in the home market now, for example is from foreign firm- they now face substantially growing competition from goods produce in India by MNC.In shorts, national market are being Internationalized by imports and foreign investment during the last centuries, marketing activities around the world witnessed and unprecedented change. It was only during the latter half of the 20th century when large US, European, and Japanese companies expanded their markets as well as production facilities beyond national boarders The breakthroughs in information and communication technology and means of transports have contributed to the convergence in tastes and preferences of the consumer around the worlds, besides consumers, competitor true have become global in the outlook and approach to business and are ready to experiment and adopt different competitive marketing strategy in various markets. All this developments have let to interdependency in International trade between nations. Income growth triggered the consumer's desired for more and newer verities of goods their by crating markets for foreign products. All this factors has reinforced one another in the International Markets. Lower trades barriers have triggered the tradition of International trade can be traced back to the days of Indus valley civilization in 3000 BC when Trade, between India Mesopotamia, And Egypt was a regular phenomenon 1.

(A.T. Kearney, measuring Globalization, foreign policy, Jan-Feb 2004, pp. 54)

The Concept of International

In the mid fifties the orientation of markets shifted from selling to marketing. Earlier, under the selling concept, the focus was on selling product through aggressive selling and sales promotion programmers leading sales maximization which in turn was expected to maximize a firms profit earnings. On the other hand, under the marketing concept, the target market is the starting point and the focus is on customers needs. The profit maximization under the marketing concept is achieved through customer satisfaction by way of integrated marketing efforts. Prof Theodore Levitt explains this distraction by stating that selling focuses on the needs of the sellers while marketing focuses on the needs of buyers. Selling is preoccupied with the seller need to convert his product in to cash "Marketing involves the idea of satisfying the needs of customers by means of products and the whole cluster of things associated with creating, delivering, and finally consuming it. However, Prof P. Druker opines that there would always be need for some selling. But the aim of marketing to make selling superfluous. The aim of marketing is to know and understand a customer so well that the product or service satisfies him and sales itself. Ideally marketing should result in a customer who is ready to buy. All that is needed then is to make the product or service available. Consequent economic liberalization, a firms operating in domestic markets can no longer rely upon its home markets because the firm home markets is now an export markets for everybody else 3. It was believed earlier that in order to compete in the International Markets a firm need to be competitive in the domestic markets. But in view of the liberal economic policies, The Indian firms are now required to compete with International firms in the domestic market also. Therefore in order to remain domestically competitive, a firms needs to be internationally competitive. A strategic response to globalization of markets, Indian firms needs to follow a proactive approach and learn to transform the emerging Marketing Threads and challenges to their benefits. It makes International Markets relevant even for firm operating solely in domestic Markets 2.

International marketing involves:

(a) Identifying needs and wants of customers in International Markets.

(b) Taking marketing Mix decision related to product. Pricing, Distribution and communication keeping in view the diverse consumers and Market behavior across different countries on one hand and firms goals towards globalization on the other hand.

(c) Penetrating into International Markets using various mode of entry,

(d) Taking decision in view of dynamic International Marketing environment. (2, Peter Druker, management: task, responsibilities, Harper and Row, new York,1973, pp. 64-65)

As the difference between International and domestic Marketing mainly arises due to the difference in the challenges a firm has to face in the Marketing environment, which are in variably much more grave than what a firm faces while operating exclusively in domestic markets. Since the environmental challenges are beyond the control of marketers, the key to success in International Markets lies in responding competitively by adopting and effecting marketing strategy.

Global marketing is expansive, extensive, and complex. It can be seen as both a business strategy and an operation, as a force for good and/or as the 'new imperialism'. It can be embodied in companies or perceived as a phenomenon (e.g. business globalization, the internet, etc.). One view of global marketing is as a giant supply chain management system or an added value system. Global giants such as Toyota Daimler Chrysler (www.daimlerchrysler.com) source their raw materials, semi-processed and processed materials, finance and human inputs from all over the world and deliver the results of the combination of these, i.e. vehicles, to numerous market segments, adding value as they do so. Defining terms in the global marketing arena is a complex issue. Marketing across political and cultural boundaries raises many questions, problems, and juxtapositions, rendering precise definitions difficult. Typical issues centre on the standardization–adaptation argument; locus of control—central or devolved; and when exactly a multinational corporation focus becomes a global one.

Domestic marketing

The focus of domestic marketing is primarily marketing carried out within a defined national or geographic boundary where the marketer is relatively free to plan, implement, and control marketing plans, including decisions on the marketing mix (i.e. the 'controllable'), within a relatively known and easily researchable marketing environment (i.e. the 'uncontrollable'). Over time, the marketer learns to anticipate the needs and wants of his/her market. There is little need to attend to the demands of the across-boundary markets, other than to monitor and meet the threat of imports. Focus and control are firmly on the domestic market.

International marketing

International marketing takes place when the marketer explores markets outside the national boundaries of the domestic market. This often begins with direct or indirect exporting to a neighboring country. The focus is to find markets which have needs similar to those in the domestic market and can be satisfy with similar products and services. Typical of these are standard product parts and computers. While the marketing environment may be different and some adjustment may have to be made to the marketing mix elements, exporting in economic terms is basically the movement of surplus production overseas.

Once again, planning, implementation, and control of the marketing mix are based in the exporting organization. When organizations begin operating across a number of national/political boundaries, they need a more cohesive and constructive approach to their engagement with their international markets. As they progress in their internationalization, organizations would increasingly recognize the importance of accounting for country-to-country differences in their international marketing planning decisions. Because they value these differences, there is the recognition that there are many distinct marketing systems, leading to the notion that international marketing can be viewed as 'a collection of more or less coordinated domestic marketing's (Perry, 1999: 45). In this sense, the characteristics of international operations are the differing effects of, and the emphases on, the uncontrollable marketing elements and hence the need for differing marketing mixes to address those differences .However, international operators may wish to minimize the effect of these differences by operating a standardized marketing mix policy by appealing to global market segments. The emphasis may still be on central production, planning, implementation, and control, with deference paid to different market conditions. When organizations begin to produce in different countries and market according to the demands of local or regional markets, with the resultant devolution of production, planning, implementation, and control ('think global, act local'), then they are evolving into a 'multinational'. Despite this devolution, most multinationals have a corporate base from which to operate through a network of subsidiaries. The media company is a typical example. The concept of global marketing begins with the notion that the world has no centre. The 'borderless' global marketplace encompasses the participation of all countries—not only the industrialized and the newly industrialized nations, but also the emergent economies such as China and India—in international competition. This new 'market internationalism 'is coupled with more integrative global structures, including free trade areas, common markets, and multilateral agreements (e.g. World Trade Organization) which link international markets more closely, even though protectionism and conflicts coexists with it. It rests upon 'the dynamic premise that consumer preferences can be, and are, constantly being reshaped by *common exogenous* (rather than *endogenous*) forces, resulting in the convergence of many consumers' wants and desires' (Perry, 1999: 48). The growing availability and spread of communication and transportation technologies are making consumers more homogeneous and foreign markets more accessible. National borders are no longer effective barriers against external influences. For instance, the internet has made it possible for foreign companies to get around local advertising restrictions. Global marketing organizations would strive exclusively to 'maximize standardization, homogenization, similarity, concentration, dependence, synchronization, and integration of marketing activities across markets' (Svenssen, 2002: 581)

On the other hand, the truly global marketing organizations would also have an enlightened recognition that global consumers differ in their consumption behavior from culture to culture. Markets are about people, not products. There may be global products, but there are not global people. There may be global brands but they are no global motivations for buying those brands. Global organization seeks to lever its resources across political and cultural boundaries to maximize opportunities and exploit market similarities and differences in search of competitive advantage. There is a proactive willingness to adopt a global perspective instead of a country-to country or region-by-region perspective in the development of a marketing strategy. It will move its resources from country to country to achieve its goals and maximize stakeholders' value by globalizing marketing activities in the organization of worldwide efforts, the research of domestic and foreign markets, the pursuit of international partnerships, the sourcing of raw materials and support services, and the managing of international transactions. Organizations would operate as if the world were one large market, ignoring superficial regional and national differences while making sure that marketing activities fit the products and services to the practices and cultural characteristics of different markets.

International Involvement

The term International Marketing refers to exchange across national boundaries for the satisfaction of human needs and wants, the extent of a firm involvement abroad is a function of its commitment to the pursuit of foreign markets.

A firm overseas involvements may fall into following categories:-

(i) Domestic- Operating exclusively win a single country

(ii) Regional Exporter- Operation a win geographically defined region, that crosses national boundaries .Markets served are economically and culture homogeneous. If activities occur out side the home region, it is opportunistic.

(iii) Exporter- Operating from a certain office in the home region and exporting finished goods to verities of countries. Some marketing, sales, and distribution are out side the home region.

(iv) International- Operating regionally in a some what autonomous fashion, but with key discussion made a coordinated from the central office in the home region. Manufacturing and assembly, Marketing, and Sales are decentralized beyond the home region. Both finished goods and intermediate products are exported outside the home region.

(v) International to Global; operating independent and mainly self sufficient subsidiaries in a range of countries. While some function, such as R& D, sourcing and financing are decentralized the home region is still the primary base for many function.

(vi) Global- Operating as a highly decentralized organization across and a broad range of countries. No geographic area including the home region"

Spastics clearly show that the International Market is much more dynamics and is growing much faster then the domestic master. On of the most important facts of this is the difference between the growth rate of the GDP and Global Trade. For a long time now International trade has been growing at almost twice the rate of Global GDP in other words, the proportion of the domestic output sold in the foreign markets has been growing faster then the growth of the domestic income or markets as a result of this the export GDP ratio (i.e. the value of export expressed as a percentage of the GDP). Has been increasing in all categories of economics. The growth was faster for the developing economy. The fastest growth was for the low income economies- from 9% in 1985 to 15% in 1990, 20% 2002 and 28% in 2007, however now lower middle income economies have a higher export GDP ratio then all other categories. Including high income economies; it increases from 18% in 1985 to 20% in 1990, 28 % in 2000 and 23.2% in 2008%. For the world as a whole its increases 14% in 1990 to 26% in 2007. The increase export GDP ratio has been very fast in respect of a number of emerging economies whose economy growth has been driven by exports. The exports dependent Chinas enviable economic growth in the last three decade is particularly note worthy. The export of goods & services – GDP ratio of the world in 2007 was about 31% this implies that, on and average every nation,sales more then 30% of its domestic production of goods and services in foreign markets and imports goods and services of all most and equal amount. The average however, conceals more important factors. For instance, The International market is highly important for all. Secondly, a number of country sell abroad much more than they buy from other nations (Singapore, China) and many countries buy from abroad much more then they sell their (India, United Kingdom, America). Thirdly, many countries which has merchandise trade surplus have services trade deficit (Germany, China, and Japan) and vise versa, Ex (India, America, and United Kingdom). That the International market is expanding much faster than the domestic market is clear from wide difference between the growth rate of the world GDP and trade that has been observe for a very long period estimate of growth rate of world GDP and trade since (1850 estimate for war disturbed period of 1914-1950 are not available) So that global trade has grown much rapidly than GDP. During 1950 – 2007, while the world GDP registered an annual growth of 3.8%, the trade growth was 6.2%. That the International market is expanding much faster than the domestic market is clear from wide difference between the growth rates of the world GDP & Merchandise exports (figure 1.1q). Foreign market are important not MNC or other large companies but also for many small firms. About half of the total USA exports are the creation of small firms more than one third of the total export of India is contributed by the small scale sector including village and cottage industries. Many of India's 100% export oriented units (EOUS) are small firms. The important of the International markets is further elaborated in the section region for /motives of International marketing (5 WTO).

World Merchandise

For a long time now global trade, both merchandise and services, has been growing much faster than global output. That trade has been growing faster than world out put means that a growing proportion of the national output is traded internationally. In 2008 the combined value of trade in goods and commercial services amounted to nearly \$20 trillion. The ratio merchandise and services in the global trade remained more and less stable at 80:20 since 1990. Much of trade takes place between the develop countries; particularly trade (USA, Western Europe and Japan). Bull of exports of the developing countries is also absorbed by the developed countries. Just three countries, Germany, USA, and China account for over a quarter of the global trade in goods. Ibid table 1.3. more than half of the world export originate in just ten count tries 50 country contribute nearly 97% of the global trade in merchandise trade .For many years, the first rank in term of value of exports was occupied by the USA with Japan and Germany in 2nd and 3rd position respectively.

Government Policies & Regulations

Government policies & regulation may also motivate Internalization there are both positive and negative factor which could cause internationalization, many government gives a number of incentive and other positive supports to domestic companies to export and to invest in foreign country. Similarly, several countries give a lot of important to import development foreign investment. Some time as was the case in India company may be oblige to earn foreign exchange to finance their import and to meet certain other foreign exchange requirements like payment go royalty dive dent etc. further, in India, permission to enter certain industries by the large company and foreign companies was subject to specific export obligation. Some company also moves foreign country because of certain regulation, like the environmental low in advanced countries. Government policies which limit the scope of business in the home country may also provoke companies to move to other countries.

Internationalization stages

Most company pass through different stages of Internationalization there are many company which has international business since there very beginning including 100% export oriented companies even in the case of many of the

100% export orient company, the development of their international business would pass through different stages of evolution. A firm which is entirely domestic in its activities normally passes through different stages of internationalization before it's become a truly global one. There is much company which enthusiastically and systematically go international as part of their corporate plan however, in the case of many firms the initial attitude towards international business is passing and they get into the international business in response to some external stimuli. A firm may start export on an experimental basis and if the result is satisfied it would enlarge the international business and in due course it would establish offices, branches or subsidiaries or joint venture abroad. The expansionary process may also be characterized by increasing the product mix and the number of market segments, Market and countries of operation. In the process the company could be expanses to become multinational and finally global. In short, in many firms oversees business internally start with a low degree of commitment or involvement" but they gradually developed a global outlook and embark upon oversee business in a big way. The important stages in the evolutionary process are the following;

(i) Domestic Company- Most International Company has their origin as domestic companies. The orientation of a domestic company essentially is ethnocentric. A purely domestic company" operates domestically because it never considers the alternative of going international. The growing stages one company, when its reaches growth limit in its primary market d diversified into new market product and technologies instance of focus sing on penetrating international marketing:. However, if factor like domestic market constraints, foreign market prospects, increasing competition etc, make the company reorient it strategy to tap foreign market potential, it would be moving to the next stage in the evolution. A domestic company may extend its products to foreign marketing, licensing and franchising .The company, however, is primarily domestic and the orientation essential is ethnocentric .

Reason for entering International markets

The reason for entering International Markets vary from firm to firm and country to country depending upon the Market Characteristic However, firms often decide to enter into International market due to the following reason:

(a) Development:- Firms enters International market when the domestic Market Potential saturate and they are force to explore alternative market opportunities overseas. However given the size of The Indian market enormous opportunity. Most of the practices exist in the domestic market itself therefore; Development is the Motive of only a few select companies to internationalize. These is also true for large market economy such as Canada and US it may also be observed that country with smaller market size, such as Malaysia, Singapore etc had no other option but to Internationalize.

(b) Profitability:- The price differential among the markets also serves as an important incentive to Internationalize. Exporters benefits from the higher profit market in the International markets, some time stuff competition in Domestic markets limits a firm profitability in that markets. Price differential and enhance profit in the International markets are some of the fundamental motives for exporting. Some of the policies incentives such as exemption from in directed taxes and duties, several incentives by Got for export oriented production, and Marketing supports schemes contribute to enhance the profitability of firm in International markets.

(c) Achieving Economic:- Large scale production capacity necessitated domestics firms to dispose of their goods in International markets once the domestic Markets become saturated.

(d) Risk: - A company operating in Domestic market is highly vulnerable to economic upheavals in the home markets. Overseas markets provide and opportunity to reduce their dependence of one markets and spread the market risk.

(e) Access to import: - The national trade policy provides for imports of inputs used for export production, which are other wise respected. Besides, there are a number of incentive schemes which provide duty emption or remission of import of inputs for export production, such as advance licensing, duty drawback, duty exemption export promotion, capital goods schemes. It helps the company accessing imported inputted and technical no how to upgrade there operation and increase there competitiveness.

(f) Uniqueness:- The products with unique attribute are unlikely to meet any competition in the overseas markets and enjoy enormous opportunity in International market Ex- Medicinal plants, Value added BPO services and Softer ware Development at competitive prices provide Indian funds and edge over other countries and smoothen there entry in to International market.

(g) Research & Development: - A firm recovers quickly the cost incurred on R&D. it is especially true for products involving higher costs of R&D,where use the price skimming strategies necessitated faster recovery of costs incurred.

The evolution of global marketing

Whether an organization markets its goods and services domestically or internationally, the definition of marketing still applies. However, the scope of marketing is broadened when the organization decides to sell across international boundaries, this being primarily due to the numerous other dimensions which the organization has to account for. For example, the organization's language of business may be "English", but it may have to do business in the "Hindi language". This not only requires a translation facility, but the Hindi cultural conditions have to be accounted for as well. Doing business "the Hindi way" may be different from doing it "the English way". This is particularly true when doing business with the Japanese or Chinese.

"The process of building lasting relationships through planning, executing and controlling the conception, pricing, promotion and distribution of ideas, goods and services to create mutual exchange that satisfy individual and organizational needs and objectives". The long held tenants of marketing are "customer value", "competitive advantage" and "focus". This means that organizations have to study the market, develop products or services that satisfy customer needs and wants, develop the "correct" marketing mix and satisfy its own objectives as well as giving customer satisfaction on a continuing basis. However, it became clear in the 1980s that this definition of marketing was too narrow. Preoccupation with the tactical workings of the marketing mix led to neglect of long term product development, so "Strategic Marketing" was born. The focus was shifted from knowing everything about the customer, to knowing the customer in a context which includes the competition, government policy and regulations, and the broader economic, social and political macro forces that shape the evolution of markets. In global marketing terms this means forging alliances (relationships) or developing networks, working closely with home country government officials and industry competitors to gain access to a target market. Also the marketing objective has changed from one of satisfying organizational objectives to one of "stakeholder" benefits - including employees, society, and government and so on. Profit is still essential but not an end in itself.

Strategic marketing according to Wensley (1982) has been defined as:

"Initiating, negotiating and managing acceptable exchange relationships with key interest groups or constituencies, in the pursuit of sustainable competitive advantage within specific markets, on the basis of long run consumer, channel and other stakeholder franchise". Whether one takes the definition of "marketing" or "strategic marketing", "marketing" must still be regarded as both a philosophy and a set of functional activities. As a philosophy embracing customer value (or satisfaction), planning and organizing activities to meet individual and organizational objectives, marketing must be internalized by all members of an organization, because without satisfied customers the organization will eventually die. As a set of operational activities, marketing embraces selling, advertising, transporting, market research and product development activities to name but a few. It is important to note that marketing is not just a philosophy or one or some of the operational activities. It is both. In planning for marketing, the organization has to basically decide what it is going to sell, to which target market and with what marketing mix (product, place, promotion, price and people). Although these trend of marketing planning must apply anywhere, when marketing across national boundaries, the difference between domestic and international marketing lies almost entirely in the differences in national environments within which the global program is conducted and the differences in the organization and programs of a firm operating simultaneously in different national markets.

It is recognized that in the "postmodern" era of marketing, even the assumptions and long standing trends of marketing like the concepts of "consumer needs", "consumer sovereignty", "target markets" and "product/ market processes" are being challenged. The emphasis is towards the emergence of the "customizing consumer", that is, the customer who takes elements of the market offerings and moulds a customized consumption experience out of these. Even further, post modernisms, posts that the consumer who is the consumed, the ultimate marketable image, is also becoming liberated from the sole role of a consumer and is becoming a producer. This reveals itself in the desire for the consumer to become part of the marketing process and to experience immersion into "thematic settings" rather than merely to encounter products. So in consuming food products for example, it becomes not just a case of satisfying hunger needs, but also can be rendered as an image - producing act. In the postmodern market place the product does not project images, it fills images. This is true in some foodstuffs. The consumption of "designer water" or "slimming foods" is a statement of a self image, not just a product consuming act.

Acceptance of postmodern marketing affects discussions of products, pricing, advertising, distribution and planning. However, given the fact that this textbook is primarily written with developing economies in mind, where the environmental conditions, consumer sophistication and systems are not such that allow a quantum leap to postmodernism, it is intended to mention the concept in passing. Further discussion on the topic is available in the accompanying list of readings.

When organisations develop into global marketing organisations, they usually evolve into this from a relatively small export base. Some firms never get any further than the exporting stage. Marketing overseas can, therefore, be anywhere on a continuum of "foreign" to "global". It is well to note at this stage that the words "international", "multinational" or "global" are now rather outdated descriptions. In fact "global" has replaced the other terms to all intents and purposes. "Foreign" marketing means marketing in an environment different from the home base, it's basic form being "exporting". Over time, this may evolve into an operating market rather than a foreign market. In "global marketing" the modus operandi is very different. Organisations begin to develop and run operations in the targeted country or countries outside of the domestic one. In practice, organisations evolve and Table 1.1 outlines a typology of terms which describes the characteristics of companies at different stages in the process of evolving from domestic to global enterprises.

The four stages are as follows:

1. *Stage one:* domestic in focus, with all activity concentrated in the home market. Whilst many organizations can survive like this, for example raw milk marketing, solely domestically oriented organisations are probably doomed to long term failure.
2. *Stage two:* home focus, but with exports (ethnocentric). Probably believes only in home values, but creates an export division. Usually ripe for the taking by stage four organisations.
3. *Stage three:* stage two organisations which realize that they must adapt their marketing mixes to overseas operations. The focus switches to multinational (polycentric) and adaption becomes paramount.
4. *Stage four:* global organizations which create value by extending products and programs and focus on serving emerging global markets (geocentric). This involves recognizing that markets around the world consist of similarities and differences and that it is possible to develop a global strategy based on similarities to obtain scale economies, but also recognizes and responds to cost effective differences. Its strategies are a combination of extension, adaptation and creation. It is unpredictable in behavior and always alert to opportunities.

There is no time limit on the evolution process. In some industries, like horticulture, the process can be very quick. In practice, global marketing hardly means complete standardization of the marketing mix decisions, but it increasingly means a strategic approach to have a global perspective to have economies of scale. Higher volume of production and sales results into reduction in cost per unit due to "experience curve" effects and increased efficiency in activities mainly related to production, resource management and marketing. Economies of scope refer to the synergy effects of global markets. The objective to find out some commonality in the customer' needs and strive for a uniform marketing strategy as far as feasible in various country markets.

Table 1.1: Stages of domestic to global evolution

Management emphasis	Stage one Domestic	Stage two International	Stage three Multinational	Stage four Global
Focus	Domestic	Ethnocentric	Polycentric	Geocentric
Marketing strategy	Domestic	Extension	Adaption	Extension
Structure	Domestic	International	Worldwide area	Adaption creation matrix/mixed
Management style	Domestic	Centralized top down	Decentralized bottom up	Integrated
Manufacturing stance	Mainly domestic	Mainly domestic	Host country	Lowest cost worldwide
Investment policy	Domestic	Domestic used worldwide	Mainly in each host country	Cross subsidization
Performance evaluation	Domestic market share	Against home country market share	Each host country market share	Worldwide

Factors which have led to internationalization

There have been many underlying forces, concepts and theories which have emerged as giving political explanation to the development of international trade. Remarkably, despite the trend to world interdependency, some countries have been less involved than others. The USA, for example, has a remarkably poor export record. About 2000 US companies only account for more than 70% of US manufacturer's exports. This has been mainly due to its huge statewide domestic market, which is almost tantamount to "international trade", for example, Californian fruit being sold three thousand kilometers away in New Jersey. Japan has risen fast to dominate the export rankings, with countries of Africa struggling to make a significant mark, mainly because of their emphasis on exporting primary products. This section will briefly examine the forces which have been instrumental in the development of world trade.

Theoretical approaches

These include the theory of comparative advantage described in the book Wealth of Nations (Adam Smith) and David Ricardo), the product trade cycle (Raymond Vernon) and The Business Orientation (Howard Perlmutter).

The theory of comparative advantage

The theory can be relatively complex and difficult to understand but stated simply this theory is a demonstration (under assumptions) that a country can gain from trade even if it has an absolute disadvantage in the production of all goods, or it can gain from trade even if it has an absolute advantage in the production of all goods. Even though a country has an absolute production advantage it may be better to concentrate on its comparative advantage.

To calculate the comparative advantage one has to compare the production ratios, and make the assumption that the one country totally specializes in one product. To maximize the wellbeing of both individuals and countries, countries are better off specializing in their area of competitive advantage and then trading and exchanging with others in the market place. Today there are a variety of spreadsheets that one can use to calculate comparative advantage, one such is that of the Food and Agriculture Organization (FAO). Calculation of comparative advantage is as follows:

Example: It may be assumed that Holland is more efficient in the production of flowers than Kenya. Yet Kenya succeeds in exporting thousands of tons of flowers to Europe every year. Kenya flower growers Sulmac and Oserian have achieved legendary reputations, in the supply of fresh cut flowers to Europe, How. Take the simple two countries - two product model of comparative advantage. Europe grows apples and India oranges, these are two products, both undifferentiated and produced with production units which are a mixture of land, labor and capital. To use the same production units India can produce 100 apples and no oranges, and Europe can produce 80 apples and no oranges. At the other extreme India can produce no apples and 50 oranges and Europe no apples and 30 oranges.

Now if the two countries specialize and trade the position is as follows:

Product	India			Europe		
	Production	**Imports**	**Consumers**	**Production**	**Imports**	**Consumers**
Apples (000's)	0	30	30	80	30	50
Oranges (000's)	50	14	36	30	14	44

The trading price is30:14 =2.14 apples= 1 orange

14:30 = 4.67 oranges = 1 apple

So in apples, India has an advantage of 1.25 (100/80) but in oranges 1.67 (50/30). So India should concentrate on the production of oranges as its comparative advantage is greatest here. Unfortunately the theory assumes that production costs remain relatively static. However, it is a well known fact that increased volumes result, usually, in lower costs. Indeed, the Boston Consulting Group observed this phenomenon, in the so called "experience curve" effect concept. And it is not only "production" related but "all experience" related; including marketing. The Boston Consulting group observed that as an organization gains experience in production and marketing the greater the reduction in costs. The theory of comparative advantage also ignores product and programme differentiation. Consumers do not buy products based only on the lowest costs of production. Image, quality, reliability of delivery and other tangible and non tangible factors come into play. Kenyans may well be prepared to pay extra for imported French or South African wines, as the locally produced paw paw wine may be much inferior.

The product trade cycle

The model describes the relationship between the product life cycle, trade and investment (see figure 1.1) and is attributable to Venon[1] (1966)

The international product trade cycle model suggests that many products go through a cycle during which high-income, mass consumption countries which are initial exporters, lose their export markets and finally become importers of the product. At the same time other countries, particularly less developed but not exclusively so, shift from being importers to exporters.

These stages are reflected in figure 1.1.

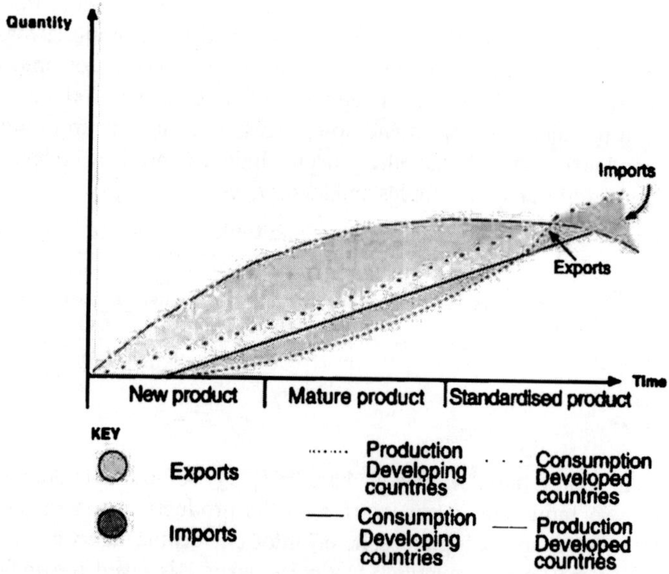

Figure 1.1 International product trade cycle

From a high income country point of view phase I. involves exporting, based on domestic product strength and surplus-to phase II when foreign production begins, to phase III when production in the foreign country becomes competitive, to phase IV when import competition begins. The assumption behind this cycle is that new products are firstly launched in high income markets because:-

(a) Most potential

(b) The product can be tested best domestically near its source of production.

Thus new products generally emanate from high income countries and, over time, orders begin to be solicited from lower income countries and so a thriving export market develops. High income country entrepreneurs quickly realize that the markets to which they are selling often have lower production costs and so production is initiated abroad for the new products, so starts the second stage.

In the second stage of the cycle, foreign and high income country production begins to supply the same export market. As foreign producers begin to expand and gain more experience, their competition displaces the high income export production source. At this point high income countries often decide to invest in foreign countries to protect their share. As foreign producers expand, their growing economies of scale make them a competitive source for third country markets where they compete with high income exporters. The final phase of the cycle occurs when the foreign producer achieves such a scale and experience that it starts exporting to the original high income producer at a production cost lower than its original high income producer at a production cost lower than its original high income supplier. High income producers, once enjoying a monopoly in their own market, now face competition at home.

Whilst the underlying assumption behind the International Product Trade Cycle is that the cycle begins with the export of new product ideas from high income countries to low income importers, and then low income countries begin production of the product etc., things do not always turn out as the cycle suggests. Sometimes a high or even low income exporter may put a product into a high/low income country which is simply unable to respond. In this case, the Trade Cycle ceases to be the underpinning concept. This may be due to a number of factors like lack of access to capital to build the facilities to respond to the import, lack of skills or that the costs of local production cannot get down to the level of costs of the imported product. In this case, product substitution between the exporter and importer may also take place. A classic example of this phenomenon is the case of Zimbabwe Sunsplash fruit juice drinks.

Management Orientation

Perlmutter 5 (1967) identified distinctive "orientations" of management of international organisations. His "EPRG" scheme identified four types of attitudes or orientations associated with successive stages in the evolution of international operations.

- Ethnocentrism - home country orientation - exporting surplus.
- Polycentrism - host country orientation - subsidiary operation.
- Regiocentrism - regional orientation - world market strategies.
- Geocentrism - world orientation - world market strategies.

The latter two are based on similarities and differences in markets, capitalising on similarities to obtain cost benefits, but recognising differences.

Market forces and development

Over the last few decades internationalism has grown because of a number of market factors which have been driving development forward, over and above those factors which have been attempting to restrain it. These include market and marketing related variables.

Many global opportunities have arisen because of the clustering of market opportunities worldwide. Organisations have found that similar basic segments exist worldwide and, therefore, can be met with a global orientation. Cotton, as an ingredient in shirting, sittings, and curtain material can be globally marketed as natural and fashionable. One can see in the streets of New York, London, Kuala Lumpar or Harare, youth with the same style and brand of basketball shirts or American Football shorts. Coca Cola can be universally advertised as "Adds Life" or appeal to a basic instinct "You can't beat the Feeling" or "Come alive" as with the case of Pepsi. One can question "what feeling?", but that is not the point. The more culturally unbounded the product is, the more a global clustering can take place and the more a standardised approach can be made in the design of marketing programmes.

This standardised approach can be aided and abetted with technology. Technology has been one of the single most powerful driving forces to internationalism. Rarely is technology culturally bound. A new pesticide is available almost globally to any agricultural organisation as long as it has the means to buy it. Computers in agriculture and other applications are used universally with IBM and Macintosh becoming household names. The need to recoup large costs of research and development in new products may force organisations to look at global markets to recoup their investment. This is certainly true of many veterinary products. Global volumes allow continuing investment in R & D, thus helping firms to improve quality. Farm machinery, for example, requires volume to generate profits for the development of new products.

Communications and transport are shrinking the global market place. Value added manufacturers like Cadbury, Nestlè, Kelloggs, Beyer, Norsk Hydro, Massey Ferguson and ICI find themselves "under pressure" from the market place and distributors alike to position their brands globally. In many cases this may mean an adaption in advertising appeals or messages as well as packaging and instructions. Nestle will not be in a hurry to repeat its disastrous experience of the "Infant formula" saga, whereby it failed to realise that the ability to find, boiled water for its preparations, coupled with the literacy level to read the instructions properly, were not universal phenomenon.

Marketing globally also provides the marketer with five types of "leverage" or "advantages", those of experience, scale, resource utilisation and global strategy. A multi-product global giant like Nestle', with over £10 billion turnover annually, operates in so many markets, buys so much raw material from a variety of outgrowers of different sizes, that its international leverage is huge. If it consumes a third of the world's cocoa output annually, then it is in a position to dominate terms. This also has its dangers.

The greatest lift to producers of raw agricultural products has been the almost universal necessity to consume their produce. If one considers the whole range of materials from their raw to value added state there is hardly a market segment which cannot be tapped globally. Take, for example, oranges. Not only are Brazilian, Israeli, South African and Spanish oranges in demand in their raw state worldwide, but their downstream developments are equally in demand. Orange juice, concentrates, segments and orange pigments are globally demanded. In addition the ancillary products and services required to make the orange industry work, find themselves equally in global demand. So insecticides, chemicals, machinery, transport services, financial institutions, warehousing, packaging and a whole range of other production and marketing services are in demand, many provided by global organisations like Beyer, British Airways and Barclays Bank. Of course, many raw materials are at the mercy of world prices, and so many developing countries find themselves at the mercy of supply and demand fluctuations. But this highlights one important global lesson - the need to study markets carefully. Tobacco producing countries of the world are finding this out. With a growing trend away from tobacco products in the west, new markets or increasing volumes into consuming markets have to be prospected and developed. Many agricultural commodities take time to mature. An orange grove will mature after five years. By that time another country may plant or have its trees mature. Unless these developments are picked up by global intelligence the plans for a big profit may be not realised as the extra volume supplied depresses prices. This happened in 1993/94 with the Malawian and Zimbabwean tobacco companies. The unexpected release of Chinese tobacco depressed the tobacco price well below expectations, leaving farms with stock and large interest carrying production loans.

A number of suppliers of agricultural produce can take advantage of "off season" in other countries, or the fact that they produce specialist products. This is the way by which many East African and South American producers established themselves in Europe and the USA respectively. In fact the case of Kenya vegetables to Europe is a classic, covering many of the factors which have just been discussed-improved technology, emerging global segments, shrinking communications gaps and the drive to diversify product ranges. Whilst the forces, market and otherwise, have been overwhelming in their push to globalization, there remain a number of negatives. Many organisations have been put off or have not bothered going into global industry due to a variety of factors. Some have found the need to adapt the marketing mix, especially in many culture bound products, too daunting. Similarly brands with a strong local history may not easily transfer to other markets. National Breweries of Zimbabwe, for example, may not find their Chibuku brand of beer (brewed especially for the locals) an easy transboundary traveler. More often than not sheer management myopia may set in and management may fail to seize the export opportunity although products may be likely candidates. Similarly organisations may refuse to devolve activities to local subsidiaries.

Other negative forces may be created by Governments. Simply by creating barriers to entry, local enterprises may be protected from international competition as well as the local market. This is typical of many developing countries, anxious to get their fledging industries off the ground.

The international economic system

Several factors have contributed to the growth of the international economy post World War II. The principal forces have been the development of economic blocs like the European Union (EU) and then the "economic pillars"- the World Bank (or International Bank for Reconstruction and Development to give its full name), the International Monetary Fund (IMF) and the evolution of the World Trade Organisation from the original General Agreement on Tariffs and Trade (GATT).

Until 1969 the world economy traded on a gold and foreign exchange base. This affected liquidity drastically. After 1969 liquidity was eased by the agreement that member nations to the IMF accept the Special Drawing Rights (SDR) in settling reserve transactions. Now an international reserve facility is available. Recently, the World Bank has taken a very active role in the reconstruction and development of developing country economies, a point which will be expanded on later.

Until the General Agreement on Tariffs and Trade (GATT) after World War II, the world trading system had been restricted by discriminating trade practices. GATT had the intention of producing a set of rules and principles to liberalize trade. The most favored nation concept (MFN), where by each country agrees to extend to all countries the most favorable terms that it negotiates with any country, helped reduce barriers. The "round" of talks began with Kennedy in the 60s and Tokyo of the 70s. The latest round, Uruguay, was recently concluded in April 1994 and ratified by most countries in early 1995. Despite these trade agreements, non tariff barriers like exclusion deals, standards and administrative delays are more difficult to deal with. A similar system exists with the European Union, - the Lomè convention. Under this deal, African and Caribbean countries enjoy favored status with EU member countries.

Relative global peace has engendered confidence in world trade. Encouraged by this and the availability of finance, global corporations have been able to expand into many markets. The breakup of the former Soviet Union has opened up vast opportunities to investors, aided by the World Bank and the European Development Bank. This atmosphere of peace has also allowed the steady upward trend of domestic growth and again opened up market opportunities domestically to foreign firms. Peace in Mozambique, the "normalization" of South Africa, and peace in Vietnam as examples have opened up the way for domestic growth and also, therefore, foreign investment. The liberation of economies under World Bank sponsored structural adjustment programmers have also given opportunities. This is very true of countries like Zambia and Zimbabwe, where in the latter, for example, over Z$2.8 billion of foreign investment in the stock exchange and mining projects have occurred in the early 1990s.

Sometimes, market opportunities open up through "Acts of God". The great drought of 1992 in Southern Africa, necessitated a large influx of foreign produce, especially yellow maize from the USA and South America.

Not only did this give a market for maize only, but opened up opportunities for transport businesses and services to serve the drought stricken areas. Speedy communications like air transportation and electronic data transmission and technology have "shrunk" the world. Costs and time have reduced enormously and with the advent of television, people can see what is happening elsewhere and this can cause desire levels to rise dramatically. Only recently has television been introduced into Tanzania, for example, and this has brought the world and its markets, closer to the average Tanzanian.

No doubt a great impetus to global trade was brought about by the development of economic blocs, and, conversely, by the collapse of others. Blocs like the European Union (EU), ASEAN, the North American Free Trade Agreement (NAFTA) with the USA, Canada and Mexico has created market opportunities and challenges. New countries are trying to join these blocs all the time, because of the economic, social and other advantages they bring. Similarly, the collapse of the old communist blocs have given rise to opportunities for organisations as they strive to get into the new market based economies rising from the ruins. This is certainly the case with the former Soviet bloc.

In the late 1980s and early 90s, the United States, along with Japan, have been playing an increasingly influential role in world affairs, especially with the collapse of the former USSR. Whilst on the one hand this is good, as the USA is committed to world welfare development, it can be at a price. The Gulf War coalition of the 90s, primarily put together by the USA as the leading player, was an example of the price 6.(WTO).

Global marketing involvement

Individuals or organisations may get involved in International Marketing in a rather unplanned way which gives the impetus to more formal and larger operations. This may happen in a following ways:

Foreign customers

Unsolicited enquiries through word of mouth, visits, exhibitions, and experience through others may result in orders. This is often typical of small scale organisations.

Importers

Importers may be looking for products unavailable in domestic markets, for example, mangoes in the UK, or products which can be imported on more favorable terms. An example of these is flowers from Kenya to Holland.

Intermediaries

These may be of four types - domestic based export merchants, domestic based export agents, export management companies or cooperative organisations. These will be expanded on later in this text. Sometimes an intermediary may provide export services in an attempt to reduce their own costs on the export of their own produce by acting as a representative for other organisations. This is called "piggybacking".

Attitudes as precursors to global involvement

Cavusgil[3] (1984) developed a three stage model of export involvement, based on the fact that the opportunity to export may arise long before exporting behaviors became manifest. See figure 1.2.

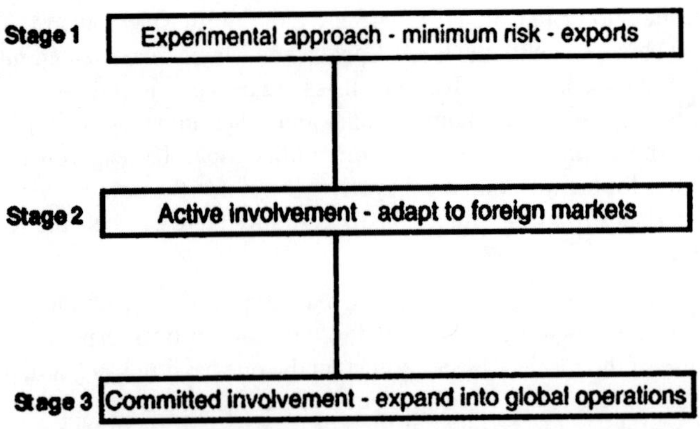

Figure 1.2: Cavusgil's three stage model of export involvement.

According to Cavusgil attitudes are determined by the operating style of the organisation and cultural norms which prevail in the domestic market. An organisation's style may be defensive or prospective. The latter type of organisation may systematically, or in an ad hoc manner, search out international opportunities.

Behavior as a global marketing impetus

We saw earlier in the internationalization process that organisations may evolve from exporting surplus or serving ad hoc enquiries to a more committed global strategy. This gradual change may involve moving from geographically adjacent markets to another, say, for example from the Southern African Development Conference (SADC) to Europe. However, not all globalization takes place like this. In the case of fresh cut flowers, these may go to major, developed country consumer centers, for example from Harare to London or Amsterdam and Frankfurt. Lusaka or Nairobi may never see Zimbabwe flowers. In analyzing behavior one has not to generalize. What is certain is that in all stages, the balance of opportunity and risk is considered.

The context of internationalization

It is essential to see in what context individual organizations view internationalization. The existing situation of the firm will affect its interest in and ability to internationalize. Such may be the low domestic quality and organisation that a firm could never export. It may not have the resources or the will.

Internationalization infrastructure

Johansson and Mattison (1984) have explored the notion of differences in tasks facing organisations which internationalize. In low and high infrastructure situations. "Early starters" are likely to experiment or depend on contacts with experienced organisations which know the process. "Late starters" may use existing contacts as a "bridge" to new opportunities. They may also be pressurized by customers, supplies or competitors to get into joint venturing. Joint venturing, with its added infrastructure, may lead to rapid progress. If the organisation faces intense competition then it may be forced to up the pace and scale of foreign investment. Rising protectionism in recent years has given impetus to late starters to establish production facilities in target markets. Infrastructure for foreign operations may also change (firms also reduce their investment as well as invest). When this happens the perceived risk changes also. This discussion on international infrastructure concludes t he factors which have led to internationalization. It is a complex focus of internal and external factors and looking carefully at risk versus opportunities.

Strategy

Whatever business we are in, haphazard organisation often leads to haphazard results. In planning for international marketing organisations need a clear picture of the steps involved. "Strategy" gives such a picture. Strategy is the response of the organisation to the realities of shareholders and the business environment. The phases in the strategy formulation process are given on figure 1.3.

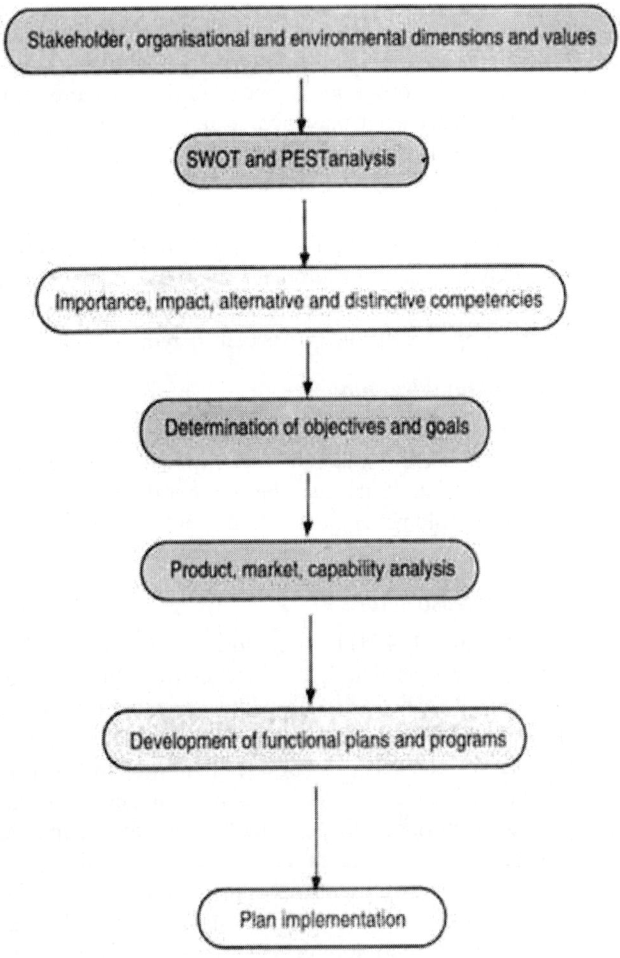

Figure 1.3 Strategy formulation

The Global environment

Of all the steps in formulating strategy, no one step is as important as the ability to assess the "environmental" factors in international marketing. Taking account of cultural, economic and political differences is a must when dealing with different markets. More will be said on these factors in later chapters. Environmental analysis allows the organisation to cluster markets according to similarities and differences, based on the environmental "uncontrollable" factors. The international "uncontrollable" are in addition to the organization's domestic "uncontrollable" so need to be treated with extra care. Figure 1.4 shows the major environmental factors to be considered. It must be noted that according to the "relationship" marketing school of thought, the so called "incontrollable" can be made more "controllable" by building relationships with the influences of these factors. For example, if an exporter of horticultural produce wishes to be able to anticipate changes in the political environment, it may build a relationship with certain politicians who may have intimate knowledge of the political system.

International environment

An analysis of the environmental uncontrollable allows the potential marketers to place products on a continuum of environmental sensitivity. At the one end are environmentally insensitive products and at the other end, those more sensitive to economic, sociocultual l, physical and other factors. The greater the sensitivity, the greater the need for the organisation to learn the way the product interacts with the environment. international analysis

In order to put together the task of finding the differences and similarities in environmental and market analysis, a framework needs to be devised. Where unifying influences are found then the marketer is able to develop more standardized plans. When there are a large number of differences, then plans

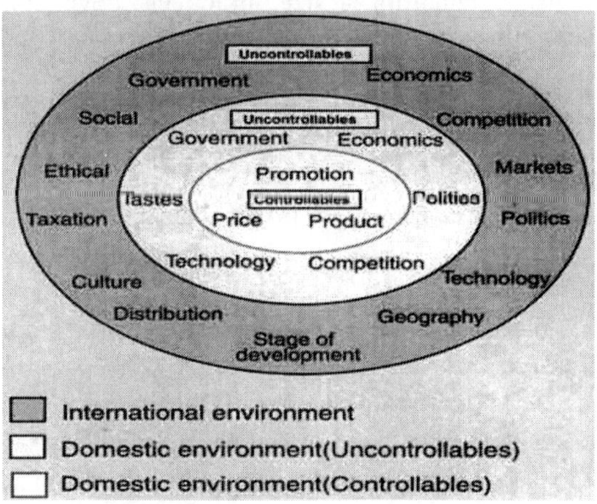

Figure 1.4: A conceptual framework for multinational marketing in constraint economies

have to be designed adapted to circumstances. Once having identified the unifying and differentiating influences and answered many questions about where one could or could not standardize the marketing planning process then a conceptual framework for multinational marketing planning can be developed. One such conceptual framework is given in figure 1.4

Key questions for analysis, planning and control of marketing in constraint economies.

(a) Principle constraint analysis
   (i) Government's attitude to employment, foreign intervention, foreign exchange, indebtedness and policies
   (ii) Government's policy of economic development, foreign exchange, barter deals, equity arrangements, remittance of funds, state intervention, private sector development and import substitution
   (iii) Government's social objectives including indigenization, subsidies, population and socialization
   (iv) Laws, tariffs, duties, trade regulations, balance of payments, licensing and labor laws
   - Leading to an economic analysis
   - Gathering *of appropriate* data on:

(b) Appropriate environmental variable data
   (i) Market characteristics-physical, cultural, size, growth rate, stage of development?
   (ii) Market institutions - distribution, media, research, services
   (iii) Industry conditions- size, practices, development stage, appropriate technology
   (iv) Resources- manpower and money

Planning

(c) Target country experts or generalist staff to plan operations
(d) What are the *authorized* target markets and the product appropriateness
(e) Market size
(f) What is the stage of development and strength of competition both state and private?
(g) What is the appropriate product/market technology
(h) What is the necessary adaptation of the marketing mix
(i) How do the government and company objectives coincide
(j) What is the trading risk
(k) What government/organisation interface is required? How are licenses agreed and obtained? Who are the principle characters

Structure

(l) How does the company have to be structured to meet the government, economic and social objectives as well as company objectives

Plan implementation

(m) Given the government's policies, attitudes and economic and social objectives how is an effective marketing plan designed, resourced and implemented? what degree of adaptation and cooperation is required at all levels? (Government marketing institutions and function)? Who will be responsible for each level"?

Controlling the market program

(n) Who is responsible and how is the plan performance measured and monitored

(o) What controls, other than profit are required? Are employment and other such objectives necessary

(p) Has the company the ability and authority to alter the parameters to bring actual results into line with desired

(q) What are the principal control parameters? Can they be easily adjusted at all

This framework is particularly relevant to developing economies where government constraints and controls tend to be more intensive than developed economies.

Product life cycle

Just as in domestic marketing the concept of the Product Life Cycle has often been cited as a useful (but often maligned!) planning concept, so it can be useful in international marketing. The traditional four stage life cycle - introduction, growth, maturity, and decline - is a well-documented phenomenon. Attempts are made in the maturity stage to extend the cycle. The market life cycle is very similar and what global marketers have to be wary of is that not all markets are at the same stage globally. It may be appropriate to have tractor mounted ditchers and diggers in Africa or the UK where labor is not too plentiful, but in India, they may be the last thing required where labor is plentiful and very cheap. So the appropriate marketing strategy will be different for each market.

It would be very easy to discuss the global marketing decision as a case of deciding whether to export or standardize or adapt your product/market offering. This is far from the case. Even the smallest nuance of change in the global environment can ruin a campaign or plan. Whilst the above discussion has tended to be theoretical in nature, most of it, if not all of it, is essential in practice. In food marketing systems many transactions and discussions take place across international boundaries. This involves a close look at all the necessary environmental factors. If one considers food marketing as the physical and economic bridge linking raw materials production and consumer purchases then a whole series of interdependent decisions, institutions, resource flows and physical and business activities take place. Food marketing stimulates and supports raw material production, balances commodity supply and demand and stimulates end demand and enhances consumer welfare. This process often transcends several different industries and markets, many of them crossing international boundaries. The product may change form, be graded, packed, transported and necessitate information flows, financial resources, invoice and retailing or wholesaling functions. In addition, quality standards designed for producers and transporters may apply as may product improvements. In other words, the bridge may involve a whole set of utilities afforded to the end user (time, place and form), and add value at each stage of the transaction. This system involves numerous independent and interdependent players and activities. To shift a perishable like strawberries 7000km from Harare, Zimbabwe to the UK requires an extraordinary complex series of activities, involving perfect timing. The detail involved in this intricate transaction will be explained in later chapters.

With commodities, physical, Government and economic environmental factors playing a major role in international marketing. So does price and quality differentiation. In later years the enormous success of the Brazilian frozen concentrated orange juice industry has been attributable not only to poor climatic conditions prevailing in its competitive countries, but the fact that its investment in large production economies of scale, bulk transport and storage technologies considerably reduced international transport costs and facilitated improved distribution of the juice to, and within, importing countries. From a cottage industry in 1970, it grew to account for 80% of world trade by the early 1990's. Its success, therefore, has been based on price and added value quality differentiation.

International marketing is, therefore, quite a complex operation, involving both an understanding of the theoretical and practical aspects involved. Prescriptions are totally inappropriate.

This concludes the discussion on the reasoning why internationalism has grown and the next chapters' took more closely at the environmental factors which have to be taken into account when considering to market internationally. Internationalization of Indian Firms By Mr. Roy we will take process also.

References

1. Vernon, R. "International Investment and International Trade in the Product Cycle." *Quarterly Journal of Economics,* May 1966, pp. 190 -207.

2. Perlmutter, H.J. "Social Architectural Problems of the Multinational Firm." *Quarterly Journal of AISEC International.* Vol. 3, No. 3, August 1967.
3. Cavusgil, S. T. "Differences among Exporting Firms based on Degree of Internationalization". *Journal of Business Research,* Vol. 12,1984.
4. Firat A. F., Dholakia N., Venkatesh A., "Marketing in a Postmodern World. European" *Journal of Marketing* Vol 29 No. 1 1995 pp. 40-56
5. Hakansson, H. (ed), "International Marketing and Purchasing of Industrial Goods." IMP Project Group, John Wiley and Sons, 1982.
6. Jaffee S. "Exporting high value food commodities." World Bank Discussion Paper No. 198. The World Bank 1993.
7. Johanson, J and Mattison, L.G. "Internationalization in Industrial Systems - A Network Approach." Paper prepared for the Prince Bertil Symposium on Strategies in Global Competition. Stockholm School of Economies, 1984.
8. Keegan, W. J. "Global Marketing Management" 4th Edition. Prentice Hall International Edition 1989.
9. Kotler, P." Marketing Management, Analysis, Planning, Implementation and Control", 6th Edition. Prentice Hall International Edition, 1988.
10. Wensley J.R.C. "PIMS and BCG New Horizons" or *False Dawns Strategic Management Journal No.* 3 April/June 1982.
11. Carter, S. "Multinational and International Marketing in Constraint Economies." The Quarterly Review of Marketing, Summer 1988, pp. 13-18.
12. Smith, P. "International Marketing." University of Hull, MBA Notes, 1990.
13. Terpstra, V. "International Marketing", 4th ed. The Dryden Press, 1987.
14. "The Business Herald " (Zimbabwe) January 19, 1995

Chapter - Two

The Global environment

International Environment

The international marketing environment is a complex constellation of demands and constraints which the firm faces as it attempts to compete and grow. Identifying customer values in international markets requires a sophisticated understanding of differentiated expressions of customer needs, many of which are influenced by culture. Similarly, the task of communicating the values provide and their delivery in international markets is complex, requiring a great deal of understanding of the environment and its influences. International marketing is characterized by the convergence of the company marketing process, usually in one country, and the customer's purchase decision process in another. This international marketing environment consists of a number of elements most of which lie outside the control of the firm. Each of these elements is discussed and integrated in the firm's decision making process. Firm in international markets Customers Culture and values Resources Technology Political economy Competitor.] The study of the international political and legal environment must therefore be broken down into several sub segments. Many researchers do this by separating the legal from the political. This separation – although perhaps analytically useful is somewhat artificial because laws are generally the result of political decisions. Here no attempt will be made to separate legal and political factors, except when such a separation is essential. The political systems of the countries served or being considered by an international marketer are an important part of the firm's macro environment. It may be noted that significant differences in the business environment may exist even within country, particularly if the country is geographically very vast, very populous and multi cultural. The differences in the level and the nature of industrialization and economic development between different states and defend regions within the states and preferences, beliefs and culture customs etc. of the different culture may vary significantly, as is the case with India also. Dissimilar weather and climate conditions, topographical factors etc. could also be decisive factors.

The basic thing is not whether the market is domestic or foreign but whether the business environment of the different markets is similar or dissimilar.

Marketing Environment

The marketing environment surrounds and impacts upon the organization. There are three key elements to the marketing environment which are the internal environment, the microenvironment and the microenvironment. Why are they important? Well marketers build both internal and external relationships. Marketers aim to deliver value to satisfied customers, so we need to assess and evaluate our internal business/corporate environment and our external environment which is subdivided into micro and macro.

In global marketing, there are five different sets of relevant global environment are:-

(i) Internal

(ii) Global

(iii) Foreign

(iv) Domestic

Internal environment THE MICRO-ENVIRONMENT influences the organization directly. Includes suppliers, consumers & customers, and other local stakeholders. ; internal environment 'include '5 Ms; Men, Money, Machinery, Materials & Markets. The internal environment has already been touched upon by other lessons on marketing teacher. For example, the lessons on internal marketing and also on the function within an organization give a good starting point to look at our internal environment. A useful tool for quickly auditing your internal environment is known as the Five MS which are Men, Money, Machinery, Materials and Markets. Here is a really quick example using British Airways. Looking internally at men, British Airways employees pilots, engineers, cabin crew, marketing managers, etc. Money is invested in the business by shareholders and banks for example. Machinery would include its aircraft but also access to air bridges and buses to ferry passengers from the terminal to the aircraft. Materials for a service business like British Airways would be aircraft fuel called kerosene (although if we were making aircraft materials would include aluminum, wiring, glass, fabric, and so on). Finally markets which we know can be both internal and external. Some might include a sixth M, which is minutes, since time is a valuable internal resource. Example of how the internal environment would impact a company such as Wal-Mart. We are looking at the immediate local influences which might include its marketing plans, how it implements customer relationship management, the influence of other functions such as strategy from its top management, research and development into new logistics solutions, how it makes sure that it purchases high-quality product at the lowest possible price, that accounting is undertaken efficiently and effectively, and of course its local supply chain management and logistics for which Wal-Mart is famous.

Microenvironment

The microenvironment is made from individuals and organizations that are close to the company and directly impact the customer experience. Examples would include the company itself, its suppliers, other marketing input from agencies, the markets and segments in which your business trades, your competition and also those around you (which public relations would call publics) who are not paying customers but still have an interest in your business. The Micro environment is relatively controllable since the actions of the business may influence such stakeholders. Walmart's Micro environment would be very much focused on immediate local issues. It would consider how to recruit, retain and extend products and services to customers. It would pay close attention to the actions and reactions of direct competitors. Walmart would build and nurture close relationships with key suppliers. The business would need to communicate and liaise with its publics such as neighbors which are close to its stores, or other road users. There will be other intermediaries as well including advertising agencies and trade unions amongst others.The global environment refers to those global factors which are relevant to business such as the WTO principles and agreements other International convention / treaties agreement/ declaration/ protocols etc. Economic and business condition impacts of major development like war, substantial fluctuations in oil prices, sentiment in other countries etc. Similarly, there are certain developments which have global impact, like substantial fluctuation in the crude oil crises, global economic melt. An Indian company which want to globalizes would have to adopt Internationally acceptable standards and practices in several respect, like accounting and reporting, governances etc., particularly if it wants to tap the International capital market or enter in to foreign collaboration. A multitude of more or less powerful groups of stakeholders from inside but sometimes also outside a country's borders influences:

Various environmental factors such as economic environment, socio-cultural environment, political, technological, demographic and international, affect the business and its working. Out of these factors economic environment is the most important factor.

1. Economic Environment:- Those Economic factors which have their effect on the working of the business is known as economic environment. It includes system, policies and nature of an economy, trade cycles, economic resources, level of income, distribution of income and wealth etc. Economic environment is very dynamic and complex in nature. It does not remain the same. It keeps on changing from time to time with the changes in an economy like change in Govt. policies, political situations.

2. Elements of Economic Environment:- It has mainly five main components:-
    1. Economic Conditions
    2. Economic System
    3. Economic Policies
    4. International Economic Environment
    5. Economic Legislations
3. Economic Conditions:- Economic Policies of a business unit are largely affected by the economic conditions of an economy. Any improvement in the economic conditions such as standard of living, purchasing power of public, demand and supply, distribution of income etc. largely affects the size of the market.

   Business cycle is another economic condition that is very important for a business unit.

   Business Cycle has 5 different stages viz. (i) Prosperity, (ii) Boom, (iii) Decline, (iv) Depression, (v) Recovery.
4. Following are mainly included in Economic Conditions of a country:-
    I. Stages of Business Cycle
    II. National Income, Per Capita Income and Distribution of Income
    III. Rate of Capital Formation
    IV. Demand and Supply Trends
    V. Inflation Rate in the Economy
    VI. Industrial Growth Rate, Exports Growth Rate
    VII. Interest Rate prevailing in the Economy
    VIII. Trends in Industrial Sickness
    IX. Efficiency of Public and Private Sectors
    X. Growth of Primary and Secondary Capital Markets
    XI. Size of Market
5. Economic Systems:- An Economic System of a nation or a country may be defined as a framework of rules, goals and incentives that controls economic relations among people in a society. It also helps in providing framework for answering the basic economic questions. Different countries of a world have different economic systems and the prevailing economic system in a country affect the business units to a large extent. Economic conditions of a nation can be of any one of the following type:-
    1. Capitalism:- The economic system in which business units or factors of production are privately owned and governed is

called Capitalism. The profit earning is the sole aim of the business units. Government of that country does not interfere in the economic activities of the country. It is also known as free market economy. All the decisions relating to the economic activities are privately taken. Examples of Capitalistic Economy:- England, Japan, America etc.

2. Socialism:- Under socialism economic system, all the economic activities of the country are controlled and regulated by the Government in the interest of the public. The first country to adopt this concept was Soviet Russia. The two main forms of Socialism are: -
   (a) Democratic Socialism:- All the economic activities are controlled and regulated by the government but the people have the freedom of choice of occupation and consumption.
   (b) Totalitarian Socialism:- This form is also known as Communism. Under this, people are obliged to work under the directions of Government.
3. Mixed Economy:- The economic system in which both public and private sectors co-exist is known as Mixed Economy. Some factors of production are privately owned and some are owned by Government. There exists freedom of choice of occupation and consumption. Both private and public sectors play key roles in the development of the country.

6. Economic Policies:- Government frames economic policies. Economic Policies affects the different business units in different ways. It may or may not have favorable effect on a business unit. The Government may grant subsidies to one business or decrease the rates of excise or custom duty or the government may increase the rates of custom duty and excise duty, tax rates for another business. All the business enterprises frame their policies keeping in view the prevailing economic policies. Important economic policies of a country are as follows:-
   1. Monetary Policy:- The policy formulated by the central bank of a country to control the supply and the cost of money (rate of interest), in order to attain some specified objectives is known as Monetary Policy.
   2. Fiscal Policy:- It may be termed as budgetary policy. It is related with the income and expenditure of a country. Fiscal Policy works as an instrument in economic and social growth of a country. It is framed by the government of a country and it deals with taxation, government expenditure, borrowings, deficit financing and management of public debts in an economy.

3. Foreign Trade Policy:- It also affects the different business units differently. E.g. if restrictive import policy has been adopted by the government then it will prevent the domestic business units from foreign competition and if the liberal import policy has been adopted by the government then it will affect the domestic products in other way.
4. Foreign Investment Policy:- The policy related to the investment by the foreigners in a country is known as Foreign Investment Policy. If the government has adopted liberal investment policy then it will lead to more inflow of foreign capital in the country which ultimately results in more industrialization and growth in the country.
5. Industrial Policy:- Industrial policy of a country promotes and regulates the industrialization in the country. It is framed by government. The government from time to time issues principals and guidelines under the industrial policy of the country.

7. Global/International Economic Environment:- The role of international economic environment is increasing day by day. If any business enterprise is involved in foreign trade, then it is influenced by not only its own country economic environment but also the economic environment of the country from/to which it is importing or exporting goods. There are various rules and guidelines for these trades which are issued by many organizations like World Bank, WTO, United Nations etc.

A brief account of important environmental factor are :-

Political Environment

The political environment including the characteristics and policies of the potical parties. The nature of the constitution system encompassing the economic and business policies and regulations are among the factors of almost importance in the markets selection and business strategy formulation. Until the political and economic changes in the late 1980s and in the early 1990s in the Eastern Europe and U.S.S.R, these countries were a separate block themselves with several common characteristics. Private enterprises were very limited and State trading, particularly counter trade, was the rule. There were a lot of restriction on import and foreign business.

In the past, public sector was assigned a very important role in many non-communist particularly the developing countries too. In, India, for instance, before the policy changes of 1991, 17 of the most important industries were exclusively reserved for the public sector., the public sector was to pay a leading role in important industries. Thus, the industrial policy of India which wanted the public sector to gain control over the commanding heights of the economy limited the scope of the private enterprise, both domestic and foreign.

There are also wide variation in the policies and regulations regarding the conduct of the business. For instance, certain trade practices or promotion methods and strategy allowed in some countries may be regarded as unfair by laws of some other countries. In many countries there is a lot of restriction on the use of the media. Radio and television in particular, are state monopoly or under strict state control in a number of countries.

No matter how attractive the economic prospects of a particular country or region are, doing business there might prove to be financially disastrous if the host government(s) inflict(s) heavy financial penalties on a company or if unanticipated events in the political arena lead to the loss of income-generating assets. The political environment in which the firm operates (or plan to operate) will have a significant impact on a company's international marketing activities. The greater the level of involvement in a foreign markets, the greater the need to monitor the political climate of the countries business is conducted. Changes in government often result in changes in policy and attitudes towards foreign business. Bearing in mind that a foreign company operates in a host country at the discretion of the government concerned, the government can either encourage foreign activities by offering attractive opportunities for investment and trade, or discourage its activities by imposing restrictions such as import quotas, etc. An exporter that is continuously aware of shifts in government attitude, will be able to adapt export marketing strategies accordingly.

Nearly all governments today play active roles in their countries' economies. Although evident to a greater or lesser extent in most countries, government ownership of economic activities is still prevalent in the former centrally planned economies, as well as in certain developing countries which lack a sufficiently well developed private sector to support a free market system

The implications of government ownership to a company marketing abroad might be that certain sectors of the foreign market are the exclusive preserve of government enterprise or that the company is obliged to sell directly to a state trading organisation. In either case, the company's influence on the market is greatly reduced. Similarly, if an exporter is seeking to establish a subsidiary in a country where there is a high degree of state influence over the factors of production, the investor should bear in mind that marketing activities in the country concerned may be restricted and that the so-called controllable elements of the marketing mix will be less controllable.

Of primary concern to an exporter should be the stability of the target country's political environment. A loss of confidence in this respect could lead to a company having to reduce its operations in the market or to withdraw from the market altogether. One of the surest indicators of political instability is a frequent change in regime. Although a change in government need not be accompanied by violence, it often heralds a change in policy towards business, particularly international business. Such a development could impact harshly on a firms long-term international marketing program me.

Reflected in a government's attitudes and policies towards foreign business are its ideas about how best to promote national interest in the light of the country's economic and political resources and objectives. Foreign products and investment seen to be vital to the growth and development of the economy often receive favorable treatment from the government in the form of reduced tax, exemption from quotas, etc. On the other hand, products considered by a government to be non-essential, undesirable, or a threat to local industry are frequently subjected to a variety of import restrictions such as quotas and tariffs. It is also important to be aware of the nature of the relationship between South Africa and the foreign target market. This was a major consideration during South Africa's political isolation. Fortunately, South Africa's international relations have normalized and today South Africa is viewed very favorably, from a political perspective, by the rest of the world.

The technological environment

Technology can be defined as the method or technique for converting inputs to outputs in accomplishing a specific task. Thus, the terms 'method' and 'technique' refer not only to the knowledge but also to the skills and the means for accomplishing a task. Technological innovation, then, refers to the increase in knowledge, the improvement in skills, or the discovery of a new or improved means that extends people's ability to achieve a given task.

Technology can be classified in several ways. For example, blueprints, machinery, equipment and other capital goods are sometimes referred to as hard technology while soft technology includes management know-how, finance, marketing and administrative techniques. When a relatively primitive technology is used in the production process, the technology is usually referred to as labor-intensive. A highly advanced technology, on the other hand, is generally termed capital-intensive.

Changes in the technological environment have had some of the most dramatic effects on business. A company may be thoroughly committed to a particular type of technology, and may have made major investments in equipment and training only to see a new, more innovative and cost-effective technology emerge. Indeed, the managing director of a multinational organisation manufacturing heavy machinery once said that the hardest part of his job had nothing to do with unions, pay or products, but with whether or not to spend money on the latest technologically improved equipment.

Computer technology has had an enormous impact on education and health care, to name but two areas affected. The advancements in medical technology, for example, have contributed to longevity in many societies. In addition, the introduction of robots in many factories has reduced the need for labor, and the use of VCR's and microcomputers has become commonplace in many homes and businesses.Unfortunately, there is a negative side to technological progress. The introduction of nuclear weapons, for example, has made the destruction of the human race a frightening possibility. In addition, factories using modern technologies have polluted both air and water and contributed to various environmental and health-related problems.

Technology is a critical factor in economic development. Because of the advances of international communication, the increasing economic interdependence of nations, and the serious scarcity of vital natural resources, the transfer of technology has become an important preoccupation of both industrialized and developing countries. For many industrialized countries, the changes in the technological environment over the last 30 years have been immense particularly in such areas as chemicals, drugs, and electronics. It is vital that organisations stay abreast of these changes - not only because this will allow them to incorporate new and innovative designs into their products, but also because it will give them a firmer base from which to anticipate and counteract competition from other organisations.

When the Gillette company developed a superior stainless steel razor blade, it feared that such a superior product might mean fewer replacements and sales. Thus, the company decided not to market it. Instead, Gillette sold the technology to Wilkinson, a British garden tool manufacturer, thinking that Wilkinson would use the technology only in the production of garden tools. When Wilkinson Sword Blades were introduced and sold quickly, Gillette understood the magnitude of its mistake.

The transfer of technology is essential for attaining a high level of industrial capability and competitiveness. Multinational corporations are playing an increasingly important role in technology transfer because they invest abroad to expand production, marketing and research activities. There is also a growing consciousness amongst governments of the need to increase technology transfer to the developing countries to help stabilize their economic and social conditions.

In spite of the many differences in social, political, cultural, geographic and economic conditions, there are some common characteristics in the technological environments of developing countries. The most common technology transfer from industrialized to developing countries has been in agriculture and health care. As a result of improved health care systems, infant mortality rates have been cut while the incidence of once common diseases such as malaria and typhoid has been reduced in Latin America, south-east Asia and Africa (although the incidents of the AIDS virus has increased alarmingly). Similarly, agricultural technology has increased agricultural productivity in Brazil, India and elsewhere. However, in most developing countries, technology has made little impact on the productive systems, income distribution and living conditions of the majority of the population.

Technology transfer is a complex, time-consuming and costly process, and the successful implementation of such a process demands continuous communication and co-operation between the parties involved. Furthermore, technology transfer cannot be effective if it experiences conflict with the economic and social needs of the recipient country. The agricultural development of north-eastern Brazil, for example, was largely financed by international banks and financial organisations in the 1960's. Much of this region had been inhabited by Brazilian aborigines but it was owned by a small number of wealthy landowners. The introduction of large-scale mechanical agricultural technology in areas of the tropical rain forest of the Amazon has caused serious environmental damage such as erosion of tropical topsoil and the destruction of the natural environment of numerous birds and animals, and has displaced a large number of the local inhabitants of the forests.

Technology transfer may become a serious source of conflict between donor and recipient countries. The recipient country may feel that the donor is trying to dominate it through technology, capital and production. Dependence on foreign technology can be viewed as a serious threat to economic independence. Countries that export technology may experience different problems. For the seller of technology, the technology transfer can result in unemployment in the home country and future loss of technological superiority. For example, Japan transferred modern steel production technology to South Korea in the early 1970's. As labor and production costs in Japan increased, the Korean steel industry began to take over a significant portion of the previously Japanese-controlled international market. Some Japanese executives are now complaining that the cost of technology transfer has been much greater than the income received through the sale of technology.

Technology can be transferred from person to person, industry to industry and government to government, although the government of any country generally plays the most important role in facilitating or impeding the transfer process. Contacts amongst students from different countries are also a means of technology transfer as are journals, books, technical and professional publications, trade magazines and product pamphlets. Furthermore, multinational corporations play an important role in technology transfer by transferring information and technology from the parent company to subsidiaries in other countries, training foreign employees, etc.

Many companies in advanced countries have considered the developing countries as a market for their obsolete technology. Several developing countries even import second hand plant and machinery.

There is often a time lag between countries in the adoption and diffusion of technologies. The developing countries generally lag behind the developed ones. Even among the developed countries the technology absorption is not simultaneous and similar. The lag has, however, been diminishing in several cases. Black and white television sets extensively penetrated households in the United States nearly a dozen years before they reached comparable number of viewers in Europe and Japan. With color television, the time lag fell to about five to six years for Japan and a few more for Europe. With video cassette recorders, the difference was only three of four years but this time Europe and Japan led the way, the United States, with its focus on cable TV followed. With the compact disc, household penetration rates even up after only one year. Now with MTV available by satellite across Europe there is no lag at all.

Technological environment of the use facilities etc. also have very important implication for business. For example, advances in the technologies of food processing packaging, and preservation, transportation etc. have facilitated product improvements and introduction and have considerably improved the marketability of products. The advent of microwave ovens has given a new dimension to food marketing. In the US by the end of 20th century nearly 90% of the households were using microwave ovens. Experts predict that by the turn of the century, in-home preparation of the main evening meal will take only fifteen minutes. In early days, anything microwaveable was OK. Now consumers are looking for more quality and even more convenience.

Intermediate technology, which often means a technology which combines elements of traditional technology with elements of modern technology gained importance in the developing countries. Thus, the sophisticated capital intensive technologies in use in the developed countries are not acceptable in some sectors in several of the developing countries.

The physical environment

Although the physical environment is not considered one of the core components of the SLEPT factors, it is an environment that can impact upon your success in exports and consequently needs to be considered.

A country's territorial size, geographical location, natural resources, climate, rivers, lakes and forests constitute its physical environment. The physical environment influences political and economic activities, shapes cultural characteristics such as language and religion, and determines land usage, transportation, and commercial flows.

When planning international marketing activities, the possible impact of the physical environment should take into account. For example:

- Population distribution will be affected by topography (i.e. a country's rivers, mountains, deserts, etc.) and climate - people tend to settle where the climate is temperate, and there is an adequate supply of water.

- Certain climatic conditions may dictate adaptations to the product - some glues and oils, for example, will not function in very cold climates.
- Climate should also influence the arrangements made in respect of packaging (in the marketing context) and protective packing for the purposes of safeguarding the product while it is in transit or in storage. Products which are particularly vulnerable to climatic conditions, are those that are adversely affected by extremes in temperature or excessive humidity changes (fruits being transported to hot climates or across the equator, for example).
- Abnormal weather conditions (e.g. typhoon season in Asia) can disrupt the transportation of export products while unforeseen changes in the weather can threaten companies which produce seasonal goods.
- Topography will influence the routing of goods and the choice of transport mode, which in turn will affect cost and thus impact on the price offered to the buyer

Social Environments

The social and cultural environment encompassing the religious aspects language; customs, tradition and beliefs, taste and preferences; social satisfaction; social institution buying and consumption habits etc are all important factors for business. What the people liked of one culture many not be liked by those of some other culture. One of the important reason for the failure of numbers of company in International markets is their failure to understand the cultural environment of these markets and it to suitably formulate their business strategies. There are also several other demographic trend which has implication for business strategic formulation . While some of these trends are confined to certain country only . The strength of other trends vary greatly between nation, instance – the number of unmarried couple living together has risen in the two decades ended 1990 from about half a million to 2.5 million in the US, such a thing is quite unheard of in several country like India. Similarly the high divorce rate created over a million single parent family in the US most of the divorced remarry, leading to the emergence of a large number of blended families. This is not the situation in several country where people attach more sanctity to marriage so that the marriage lasts lifelong. In countries where the culture is that a marriage relationship is to last life long, a company may advertise that its durable product will be a lifelong companion like one's life partner, but to use such a promotional theme in a culture where divorce rate is high and even un married partnership which normally last for only for short period is common, will a blunder, The social environment markets differ vastly. Even within a nation, culture diversity may be very significant. It is essential to understand these differences to formulate successful business strategies

Trading Environment

International trade accounts for the major part of the international business. Certain other forms of international business, like international investment, may also be affected by international trade. The international environment is, therefore, a very important factor affecting international business. The trading environment affects not only the exports and imports but also other factors such as international investment and financial flows. The international trading environment includes important factors such as trade barrier, trade agreement, trading blocs, cartels and multinational trade negotiations.

Trade Barriers

One of the most important features of the International trading environment is the proliferation of the trade barrier. The main objective of imposing trade barrier are to protect domestic industries from foreign competition, to promote indigenous research and development to conserve the foreign exchange resources of the country, to make the balance of payment position favorable to curve conspicuous consumption, to mobilized revenue for the government and to discriminate against certain countries. After the second world war there was progressive liberalization of trade by the developed countries. Successive round of negotitiation in the GATT have cut tariff on trade in manufacturers from an average level of 40 % in 1947 to about 3% in the 1990s in the industrial countries. Even though the process of elimination of the tariff barriers has continued, since around the mid 1970s the liberalization trend in the developed countries has been replaced by a growing protect ionism. A number of problems l ike the currency crises, oil crises, debt crises recession, high unemployment and trade deficits produced and atmosphere in which demands for protection increase dramatically. Added to this has been the growing competition from Japan and the newly industrializing countries. As response to this the developed countries have increased their non-tariff barriers (NTBs) . In addition to the hard core NTBs such as quotas ,voluntary exports restraints, multifibre arrangement (MFA etc), this includes measures such as price restraint and health and safety regulation .The exports of developing countries have been hit much more than those of the developed ones by such protectionism.

Barriers to exporting

There are some traders that would argue that exporting is no different to doing business in the local market. It is all about doing good business and making the right decisions. The reality is, however, that the foreign marketplace is often very different from that in South Africa.

Foreign environment as a barrier to trade

To begin with, there are social, cultural, economic, legal, political, technical and physical differences between South African and the rest of the world. After all, other countries speak different languages (e.g. German, French or Chinese), they use different currencies (such as the dollar or the yen), they adhere to different standards (think of the 110V power supply in the US), they follow different laws (such as Islamic law) and they are often governed by different politics (such as communism or socialism). These factors all contribute to making exporting more difficult - that is, they are barriers to exporting. These factors are all related to the different environments that you will encounter abroad and we have discussed them in more detail a separate section -

Besides for the different environments that you will encounter abroad (which we have said are barriers to trade in their own right), there are also tariff and non-tariff barriers to trade that you should be aware of. These are discussed below:

Tariff barriers

International trade increases the number of goods that domestic consumers can choose from, decreases the cost of those goods through increased competition, and allows domestic industries to ship their products abroad. While all of these seem beneficial, free trade isn't widely accepted as completely beneficial to all parties. This article will examine why this is the case, and look at how countries react to the variety of factors that attempt to influence trade.

The main objectives of imposing trade barriers are to protect domestic industries from foreign competition, to promote indigenous research and development, to conserve the foreign exchange resources consumption, to mobilise revenue for the government and to discriminate against certain countries.

Tariff

In simplest terms, a tariff is a tax. It adds to the cost of imported goods and is one of several trade policies that a country can enact. Tariff in international trade refers to the duties or taxes imposed on internationally traded goods when they cross the national boarders. With the recent economic liberalization across the world, many developing countries has reduced the tariff rate and NTBs as part of their trade libralisation. India has had one of the highest tariff in the world. The government, following the recommendation of the tax reforms committee steadily reduced the peak level of tariffs from over 300 % in 1991 in 50 in 1995, further imports duties on capital goods project imports basic feeds stocks for petrochemical etc. The government proposes the further reduce the average and maximum tariff and simplify and rationalize the tariff structure in order to bring the country tariff structure in line with those of other developing countries.

Tariffs and Trade Barriers Used

Tariffs are often created to protect infant industries and developing economies, but are also used by more advanced economies with developed industries. Here are five of the top reasons tariffs are used:

- *Protecting Domestic Employment*

  The levying of tariffs is often highly politicized. The possibility of increased competition from imported goods can threaten domestic industries. These domestic companies may fire workers or shift production abroad to cut costs, which means higher unemployment and a less happy electorate. The unemployment argument often shifts to domestic industries complaining about cheap foreign labor, and how poor working conditions and lack of regulation allow foreign companies to produce goods more cheaply. In economics, however, countries will continue to produce goods until they no longer have a comparative advantage (not to be confused with an absolute advantage).

- *Protecting Consumers*

  A government may levy a tariff on products that it feels could endanger its population. For example, South Korea may place a tariff on imported beef from the United States if it thinks that the goods could be tainted with disease.

- *Infant Industries*

  The use of tariffs to protect infant industries can be seen by the Import Substitution Industrialization (ISI) strategy employed by many developing nations. The government of a developing economy will levy tariffs on imported goods in industries in which it wants to foster growth. This increases the prices of imported goods and creates a domestic market for domestically produced goods, while protecting those industries from being forced out by more competitive pricing. It decreases unemployment and allows developing countries to shift from agricultural products to finished goods.

  Criticisms of this sort of protectionist strategy revolve around the cost of subsidizing the development of infant industries. If an industry develops without competition, it could wind up producing lower quality goods, and the subsidies required to keep the state-backed industry afloat could sap economic growth.

- *National Security*

  Barriers are also employed by developed countries to protect certain industries that are deemed strategically important, such as those supporting national security. Defense industries are often viewed as vital to state interests, and often enjoy significant levels of protection. For example, while both Western Europe and the United States are industrialized, both are very protective of defense-oriented companies.

- *Retaliation*

  Countries may also set tariffs as a retaliation technique if they think that a trading partner has not played by the rules. For example, if France believes that the United States has allowed its wine producers to call its domestically produced sparkling wines "Champagne" (a) name specific to the Champagne region of France) for too long, it may levy a tariff on imported meat from the United States. If the U.S. agrees to crack down on the improper labeling, France is likely to stop its retaliation. Retaliation can also be employed if a trading partner goes against the government's foreign policy objectives.

Types of Tariffs and Trade Barriers

The NTBs are two categories the first categories includes those which are generally used by developing countries to prevent foreign exchange out flow or result from their chosen strategy for their economic development. These are mostly traditional NTBs such as import licensing, import quotas, foreign exchange regulation and canalization of imports .

The second categories are those which are mostly used by developed economies to protect domestic industries which has lost international competitiveness and which are politically sensitive for governments of these countries.

There are several types of tariffs and barriers that a government can employ:

- Specific tariffs
- Ad valorem tariffs
- Licenses
- Import quotas
- Voluntary export restraints
- Local content requirements

Specific Tariffs

A fixed fee levied on one unit of an imported good is referred to as a specific tariff. This tariff can vary according to the type of good imported. For example, a country could levy a $15 tariff on each pair of shoes imported, but levy a $300 tariff on each computer imported.

Ad Valorem Tariffs

The phrase *ad valorem* is Latin for "according to value", and this type of tariff is levied on a good based on a percentage of that good's value. An example of an ad valorem tariff would be a 15% tariff levied by Japan on U.S. automobiles. The 15% is a price increase on the value of the automobile, so a $10,000 vehicle now costs $11,500 to Japanese consumers. This price increase protects domestic producers from being undercut, but also keeps prices artificially high for Japanese car shoppers.

Non-tariff barriers to trade include

Licenses

A license is granted to a business by the government, and allows the business to import a certain type of good into the country. For example, there could be a restriction on imported cheese, and licenses would be granted to certain companies allowing them to act as importers. This creates a restriction on competition, and increases prices faced by consumers.

Import Quotas

An import quota is a restriction placed on the amount of a particular good that can be imported. This sort of barrier is often associated with the issuance of licenses. For example, a country may place a quota on the volume of imported citrus fruit that is allowed.

Voluntary Export Restraints (VER)

This type of trade barrier is "voluntary" in that it is created by the exporting country rather than the importing one. A voluntary export restraint is usually levied at the behest of the importing country, and could be accompanied by a reciprocal VER. For example, Brazil could place a VER on the exportation of sugar to Canada, based on a request by Canada. Canada could then place a VER on the exportation of coal to Brazil. This increases the price of both coal and sugar, but protects the domestic industries.

Local Content Requirement

Instead of placing a quota on the number of goods that can be imported, the government can require that a certain percentage of a good be made domestically. The restriction can be a percentage of the good itself, or a percentage of the value of the good. For example, a restriction on the import of computers might say that 25% of the pieces used to make the computer are made domestically, or can say that 15% of the value of the good must come from domestically produced components.

In the final section we'll examine who benefits from tariffs and how they affect the price of goods.

The benefits of tariffs are uneven. Because a tariff is a tax, the government will see increased revenue as imports enter the domestic market. Domestic industries also benefit from a reduction in competition, since import prices are artificially inflated. Unfortunately for consumers - both individual consumers and businesses - higher import prices mean higher prices for goods. If the price of steel is inflated due to tariffs, individual consumers pay more for products using steel, and businesses pay more for steel that they use to make goods. In short, tariffs and trade barriers tend to be pro-producer and anti-consumer.

The effect of tariffs and trade barriers on businesses, consumers and the government shifts over time. In the short run, higher prices for goods can reduce consumption by individual consumers and by businesses. During this time period, businesses will profit and the government will see an increase in revenue from duties. In the long term, businesses may see a decline in efficiency due to a lack of competition, and may also see a reduction in profits due to the emergence of substitutes for their products. For the government, the long-term effect of subsidies is an increase in the demand for public services, since increased prices, especially in foodstuffs, leave less disposable income.

How Do Tariffs Affect Prices

Tariffs increase the prices of imported goods. Because of this, domestic producers are not forced to reduce their prices from increased competition, and domestic consumers are left paying higher prices as a result. Tariffs also reduce efficiencies by allowing companies that would not exist in a more competitive market to remain open.

Figure 2.1 illustrates the effects of world trade without the presence of a tariff. In the graph, DS means domestic supply and DD means domestic demand. The price of goods at home is found at price P, while the world price is found at P*. At a lower price, domestic consumers will consume Qw worth of goods, but because the home country can only produce up to Qd, it must import Qw-Qd worth of goods.

When a tariff or other price-increasing policy is put in place, the effect is to increase prices and limit the volume of imports. In Figure 2.2, price increases from the non-tariff P* to P'. Because price has increased, more domestic companies are willing to produce the good, so Qd moves right. This also shifts Qw left. The overall effect is a reduction in imports, increased domestic production and higher consumer prices. (To learn more about the movement of equilibrium due to changes in supply and demand,

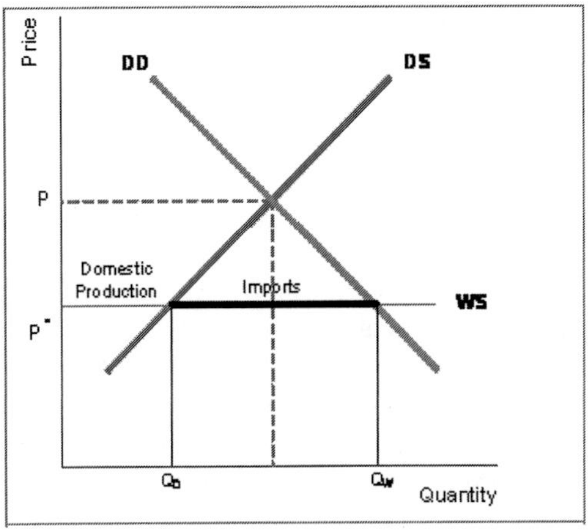

Figure 2.1. Price without the influence of a tariff

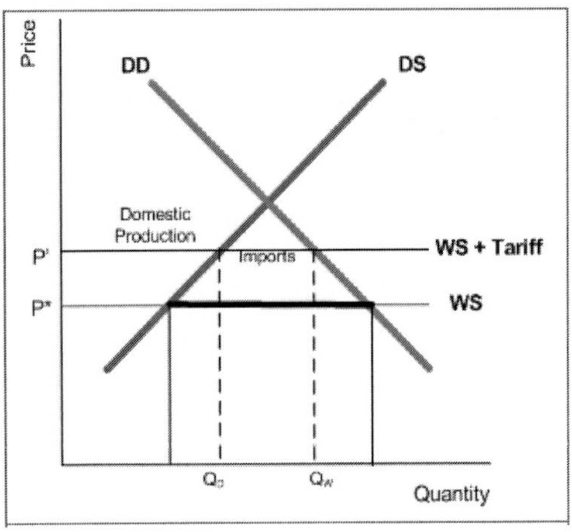

Figure 2.2. Price under the effects of a tariff

A tariff is a tax that is placed on imported goods by governments. Governments do this for several reasons:

- They may wish to restrict the amount of imported goods coming into the country in order to protect or encourage a positive trade balance. If a country imports more than it exports, it will have to use valuable foreign exchange to pay for these goods - this is referred to as a negative trade balance or a trade deficit. Since a country's foreign exchange holdings represents direct wealth to the country, as more foreign exchange leaves the country to pay for imported goods so the country becomes relatively poorer. Governments try to prevent this by placing tariffs (taxes) on imported goods.

- They may wish to protect a local industry from foreign competition. This is often done where the industry in question is still very young and susceptible to foreign competition. The government will then place a tax on imported goods that compete with goods being produced by that industry, thus making these imported goods more expensive compared with locally produced goods. In so doing, the expectation is that consumers will buy more of the locally produced goods thereby helping the industry to grow. Once the industry is better established the intention is normally to withdraw the tariff so that the local industry can compete normally with foreign competitors.
- Some countries introduce tariffs in order to generate additional revenues for the country. This is often done in the case of luxury goods.

Duties are calculated

Tariffs may be calculated in different ways. They are usually either ad valorem duties or specific duties.

Specific duty - A specific duty is usually levied on the quantity (measured by weight or volume) of imported goods (e.g. R1/kg or R1/cubic meter)

Ad valorem duty - An ad valorem duty is levied as a percentage duty on the value of imported goods (e.g. 15% on the CIF value of the imported goods).

The duties levied in a particular country

Clearly, every country applies a different set of tariffs on its imported goods. Some countries have very low overall duties, others a very high set of duties. Unfortunately, there is still no readily available source of country import tariffs available on the Web. Nevertheless, we have listed the best sources of country tariffs currently available on the Web for you to visit. There is also a link to the South African duty structure for your reference.

Tariffs and Modern Trade

The role tariffs play in international trade has declined in modern times. One of the primary reasons for the decline is the introduction of international organizations designed to improve free trade, such as the World Trade Organization (WTO). Such organizations make it more difficult for a country to levy tariffs and taxes on imported goods, and can reduce the likelihood of retaliatory taxes. Because of this, countries have shifted to non-tariff barriers, such as quotas and export restraints. Organizations like the WTO attempt to reduce production and consumption distortions created by tariffs. These distortions are the result of domestic producers making goods due to inflated prices, and consumers purchasing fewer goods because prices have increased. (To learn about the WTO's efforts,

Since the 1930s, many developed countries have reduced tariffs and trade barriers, which has improved global integration and brought about globalization. Multilateral agreements between governments increase the likelihood of tariff reduction, while enforcement on binding agreements reduces uncertainty.

The Bottom Line

Free trade benefits consumers through increased choice and reduced prices, but because the global economy brings with it uncertainty, many governments impose tariffs and other trade barriers to protect industry. There is a delicate balance between the pursuit of efficiencies and the government's need to ensure low unemployment.

NTBS impact

Today they are not confines to the labor intensive products where the developing countries have advantage but also cover sophisticated products. Japan and the newly industrializing countries like Mangolia, S.Korea are among the most affected countries by NBTs. The developing country export are also significantly affected by them. However, the NTBs have come to affect the intra- OECA (i.e, trade between developed economics) also. The NTBs tend to offset favorable effects of the GATT/WTO negotiations on trade liberalizations like reductions in the average level of tariffs.

As a matter of fact, several advanced countries like the USA who were high priests of free trade increasingly resort to several NTBs, particularly against the developing countries and certain countries like Japan. NTBs seriously affect many exporting countries . As mention above, developing country export to developed countries face considerable NTBs. In several cases, the impact is very sever. Ntbs also cause diversion of production and exports. For instance, some Indian Textile firms decided to set up manufacturing Unit in Nepal in order to circumvent MFA quota control on their exports from India and to avoid the local costs of purchasing added quota right.

Non-tariff barriers

Any barrier to doing business over international borders and that is not a tariff barrier, is classified as a non-tariff barrier. As the various environments that you are likely to encounter in foreign markets represent barriers in their own right, they are also therefore a form of non-tariff barrier

Non-tariff barriers to trade (NTBs) are trade barriers that restrict import but are not in the usual form of a tariff. Some common examples of NTB's are anti-dumping measures and countervailing duties, which, although they are called "non-tariff" barriers, have the effect of tariffs once they are enacted.

Their use has risen sharply after the WTO rules led to a very significant reduction in tariff use. Some non-tariff trade barriers are expressly permitted in very limited circumstances, when they are deemed necessary to protect health, safety, or sanitation, or to protect depletable natural resources. In other forms, they are criticized as a means to evade free trade rules such as those of the World Trade Organization (WTO), the European Union (EU), or North American Free Trade Agreement (NAFTA) that restrict the use of tariffs.

Some of non-tariff barriers are not directly related to foreign economic regulations, but nevertheless they have a significant impact on foreign-economic activity and foreign trade between countries.

Trade between countries is referred to trade in goods, services and factors of production. Non-tariff barriers to trade include import quotas, special licenses, unreasonable standards for the quality of goods, bureaucratic delays at customs, export restrictions, limiting the activities of state trading, export subsidies, countervailing duties, technical barriers to trade, sanitary and phyto-sanitary measures, rules of origin, etc. Sometimes in this list they include macroeconomic measures affecting trade.

Six Types of Non-Tariff Barriers to Trade

1. Specific Limitations on Trade:
    1. Quotas
    2. Import licensing requirements
    3. Proportion restrictions of foreign to domestic goods (local content requirements)
    4. Minimum import price limits
    5. Embargoes
2. Customs and Administrative Entry Procedures:
    1. Valuation systems
    2. Anti-dumping practices
    3. Tariff classifications
    4. Documentation requirements
    5. Fees
3. Standards:
    1. Standard disparities

   2. Intergovernmental acceptances of testing methods and standards
   3. Packaging, labeling, and marking
4. Government Participation in Trade:
   1. Government procurement policies
   2. Export subsidies
   3. Countervailing duties
   4. Domestic assistance programs
5. Charges on imports:
   1. Prior import deposit subsidies
   2. Administrative fees
   3. Special supplementary duties
   4. Import credit discrimination
   5. Variable levies
   6. Border taxes
6. Others:
   1. Voluntary export restraints
   2. Orderly marketing agreements

Non-Tariff Barriers to Trade

Non-tariff barriers to trade can be:

- Import bans
- General or product-specific quotas
- Rules of Origin
- Quality conditions imposed by the importing country on the exporting countries
- Sanitary and phyto-sanitary conditions
- Packaging conditions
- Labeling conditions
- Product standards
- Complex regulatory environment
- Determination of eligibility of an exporting country by the importing country
- Determination of eligibility of an exporting establishment (firm, company) by the importing country.
- Additional trade documents like Certificate of Origin, Certificate of Authenticity etc.
- Occupational safety and health regulation

- Employment law
- Import license
- State subsidies, procurement, trading state ownership
- Export subsidies
- Fixation of a minimum import price
- Product classification
- Quota shares
- Foreign exchange market controls and multiplicity
- Inadequate infrastructures
- "Buy national" policy
- Over-valued currency
- Intellectual property laws (patents, copyright)
- Restrictive licenses
- Seasonal import regimes
- Corrupt and/or lengthy customs procedures

Types of Non-Tariff Barriers

There are several different variants of division of non-tariff barriers. Some scholars divide between internal taxes, administrative barriers, health and sanitary regulations and government procurement policies. Others divide non-tariff barriers into more categories such as specific limitations on trade, customs and administrative entry procedures, standards, government participation in trade, charges on import, and other categories. We choose traditional classification of non-tariff barriers, according to which they are divided into 3 principal categories.

The first category includes methods to directly import restrictions for protection of certain sectors of national industries: licensing and allocation of import quotas, antidumping and countervailing duties, import deposits, so-called voluntary export restraints, countervailing duties, the system of minimum import prices, etc. Under second category follow methods that are not directly aimed at restricting foreign trade and more related to the administrative bureaucracy, whose actions, however, restrict trade, for example: customs procedures, technical standards and norms, sanitary and veterinary standards, requirements for labeling and packaging, bottling, etc. The third category consists of methods that are not directly aimed at restricting the import or promoting the export, but the effects of which often lead to this result.

The non-tariff barriers can include wide variety of restrictions to trade. Here are some examples of the "popular" NTBs.

- Licenses

Licensing requirements - Some goods may only be imported only if they have been issued with import licences by the authorities (such as in the case of armaments). While licensing in itself should not hinder the export process, some countries issue only a limited number of licenses (thereby excluding late entrants from the market), or they may make the licensing process so cumbersome as to make it impossible or extremely difficult to obtain the license.

The most common instruments of direct regulation of imports (and sometimes export) are licenses and quotas. Almost all industrialized countries apply these non-tariff methods. The license system requires that a state (through specially authorized office) issues permits for foreign trade transactions of import and export commodities included in the lists of licensed merchandises. Product licensing can take many forms and procedures. The main types of licenses are general license that permits unrestricted importation or exportation of goods included in the lists for a certain period of time; and one-time license for a certain product importer.(exporter) to import (or export). One-time license indicates a quantity of goods, its cost, its country of origin (or destination), and in some cases also customs point through which import (or export) of goods should be carried out. The use of licensing systems as an instrument for foreign trade regulation is based on a number of international level standards agreements. In particular, these agreements include some provisions of the General Agreement on Tariffs and Trade and the Agreement on Import Licensing Procedures, concluded under the GATT (GATT).

Quotas

Quotas are defined as a specific unit or currency limit applied to a particular type of good. Quotes are thus quantitative restrictions applied to the import of goods and have the effect of either barring goods from a market altogether, or increasing the price of the goods in that market. Licensing of foreign trade is closely related to quantitative restrictions – quotas - on imports and exports of certain goods. A quota is a limitation in value or in physical terms, imposed on import and export of certain goods for a certain period of time. This category includes global quotas in respect to specific countries, seasonal quotas, and so-called "voluntary" export restraints. Quantitative controls on foreign trade transactions carried out through one-time license. Quantitative restriction on imports and exports is a direct administrative form of government regulation of foreign trade. Licenses and quotas limit the independence of enterprises with a regard to entering foreign markets, narrowing the range of countries, which may be entered into transaction for certain commodities, regulate the number and range of goods permitted for import and export. However, the system of licensing and quota imports and exports, establishing firm control over foreign trade in certain goods, in many cases turns out to be more flexible and effective than economic instruments of foreign trade regulation. This can be explained by the fact, that licensing and quota systems are an important instrument of trade regulation of the vast majority of the world.

The consequence of this trade barrier is normally reflected in the consumers' loss because of higher prices and limited selection of goods as well as in the companies that employ the imported materials in the production process, increasing their costs. An import quota can be unilateral, levied by the country without negotiations with exporting country, and bilateral or multilateral, when it is imposed after negotiations and agreement with exporting country. An export quota is a restricted amount of goods that can leave the country. There are different reasons for imposing of export quota by the country, which can be the guarantee of the supply of the products that are in shortage in the domestic market, manipulation of the prices on the international level, and the control of goods strategically important for the country. In some cases, the importing countries request exporting countries to impose voluntary export restraints.

Voluntary export restraint

In the past decade, a widespread practice of concluding agreements on the "voluntary" export restrictions and the establishment of import minimum prices imposed by leading Western nations upon weaker in economic or political sense exporters. The specifics of these types of restrictions is the establishment of unconventional techniques when the trade barriers of importing country, are introduced at the border of the exporting and not importing country. Thus, the agreement on "voluntary" export restraints is imposed on the exporter under the threat of sanctions to limit the export of certain goods in the importing country. Similarly, the establishment of minimum import prices should be strictly observed by the exporting firms in contracts with the importers of the country that has set such prices. In the case of reduction of export prices below the minimum level, the importing country imposes anti-dumping duty which could lead to withdrawal from the market. "Voluntary" export agreements affect trade in textiles, footwear, dairy products, consumer electronics, cars, machine tools, etc.

Problems arise when the quotas are distributed between countries, because it is necessary to ensure that products from one country are not diverted in violation of quotas set out in second country. Import quotas are not necessarily designed to protect domestic producers. For example, Japan, maintains quotas on many agricultural products it does not produce. Quotas on imports is a leverage when negotiating the sales of Japanese exports, as well as avoiding excessive dependence on any other country in respect of necessary food, supplies of which may decrease in case of bad weather or political conditions.

Export quotas can be set in order to provide domestic consumers with sufficient stocks of goods at low prices, to prevent the depletion of natural resources, as well as to increase export prices by restricting supply to foreign markets. Such restrictions (through agreements on various types of goods) allow producing countries to use quotas for such commodities as coffee and oil; as the result, prices for these products increased in importing countries.

Embargo

Embargo is a specific type of quotas prohibiting the trade. As well as quotas, embargoes may be imposed on imports or exports of particular goods, regardless of destination, in respect of certain goods supplied to specific countries, or in respect of all goods shipped to certain countries. Although the embargo is usually introduced for political purposes, the consequences, in essence, could be economic.

Standards

Sanctions/embargoes/boycotts - Sanctions, embargoes and boycotts represent an absolute prohibition on the purchase and import of goods from the sanctioned/embargoed/boycotted country. In the apartheid era, South Africa was subject to sanctions and boycotts from many of its former trading partners.

Standards take a special place among non-tariff barriers. Countries usually impose standards on classification, labeling and testing of products in order to be able to sell domestic products, but also to block sales of products of foreign manufacture. These standards are sometimes entered under the pretext of protecting the safety and health of local populations.

Other non-tariff barriers include the following:

Customs and administrative entry procedures - These procedures, while they may be applied uniformly, are often so cumbersome and complex that they represent a major trade restriction in their own right. What is more, local manufacturers within the target market are generally not subject to the same procedures (except in instances where they may be using imported raw materials or components), and this places the exporter at a disadvantage compared to local firms.

Government participation in trade - It is quite common for governments to follow discriminatory public purchasing activities (i.e. that favor buying local) as an effective way to lock out international competitors.

Charges on imports – A few countries may apply port-of-entry taxes or levies on imported goods. The purpose of such a tax is usually to offset infrastructure costs at a port, for example, but such levies often stay in place long after their intended purpose has been achieved.

Exchange controls - One of the more complete forms of non-tariff barriers, exchange controls represent a government monopoly on all dealings in foreign exchange. South Africa is an example of a country that still applies exchange controls on its trading community. Local firms therefore have to obtain permission to buy the foreign exchange they need to import goods and services and exporters also need to pay their foreign exchange earnings back to the commercial banks within seven days of receiving such income. No company is allowed to hold foreign exchange without permission from the Reserve Bank.

Voluntary export restraints (VER) - A VER is a 'voluntary' agreement between an importing country (such as the US) and an exporting country (such as Japan, in the case of motor vehicles) that the exporting country will restrict the volume of exports of the goods in question (in this instance, motor vehicles). Although such agreements are supposedly voluntary (a "gentlemen's agreement"), they are generally agreed to under threat of stiffer quotas and/or tariffs being applied to the exporting country by the importing country. VERs may sometimes be referred to as orderly marketing agreements (OMA).

Differing product classification - Since the classification of a product according to the various customs' product categories will almost certainly impact on the duty that is applied to that imported good, exporters may occasionally be frustrated by customs authorities (who always have the final say) who classify their goods into a category that they exporter does not agree with. This classification may render the goods completely uncompetitive in the market.

Administrative and bureaucratic delays at the entrance

Among the methods of non-tariff regulation should be mentioned administrative and bureaucratic delays at the entrance which increase uncertainty and the cost of maintaining inventory.

Import deposits

Another example of foreign trade regulations is import deposits. Import deposits is a form of deposit, which the importer must pay the bank for a definite period of time (non-interest bearing deposit) in an amount equal to all or part of the cost of imported goods.

At the national level, administrative regulation of capital movements is carried out mainly within a framework of bilateral agreements, which include a clear definition of the legal regime, the procedure for the admission of investments and investors. It is determined by mode (fair and equitable, national, most-favored-nation), order of nationalization and compensation, transfer profits and capital repatriation and dispute resolution.

Foreign exchange restrictions and foreign exchange controls

Foreign exchange restrictions and foreign exchange controls occupy a special place among the non-tariff regulatory instruments of foreign economic activity. Foreign exchange restrictions constitute the regulation of transactions of residents and nonresidents with currency and other currency values. Also an important part of the mechanism of control of foreign economic activity is the establishment of the national currency against foreign currencies.

The transition from tariffs to non-tariff barriers

One of the reasons why industrialized countries have moved from tariffs to NTBs is the fact that developed countries have sources of income other than tariffs. Historically, in the formation of nation-states, governments had to get funding. They received it through the introduction of tariffs. This explains the fact that most developing countries still rely on tariffs as a way to finance their spending. Developed countries can afford not to depend on tariffs, at the same time developing NTBs as a possible way of international trade regulation. The second reason for the transition to NTBs is that these tariffs can be used to support weak industries or compensation of industries, which have been affected negatively by the reduction of tariffs. The third reason for the popularity of NTBs is the ability of interest groups to influence the process in the absence of opportunities to obtain government support for the tariffs.

Non-tariff barriers today

With the exception of export subsidies and quotas, NTBs are most similar to the tariffs. Tariffs for goods production were reduced during the eight rounds of negotiations in the WTO and the General Agreement on Tariffs and Trade (GATT). After lowering of tariffs, the principle of protectionism demanded the introduction of new NTBs such as technical barriers to trade (TBT). According to statements made at United Nations Conference on Trade and Development (UNCTAD, 2005), the use of NTBs, based on the amount and control of price levels has decreased significantly from 45% in 1994 to 15% in 2004, while use of other NTBs increased from 55% in 1994 to 85% in 2004.

Increasing consumer demand for safe and environment friendly products also have had their impact on increasing popularity of TBT. Many NTBs are governed by WTO agreements, which originated in the Uruguay Round (the TBT Agreement, SPS Measures Agreement, the Agreement on Textiles and Clothing), as well as GATT articles. NTBs in the field of services have become as important as in the field of usual trade.

Most of the NTB can be defined as protectionist measures, unless they are related to difficulties in the market, such as externalities and information asymmetries information asymmetries between consumers and producers of goods. An example of this is safety standards and labeling requirements.

The need to protect sensitive to import industries, as well as a wide range of trade restrictions, available to the governments of industrialized countries, forcing them to resort to use the NTB, and putting serious obstacles to international trade and world economic growth. Thus, NTBs can be referred as a "new" of protection which has replaced tariffs as an "old" form of protection.

India is actively pursuing bilateral /regional free trade arrangements as part of its trade policy. India has signed a Free Trade Agreement (FTA) with Singapore and with Thailand in 2003. It has also simultaneously signed a Free Trade Agreement with ASEAN. India signed a bilateral Free Trade Agreement with Sri Lanka in 2000. It is currently in the process of extending the existing Free Trade Agreement that would address the anomalies in the existing agreement and also broaden the scope of the FTA by including trade in services. India and Sri Lanka are also Members of the South Asian Association for Regional Co-operation (SAARC) which envisages the formation of a South Asian Free Trade Arrangement by 2006.How important are ASEAN and Sri Lanka in India's export basket? ASEAN has been a relatively small market for India. Since 1997-98 India's exports to ASEAN (six major countries) increased from US $ 2410 million to US $ 4518 in 2002-03. During this period India's exports to ASEAN almost doubled. However, the share of exports to ASEAN countries in India's total trade increased only marginally from 6.9% in 1997-98 to 8.6% in 2002-03. Each of the ASEAN countries accounts for a very small share of India's exports. In 2002-03, Vietnam had the smallest share of 0.6% while Singapore had the largest share of 2.7%. Sri Lanka's share in India's total exports has also increased only marginally from 1.4% in 1997-98 to 1.7% in 2002-03. (see Table 1)

While Free Trade Arrangements would certainly imply a reduction in tariffs, the gains from such trade would be limited in the presence of non-tariff barriers.

Table 1: India's Exports to Six Major ASEAN Countries and Sri Lanka from 1998-99 to 2002-03 (US $ million)

India's Exports (US $ million)

Country	*1997-98*	*1998-99*	*1999-00*	*2000-01*	*2001-02*	*2002-03*
Indonesia	437.3	**185.3**	**325.6**	**399.8**	**533.7**	**826.1**
Malaysia	490.0	**321.7**	**447.1**	**608.2**	**773.7**	**749.4**
Philippines 2	238.7	**118.7**	**143.5**	**202.6**	**247.8**	**472.0**
Singapore	774.5	**517.5**	**672.7**	**877.1**	**972.3**	**1421.6**
Thailand	342.9	**321.0**	**449.6**	**530.1**	**633.1**	**711.2**
Vietnam	**126.6**	**125.4**	**154.4**	**225.9**	**218.2**	**337.4**

Total (ASEAN 6) 2410.0 1589.7 2192.9 2843.6 3378.8 4517.6

Sri Lanka 489.2 437.1 499.3 640.1 630.9 921.0

Total (world) 34785.0 33218.7 36822.5 44560.3 43826.7 52719.4

Non-Tariff Measures

While market access would improve on account of reduction of import duties, it may be thwarted due to the application of non-tariff measures. It is important to define non-tariff barriers. Any restriction imposed on the free flow of trade is a trade barrier. Trade barriers can either be tariff barriers, that is levy of ordinary customs duties within the binding commitments undertaken by the concerned country in accordance of GATT or non tariff barriers, that is any trade barriers other than the tariff barriers. Non-tariff barriers can take various forms. Broadly these can be categorized as under:

- Import Policy Barriers
- Standards, Testing, Labeling and Certification requirements
- Anti-dumping & Countervailing Measures
- Export Subsidies and Domestic Support
- Government procurement

(i) Import Policy Barriers

One of the most commonly known non-tariff barriers is the prohibition or restrictions on imports maintained through the import licensing requirements. Article XI of the GATT Agreement requires Members not to impose any prohibitions or restrictions other than duties, taxes or other charges, whether made effective through quotas, import or export licenses or other measures. Any form of import licensing (other than an automatic license) is, therefore, to be considered as an import restriction. Certain restrictions on imports, however, can be imposed in accordance with various provisions of the GATT. These include restrictions on grounds of safety, security, health, public morals etc. Article XX of the GATT Agreement provides for certain general exceptions on grounds of protection of:

- public morals,
- human, animal or plant life or health,

This type of gelatin is derived from animal hide and bone, hence there are problems with regard to kosher and Halal status. It was found in the course of the survey that for exports of capsules to ASEAN countries such as Indonesia, Malaysia and Thailand the exporter needs to procure the Halal certificate from the Government of India (Ministry of health) mentioning that the gelatin is derived from Halal animal. While the time and cost involved in obtaining such certification is not much, it is an irritant for exporters, as it is required only for three ASEAN countries. One way to overcome this irritant is to accept the certification for Halal only once and not repeatedly for every consignment.

(a) Barriers Related to Process Standards

Many countries link up quality of the product with production processes also. Thus, what is under surveillance is not just the end - product but also the process of production of end - product. In India, where most primary production takes place at much unorganized, small - scale units, such primary-level quality assurances are hard to give. PPMs are a major issue between Indian exporters and importing countries. The exporting country contention is that the importing countries should be bothered about quality of the final product not the manufacturing process. It is because every country has different natural resources and method of production. The importing countries method of production cannot be applied in importing countries. Thus Indian exporters face lot of barriers on PPM account.

For example, Philippines and Malaysia, in addition to specifications on the meat portion have brought out another regulation, which states that, any exporter interested in exporting to these countries must have an integrated slaughterhouse of his own which should be HACCP certified. An integrated slaughterhouse would include slaughtering, cutting into pieces and packaging facilities failing which they are not eligible to export. With this requirement the Indian exporter loses out on two counts. Firstly, to set up an integrated slaughter house (with HACCP certification) in India an exporter would have to incur a cost around Rs. 20 million. Secondly, even if he is able to set up an integrated plant, getting a license to set up such a plant is extremely difficult. Not only are there multiple agencies involved but since slaughtering has a religious connotation, getting a license becomes doubly difficult. Yet another barrier has been identified through a case study. Import of Indian meat is banned in Singapore and Indonesia. Indonesia has banned the Indian meat on the pretext of the foot and mouth disease prevalent in India. Even after numerous certificates and declaration from the Ministry of Health, Indian meat is banned in these countries on a false allegation of foot and mouth disease. Indian exporters export frozen de-boned and degraded meat to countries in the Middle East and South East Asia (Philippines and Malaysia), as per the guidelines stipulated by the OIE (Office International des Epizooties2).In spite of obtaining all the relevant certifications, Indian exporters are often held on various grounds such as ill-maintained and unhygienic slaughtered houses. The grounds they hold are ill defined and change every time with orders. Hence the volatility of the norms actually causes Indian exporters to lose out on orders many a times.

(b) Barriers Related to Certification

Jute exporters exporting to ASEAN countries faced minor irritants. IJIRA (Indian Jute Industries Research Association)3 certificate is one certification, which is recognized and accepted by many of the importers. The exporters exporting to these countries need to undertake the tests and have to supply the certificate during the trade process. Due to this the exporters lose out time and money. Though the amount is not exorbitant but it is an irritant. Indian Jute Industries Research Association [IJIRA] was established in 1937, the first cooperative R & D organization rendering services to the Indian Jute Industry. IJIRA offers quality assurance services for various chemical inputs and chemically processed textiles, their certification for export quality jute product is accredited globally, IJIRA has sophisticated state of art labs to test dyes, chemicals, and auxiliaries for jute. Tests for checking the properties of jute is done by this organization. They do various tests like Grist (Count), Strength, Twist, Imperfections, Knots / 100 yards. Imperfection tests are done to check the thickness and thinness of yarn.

Hot and cold rolled coil

imported into Thailand requires a registration with the customs of Thailand. This registration is required each time a consignment is sent to Thailand. In order to register with the customs the exporter has to send various documents like plant information, production flowchart, quality system, and other firm details. The cost for this registration is not high but the time involved in getting the registration done could take anything between 2 weeks to 2 months.

Bulk Drugs

Similar to the case of cosmetics, the imports of bulk drugs by Vietnam also requires registration with the Government of Vietnam. The registration is done by the importers who ask for information on manufacturing process, the raw material mixture and other important and confidential information, which the Indian exporter is reluctant to supply.

Mango pulp

In case of mango pulp most importing countries have standard specifications but in order to export to Sri Lanka, Indian exporters are required to obtain a Health certificate from the Ministry of Health of Sri Lanka. However for the other countries they also accept the certificate from the Government of India (Ministry of Health). In addition, the exporter also needs to get a thread bare analysis done. This test is conducted in order to specify the exact contents of the product. This test is conducted over a period of 2 days and costs about Rs.5000- Rs.7000 per consignment. According to the exporters it is a test, which they do, and they integrate this in the cost of the products. The Ministry of Agriculture and Rural Development (MARD) in Vietnam is responsible for approving pesticides to be registered in Vietnam on the basis of recommendations made by the Advisory Committee for Pesticide.

Mango pulp/ Fruit pulp

All edible products to be exported to Malaysia must be supported by the Halal certificate.6 Although the cost for obtaining this certificate is not high it is a requirement imposed only by Malaysia and no other country. The exporter needs to certify that the product does not contain any animal products or derivatives. The test is required since gelatine is often used as a thickener for mango pulp. Even though getting the certificate is not difficult, it is definitely an irritant for the importer.

Textile products

Textile products require quality certification for exports. Most importing countries accept the quality certification from ISO and Bureau Veritas. However, Sri Lanka asks for certification from its own agencies like Sri Lanka Standards Institution (SLSI).7 This is a problem for Indian exporters as they have to get this certificate and incur the cost and the time even though they have an ISO certificate from a recognised agency in India. Hence, exporters exporting to Sri Lanka have to get the additional certificate, without which export is not possible.

(c) Barriers Related to Testing

Bamboo baskets in India is exporting various food products to different countries in the world. Although all countries have uniform packaging requirements, some countries demand special packaging. Malaysia and Singapore demand packaging of tamarind and onion products in bamboo baskets. They demand for this kind of packaging because it is environment friendly. As result the Indian exporter incurs 10% extra cost which makes their products economically unviable in the international market. This is a non-tariff barrier. Normally the packaging for powder dyes is done in polythene and liquid is in plastic bottles which is then put in metallic drums for export. This type of packaging is done for U.S and European countries. Indonesia requires paper and high density polyethylene drums packaging for dyes. To pack the dyes in the Indonesian format, Indian exporters incur 2-3% additional cost in packaging. This makes the product less competitive in the international market and is a non-tariff barrier.

Labeling

Halal logo:

Countries such as Malaysia demand the Halal logo on products like toothpastes. This is to certify that the products do not contain pork derivatives. The animal derivatives used are as per Halal specification. To meet these requirements, exporters are compelled to do a special line of printing, which increases the cost of exporting. This is a clear case on a non-tariff barrier. Bulk drugs need to be registered in the importing country. But while exporting to Philippines and Thailand each product pack, individually, should have the registration number mentioned on it. The samples are sent to these countries and the agents get the products registered with the government of the importing countries. Exporters have to incur additional costs and time to get the registration number and then print them on the products. In addition exporters give bribes to get these certificates, which again increase the cost to a considerable amount. In the survey it was also found that for marine product exports to Indonesia there were strict food labeling law that require labels written only in Bhasa Indonesian on all consumer products.

(d) Environmental Barriers

In case of the non-processed foods like onions and tamarind it was found that Malaysian buyers prefer packaging in bamboo baskets on the pretext that bamboo baskets are considered environmentally friendly. Exporters incur incremental cost for such specification.

Customs Classification Procedures: Countries are required to use internationally harmonized methods of classification rather than national methods of custom classification. Very often classification of items is done indiscriminately posing as a nontariff barrier. Countries mis-classify items which leads to higher duty levies. In case of jute products it was seen that special duty was being levied depending upon the type of product mentioned on the consignment. On the export of "Jute Bags" to Malaysia a duty of 10% was levied however on the export of "Jute Shopping Bag" a duty of 25% was being levied. Both the products are exactly the same and do not differ from each other in any aspect. Exporters often have to pay bribes in order to get the item classified in a manner that it would attract lower customs duties.

Anti-dumping duties: Dumping is said to occur when the goods are exported by a country to another country at a price lower than its normal value. In our survey there was no evidence of any anti-dumping cases. However, the Ministry of Commerce, Government of India, Annual Report indicates that Indonesia has initiated 6 cases against India in products such as ampicillin, black carbon, hot rolled coils, phallic anhydride, Ferro manganese and silicon manganese and wire rods. None of the other ASEAN countries or Sri Lanka has initiated any anti-dumping cases against India.

Impact of Non-Tariff barriers

The NTBs (Non-tariff barriers) are less transparent, difficult to identify and their impact on exporting countries is almost impossible to quantify. It contravenes widely accepted principles of non-discrimination and transparency in measures to restrict trade principles which remain sound. NTBs usually discriminate against the lowest cost sources of imports. Over the years, the NTBs have been becoming more and more extensive and intensive. Today they are not confined to the labor intensive products where the developing countries have an advantage but also cover sophisticated products. Japan and the newly industrializing countries (NICs) like S. Korea are among the most affected countries by NTBs. Developing country exports are also significantly affected by them. However, the NTBs have become to affect the intra-OECD (i.e. trade between developed economies) also. The NTBs tend to offset favorable of the GATT/WHO negotiations on trade liberalizations like the reductions in the average levels of tariffs. As a matter of fact, several advanced countries like USA who were high priest of free trade increasingly resort to several NTBs particularly against the developing countries and certain countries like Japan. NTBs seriously affect many exporting countries. As pointed out earlier, developing country exports to developed countries face considerable NTBs. In several cases, the impact is very severe. For example, the VER covering the tapioca exports of Thailand to the European Community, established in 1982, caused its tapioca exports to decline by 40% and its export earnings to fall by about $300 million (representing somewhat over 10% of Thailandâ€™s total export earnings from the EC). However, such draconic VERs which not only reduce the growth rate but also the level of exports has not been widely applied to non-apparel exports of developing Asian countries other than Korea. As the Asian Development Bank study points out, with the reduction of the average tariff levels in the industrial countries, non-tariff barriers to imports of manufactures have increased in relative importance in these countries, including in categories of labor intensive and other products for which less developed countries have a strong comparative advantage. Moreover, through the exercise of various forms of administrative protection, non-tariff have increased kin importance in absolute terms and have been applied with increasing discrimination, causing bilateral trade arrangement in many cases to reign over more globally efficient multilateral trade arrangements and threatening the gains, especially to less developed countries, of negotiated tariff reductions. Apparel exports are the most affected of the developing countries because of such barriers. This has been done mostly by the Multi-Fiber Arrangement (MFA) which constitutes a restrictive system, imposing economic costs on the economies of developing as well as industrial countries. Several of the country studies cite instances of lost apparel exports, production and employment due to reporting, certification and other problems involved in administering bilateral MFA agreements, whereby the system of administrative controls creates such uncertainties, especially for new exporters or financially weak firms, that export production must be curtailed or abandoned by many firms. Another important cost of the MFA is rent seeking i.e. established exporters tend to enjoy greater than perfectly competitive returns from their export sales since quota rights enable them to sell in protected markets. NTBs also cause diversion of production and exports. For example, some Indian textile and apparel firms decided to set up manufacturing facilities in Nepal in order to circumvent MFA quota controls on their exports from India and to avoid the local costs of purchasing added quota rights. Similarly, exporters have attempted to diversify their exports to non-quota countries.

State trading of India

There is no precise definition of State trading. There are various types of government participation in foreign trade, all of which can be defined as State trading. For example, in the centrally planned economies the entire foreign trade is nationalized and is, therefore conducted directly by government departments or government owned corporations. On the other hand, there are countries which are essentially free enterprise economies but export and import of specific commodities are entrusted to government trading organizations or departments. For example, imports of un-manufactured tobacco is a State monopoly in France. The Government Food Agency of Japan regulates the import, export and internal distribution of rice, wheat and barley. Similarly, Japan Monopoly Corporation which is a State body has the exclusive rights of tobacco importation. The Australian Wheat Board has the exclusive rights for exports of wheat. There are many such instances all over the world. The third variety of State trading is found in mixed economies like India. In India, State participation in foreign trade is mostly done through government departments. The government owned trading corporations are, however, commercial entities registered under the Companies Act and have the same rights and obligations as any private sector firm.

Rationale of State Trading

State trading is resorted to for a number of reasons. In the centrally planned economies, foreign trade as a matter of State policy is nationalized. Foreign trade in those countries is to be conducted by State trading organizations because otherwise the central planning mechanism will not function properly. In the developed free enterprise economies, State trading sometimes is practiced as a source of revenue. That is why it is found that trade in products like alcohol and tobacco is subject to State monopoly. Similarly, trade in drugs and arms and ammunition is managed through State bodies in the interest of health and national security of the country. State trading in a number of agricultural products is quite common because State intervention is necessary to avoid fluctuations in the prices and preventing deterioration in the income of the agricultural producers. State trading however, is more commonly practiced in the developing economies. The reasons behind this are varied. First, such countries may not have adequately developed private sector trading bodies which can effectively participate in international commerce and also protect the national interest. Secondly, the private sector bodies, though possessing adequate trading expertise, will be solely motivated by profit consideration. However, it may be necessary from the national standpoint to promote new export items and cultivate new export markets even by sustaining short terms losses. This can be done only by government bodies having a development role and which are backed by the government so that the financial losses do not hamper the pursuit of long term objectives. Thirdly, the centrally planned economies have emerged as important export markets for a large number of developing countries including India. Since the foreign trade of these countries is invariably conducted through State trading organizations, it is found that government trading bodies are in a better position to negotiate with their counterparts in the certainly planned economies.

Canalization of Imports

State participation in imports is generally motivated by some other considerations. These are: (1) to reap the advantage of bulk buying, (2) to mop up any excess profit which the private sector firms might enjoy in import business, and (3) to ensure proper internal distribution of the imported items and to maintain stable domestic price level.

Advantage of Bulk Buying

There are essentially three elements which can be associated with the advantage of bulk purchase. First, a bulk purchaser may get better discount and trading terms. Secondly, since the bulk purchaser will be monopolist, the possibility that prices of commodities in short supply can be pushed up by competitive bidding by the Indian importers, is eliminated. Thirdly, since the international markets of many importable items are monopolistic, State trading will give rise to countervailing power which may mitigate to some extent the ill effects of the monopolistic market structure.

Other Barriers and Constraints

Some barriers could find an indirect relevance to the study. For instance, many buyers in Sri Lanka demand under invoicing in order to save themselves from import duties. This causes exporters undue harassment. Also Indian banks like the State Bank of India do not confirm the Letter of credit issued by Banks of Thailand and most banks of Vietnam. Due to this, the exporter has to take all the risk of default by the bank. Sometimes it may happen that these banks may not pay the Indian exporter. Due to non-confirmation of the Letter of Credit the exporters are not able to take orders. On the other hand, some of the private banks like Citibank, HSBC do confirm the Letter of Credit. Some exporters have also faced problems with some of the banks in Brunei and Cambodia which issue false Letter of Credit because such banks in reality do not exist. Therefore, the Indian banks generally do not confirm the Letter of Credit issued by the banks of these countries. In the course of the survey several exporters opined that they faced hindrances in exporting their products. Exporters felt that the Indian Government did not provide enough subsidies. Other countries provide far greater subsidies which places Indian export products at a disadvantage. In particular exporters feel that the withdrawal of the DEPB scheme is likely to affect Indian exports adversely. Also, export procedures are very lengthy and cumbersome leading to huge transaction costs in terms both time and money. Bribes are rampant at lower levels of government officials adding further to transaction costs. India does not have a hub port and transshipment of products through a hub port often delays exports. Basic infrastructure facilities like logistics are subjected to strikes and lockouts due to poor labor laws. Exporters face problems due to lack of prompt and accurate changes in government policy from time to time. The Indian Government does not take enough initiative to promote Indian goods abroad. It may be reiterated that these are constraints that were pointed out by the exporters in the course of the survey.

World trade

Economic progress is linked to world trade and those who preach trade restrictions are denying this fact. Countries like the old communist bloc (Russia, East Germany, etc.) have not developed as fast as those with more outward orientation. The same can be said of African nations, where the inability to industrialise and export in volume has locked them into, generally, primary product producers. Economic Structural Adjustment Programmes (ESAP) are supposed to remedy this situation by giving "command economies" a market oriented focus. Another argument concerns whether marketing has relevance to the process of economic development. Less developed countries (LDCs) have traditionally focused on production and domestic income generation. Also, marketing addresses itself to needs and wants and it could be argued that where LDCs' productive capabilities are far less than unsatisfied needs and wants, then marketing is superfluous. However, adopting "marketing" could lead to the more efficient and effective use of productive and marketing resources and it may be able to focus on current needs and find better solutions. For example, techniques developed in the West for optimising transport resources could well be transferred to effect. Similarly, adopting new methods of marketing may give better results. A good example is the Cold Storage Company of Zimbabwe (CSC). By changing from the current system of marketing cattle (the CSC takes in cattle, at fixed prices and slaughters) to an auction system by description, all actors in the system could benefit. Decisions in product, price, communications and merchandising can stimulate economic development. Changing from fixed price systems to market based pricing could lead to the faster achievement of development objectives (for example "higher incomes"). In current drought conditions in Africa, governments could well benefit from advertising other forms of nutritious food, for example, fish, rather than let the populace be left uninformed and disgruntled about the lack of maize.

Composition of world trade

Agriculture, minerals, fuels and manufactured goods figure most in world trade. However shifts are occurring (see table 2.1)[6].

Table 2.1 Shift in commodity trade - % of world trade

Product	*1980*	*1985%*	*1988%*
Agriculture	22.5	1	14
Minerals	14	-5	14
Fuel	41	-3.5	1
Manufactures	17	4.5	1

Interestingly enough, those economies which have divested themselves of agriculture (or made it more efficient) and invested in manufacturing are those which have shown spectacular growth. Table 2.2 compares Zimbabwe with Thailand[6].

Patterns of trade

Most industrialised nations trade with each other. This had led to their continued domination. particularly the USA, Western Europe and Japan which between them have 66% of world GNP and trade. In 1985 industrialised trade to other industrialised countries accounted for 47% of trade, next came developing countries to industrialised (15%), and finally industrialised to developing countries (13%). Political influences can also be seen between trading partners, for example Zimbabwe's trade with China. Marketers need to identify trading patterns between nations and product trading patterns. East-West trade and West to the former communist bloc is likely to grow at the expense of North-South trade.

Table 2.2: Structure of production

Country	*GDP $ m*		*Distribution of GDP %*							
			Agriculture		*Industry*		*Manufacturing*		*Services*	
	1970	*1992*	*1970*	*1992*	*1970*	*1992*	*1970*	*1992*	*1970*	*1992*
Zimbabwe	1415	5350	15	22	36	35	21	30	49	43
Thailand	7087	110337	26	12	25	39	16	28	49	49

This pattern is repeated throughout Africa and Asia in general.

Comparative costs - comparative advantage

As discussed in chapter one, price has been called the immediate basis for international trade - cheaper prices based on different cost structures, especially labour. Countries trade because they produce and export goods in which they enjoy a greater comparative advantage and import goods in which they have a least comparative advantage. A further refinement of this is the international product cycle discussed fully in chapter one.

Balance of payments

This is the measure of all economic transactions between one nation and another. The balance of payments is made up of the current account, showing trade in goods and services; and the capital account, which shows financial transactions. In 1989, after official transfers, the USA had a US$ 109,242 million deficit on its current account, Japan had a $ 131,400 million surplus, Tanzania a $ 778,5 million deficit and Zimbabwe a $ 2,783 million deficit.

The balance of payments account helps marketers select the location of supply for foreign markets and the selection of markets. The capital account may show the nations which have control restrictions and hence be difficult to deal with. In this regard, African nations are generally disadvantaged.

Government policy

This refers to the government measures and regulations which have a bearing on trade - tariffs, quotas, exchange controls and invisible tariffs. These can cause formidable barriers to marketers and will be dealt with at length later.

World Institutions

Institutions like GATT and the United Nations Conference on Trade and Development (UNCTAD) have been of help to countries in their development. GATT had over 120 members and associated and accounted for 80% of world trade. Its intention was to create a general system of preferences and negotiate tariffs for members' products on a nondiscriminant basis and provide a forum for consultation. The Kennedy Round of the 1960s was superseded by the Tokyo round of the 1970s and that by the current Uruguay round signed in 1994.

UNCTAD furthers the development of emerging nations. It seeks to improve the prices of primary goods exports through commodity agreements. It also established a tariff preference system favouring developing nations.

Regionalism

Regionalism is a major and important trade development. Some regional groupings have either market (EU) or command (China) or mixed economies (former communist countries and The Preferential Trade Area (PTA) and The Southern African Development Community (SADC). With these developments, free trade zones have occurred (all internal barriers abolished) economic unions (the EU), export pricing zones (Mauritius) and other schemes. The major regional economic organisations are: Acuerdo de Cartegna (Andean Group), Association of South East Nations (ASEAN), Asian Pacific Rim countries (APC), Caribbean Community and Common Market (CARICOM), Central American Common Market (Mercado Comùn Centro Americano), Council of Arab Economic Unity, Economic Community of West African States (ECOWAS), the European Union (EU), Latin American Integration

Association, Organisation Commune Africans et Mauricienne, Preferential Trade Area (PTA) and the Southern African Development Conference (SADC). A principal collapse has been the Council for Economic Assistance (COMECON) with the disappearance of the communist bloc in Eastern Europe. Of these blocs, the EU (reporting 33% of world trade) and EFTA are very important. To counteract the growing power of the EU, the USA and Canada have entered into an agreement with Mexico as a willing partner and created the North American Free Trade Agreement (NAFTA). These blocs are of various form, power, influence and success. ASEAN is a collaboration of industry and agriculture, PTA in tariffs. SADC and PTA have had historically little impact but are now beginning to grow in importance in view of the normalization of South Africa. The EU, North American Union and the Pacific Rim Union will pose the greatest power blocs in future years. Many developing countries have entered into trading blocks as a reaction against loss of developed country markets or as a base to build economic integration and markets. The development of trading blocs can bring headaches and advantages to trade. It is worth comparing the European Union, a relatively well developed bloc, with SADC and the PTA which are well developed.

The international financial system

Global financing operations based on the gold standard gave rise to instability, so Bretton Woods, post-World War II, saw the nascence of the International Monetary Fund (IMF) and World Bank. The IMF deals with the International Monetary System. Involved countries joined IMF to establish a par value for other countries in terms of the US dollar and maintain it with +/ - one percent of that value. The system fell down because large corporations were holding more funds than banks and so a "float" set in. IMF began to fade somewhat. However it still lends, on a short term basis, to countries with payment problems to help them continue trading. The World Bank, or International Bank for Reconstruction and Development (IBRD) deals with international capital. It provides long term capital to aid economic development. Currently it has about US$ 22 billion annually for this operation. The role of the World Bank has often been criticized especially on its conditionality's for loans to Africa in funding structural adjustment and trade liberalization programs. However many developing countries require institutional funding to help them with trade and balance payment problems. Other major lenders include the EU and bilateral donors and agencies who have provided money for developmental projects. A principal donor is the United States Agency for International Development (USAID).

The United States of America

Since the Gulf War of 1991, the USA has played an increasingly important role in the economic affairs of the world. Since that time, itself, and its agency

USAID, have increasingly flexed their muscles. However, the balance of economic power in recent years, has shifted towards the Pacific rim, especially Japan and the Asian Tigers.

Individual economies

Whilst the global factors listed above have aided the development of a world economy, marketers must consider carefully individual economies. A study of these helps answer the questions - how big is the market and what is it like? Currently there are over 200 individual countries in the world.

Size of market

General indications of market size include population (growth rates and distribution) and income (distribution, per capita, GNP).

(a) **Population:** In general, the larger the population, the bigger the market. However there is no correlation between income level and population. China has 2 billion plus people, India 1 billion, Zimbabwe 8 million. However, they do not have the same income per capita as the USA or UK. In 1993 the USA population of 252.2 million, the UK 57.4 million and Africa 400 million, were respectively 6%, 1.5% and 9% of the world's population. However the USA and UK had an infinitely higher GNP per capita income than Africa, US$ 22,520, UK $17,300 and Africa $ 270 respectively (1989).

Different countries experience different population growth rates. In the early 90s, the UK had an annual growth rate of 0.1%, the Ivory Coast 6%, and Africa in general, 3% per annum. Low income countries and oil rich countries have the largest growth rates. Growth rates have a dual edge - they are good for sales but bad for world resources. The world population, currently standing at 5 billion is experiencing a rapid growth rate. It is expected to reach 7 billion by the end of the century. The strain on world resources is likely to be very large. The distribution of the population is also important. Different age groups have different needs and population density should mean good market potential, the higher the better. The Netherlands have 1000 persons per square mile, Bangladesh 1,791 but the USA only 65 persons per square mile. However, the USA spends more per capita than Bangladesh

(b) **Income:** No one has yet been able to assess accurately the impact of the AIDS pandemic on world population and economic activity. South Africa estimates AIDS will cost South African industry R16.7 billion by the year 2000 (Business Herald - Nov. 24.1994). Suffice to say, unless a cure or prevention is found, it could be serious, especially in Africa and South East Asia, the world's "hot spots"

Income is the most important variable affecting market potential. Markets are not markets without money to spend. Interestingly, there is an inverse correlation between GNP per capita and income elasticity of demand for food. Asia has a 0.9 income elasticity of demand and the USA 0.16. The distribution of income is very uneven. In Kenya the lowest 20% of the population receive less than 3% of national resource. This bimodal distribution of income means marketers must analyze two economies in a country. Per capita measures have therefore, many limitations. Per capita judges a country's level of economic development and its degree of modernization and progress in health, education and welfare. Half of the world's population lives with an average per capita income of only US$ 270. Per capita is usually reflected in US dollars and is only valid for comparison if exchange rates are equal. Exchange rates reflect international goods and services in a country but not domestic consumption. Another limitation of per capita measures is the lack of comparability with the figures themselves. The US budget contains food, clothing and shelter. In many of the less developed nations these items may be largely self-provided and therefore not reflected in national income tables. Also in the UK, snow equipment is included, and this is not, obviously, in Africa and parts of Asia. Other limitations are that sales of goods are not well correlated with per capita income and if there is great unevenness in income distribution, per capita figures are less meaningful. Product saturation can be equally troublesome in affecting market potential. A vacuum cleaner in the Netherlands has a 95% household penetration rate, but only 7% in Italy. Gross National Product is a better indicator of potential than Gross Domestic Product as GDP includes more than "product". World GNP figures reveal the concentration of wealth in the three nations, the USA, Japan and Western Europe. Africa trails far behind (see table 2.3)· However, when evaluating markets it is wise to consider individual product areas. For example, Belgium's GNP is better than India's but India's, consumption of steel is 3 times that of Belgium's.

Table 2.3: GDP and GNP of selected countries

	GDP US$ bn	% of World	GNP US$ bn	% of World
USA	5670	35	3000	29
UK	903	6	540	5
Africa	322	3	220	3

The United Nations International Comparison Project (ICP) developed a sophisticated method for measuring total expenditure, which has been used to derive more reliable and directly comparable estimates of per capita income. The World Bank has published a comparison of ICP findings with its own Atlas figures based on the exchange rate conversion. The use of exchange rates tends to distort real income or standard of living measures.

The nature of economy

More than money makes up an economy's economic environment. Natural resources -raw materials now and in the future are important. If synthetic gold or tobacco were developed or, in the case of the latter, became unfashionable, Zimbabwe's economy would be ruined. Topography may produce two, three or more submarkets in a country. Zambia, for example, has "rural" and "urban" areas with different needs and wants. Extremes of climate - like the Southern African drought in 1992 can devastate economies and derail any economic development plans and exports. Simply, products are not available to export, because they are being consumed by the domestic economy.

The nature of economic activity

Economic activity is often correlated to the type of economic activity. Various methods have been derived to classify economies. These are:

Stages of market development

Global markets are at different stages of development which can be divided into five categories based on the criterion of gross national product per capita.

(i) *Preindustrial countries* - incomes less than US$ 400 GNP per capita. Limited industrialization, low literacy rates, high birth rates, heavy reliance on foreign aid, political instability. Parts of Sub-Saharan Africa. Little market potential.

(ii) *Less developed countries* - per capita between US$ 401 and US$ 1,635. Early stages of industrialisation, growing domestic market, mature product markets, increasing competitive threat.

(iii) *Developing countries* - per capita income between US$ 1,636 and US $ 5,500. Decrease in percentage of agricultural workers, industrialisation, rising wages, high literacy rates, lower wage rates than developed countries, formidable competitors.

(iv) *Industrialized countries* - per capita income between US$ 5,501 and US$ 10,000. Moving towards post industrialisation, high standard of living.

(v) *Advanced countries* - per capita income in excess of US$ 10,000. Post industrialisation, information processors, knowledge based, less machine based. Product opportunities are in new products, innovations and raw materials plus fresh foods.

The World Bank classification

The World Bank has drawn up a classification of economies based on GNP per capita.

(i) Low income economies, China and India, other low-income-GNP per capita income of between US$ 675 or less, 41 nations including Tanzania, Kenya, Zambia and Malawi.

(ii) Middle income economies, lower middle income, GNP per capita of between US$ 676 and US$ 2,695, 40 nations including Zimbabwe, Mexico and Thailand.

(iii) Upper middle income, GNP per capita of between US$ 2,676 and US$ 8,355, 17 nations including Brazil, Portugal and Greece.

(iv) High income economies, OECD members and others, GNP per capita of between US$ 8,356 or more, 24 nations including UK and the USA.

(v) Other economies - communist bloc.Mozambique and Switzerland are the two extreme ends of the spectrum with US$ 80 per capita and US$ 29,880 per capita respectively.

Rostow: Whilst economic in nature, Rostow (1971) produced a five stage model of economic takeoff:

- Stage 1 traditional society, little increase in productivity, no modern science application systematically, low level of literacy
- Stage 2 the preconditions of takeoff, modern techniques in agriculture and production, developments in infrastructure and social institutions
- Stage 3 the takeoff, normal growth patterns, rapid agricultural and industrial modernization, good social environment.
- Stage 4 the drive to maturity, modern technology applied to all fronts, international involvement, can produce anything
- Stage 5 the age of high mass consumption, production of durable goods and services, large amounts of

These classifications enable marketers to assess where and how to operate in countries which may display the stage characteristics. For example African exporters would look to stage 4 and 5 economies to obtain the greatest revenue opportunities for other produce.

Another way to assess the market alternatives to a potential global marketer is to look at the origin of its national product - is it farm or factory generated? Farm workers tend to have low incomes. Input-output tables provide other insights into a country's potential, that is, what inputs go into a particular industry's output? What combination of labour, materials and equipment?

Infrastructure

Infrastructure is a very important element in considering whether to market in a country or not. Transportation, for example, is vital. Zambia and Zimbabwe are landlocked and have relatively poor transport facilities. Tanzania, whilst having direct access to the coast, has also a relatively poor internal rural infrastructure. Chaos can therefore ensue, especially during the rainy season. Without being able to get produce to the point of exportation, countries will suffer poor export performance accordingly. Energy consumption shows the overall industrialisation of a society as does its infrastructure. The less energy is consumed, the less likely the development of the market resulting in a not too attractive market proposition. Communications are essential. India has only some 10 million telephones to a population of 1 billion people. Media availability is important. Zambia has 680 radios per 1000 population, France 2,059 per 1000. Malawi has no domestic television service but access to satellite television. Commercial infrastructure is also vital - banks, accountants, advertising agencies and other services. Without these " transaction " facilities, exporting cannot take place.

Urbanization

Differences exist between "urban" and "country" dwellers. City dwellers may have more income, more developed communications and access to new products. Developing countries tend to suffer from rural drift, but without the accompanying incomes characteristic of developed countries. So when assessing market opportunities widespread urbanisation is no guarantee of a good market potential. Inflation causes havoc with economies and foreign exchange. For example Zambia has an unofficial inflation rate of over 100%, which makes it difficult and expensive to access capital for investment and obtain pre-export finance. The role of Government is essential. Some encourage joint ventures and investment, others do not. The number of international companies operating in an economy can be both good and bad. Japan's investment in the USA and UK is high, creating jobs, but gives rise to negative feelings because access to Japan is not so easy. This has led to calls for protectionism. Similarly, flows from developed countries to less developed ones are generally one way. This leads to instability in the underdeveloped country because it has no "hostage" leverage.

Repatriation or transfer of dividends can be an issue which can detract from investment if negative facilities exist. This can seriously undermine economic development and trade. Many African countries are undergoing structural adjustment and trade liberalisation programmes. In some cases, these have met with limited success. They can create market opportunities, but they also can cause internal economic upheavals for long periods of time, detracting from investment by outsiders and limiting the export opportunities, especially if interest rates rise, as is often the case. The economic environment is one of the major determinants of market potential and opportunity. Careful analysis of this, particularly income and the stage of economic development are essential. Failure to do so will lead, at best, to sub optimal opportunity and, at worst, to disaster. Less developed countries like Africa, are at a disadvantage, due to their primary material export dependence. It behaves these nations in the continent to derive policies and strategies for rapid industrialization, or forever to be at the mercy of world demand and prices.

Economic Integration

Economic theory shows free trade on a worldwide basis as the first best outcome, in as much as it allows specialization and exchange to take place globally, thus leading to greater world output and welfare. PTAs among a subset of countries are therefore a second best solution. They create trade among their members as trade barriers fall, and they divert trade from efficient non-member producers to members because of their privileged market access. It should be noted that PTAs can take a variety of forms. These range from low-level integration by means of FTAs or CUs to higher levels of integration, such as a common market, economic (and monetary) union, or even economic and political union. A PTA also refers to two or more countries forming a union with lower tariffs (and other trade barriers) for goods and services from member countries. FTAs eliminate tariffs on goods from members entirely, and CUs are FTAs with a common external tariff. More specifically, economic integration proceeds by agreements to:

- abolish tariffs and import quotas among members (FTAs and sectoral FTAs).
- establish common external tariffs and quotas (CUs).
- allow free movement of goods, services and workers (Common Market).
- harmonize competition, structural, fiscal, monetary and social policies (Economic Union).
- unify economic policies and establish supra-national institutions (Economic and Political Union).

Thus three progressively higher levels of integration can be distinguished. The first level entails modest integration by means of an agreement to apply symmetric preferential treatment of imports and assign supporting functions and instruments to jointly operated institutions. Examples would be NAFTA's commitment to eliminate tariffs among its members, its dispute settlement provisions, and the various working groups and committees that serve to facilitate trade and investment among the three partners. In the case of a CU, the agreement would additionally involve a common external tariff applicable to non-members, which, in turn, requires an understanding on how to apportion among the partners the tariff revenue collected. The second level of economic integration would be the harmonization of instruments over which the parties retain control, and through which, due to different national approaches, obstacles to a common market exist. This could be the case in the area of migration of workers, competition policy, and production standards. One example of such harmonization is the European Single Act. Among other provisions this act applied the "principle of mutual recognition" to product standards. More co-operation and supranational institutions, such as a joint tribunal on competition policy, are also characteristic of this second level. The third and highest level of economic integration adds coordination of national policies and the creation of further supranational bodies which entail not only economic but increasingly political integration. Examples here are the creation of a common currency and central bank, and even a supranational parliament as in the case of the EU.

(i) Free Trade Area: This is the preferred option for countries embarking on economic integration and for those unwilling or unable to engage in higher levels of integration. An FTA can be limited to particular sectors, thus retaining a high level of control at the national level and preventing exposure to competition for the other sectors. The authority to decide how third countries are to be treated remains unaffected (independent trade policy) in an FTA. However, rules of origin (ROO) have to be agreed upon among members so as to determine which products can be transferred duty-free. In the case of NAFTA a product has to have been substantially transformed so that a change in tariff classification has occurred, or it must have 50% (62.5% for cars) member-country content1 to qualify for duty-free treatment. There are extensive and complex provisions on how such content is arrived at and what documentation is necessary at the border. If there were no such ROO third country, products could be landed in the lower duty jurisdiction and then transferred duty-free to the higher tariff member thereby circumvent its tariff. As a result, in an FTA border controls are necessary for commerce among members, and arguments over interpretation of ROO can lead to delays and disputes. These restrictive effects of ROO have led one eminent economist to observe: "It is reported that Canadian producers have on occasion chosen to pay the relevant duties rather than incur costs of proving origin." (Krueger, 1995)

(ii) Customs Union: When two or more countries agree to remove (essentially) all restrictions on mutual trade and set up a common system of tariffs and import quotas vis-à-vis non-members, the result is referred to as a CU. The adoption of a common external tariff (CET) and joint quotas necessitates closer co-operation with respect to the sharing of customs revenues collected on non-member imports. Rules of origin are no longer necessary: when a common external tariff exists, imports into the CU–area face the same tariff in each CU-member country, hence there is no incentive for trans-shipment of imports between members. The CET effectively creates "destination-neutrality" for imports into the CU. Both FTAs and CUs imply that the member countries remain nation states, yet when viewed in the historical context there are some subtle differences between the agreements. The German Zollverein and the European Community for Coal and Steel are examples of successful CUs. The Zollverein preceded the formation of Germany in 1870 and thus holds fewer lessons for today. The European Community for Coal and Steel, a sectoral CU created in 1951, was not expected to be a precursor to eventual European political union. Nevertheless, it was recognized at the time that free trade and the consequent rationalization and specialization of production in coal and steel products would require a supranational body to regulate pricing practices and commercial policies. This historical precedent therefore suggests that a successful CU implies a common competition policy. Subsequently the European Common Market naturally adopted and extended this competition policy. A common competition policy would replace the need for, and the application of, trade remedy laws among the CU-members. Predatory pricing (dumping) would be dealt with by the common competition watchdog, and Article 19 of the GATT/WTO could be relied upon to obtain temporary relief from import surges that threaten an industry's survival. That said, the key feature of a CU remains the CET. Derivative issues are a matter of negotiation and will determine how successful the CU is.

(iii) Market: A common market (CM) can be considered the first stage of deep economic integration. Free mobility of the key participants in the process of production is its characteristic. In addition to goods and services, capital and people move freely inside a common market. The benefits expected consist of further gains in efficiency through a more appropriate allocation of resources: capital moves to where skills are and people move to where opportunities beckon.

In addition to the common external tariff that defines a CU and to ensure the viability of a common market, uniform regulations have to be worked out among the members regarding the movement of people and capital. This is a major task that requires, at least over time, agreement on qualifications and certifications of workers from different member countries.

For a common market to become effective, therefore, co-operation in decision-making is required in yet more areas. Non-tariff barriers have to be dismantled, structural adjustment policies have to be jointly reassessed, distribution policies will face harmonization pressures, and fiscal and monetary policies, as a dynamic consequence or by design, will show greater convergence. This convergence results from the increased economic interdependence among the members and necessitates that greater consideration be given to the effects of national policies on the welfare of CM partners.

(iv) European Union: The European Union, or EU, is a collaborative effort between 27 European countries to form a mutually beneficial economic and policy community. Since 1993, the EU has worked to increase economies and spread human rights advances worldwide. The goals of the European Union include uniting Europe toward common goals and providing aid to developing nations. After World War II, Europe was a fractured area, divided by political and cultural differences. Several attempts to promote a regional governing body met with varying success, including the European Coal and Steel Community and the european community. Because of the power ideological and political differences between Western and Eastern Europe, a true community could not be formed until after the end of the cold war. In 1992, the Maastricht Treaty was signed by member nations, bringing the European Union into effect. The treaty outlined three pillars of the union: European Communities, Common Foreign and Security Policy, and Justice and Home Affairs. The treaty also made provisions to admit many of the nations of Eastern Europe. In 2001, the Treaty of Nice further expanded provisions for new nations. To become a member of the European Union, a nation must be in conformance with a series of standards called the Copenhagen criteria. These detail geographic and political necessities for member nations. Included standards dictate human rights laws, democracy, protective law for minorities, and a market economy. As of 2008, three states are candidates undergoing review: Turkey, Croatia, and the Republic of Macedonia. Several other nations are identified as potential candidates for future admission, including Albania and Serbia. One of the greatest achievements of the European Union is the establishment of a single market economy. Between member nations, trade is largely unrestricted. While nations maintain separate laws on taxation and trade standards, EU members agree to basic trade laws between their countries. Almost all products created by one nation are legal for trade in all of the other countries. Most nations belonging to the EU have adopted a common currency, called the Euro. The Euro is overseen by the European Central Bank, in an effort to promote all economies that incorporate the use of the currency. As of 2008, 15 nations use the Euro, collectively called the Eurozone. Other EU members must meet specific financial and economic standards before being allowed to adopt the currency. Slovenia was the first of the countries from the 2004 expansion to meet euro criteria. In addition to increasing economic stability, the European Union sets member policy on a variety of social and political issues. Agriculture, energy policy, anti-terrorism efforts, environmental issues, and education are among the serious areas covered by various EU committees. The EU's goal of creating a neighborhood community of nations is still in its infancy, but measurable impacts are already apparent in the economic and social arenas. The European Union (EU) is a union of twenty-seven independent states based on the European Communities and founded to enhance political, economic and social co-operation. Formerly known as European Community (EC) or European Economic Community (EEC).

Date of foundation: 1st November, 1993.

Member states (EUR: Euro currency):

- Austria *(since 1995-01-01)* (EUR)
- Belgium (EUR)
- Bulgaria *(since 2007-01-01)*
- Cyprus (Greek part) *(since 2004-05-01)* (EUR: 2008-01-01)
- Czech Republic *(since 2004-05-01)*
- Denmark
- Estonia *(since 2004-05-01)*
- Finland *(since 1995-01-01)* (EUR)
- France (EUR)
- Germany (EUR)
- Greece (EUR)
- Hungary *(since 2004-05-01)*
- Ireland (EUR)
- Italy (EUR)
- Latvia *(since 2004-05-01)*
- Lithuania *(since 2004-05-01)*
- Luxembourg (EUR)
- Malta *(since 2004-05-01)* (EUR: 2008-01-01)
- Netherlands (EUR)
- Poland *(since 2004-05-01)*
- Portugal (EUR)
- Romania *(since 2007-01-01)*
- Slovakia *(since 2004-05-01)* (EUR: 2009-01-01)
- Slovenia *(since 2004-05-01)* (EUR)
- Spain (EUR)
- Sweden *(since 1995-01-01)*
- United Kingdom of Great Britain and Northern Ireland

Euro

The euro, often signified by €EUR, is the currency used in 12 members of the European Union, as well as regions such as Montenegro, Kosovo, Andorra and more. The euro is the result of the most significant monetary reform in Europe since the Roman Empire. While creation of this currency is most obviously a channel through which Europe may perfect a single market (by facilitating free trade between members of the Eurozone), the euro is just as importantly a means through which Europe may achieve political integration. Although the euro was only formally put into circulation on January 1, 2002, the idea of creating "an ever closer union among the peoples of Europe" has been around for decades-as stated in the Treaty of Rome in 1957. In 1979, the European Monetary System (EMS) was introduced and locked exchange rates among participating countries, which aided efforts to stabilize the economy. In 1992, the Economic and Monetary Union (EMU) was formed which set the basics for the creation of the single currency. Seven years later on January 1, 1999-the euro was born when the participating countries established exchange rates between their own currencies and the euro creating a monetary union. It took three years of transition, where the euro was only used as electric money, until actual euro notes and coins were used. Now, the 12 euro area member states have a single currency, a common interest rate, and a common central bank (European System of Central Banks.) It is the largest monetary replacement the world has ever seen.

The euro is administered by the European System of Central Banks (ESCB), which is comprised of the European Central Bank (ECB) and the Eurozone central banks. Headquartered in Frankfurt, Germany, the ECB has the sole authority to set monetary policy; other members of the ESCB participate through printing, minting, and distributing notes and coins.

The countries in the European Union that use the euro are: Belgium, Germany, Greece, Spain, France, Ireland, Italy, Luxembourg, The Netherlands, Austria, Portugal, Finland. EU countries not using the euro are: Denmark, Sweden, and the U.K .Other territories using the euro are: Andorra, Monaco, San Marino, The Vatican, Martinique, Guadalupe (Caribbean), Reunion (Indian Ocean), Montenegro, Kosovo.

Political Structure

The European Union (EU) is comprised of 25 democratic states. It was established in 1992 by the Treaty on European Union and is headquartered in Brussels. The members of the EU are: Austria, Belgium, Cyprus, Czech Republic, Denmark, Estonia, Finland, France, Germany, Greece, Hungary, Ireland, Italy, Latvia, Lithuania, Luxemburg, Malta, Poland, Portugal, Slovakia, Slovenia, Spain, Sweden, The Netherlands and the United Kingdom. All decisions and procedures in the EU are based on treaties agreed upon by these countries. Since its establishment, people, goods, services and money are free to move throughout the union as if it were one country.

WTO

The World Trade Organization (WTO) is the only global international organization dealing with the rules of trade between nations. At its heart are the WTO agreements, negotiated and signed by the bulk of the world's trading nations and ratified in their parliaments. The goal is to help producers of goods and services, exporters, and importers conduct their business.

The WTO successor of general agreement on tariff and trade (GATT) establish in 1948, came in to being in 1948. A very short account of the GATT is given below to provide a background of WTO.

GATT

The general agreement on tariff and trade (GATT), The predecessor of WTO was born in 1948 as result of International desired to liberalize trade the establishment of an International trade organization (ITO) has also been recommended by Britain woods conference of 1944 which had recommended the IMF and world bank. Although the IMF and World Bank were established in 1946 because of objection that that its enforcement provisions would interfere with the autonomy of domestic policy making, The ITO charter was never ratified. Instead the GATT which had been drown up only as an interim agreement to fill the gap until the ITO charter was rectified, became the framework for International trading system since into being 1948. The international trading system since 1948 was at least in principle, guided by the rules and procedure agreed to by the signatories to the GATT which was an agreement signed by the contracting nations which were admitted on the basis of their willingness to accept the GATT disciplines.

Objectives of GATT

The earlier objective was-

(i) Reaising standard of living

(ii) Ensuring full employment and a large and steadily growing volume of real income and effective demand.

(iii) Developing full use of the resources of the world

(iv) Expansion of production and International trade

GATT embodied certain conventions and general principles governing international trade among countries that adhere to the agreement. The rules or conventions of GATT required that :

(a) Any proposed change in the tariff, or other type of commercial policy of a member country should not be undertaken without consultation of other parties to the agreement.

(b) The countries that adhere to GATT should work towards the reduction of tariffs and other barriers to international trade, which should be negotiated within the framework of GATT.

Principles of GATT are following:-

(i) Non-discrimination- The principle of Non-discrimination required that no member country shall discriminated between the member of GATT in the conduct of International trade . To ensure non-discrimination the member of GATT agree to apply the principles of most favored nation (MFM) to all import and export duties.

(ii) Prohibition of quantitative restriction- Gatt rules seek to prohibits quantitative restriction as for as possible and limit restriction on trade to the less rigid tariff. However certain exception to this prohibition are granted to countries confronted with balance of payment difficulties and to developing countries. Further, import restriction were allowed to apply to agricultural and fishery products if domestic production of these articles was subject to equally restricted production of marketing control

(iii) Consultation- by providing a forum for continuing consultation it sought to resolve this agreement through consultation. So far eight round of trade negotiation were held under the auspicious of the GATT. Is round took several year.

Bibliography

- Evans, G., Newnham, J., Dictionary of International Relations; Penguin Books, 1998
- Filanlyason, J., Zakher M., The GATT and the regulation of Trade Barriers: Regime Dynamic and Functions; International Organization, Vol. 35, No. 4, 1981
- Frieden, J., Lake, D., International political economy: perspectives on global power and wealth, London: Routledge, 1995
- Mansfield, E., Busch, M., The political economy of Non-tariff barriers: a cross national analysis; International Organization, Vol. 49, No. 4, 1995
- Oatley,T., International political economy: interests and institutions in the global economy; Harlow: Longman, 2007
- Roorbach, G., Tariffs and Trade Barriers in Relation to International Trade; Proceedings of the Academy of Political Science, Vol. 15, No 2, 1993
- Yu, Zhihao, A model of Substitution of Non-Tariff Barriers for Tariffs; The Canadian Journal of Economics, Vol. 33, No. 4, 2000
- World Trade Organization Website, Non-tariff barriers: red tape, etc

Chapter - Three

Entry of International Market

Once a firm has decided to establish itself in the global markets, it become necessary for the marketing research to analyses the various option available to enter the international markets and choose the suitable one. The selection of the entry mode is one of the most significant decision a firm takes in the process of Internalization, as it involves commitment of resources with long term financial and structural implication.

The Important strategic decision in international business is the mode of entry the foreign markets on the one extreme, a company may do the complete manufacturing of the product domestically and export it to the foreign market. On the other extreme a company may do by itself, the complete manufacturing of product to the marketed in the International market their itself. These are several alternative between these two extremes. The choice of the most suitable alternative is based on the relevant factors related to the company and the foreign market. There are various mode of entry available to a firm to enter International Markets. A firm may have production facilities in its home countries or locate it in a foreign country. It has to choose the alternative most suited to its needs and requirement. Selling goods and services produced in home countries to overseas customers is the most common form of International marketing activities. Production in the home country required relatively lower levels of commitments of resources of and minimum risk for entering International markets. Moreover its provide domestic firms and opportunity to enter international markets. The following are the strategies to enter –

(i) Licensing

(ii) Exporting

(iii) Piggybacking (Complementary Exporting)

(iv) Contract manufacturing

(v) Management contract

(vi) Assemblée operation

(vii) Fully own manufacturing facilities

(viii) Joint venturing
(ix) Counter trade
(x) Merger and acquisition
(xi) Strategic alliance
(xii) Third country location
(xiii) Operation

When an organization has made a decision to enter an overseas market, there are a variety of options open to it. These options vary with cost, risk and the degree of control which can be exercised over them. The simplest form of entry strategy is exporting using either a direct or indirect method such as an agent, in the case of the former or counter trade, in the case of the latter. More complex forms include truly global operations which may involve joint ventures, or export processing zones. Having decided on the form of export strategy, decisions have to be made on the specific channels. Many agricultural products of a raw or commodity nature use agents, distributors or involve Government, whereas processed materials, whilst not excluding these, rely more heavily on more sophisticated forms of access. An organization wishing to "go international" faces three major issues:

(i) Marketing - which countries, which segments, how to manage and implement

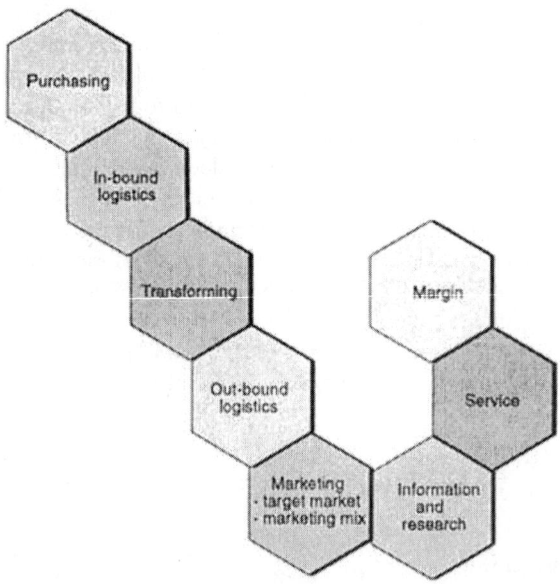

Figure 3.1: The value chain -marketing function detail

(ii) Marketing effort, how to enter - with intermediaries or directly, with what information?

(iii) Sourcing- whether to obtain products, make or buy

(vi) Investment and control - joint venture, global partner, acquisition

Decisions in the marketing area focus on the value chain (see figure 3.1). The strategy or entry alternatives must ensure that the necessary value chain activities are performed and integrated.

In making international marketing decisions on the marketing mix more attention to detail is required than in domestic marketing. Table 3.1 lists the detail required.

Table 3.1 Examples of elements included in the export marketing mix

1. Product support
- Product sourcing
- Match existing products to markets
- air, sea, rail, road, freight
- New products
- Product management
- Product testing
- Manufacturing specifications
- Labelling
- Packaging
- Production control- Market information
2. Price support
- Establishment of prices
- Discounts
- Distribution and maintenance of pricelists
- Competitive information
- Training of agents/customers
3. Promotion/selling support
- Advertising
- Promotion
- literature
- Direct mail
- Exhibitions, trade shows
- Printing
- Selling (direct)
- Sales force
- Agents commissions
- Sale or returns
4. Inventory support
- Inventory management
- Warehousing- Distribution

(Contd...)

- Parts supply
- Credit authorization
5. Distribution support
- Funds provision
- Raising of capital
- Order processing
- Export preparation and documentation
- Freight forwarding
- Insurance
- Arbitration
6. Service support
- Market information/intelligence
- Quotes processing
- Technical aid assistance
- After sales
- Guarantees
- Warranties/claims
- Merchandising
- Sales reports, catalogues literature
- Customer care
- Budgets
- Data processing systems
- Insurance
- Tax services
- Legal services
- Translation
7. Financial support
- Billing, collecting invoices
- Hire, rentals
- Planning, scheduling budget data
- Auditing

Details on the sourcing element have already been covered in the chapter on competitive analysis and strategy. Concerning investment and control, the question really is how far the company wishes to control its own fate. The degree of risk involved, attitudes and the ability to achieve objectives in the target markets are important facets in the decision on whether to license, joint venture or get involved in direct investment.

Cunningham[1] (1986) identified five strategies used by firms for entry into new foreign markets:

(i) Technical innovation strategy - perceived and demonstrable superior products

(ii) Product adaptation strategy - modifications to existing products

(iii) Availability and security strategy - overcome transport risks by countering merceived risks

(iv) Low price strategy - penetration price and,

(v) Total adaptation and conformity strategy - foreign producer gives a straight copy.

In marketing products from less developed countries to countries point iii) poses major problems. Buyers in the interested foreign country are usually very careful as they perceive transport, currency, quality and quantity problems. This is true, say, in the export of cotton and other commodities.

Because, in most agricultural commodities, production and marketing are interlinked, the infrastructure, information and other resources required for building market entry can be enormous. Sometimes this is way beyond the scope of private organisations, so Government may get involved. It may get involved not just to support a specific commodity, but also to help the "public good". Whilst the building of a new road may assist the speedy and expeditious transport of vegetables, for example, and thus aid in their marketing, the road can be put to other uses, in the drive for public good utilities. Moreover, entry strategies are often marked by "lumpy investments". Huge investments may have to be undertaken, with the investor paying a high risk price, long before the full utilization of the investment comes. Good examples of this include the building of port facilities or food processing or freezing facilities. Moreover, the equipment may not be able to be used for other processes, so the asset specific equipment, locked into a specific use, may make the owner very vulnerable to the bargaining power of raw material suppliers and product buyers who process alternative production or trading options. Zimfreeze, Zimbabwe is experiencing such problems. It built a large freezing plant for vegetables but found itself without a contract. It has been forced, at the moment, to accept sub optional volume product materials just in order to keep the plant ticking over.

In building a market entry strategy, time is a crucial factor. The building of an intelligence system and creating an image through promotion takes time, effort and money. Brand names do not appear overnight. Large investments in promotion campaigns are needed. Transaction costs also are a critical factor in building up a market entry strategy and can become a high barrier to international trade. Costs include search and bargaining costs. Physical distance, language barriers, logistics costs and risk limit the direct monitoring of trade partners. Enforcement of contracts may be costly and weak legal integration between countries makes things difficult. Also, these factors are important when considering a market entry strategy. In fact these factors may be so costly and risky that Governments, rather than private individuals, often get involved in commodity systems. This can be seen in the case of the Citrus Marketing Board of Israel. With a monopoly export marketing board, the entire system can behave like a single firm, regulating the mix and quality of products going to different markets and negotiating with transporters and buyers. Whilst these Boards can experience economies of scale and absorb many of the risks listed above, they can shield producers from information about, and from. buyers. They can also become the "fiefdoms" of vested interests and become political in nature. They then result in giving reduced production incentives and cease to be demand or market orientated, which is detrimental to producers.

Normal ways of expanding the markets are by expansion of product line, geographical development or both. It is important to note that the more the product line and/or the geographic area is expanded the greater will be the managerial complexity. New market opportunities may be made available by expansion but the risks may outweigh the advantages, in fact it may be better to concentrate on a few geographic areas and do things well. This is typical of the horticultural industry of Kenya and Zimbabwe. Traditionally these have concentrated on European markets where the markets are well known. Ways to concentrate include concentrating on geographic areas, reducing operational variety (more standard products) or making the organizational form more appropriate. In the latter the attempt is made to "globalize" the offering and the organisation to match it. This is true of organisations like Coca Cola and MacDonald's. Global strategies include "country centered" strategies (highly decentralized and limited international coordination), "local market approaches" (the marketing mix developed with the specific local (foreign) market in mind) or the "lead market approach" (develop a market which will be a best predictor of other markets). Global approaches give economies of scale and the sharing of costs and risks between markets.

Entry strategies

Mode of entry may be defined as an institutional mechanism by which a firm makes its products or services available to consumers in international market. Root (1994) defines the market entry strategy for international market as a comprehensive plan which sets forth the objectives, goals, resources, and policies that guide a company's international business operations over a future period long enough to achieve sustainable growth in world markets 2.(Franklin R. Root, entry strategy for international markets, New York, 1994, p-4-16). In order to succeed in international markets, the decision to select an appropriate entry mode is a crucial and integral part of a firm's international strategy. There are a variety of ways in which organizations can enter foreign markets. The three main ways are by direct or indirect export or production in a foreign country (see figure 3.2).

Exporting

In case exports as a mode of entry, production is carried out in home country and finished goods are shipped to the overseas market for sale.

Although exporting is low risk mode of entry in international markets, which required minimum foreign markets operational experience, it generate the lowest level of profits .Exporting is the most traditional and well established form of operating in foreign markets. Exporting can be defined as the marketing of goods produced in one country into another. Whilst no direct manufacturing is required in an overseas country, significant investments in marketing are required. The tendency may be not to obtain as much detailed marketing information as compared to manufacturing in marketing country; however, this does not negate the need for a detailed marketing strategy.

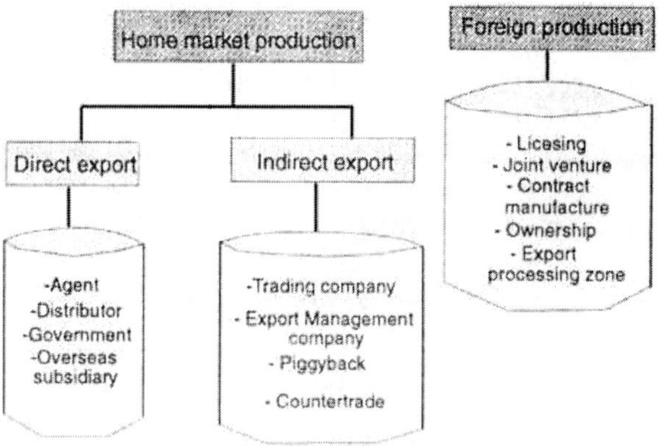

Figure 3.2 Methods of foreign market entry

The advantages of exporting are:

- manufacturing is home based thus, it is less risky than overseas based
- gives an opportunity to "learn" overseas markets before investing in bricks and mortar
- reduces the potential risks of operating overseas.

The disadvantage is mainly that one can be at the "mercy" of overseas agents and so the lack of control has to be weighed against the advantages. For example, in the exporting of African horticultural products, the agents and Dutch flower auctions are in a position to dictate to producers.

A distinction has to be drawn between passive and aggressive exporting. A passive exporter awaits orders or comes across them by chance; an aggressive exporter develops marketing strategies which provide a broad and clear picture of what the firm intends to do in the foreign market. Pavord and Bogart (1975) found significant differences with regard to the severity of exporting problems in motivating pressures between seekers and non-seekers of export opportunities. They distinguished between firms whose marketing efforts were characterized by no activity, minor activity and aggressive activity.

Those firms who are aggressive have clearly defined plans and strategy, including product, price, promotion, distribution and research elements. Passiveness versus aggressiveness depends on the motivation to export. In countries like Tanzania and Zambia, which have embarked on structural adjustment programmes, organisations are being encouraged to export, motivated by foreign exchange earnings potential, saturated domestic markets, growth and expansion objectives, and the need to repay debts incurred by the borrowings to finance the programmes. The type of export response is dependent on how the pressures are perceived by the decision maker. Piercy (1982)[3] highlights the fact that the degree of involvement in foreign operations depends on "endogenous versus exogenous" motivating factors, that is, whether the motivations were as a result of active or aggressive behaviour based on the firm's internal situation (endogenous) or as a result of reactive environmental changes (exogenous).

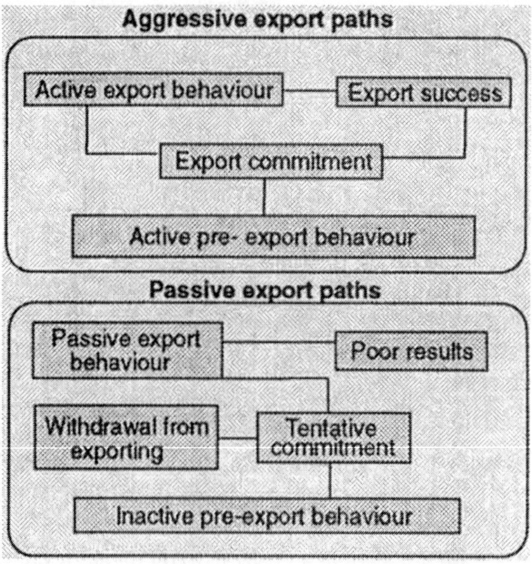

Figure 3.3: Aggressive and passive export paths

If the firm achieves initial success at exporting quickly all to the good, but the risks of failure in the early stages are high. The "learning effect" in exporting is usually very quick. The key is to learn how to minimize risks associated with the initial stages of market entry and commitment - this process of incremental involvement is called "creeping commitment" (see figure 3.3).

Exporting methods include direct or indirect export. In direct exporting the organization may use an agent, distributor, or overseas subsidiary, or act via a Government agency. In effect, the Grain Marketing Board in Zimbabwe, being commercialized but still having Government control, is a Government agency. The Government, via the Board, are the only permitted maize exporters. Bodies like the Horticultural Crops Development Authority (HCDA) in Kenya may be merely a promotional body, dealing with advertising, information flows and so on, or it may be active in exporting itself, particularly giving approval (like HCDA does) to all export documents. In direct exporting the major problem is that of market information. The exporter's task is to choose a market, find a representative or agent, set up the physical distribution and documentation, promote and price the product. Control, or the lack of it, is a major problem which often results in decisions on pricing, certification and promotion being in the hands of others. Certainly, the phytosanitary requirements in Europe for horticultural produce sourced in Africa are getting very demanding. Similarly, exporters are price takers as produce is sourced also from the Caribbean and Eastern countries. In the months June to September, Europe is "on season" because it can grow its own produce, so prices are low. As such, producers are better supplying to local food processors. In the European winter prices are much better, but product competition remains. According to Collett[4] (1991)) exporting requires a partnership between exporter, importer, government and transport. Without these four coordinating activities the risk of failure is increased. Contracts between buyer and seller are a must. Forwarders and agents can play a vital role in the logistics procedures such as booking air space and arranging documentation. A typical coordinated marketing channel for the export of Kenyan horticultural produce is given in figure 3.4. In this case the exporters can also be growers and in the low season both these and other exporters may send produce to food processors which is also exported.

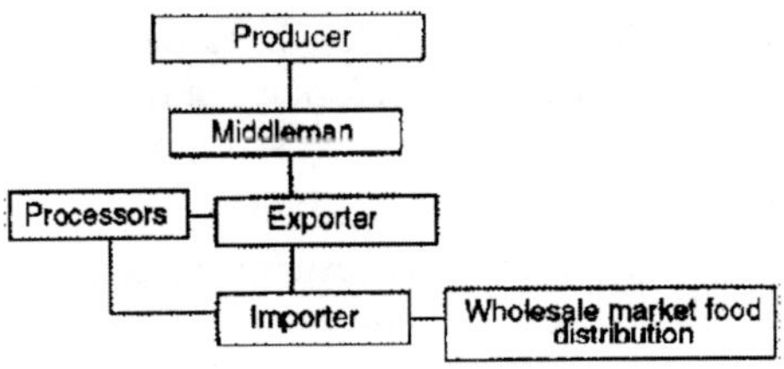

Exporting can be very lucrative, especially 'if it is of high value added produce. For example in 1992/93 Zimbabwe exported 5 338,38 tons of flowers, 4 678,18 tons of horticultural produce and 12 000 tons of citrus at a total value of about US$ 22 016,56 million. In some cases a mixture of direct and indirect exporting may be achieved with mixed results. For example, the

Grain Marketing Board of Zimbabwe may export grain directly to Zambia, or may sell it to a relief agency like the United Nations, for feeding the Mozambican refugees in Malawi. Payment arrangements may be different for the two transactions.

It is interesting to note that Korey[5] 1986 warned that direct modes of market entry may be less and less available in the future. Growing trading blocks like the EU or EFTA means that the establishment of subsidiaries may be one of the only ways forward in future. Indirect methods of exporting include the use of trading companies (very much used for commodities like cotton, soya, cocoa), export management companies, piggybacking and countertrade.

Indirect methods offer a number of advantages including:

Contracts - in the operating market or worldwide

Commission sates give high motivation (not necessarily loyalty) Manufacturer/exporter needs little expertise

Credit acceptance takes burden from manufacturer.

Complimentary exporting (Piggybacking)

Piggybacking is an interesting development. The method means that organisations with little exporting skill may use the services of one that has. Another form is the consolidation of orders by a number of companies in order to take advantage of bulk buying. Normally these would be geographically adjacent or able to be served, say, on an air route. The fertilizer manufacturers of Zimbabwe, for example, could piggyback with the South Africans who both import potassium from outside their respective The limitation of Piggybacking arrangement for the carrier include its concern about the quality and warranty of the product and continuity of supply for the rider, piggybacking arrangement in overseas markets means handing over control of its sales and distribution activities to the carrers, which may not be compatible with the firm 's long term marketing goals. Besides, the carrier's commitment to selling the riders goods is also a matter of concern to the rider countries.

Countertrade

By far the largest indirect method of exporting is countertrade. Competitive intensity means more and more investment in marketing. In this situation the organisation may expand operations by operating in markets where competition is less intense but currency based exchange is not possible. Also, countries may wish to trade in spite of the degree of competition, but currency again is a problem. Countertrade can also be used to stimulate home industries or where raw materials are in short supply. It can, also, give a basis for reciprocal trade.

Forms of Countertrade

The following are the most common among them

(i) Barter refers to directs exchange of goods equal value, with no many and no third party involved in it. For ex- a countertrade deal with mineral and metals trading corporation of India MMTC

(ii) Buy back- under the buyback agreement, the supplier of plant, equipment or technology agrees to purchase goods manufactured with that equipment, or technology. Under this scheme the full payment may be made in kind or a part may made in kind and the balance in cash.

(iii) Compensation deal- Under this arrangement, the seller receives a part of the payment in cash and their rest in products.

Counter purchase- Under this agreement the seller receives full payment in cash but agrees to expand and equivalent amount of money in that country within a specified period.

Estimates vary, but countertrade accounts for about 20-30% of world trade, involving some 90 nations and between US $100-150 billion in value. The UN defines countertrade as "commercial transactions in which provisions are made, in one of a series of related contracts, for payment by deliveries of goods and/or services in addition to, or in place of, financial settlement".

Countertrade is the modem form of barter, except contracts are not legal and it is not covered by GATT. It can be used to circumvent import quotas.

Countertrade can take many forms. Basically two separate contracts are involved, one for the delivery of and payment for the goods supplied and the other for the purchase of and payment for the goods imported. The performance of one contract is not contingent on the other although the seller is in effect accepting products and services from the importing country in partial or total settlement for his exports. There is a broad agreement that countertrade can take various forms of exchange like barter, counter purchase, switch trading and compensation (buyback). For example, in 1986 Albania began offering items like spring water, tomato juice and chrome ore in exchange for a contract to build a US $60 million fertilizer and methanol complex. Information on potential exchange can be obtained from embassies, trade missions or the EU trading desks. Barter is the direct exchange of one good for another, although valuation of respective commodities is difficult, so a currency is used to underpin the item's value.

Barter trade can take a number of formats. Simple barter is the least complex and oldest form of bilateral, non-monetarised trade. Often it is called "straight", "classical" or "pure" barter. Barter is a direct exchange of goods and services between two parties. Shadow prices are approximated for products flowing in either direction. Generally no middlemen are involved. Usually contracts for no more than one year are concluded, however, if for longer life spans, provisions are included to handle exchange ratio fluctuations when world prices change. Closed end barter deals are modifications of straight barter in that a buyer is found for goods taken in barter before the contract is signed by the two trading parties. No money is involved and risks related to product quality are significantly reduced. Clearing account barter, also termed clearing agreements, clearing arrangements, bilateral clearing accounts or simply bilateral clearing, is where the principle is for the trades to balance without either party having to acquire hard currency. In this form of barter, each party agrees in a single contract to purchase a specified and usually equal value of goods and services. The duration of these transactions is commonly one year, although occasionally they may extend over a longer time period. The contract's value is expressed in non-convertible, clearing account units (also termed clearing dollars) that effectively represent a line of credit in the central bank of the country with no money involved.

Clearing account units are universally accepted for the accounting of trade between countries and parties whose commercial relationships are based on bilateral agreements. The contract sets forth the goods to be exchanged, the rates of exchange, and the length of time for completing the transaction. Limited export or import surpluses may be accumulated by either party for short periods. Generally, after one year's time, imbalances are settled by one of the following approaches: credit against the following year, acceptance of unwanted goods, payment of a previously specified penalty or payment of the difference in hard currency.

Trading specialists have also initiated the practice of buying clearing dollars at a discount for the purpose of using them to purchase saleable products. In turn, the trader may forfeit a portion of the discount to sell these products for hard currency on the international market. Compared with simple barter, clearing accounts offer greater flexibility in the length of time for drawdown on the lines of credit and the types of products exchanged.

Counter purchase, or buyback, is where the customer agrees to buy goods on condition that the seller buys some of the customer's own products in return (compensatory products). Alternatively, if exchange is being organized at national government level then the seller agrees to purchase compensatory goods from an unrelated organisation up to a pre-specified value (offset deal). The difference between the two is that contractual obligations related to counter purchase can extend over a longer period of time and the contract requires each party to the deal to settle most or all of their account with currency or trade credits to an agreed currency value.

Where the seller has no need for the item bought he may sell the produce on, usually at a discounted price, to a third party. This is called a switch deal.

In the past a number of tractors have been brought into Zimbabwe from East European countries by switch deals.

Compensation (buy-backs) is where the supplier agrees to take the output of the facility over a specified period of time or to a specified volume as payment. For example, an overseas company may agree to build a plant in Zambia, and output over an agreed period of time or agreed volume of produce is exported to the builder until the period has elapsed. The plant then becomes the property of Zambia.

Khoury[6] (1984) categorizes countertrade as follows (see figure 3.5):

One problem is the marketability of products received in countertrade. This problem can be reduced by the use of specialized trading companies which, for a fee ranging between 1 and 5% of the value of the transaction, will provide trade related services like transportation, marketing, financing, credit extension, etc. These are ever growing in size.

Countertrade has disadvantages:

- Not covered by GATT so "dumping" may occur
- Quality is not of international standard so costly to the customer and trader
- Variety is low so marketing is limited

Difficult to set prices and service quality

Inconsistency of delivery and specification,

Difficult to revert to currency trading - so quality may decline further and therefore product is harder to market.

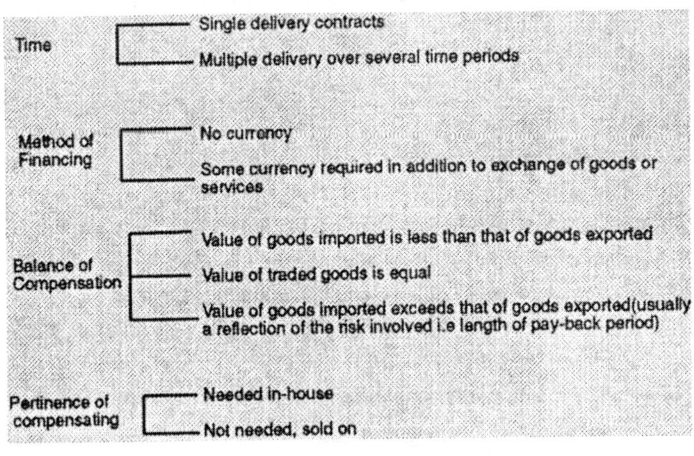

Figure 3.5 Classification of countertrade.

Shipley and Neale[7] (1988) therefore suggest the following:

Ensure the benefits outweigh the disadvantages

Try to minimize the ratio of compensation goods to cash - if possible inspect the goods for specifications

Include all transactions and other costs involved in countertrade in the nominal value specified for the goods being sold

Avoid the possibility of error of exploitation by first gaining a thorough understanding of the customer's buying systems, regulations and politics,

Ensure that any compensation goods received as payment are not subject to import controls.

Despite these problems countertrade is likely "to grow as a major indirect entry method, especially in developing countries

India's economic integration with the rest of the world was very limited because of the restrictive economic policies followed until 1991. Indian firms confined themselves, by and large, to the home market. Foreign investment by Indian firms was very insignificants with the new economic policy used in 1991 there has however been a change. Globalization has in fact become a buzzword with Indian firms now and many are expanding their overseas business by different strategies. Indian industries can move towards globalization by different strategies such as developing exports foreign investment including joint venture and acquisition, strategic alliance, licensing and etc.

Foreign production

Besides exporting, other market entry strategies include licensing, joint ventures, contract manufacture, ownership and participation in export processing zones or free trade zones.

Licensing

Licensing is defined as "the method of foreign operation whereby a firm in one country agrees to permit a company in another country to use the manufacturing, processing, trademark, know-how or some other skill provided by the licensor". It is quite similar to the "franchise" operation. Coca Cola is an excellent example of licensing. In Zimbabwe, United Bottlers have the license to make Coke.

Licensing involves little expense and involvement. The only cost is signing the agreement and policing its implementation.

Licensing gives the following advantages:

Good way to start in foreign operations and open the door to low risk manufacturing relationships

Linkage of parent and receiving partner interests means both get most out of marketing effort

Capital not tied up in foreign operation and

Options to buy into partner exist or provision to take royalties in stock.

The disadvantages are:

Limited form of participation - to length of agreement, specific product, process or trademark Potential returns from marketing and manufacturing may be lost Partner develops know-how and so license is short Licensees become competitors - overcome by having cross technology transfer deals and Requires considerable fact finding, planning, investigation and interpretation. Those who decide to license ought to keep the options open for extending market participation. This can be done through joint ventures with the licensee.

Joint ventures

Joint ventures can be defined as "an enterprise in which two or more investors share ownership and control over property rights and operation". Joint ventures are a more extensive form of participation than either exporting or licensing. In Zimbabwe, Olivine industries has a joint venture agreement with HJ Heinz in food processing.

Joint ventures give the following advantages:

- Sharing of risk and ability to combine the local in-depth knowledge with a foreign partner with know-how in technology or process
- Joint financial strength
- May be only means of entry and
- May be the source of supply for a third country.

They also have disadvantages

Partners do not have full control of management

May be impossible to recover capital if need be

Disagreement on third party markets to serve and

Partners may have different views on expected benefits. If the partners carefully map out in advance what they expect to achieve and how, then many problems can be overcome.

Ownership: The most extensive form of participation is 100% ownership and this involves the greatest commitment in capital and managerial effort. The ability to communicate and control 100% may outweigh any of the disadvantages of joint ventures and licensing. However, as mentioned earlier, repatriation of earnings and capital has to be carefully monitored. The more unstable the environment the less likely is the ownership pathway an option.

These forms of participation: exporting, licensing, joint ventures or ownership, are on a continuum rather than discrete and can take many formats. Anderson and Coughlan[8] (1987) summarize the entry mode as a choice between company owned or controlled methods - "integrated" channels - or "independent" channels. Integrated channels offer the advantages of planning and control of resources, flow of information, and faster market penetration, and are a visible sign of commitment. The disadvantages are that they incur many costs (especially marketing), the risks are high, some may be more effective than others (due to culture) and in some cases their credibility amongst locals may be lower than that of controlled independents. Independent channels offer lower performance costs, risks, less capital, high local knowledge and credibility. Disadvantages include less market information flow, greater coordinating and control difficulties and motivational difficulties. In addition they may not be willing to spend money on market development and selection of good intermediaries may be difficult as good ones are usually taken up anyway.

Once in a market, companies have to decide on a strategy for expansion. One may be to concentrate on a few segments in a few countries - typical are cashew nuts from Tanzania and horticultural exports from Zimbabwe and Kenya - or concentrate on one country and diversify into segments. Other activities include country and market segment concentration - typical of Coca Cola or Gerber baby foods, and finally country and segment diversification. Another way of looking at it is by identifying three basic business strategies: stage one - international, stage two - multinational (strategies correspond to ethnocentric and polycentric orientations respectively) and stage three - global strategy (corresponds with geocentric orientation). The basic philosophy behind stage one is extension of programmes and products, behind stage two is decentralization as far as possible to local operators and behind stage three is an integration which seeks to synthesize inputs from world and regional headquarters and the country organisation. Whilst most developing countries are hardly in stage one, they have within them organizations which are in stage three. This has often led to a "rebellion" against the operations of multinationals, often unfounded.

Export processing zones (EPZ) Whilst not strictly speaking an entry-strategy, EPZs serve as an "entry" into a market. They are primarily an investment incentive for would be investors but can also provide employment for the host country and the transfer of skills as well as provide a base for the flow of goods in and out of the country. One of the best examples is the Mauritian EPZ[12], founded in the 1970s. References Organizations are faced with a number of strategy alternatives when deciding to enter foreign markets. Each one has to be carefully weighed in order to make the most appropriate choice. Every approach requires careful attention to marketing, risk, matters of control and management. A systematic assessment of the different entry methods can be achieved through the use of a matrix (see table 3.2).

Table 3.2 Matrix for comparing alternative methods of market entry

	Entry mode							
Evaluation criteria	**Indirect export**	**Direct export**	**Marketing subsidiary**	**Counter trade**	**Licensing**	**Joint venture**	**Wholly owned operation**	**EPZ**
(a) Company goals								
(b) Size of company								
(c) Resources								
(d) Product								
(e) Remittance								
(f) Competition								
(g) Middlemen characteristics								
(h) Environmental characteristics								
(i) Number of markets								
(j) Market								
(k) Market feedback								
(l) International market learning								
(m) Control								
(n) Marketing costs								
(o) Profits								
(p) Investment								
(q) Administration personnel								
(r) Foreign problems								
(s) Flexibility								
(t) Risk								

Institutional links between producers and processors/exporters

One of the most important factors is contract coordination. Whilst many of the details vary, most contracts contain the supply of credit/production inputs, specifications regarding quantity, quality and timing of producer deliveries and a formula or price mechanism. Such arrangements have improved the flow of money, information and technologies, and very importantly, shared the risk between producers and exporters.

Most arrangements include some form of vertical integration between producers and downstream activities. Often processors enter into contracted out grower arrangements or supply raw inputs. This institutional arrangement has now, incidentally, spilled over into the domestic market where firms are wishing to target higher quality, higher priced segments.

Producer trade associations, boards or cooperatives have played a significant part in the entry strategies of many exporting countries. They act as a contact point between suppliers and buyers, obtain vital market information, liaise with Governments over quotas etc. and provide information, or even get involved in quality standards. Some are very active, witness the Horticultural Crops Development Authority (HCDA) of Kenya and the Citrus Marketing Board (CMD) of Israel, the latter being a Government agency which specifically got involved in supply quotas. An example of the institutional arrangements[13] involved is given in table 3.3.

Table 3.3 Institutional arrangements linking producers with processors/exporters

Commodity	*Market co-ordination*	*Contract co-ordination*	*Ownership interaction*	*Association co-ordination*	*Government co-ordination*	*Marketing risk reduction*
Kenya vegetables	X	X	X			X
Zimbabwe horticulture	X			X	X	X
Israel fresh fruits						
Thailand tuna		XX		X	X	X
Argentina beef		X		X		X

XX = Dominant linkage

Institutional links between exporters and foreign buyers/agents

Linkages between exporters and foreign buyers are often dominated by open market trade or spot market sales or sales on consignment. The physical distances involved are also very significant.

Most contracts are of a seasonal, annual or other nature. Some products are handled by multinationals, others by formal integration by processors, building up import/distribution firms. In the case of Indian fresh vegetables familial ties are very important between exporters and importers. These linkages have been very important in maintaining market excess, penetrating expanding markets and in obtaining market and product change information, thus reducing considerably the risks of doing business. In some cases, Government gets involved in negotiating deals with foreign countries, either through trade agreements or other mechanisms. Zimbabwe's imports of Namibian mackerel were the result of such a Government negotiated deal. Table 3.4 gives examples of linkages between exporters and foreign buyers/agents.

Table 3.4 Linkages between exporters and foreign buyers/agents

Commodity	*Market co-ordination*	*Contract co-ordination*	*Ownership interaction*	*Association co-ordination*	*Government co-ordination*	*Marketing risk reduction*
Kenya vegetables	X	X	X			X
Zimbabwe horticulture		X		X	X	X
Israel fresh fruits	X	X				X
Thailand tuna	X	XX	XX	X		X
Argentina beef	XX	X	XX	X	X	X

XX = Dominant linkage

Once again, it cannot be over-emphasized that the smooth flow between producers, marketers and end users is essential. However it must also be noted that unless strong relationships or contracts are built up and product qualities maintained, the smooth flow can be interrupted should a more competitive supplier enter the market. This also can occur by Government decree or by the erection of non-tariff barriers to trade. By improving strict hygiene standards a marketing chain can be broken, however strong the link, by say, Government. This, however, should not occur, if the link involves the close monitoring and action by the various players in the system, who are aware, through market intelligence, of any possible changes.

Factors affecting the selection of entry mode

External Factors are:-

(i) Market size
(ii) Market growth
(iii) Government Regulation
(iv) Level of Competition
(v) Physical infrastructure
(vi) Level of risk

Market Size is one of the key factors an International marketer has to keep in mind when selecting an entry mode. Countries with a large market size justify the modes of entry with long- term commitment higher level of investment, such as wholly owned subsidiaries or equity participation. Most of the large, established markets, such as the US, Europe, and Japan, have more or less reached a point of saturation for consumer goods such as automobiles, consumer electronics, i.e. refrigerators, washing machine, TV s etc.

Government Regulation

Most of a market entry mode is to a great extent affected by the legislative frame work of the overseas market. The government of most of the Gulf countries has made it mandatory for foreign firms to have a local partner. For example, the UAE is a lucrative market for Indian firms but most firms operate there with a local partner. Trade barriers such as ecological regulation and local content requirements also affect the mode of entry .It has been a major reason for increased foreign investment in Mexico, which is a part of the North America Free Trade Agreement (NAFTA), in order to cater to the US market.

Competition Level

Presence of competition and their level of involvement in an overseas market is another crucial factor in deciding on an entry mode so as to effectively respond to competitive market forces.

Physical infrastructure

The level of development of physical infrastructure such as roads, railways, telecommunications, financial institutions and marketing channels is a pre-condition for a company to commit more resources to overseas markets. The level of infrastructure development (both physical and institutional) has been responsible for major's investment in Singapore, Dubai and Hong Kong. As a result, these places have developed as International marketing hubs in the Asian region.

Level of Risk

From the point of view of entry mode selection, firms should evaluate the following risks

- Political Risk- Political in instability and turmoil dissuades firms from committing more resources to market. Company has grater inclination to invest resources in countries with stable government and transparent legal system. Broadly, the political system in developed countries such as the US ,UK, Japan and Australia is more and less stable. Besides, the judiciary is largely independent of political interference in developed countries. On the other hand, the political system is unstable and turbulent in many developing countries such as Brazil, Pakistan, Argentina, Fuji etc. The legal system is highly influenced by those in power autocratic forms of government.
- Economics Risk- It may arise due to volatility of exchange rates of the target market's currency, upheavals in balance of payment situations that may affect the cost of other in puts for production, and marketing activities in foreign markets. International companies find it difficult to manage their operation in markets where in the inflation rate is extremely high.
- Operational risks- In case the marketing system in an overseas countries is similar to that of the firm's home countries, the firm has better understanding of operational problems in the foreign market in question. Ex- the absence of an organized retailing system in India provides Indian exporters strategic edge when operating in other developing countries, which do not have organized retailing system. This is also true for marketing promotion and communication strategy in countries with less developed marketing system .Production and shipping costs.

Markets with substantial costs of shipping as in the case of low value high volume goods may increase the logistics cost. The increased shipping cost may not only due to the due to the longer distance but also because of the availability competitive shipping lines as in case of shipping goods from India to most African and Latin American countries. Lower cost of production may also be one of the key factors in firms deciding to establish manufacturing operation in foreign countries. Many transactional companies establish their manufacturing in developing countries, such as India, China, Brazil etc., in order to take advantage of lower production cost.

Internal factors are-

(a) Company objectives- Company operating in domestic markets with limited aspiration generally enter foreign markets as a result of a reactive approach to international marketing opportunities. In such cases, companies received unsolicited orders from acquaintances, firms, and relatives based abroad, and they attempt to fulfill these export orders. This casual approach to entry international markets by way of producing in the home markets and exporting overseas translates into regular exporting if the firms have positive experience in its exports operation.

(b) Availability of company resources- Venturing into international markets needs substantial commitments of financial and human resources and therefore choice of an entry mode depends upon the financial strength of a firm. It may be observed that Indian firms with good financial strength have enter international markets by way of wholly owned subsidiaries or equity participation.

(c) Level of Commitment- In view of market potential the willingness of the company to commit resources in particular markets also determines the entry mode choice. A company needs to evaluate various investment alternatives for allocating scares resources.

(a) International experience

A company well exposed to the dynamics of the international marketing environment would be at ease when making a decision regarding entry into international markets with a highly intensive mode of entry such as joint venture and wholly owned subsidiaries. It may be observed that only those Indian companies, such Ranbaxy, Tata Tea; Asian paints etc. which have substantial experience in foreign markets have opted for equity participation or wholly on subsidiaries.

Product strategy for International Markets

Product Decision

A firm operating in International should not only identify the products for various markets but should also evolve suitable strategy for developing such products. Whether a single standardize product can be offered worldwide or a customized product needs to be developed for each market is the most significant product decision that a firm has to make while operating in International markets. In international markets decision related to quality, packaging, and labeling of products required special attention and consideration.

Decisions regarding the product, price, promotion and distribution channels are decisions on the elements of the "marketing mix". It can be argued that product decisions are probably the most crucial as the product is the very epitome of marketing planning. Errors in product decisions are legion. These can include the imposition of a global standardized product where it is inapplicable, for example large horsepower tractors may be totally unsuitable for areas where small scale farming exists and where incomes are low; devolving decisions to affiliated countries which may let quality slip; and the attempt to sell products into a country without cognizance of cultural adaptation needs. The decision whether to sell globally standardized or adapted products is too simplistic for today's market place. Many product decisions lie between these two extremes. Cognizance has also to be taken of the stage in the international life cycle, the organization's own product portfolio, its strengths and weaknesses and its global objectives. Unfortunately, most developing countries are in no position to compete on the world stage with many manufactured value-added products. Quality, or lack of it, is often the major letdown. As indicated earlier, most developing countries are likely to be exporting raw materials or basic and high value agricultural produce for some time to come.

A product can be defined as a collection of physical, service and symbolic attributes which yield satisfaction or benefits to a user or buyer. A product is a combination of physical attributes say, size and shape; and subjective attributes say image or "quality". A customer purchases on both dimensions. As cited earlier, an avocado pear is similar the world over in terms of physical characteristics, but once the label CARMEL, for example, is put on it, the product's physical properties are enhanced by the image CARMEL creates. In "postmodernisation" it is increasingly important that the product fulfills the image which the producer is wishing to project. This may involve organisations producing symbolic offerings represented by meaning laden products that chase stimulation-loving consumers who seek experience - producing situations. So, for example, selling mineral water may not be enough. It may have to be

"Antarctic" in source, and flavored. This opens up a wealth of new marketing opportunities for producers.

A product's physical properties are characterized the same the world over. They can be convenience or shopping goods or durables and nondurables; however, one can classify products according to their degree of potential for global marketing:

(i) local products - seen as only suitable in one single market.

(ii) International products - seen as having extension potential into other markets.

(iii) Multinational products - products adapted to the perceived unique characteristics of national markets.

(iv) Global products - products designed to meet global segments.

Quality, method of operation or use and maintenance (if necessary) are catchwords in international marketing. A failure to maintain these will lead to consumer dissatisfaction. This is typified by agricultural machinery where the lack of spares and/or foreign exchange can lead to lengthy downtimes. It is becoming increasingly important to maintain quality products based on the ISO 9000 standard, as a prerequisite to export marketing.

Consumer beliefs or perceptions also affect the "world brand" concept. World brands are based on the same strategic principles, same positioning and same marketing mix but there may be changes in message or other image. World brands in agriculture are legion. In fertilizers, brands like Norsk Hydro are universal; in tractors, Massey Ferguson; in soups, Heinz; in tobacco, BAT; in chemicals, Bayer. These world brand names have been built up over the years with great investments in marketing and production. Few world brands, however, have originated from developing countries. This is hardly surprising given the lack of resources. In some markets product saturation has been reached, yet surprisingly the same product may not have reached saturation in other similar markets. Whilst France has long been saturated by avocadoes, the UK market is not yet, hence raising the opportunity to enter deeper into this market.

Developing products for International markets

Various approaches followed for developing products for International markets are as follows:-

(i) Ethnocentric Approach

(ii) Polycentric Approach

(iii) Aegiocentric Approach

(iv) Geocentric Approach

Ethnocentric Approach –

This approach is based on the assumption that consumer needs and market condition are more and less homogeneous in international market as result of globalization. A firm markets its products developed for the home market with little adaptation . Generally an exporting firm in the initial phases of industrialization relies two heavily on product expansion in international markets. This market extension approach of product development facilitates cost minimization in various functional areas and a firm gains rapid entry into international markets. However, the Ethnocentric Approach does not always lead to maximization of market share and profits in international markets since the local competitor are in a relatively in a better position to satisfied customers' needs.

(i) Polycentric Approach- AN INTERNATIOANL FIRM IS AWARE OF THE FACT THAT EACH COMPANY COUNTRY MARKET IS SIGNIFICANTLY DIFFENT FROM THE OTHERS. IT THERE FORE ADOPTS SEPARATE APPROACH FOR DIFFERENT MARKETS. IN Polycentric Approach products are developed separately for different markets to suit local marketing condition.

(ii) Regiocentric Approach- Ones an international firms establishes itself in various markets the world over, it attempts to consolidates its gains and tries to ascertain product similarity within market cluster. Generally, such market cluster mare based on geographical and psychic proximity.

(iii) Geocentric Approach- Instead of extending the domestic products into international markets, a firm tries to identify similarities in consumption pattern that can be targeted with standard products around the world. Psychographic segmentation is helpful in identifying consumer profiles beyond national boarders. in a Geocentric Approach

To product development, there is a high degree of centralization and coordination of marketing and production activities resulting in higher economic of scale in the various constituent of the marketing mix. However, it needs meticulous and consistent researching of international markets.

Product life Cycle

International markets follows a cyclical pattern over a period of time due to a variety of factors. Factors like level of innovational and technology, resources, size of market and competitive structure in influence the market pattern. The product life cycle foe International markets has the following four distinct stages are –

(i) Introduction

(ii) Growth

(iii) Maturity

(iv) Decline

(v)

(i) Introduction- a majority of new product invention is made in highly industrializes and developed countries. Since product invention required substantial resources for R&D activities, market skimming pricing strategies is needed for speedy recovery of initial cost incurred. Since, in the initial stages, the price of new product is relatively high, it is only within the means and capability of the customer in high income countries to buy the products. Therefore, a firm finds markets for new product in other developed countries in the initial stages to growth.

(ii) Growth- The demand in the international market exhibit are increasing trend and an innovating firm gets better opportunities for exports. Moreover, as the markets begin to mature in the develop countries, and innovative firm faces increase international competition in the target markets. In order to defend its position in international markets, the firm establishes its production location in the developed countries.

(iii) Maturity- The technical know how often innovative process become widely known, a firm begins to establish its operation in middle and low income countries in order to take advantage of resources available at competitive prices.

(iv) Decline- The major thrust of the marketing strategy at this stages shift to price and cost competitiveness, as technical know how become widely available. Therefore the emphasis of the firm is on the most cost effective locations rather than on production. Besides developing countries, production also intensifies in least developed countries. As a result a has been observed that the innovating country begins to imports such goods from other developing countries rather than manufacturing them itself. The UK, which was once the largest manufacture and exports of bi-cycle, now imports them large volume. Bicycle are at the declining stages of the product life cycle in industrialized countries where as they are still at a growth or maturity stages in a number of developing countries . besides, chemical and hazardous industries are shifting from high income countries to low incomes countries, as the former become increasingly concern over environmental issues.

The firm may adopt the strategy of positioning its products at different stages of the life cycle in different countries.

Product design

Changes in design are largely dictated by whether they would improve the prospects of greater sales, and this, over the accompanying costs. Changes in design are also subject to cultural pressures. The more culture-bound the product is, for example food, the more adaptation is necessary. Most products fall in between the spectrum of "standardization" to "adaptation" extremes. The application the product is put to also affects the design. In the UK, railway engines were designed from the outset to be sophisticated because of the degree of competition, but in the US this was not the case. In order to burn the abundant wood and move the prairie debris, large smoke stacks and cowcatchers were necessary. In agricultural implements a mechanized cultivator may be a convenience item in a UK garden, but in India and Africa it may be essential equipment. As stated earlier "perceptions" of the product's benefits may also dictate the design. A refrigerator in Africa is a very necessary and functional item, kept in the kitchen or the bar. In Mexico, the same item is a status symbol and, therefore, kept in the living room.

Factors encouraging standardization are:

(i) economies of scale in production and marketing

(ii) consumer mobility - the more consumers travel the more is the demand

(iii) technology

(iv) image, for example "Japanese", "made in".

The latter can be a factor both to aid or to hinder global marketing development. Nagashima[1] (1977) found the "made in USA" image has lost ground to the "made in Japan" image. In some cases "foreign made" gives advantage over domestic products. In Zimbabwe one sees many advertisements for "imported", which gives the product advertised a perceived advantage over domestic products. Often a price premium is charged to reinforce the "imported means quality" image. If the foreign source is negative in effect, attempts are made to disguise or hide the fact through, say, packaging or labeling. Mexicans are loathe to take products from Brazil. By putting a "made in elsewhere" label on the product this can be overcome, provided the products are manufactured elsewhere even though its company maybe Brazilian.

Factors encouraging adaptation are:

(i) Differing usage conditions. These may be due to climate, skills, level of literacy, culture or physical conditions. Maize, for example, would never sell in Europe rolled and milled as in Africa. It is only eaten whole, on or off the cob. In Zimbabwe, kapenta fish can be used as a relish, but lt always be eaten as a "starter" to a meal in the developed countries.

(ii) General market factors - incomes, tastes etc. Canned asparagus may be very affordable in the developed world, but may not sell well in the developing world.

(iii) Government - taxation, import quotas, non-tariff barriers, labeling, health requirements. Non-tariff barriers are an attempt, despite their supposed impartiality, at restricting or eliminating competition. A good example of this is the Florida tomato growers, cited earlier, who successfully got the US Department of Agriculture to issue regulations establishing a minimum size of tomatoes marketed in the United States. The effect of this was to eliminate the Mexican tomato industry which grew a tomato that fell under the minimum size specified. Some non-tariff barriers may be legitimate attempts to protect the consumer, for example the ever stricter restrictions on horticultural produce insecticides and pesticides use may cause African growers a headache, but they are deemed to be for the public good.

(iv) History. Sometimes, as a result of colonialism, production facilities have been established overseas. Eastern and Southern Africa is littered with examples. In Kenya, the tea industry is a colonial legacy, as is the sugar industry of Zimbabwe and the coffee industry of Malawi. These facilities have long been adapted to local conditions.

(v) Financial considerations. In order to maximize sales or profits the organisation may have no choice but to adapt its products to local conditions.

(vi) Pressure. Sometimes, as in the case of the EU, suppliers are forced to adapt to the rules and regulations imposed on them if they wish to enter into the market.

Production decisions

In decisions on producing or providing products and services in the international market it is essential that the production of the product or service is well planned and coordinated, both within and with other functional area of the firm, particularly marketing. For example, in horticulture, it is essential that any supplier or any of his "out grower" (sub-contractor) can supply what he says he can. This is especially vital when contracts for supply are finalized, as failure to supply could incur large penalties. The main elements to consider are the production process itself, specifications, culture, the physical product, packaging, labeling, branding, warranty and service.

Production process

The key question is, can we ensure continuity of supply? In manufactured products this may include decisions on the type of manufacturing process -

artisanal, job, batch, and flow line or group technology. However in many agricultural commodities factors like seasonality, perishability and supply and demand have to be taken into consideration.

Specification

Specification is very important in agricultural products. Some markets will not take produce unless it is within their specification. Specifications are often set by the customer, but agents, standard authorities (like the EU or ITC Geneva) and trade associations can be useful sources. Quality requirements often vary considerably. In the Middle East, red apples are preferred over green apples. In one example French red apples, well boxed, are sold at 55 dinars per box, whilst not so attractive Iranian greens are sold for 28 dinars per box. In export the quality standards are set by the importer. In Africa, Maritime (1991)[2], found, generally, that there are no consistent standards for product quality and grading, making it difficult to do international trade regionally.

Culture

Product packaging, labeling, physical characteristics and marketing have to adapt to the cultural requirements when necessary. Religion, values, aesthetics, language and material culture all affect production decisions. Effects of culture on production decisions have been dealt with already in chapter three.

Physical product

The physical product is made up of a variety of elements. These elements include the physical product and the subjective image of the product. Consumers are looking for benefits and these must be conveyed in the total product package. Physical characteristics include range, shape, size, color, quality, quantity and compatibility. Subjective attributes are determined by advertising, self-image, labeling and packaging. In manufacturing or selling produce, cognizance has to be taken of cost and country legal requirements.

Again a number of these characteristics is governed by the customer or agent. For example, in beef products sold to the EU there are very strict quality requirements to be observed. In fish products, the Japanese demand more "exotic" types than, say, would be sold in the UK. None of the dried fish products produced by the Zambians on Lake Kariba, and sold into the Lusaka market, would ever pass the hygiene laws if sold internationally. In sophisticated markets like seeds, the variety and range is so large that constant watch has to be kept on the new strains and varieties in order to be competitive.

Packaging

Packaging serves many purposes. It protects the product from damage which could be incurred in handling and transportation and also has a promotional aspect. It can be very expensive. Size, unit type, weight and volume are very important in packaging. For aircraft cargo the package needs to be light but strong, for sea cargo containers are often the best form. The customer may also decide the best form of packaging. In horticultural produce, the developed countries often demand blister packs for mange touts, beans, strawberries and so on, whilst for products like pineapples a sea container may suffice. Costs of packaging have always to be weighed against the advantage gained by it.

Increasingly, environmental aspects are coming into play. Packaging which is non-degradable - plastic, for example - is less in demanded. Bio-degradable, recyclable, reusable packaging is now the order of the day. This can be both expensive and demanding for many developing countries.

Labeling

Labeling not only serves to express the contents of the product, but may be promotional (symbols for example Cashel Valley Zimbabwe; HJ Heinz, Afri cafe, Tanzania). The EU is now putting very stringent regulations in force on labeling, even to the degree that the pesticides and insecticides used on horticultural produce have to be listed. This could be very demanding for producers, especially small scale, ones where production techniques may not be standardised. Government labeling regulations vary from country to country. Bar codes are not widespread in Africa, but do assist in stock control. Labels may have to be multilingual, especially if the product is a world brand. Translation could be a problem with many words being translated with difficulty. Again labeling is expensive, and in promotion terms non-standard labels are more expensive than standard ones. Requirements for crate l labelling, etc. for international transportation will be dealt with later under documentation.

Branding and trademarks

As mentioned in chapter four, it is difficult to protect a trademark or brand, unless all countries are members of a convention. Brand "piracy" is widespread in many developing countries.

Other aspects of branding include the promotional aspects. A family brand of products under the Zeneca (ex ICI) label or Sterling Health are likely to be recognized worldwide, and hence enhance the "subjective" product characteristics.

Warranty

Many large value agricultural products like machinery require warranties.

Unfortunately not everyone upholds them. It is common practice in Africa that if the original equipment has not been bought through an authorized dealer in the country, that dealer refuses to honor the warranty. This is unfortunate, because not only may the equipment have been legitimately bought overseas; it also actually builds up consumer resistance to the dealer. When the consumer is eventually offered a choice, the reticent. dealer will suffer. For example when new dealers spring up.

Service

In agricultural machinery, processing equipment and other items which are of substantial value and technology, service is a prerequisite. In selling to many developing countries, manufacturers have found their negotiations at stake due to the poor back-up service. Often, this is no fault of the agent, distributor or dealer in the foreign country, but due to exchange regulations, which make obtaining spare parts difficult. Many organisations attempt to get around this by insisting that a Third World buyer purchases a percentage of parts on order with the original items. Allied to this problem is the poor quality of service due to insufficient training. Good original equipment manufacturers will insist on training and updating as part of the agency agreement. In order to illustrate the above points, cotton can be used as an example. Cotton is a major foreign exchange earner for Zimbabwe. In 1990/91, 52,000 tonnes were sold overseas at a value of Zim$ 238 million. As the spinners, particularly those in the export market, are in a highly competitive industry, it is essential that the raw material is as clean as possible. Also today's spinning equipment is highly technical and the spinner wishes to avoid costly breakdowns by all means.

Product strategies

There are five major product strategies in international marketing.

Product communications extension

This strategy is very low cost and merely takes the same product and communication strategy into other markets. However it can be risky if misjudgments are made. For example CPC International believed the US consumer would take to dry soups, which dominate the European market. It did not work.

Extended product - communications adaptation

If the product basically fits the different needs or segments of a market it may need an adjustment in marketing communications only. Again this is a low cost strategy, but different product functions have to be identified and a suitable communications mix developed.

Product adaptation - communications extension

The product is adapted to fit usage conditions but the communication stays the same. The assumption is that the product will serve the same function in foreign markets under different usage conditions.

Product adaptation - communications adaptation

Both product and communication strategies need attention to fit the peculiar need of the market.

Product invention

This needs a totally new idea to fit the exclusive conditions of the market. This is very much a strategy which could be ideal in a Third World situation. The development costs may be high, but the advantages are also very high.

Product decisions epitomize marketing planning and are the manifestation of marketing strategy. These decisions are not to be taken lightly. The end consumer and channel considerations have to be taken into account and the product extended or adapted accordingly.

New product diffusion is the process by which innovation spread throughout a social system over time. The rate of product diffusion is influence significantly by the cultural contexts. As shown in fig 3.1 among the countries with high context culture the new product diffusion is faster in Japan and south –east Asian countries compared to India and the rest of the Asia. The US, Canada, and the Scandinavian countries have faster rate of new product diffusion among the low context countries as compared to the UK, and Eastern Europe. While designing new product launch strategies, a firm should take care of the following cultural differences.

High context/fast diffusion High Context/Slow diffusion

South-east Asia India

Japan Asia

Low context/fast diffusion Low context/Slow diffusion

Scandinavia UK

USA Eastern Europe

Canada

It has been observed that in the oriental countries the response patterns of the consumers differ widely as compared to their counterparts in the west. Under the influence of the peer group, the customers are cautions while buying new products, which lead to a slight delay in new product diffusion as compared to Western markets. Similarly, at the maturity stage of the product in Oriental countries, consumers discontinue the product use at a relatively rapid pace 3 (Ministry of commerce, Export Import policy).

As a company expands its operation into overseas locations it finds that market condition, such as market size, growth potentiallations, compet, government gulations, competitive intensity, physical infrastructure, -politcal, economic, and operational risks. Therefore, companies adopt various mode of entry for different markets.

Refrences

1. Nagashima A., A comparative "Made - In Product Image Survey Among Japanese Dimension Sound of Marketing", July 1977 pp. 95-100.
2. Maritim H., "Post Harvest Handling Produce in Eastern and Southern Africa" in S. Carter (Ed) "Horticultural Marketing. Proceedings of the Sound Regional Workshop on Horticultural Marketing" 1991, pp. 187-127.
3. Bischofberger, J., "What Spinners Want. In Training Manual on Cotton Trading Operations", International Trade Centre UNCTAD/GATT, Geneva, 1989, pp. 31-53.
4. Jaffee S. (1993) "Exporting High Value Added Commodities". "World Bank Discussion Paper" 198, the World Bank, Washington
5. Sunsplash. "Business Herald", Thursdays, January 19 1995
6. Dixie, G.B.R., "Horticultural Marketing", FAO Agricultural Services Bulletin 76,1989.
7. Keegan, W.J.," Global Marketing Management", Prentice Hall, 1989.

   Cunningham, M.T. "Strategies for International Industrial Marketing". In D.W. Turnbull and J.P. Valla (eds.) Croom Helm 1986, p 9.
8. Pavord and Bogart. "Quoted in The Export Marketing Decision" S.A. Hara in S. Carter (Ed) "Export Procedures", Network and Centre for Agricultural Marketing Training in Eastern and Southern Africa 1991.
9. Piercy, N. "Company Internationalisation: Active and Reactive Exporting". *European Journal of Marketing,* Vol. 15, No. 3, 1982, pp. 26-40.
10. Collett, W.E. "International Transport and Handling of Horticultural Produce" in S. Carter (ed.) "Horticultural Marketing". Network and Centre for Agricultural Marketing Training in Eastern and Southern Africa, 1991.
11. Korey, G. "Multilateral Perspectives in International Marketing Dynamics". *European Journal of Marketing,* Vol. 20, No. 7, 1986, pp. 34-42.
12. Khoury, S.J "Countertrade: Forms, Motives, Pitfalls and Negotiation Requisites". *Journal of Business Research,* Vol. 12, 1984, pp. 257-270.
13. Shipley, D.D. and Neale, C.W. "Successful Countertrading. Management Decision", Vol. 26, No. 1, pp. 49-52.
14. Anderson, E. and Coughlan, A.T. "International Market Entry and Expansion via Independent or Integrated Channels of Distribution". *Journal of Marketing,* Vol. 51. January 1987, pp. 71-82.
15. Keegan, W.J. "Global Marketing Management", 4th ed. Prentice Hall International Editions, 1989.

16. Khoromana, A.P. "The Experience and Problems in Exporting Spices". In S. Carter (ed.) Export Procedures Network and Centre for Agricultural Marketing Training in Eastern and Southern Africa, August 1991.
17. Basche, J.R. Jr. "Export Marketing Services and Costs". New York: The Conference Board, 1971, p. 4.
18. Bheenich, R. and Shapiro, M.O. Mauritius: "A Case Study of the Export Processing Zone. In Successful African Development", EDI Development Policy Case Series, No. 1, 1989, pp. 97-127.
19. Jaffee S. "Exporting High Value Food Commodities". "World Bank Discussion Paper" pp. 198, 1993.

Chapter - Four

International Pricing and Financing

Pricing And Financing

Pricing is the only component of a marketing mix decision that is often adopted in international markets with least commitment of firm's resources. Price is the sum of value received from the customer for the product or services. We generally refer to price in terms of amount of money, but it may also include other tangible and intangible item of utility. Pricing decision become crucial for international marketing firms from developing countries primarily because of their inability to influence price in international markets. Pricing products or services in international marketing is not an easy decision. Price is, in part, a function of cost, and the foreign exchange rate is an important determinant of a company's cost of production. When borrowing capital to do business the cost of that capital can be very influential in the price decision. Take, for example, the export of maize. Firstly the crop has to be bought from the producers. If we assume that the system is state owned, or administered by a Board, money has to be raised. The money may be raised locally, say by the issue of bills, or on the international market. The cost of capital has to be included in the price as well as the possible effect of changes in exchange rates if the capital is raised internationally. When the maize is bought, part of the surplus may be sold on the international market. If it is not sufficient to cover the whole of the production, financing and marketing costs, then the system is in trouble. Pricing decision became crucial for international marketing firms from developing countries primarily because of inability to influence prices in international markets.

Pricing decision

As environmental influences are far more complex in international markets, price determination become even more complex.. The demand in International markets is affected by a number of factors .Pricing decision in international markets are extremely significant for developing and lest developed countries primarily because of following reason:-

(i) The lower production and technology base often results in higher cost of production.

(ii) As the market share of developing countries is relatively lower and these countries are marginal suppliers in most product categories, they have little bargaining power to negotiate .This compels to sale their product in International market often below the total cost of production.

(iii) Since the majority of product from developing and least developed countries are sold in international market as commodity with marginal values addition, there is limited scope for realizing optimal prices in view of fiercely competitive markets and complex pricing strategies adopted by multinational marketers, formulation of appropriate pricing strategy with innovation becomes a precondition for success in international markets.

The international financial system

When conducting business across international boundaries, and dealing with foreign exchange, the risks rise enormously, especially the impact on financial resources and decisions, and particularly on pricing strategy. Foreign exchange is the way business can be conducted across national boundaries. Customers buy value, reflected in the price and intangible attributes of the product. Price is a function of cost in part, and foreign exchange affects the cost position. Foreign exchange rates, therefore, directly impact on the production quality and effectiveness of a company's marketing effort.

Post war Europe

In 1944, the Allies met at Bretton Woods to create an international monetary framework that would support post war construction and economic growth. Subsequently two organisations developed, the International Bank for Reconstruction and Development (IBRD or World Bank) which was chartered to help war-torn countries' economic reconstruction and the International Monetary Fund (IMF) which was chartered to oversee the management of the international financial system. The main elements were fiscal exchange rates for all currencies, tight bands of fluctuation around the pegged rates, a dollar defined in gold equivalent and controlled adjustment in fixed exchange values. In 1971 the gold system collapsed because of the US balance of payments deficit. Particularly, the Third World was accumulating dollars and they far exceeded the US supply of gold.

Today's system

What emerged from the collapse was a managed dirty float (due to supply and demand) with special drawing rights (SDR). "Dirty" refers to actions by governments participating in exchange rates to influence rates, "managed" refers to the effort by governments to influence exchange rates with fiscal or monetary policy instruments. SDRs were created by the IMF to supplement the dollar and gold reserves. Its allocation is based on a formula which takes into account factors such as share of world trade and can be used to help balance of payments situations or settle financial obligations like swaps, donations and security for financial obligations.

Most countries of the world are members of the IMF which, amongst its many functions, exercises surveillance over exchange rate policies of members, manages the SDR, provides temporary balance of payment assistance and technical assistance.

Foreign exchange

Foreign exchange is currency bought or sold in the foreign exchange market. The "market" is the total of persons who buy and sell and involves various financial and other institutions. The "spot" market is for the immediate delivery, or in the interbank market within two business days, of foreign exchange. The forward market is for future delivery. The principal players are the banks (interbank market) and others including the London International Futures Exchange (LIFE). London, New York and Tokyo are the major markets with a turnover worldwide in excess of US$ 200 billion per day. The foreign exchange market is very dynamic. The price of one currency in any other currency is the result of forces of supply and demand in the foreign exchange market. The demand for one currency may be due to consumers wishing to buy from overseas or a belief that one country's currency is stronger than another's. In Africa, where exchange controls occur in some countries, this can lead to an official or unofficial black market. Also currency allocation is a feature which tends to slow down business or hinder its development.

If a country sells more than it buys, its currency value will rise and vice versa. If foreign exchange rates were set simply by money exchanged for goods and services then forecasting exchange rates would be easy. However, short and long term capital flows, speculative purchases and sales distort the picture.

Governments intervene to dampen fluctuation in exchange rates. Often they get involved in extensive trading to stem the rise in currency value so exports are not harmed.

Forecasting exchange rates

Exchange rates are very difficult to forecast due to a multitude of factors. Forecasts are, therefore, a continuation of economic analysis and judgment. In forecasting foreign exchange rates it is important to take account of purchasing power parity (PPP), that is, one unit of currency should buy the same amount of goods and services as it bought in an equilibrium period, despite differential rates of inflation. The lower the level of inflation, the greater will be the PPP effect. If prices in local currency rise faster or more slowly than prices in the rest of the world, an equal adjustment of the exchange value of the currency in the opposite direction will restore equilibrium to relative price levels. The formula to calculate the PPP impact and exchange rate is:

$$S_t + 1 = (S_1) \times \frac{1 + i_n}{1 + i_r}$$

Where;

S = the spot rate of exchange in the number of units of the home currency equal to one unit of the foreign currency

i_n = the inflation rate in the home country

i_r = the inflation rate in the foreign country

T = the base period or the present time

t+1 = the future time period as defined.

For example assume that the exchange rate between Zimbabwe and the UK is Zim$ 10 = UK£ 1. Assume that the rate of inflation in the UK is 5% per annum, and that the rate of inflation in Zimbabwe is 30% per annum. Applying the above formula, the exchange rate after one year is (UK home country):

Sti = 0.08

or UK£ = Zim$ 1

or UK£ 1 = Zim$ 12.5

Unfortunately as levels of inflation are difficult to predict and foreign exchange transactions are other than solely for purchasing goods and services, the PPP is not a very reliable forecasting technique. Other factors affect the foreign rate of exchange other than just PPP. These are:

- Economic factors - balance of payments, monetary and fiscal policy, inflation, real and nominal interest rates, government controls and incentives, etc.
- political factors - philosophy of leaders, elections
- Psychological factors - expectations, forward market prices, traders' attitudes.

One of the issues in analyzing a country's competitive position is the critical adjustment of the exchange value of a country's currency. The index is a trade weighted index (based on world trade share). Indices are issued by various bodies like the IMF.

Pricing products

Three basic factors determine the boundaries of the pricing decision - the price floor, or minimum price, bounded by product cost, the price ceiling or maximum price, bounded by competition and the market and the optimum price, a function of demand and the cost of supplying the product. In addition, in price setting cognisance must be, taken of government tax policies, resale prices, dumping problems, transportation costs, middlemen and so on. Whilst many agricultural products are at the mercy of the market (price takers) others are not. These include high value added products like ostrich, crocodile products and hardwoods, where demand outstrips supply at present.

In setting prices, it must be made clear what the objectives and policy are. Few organizations can now be pure profit maximizes - there is hardly a sector of industry where competition or potential competition is not prevalent. Three frequently encountered price polices are market penetration, skimming and holding. A low price (penetration) is a volume policy. A high price (skimming) is used if the product is fairly unique, development costs are high and demand is relatively inelastic. Market holding is a strategy intended to hold share. Here products are not based on straight exchange rates at current rates but on what the market can bear. The three price policies are illustrated in figure 4.1.

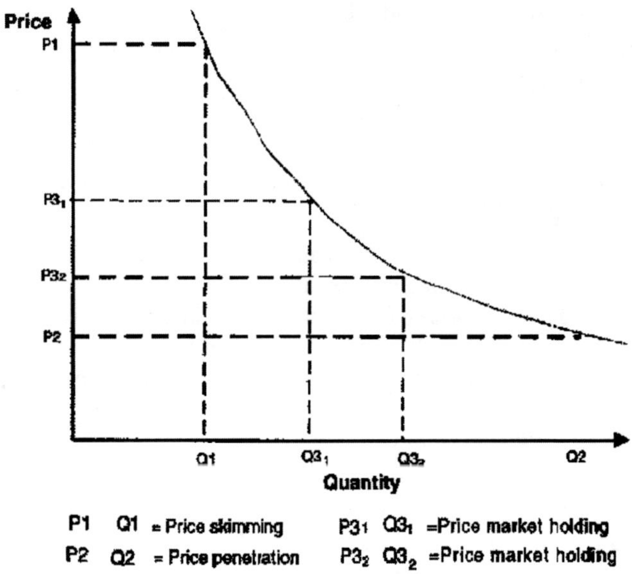

Figure 4.1 Pricing policies.

The assumption behind all three pricing policies is that the underlying conditions governing supply and demand apply. In reality, these do not always do so, if indeed ever.

Export pricing

Actual pricing methods are usually cost, market, or competition oriented. However, in the international arena, other factors come into play.

Cost plus pricing: There are basically two types under this heading, the historical accounting cost method and the estimated future cost method. The former includes direct and indirect costs and has the disadvantage of ignoring demand and competitive position in the target market. Estimated cost approaches are based on assumptions of production volume (depending on process) which will be a principal factor determining costs. Again difficulties may lie in trying to estimate production levels. In reality, costs may be a useful starting point but should never be used as a final arbiter.

Competitive pricing: Whilst costs are important they should be looked at alongside the prices of competitive products in the target markets. Once these price levels have been established the base price, or price that the buyer will pay for the product, can be determined. This involves four steps:

(i) Estimation of demand schedules

(ii) Estimation of incremental and full manufacturing and marketing costs to achieve projected sales volumes

(iii) Selection of price which offers the highest contribution

(iv) Inclusion of other elements of the marketing mix. These steps are by no means easy. Costs are difficult to assess properly as are demand conditions.

In products of a raw commodity nature or those traded on the international market subject to world prices, often the producer has no alternative but to take the going price - a price governed by competition, especially on the supply side. In Malawi, for example, although tobacco prices internationally may be encouraging, if too many farmers grow it, the price will be suppressed for all.

Market pricing

In certain products one can charge "what the market can bear". If the supplier is one of a few, despite all the problems associated with price fixing, the market may be able to bear a high price. If, as in Africa, an export crop fails, then other suppliers can take advantage of this to charge higher prices for a similar export crop. This was the case, a few years ago, with the Kenyan avocado market. An Israeli crop failure gave an unprecedented boost to Kenya's price and production.

In other cases the product may be so unique that the company should capitalize on its rarity by charging a high price. At one time exotic produce like Malaysian star fruit and rambutans could command a high price due to their scarcity. The problem is, encouraged by the profit margins; more entrants are drawn into the market.

Price escalation

One major feature of international pricing is the increase on the price due to the application of duties and so on (see table 4.1).

Table 4.1 Price escalation

Target price in foreign markets	25.00
Less 40% retail margin on selling price	10.00
Retailer cost	15.00
Less 75% importer/distributor marking up cost	1.96
Distributor cost	13.04
Less 12% value added tax on landed value and duty	1.40
CIF value plus duty	11.64
Less 9% duty on CIF value	0.96
Landed CIF value	10.68
Less ocean freight and insurance	1.40
Required FOB price to achieve target price	9.26

If 9.26 is less than the domestic price, the firm has alternatives:

(i) forget about exporting

(ii) consider marginal pricing

(iii) shorten the distribution channel

(iv) modify or simplify product if possible

(v) find an alternative source of supply with lower cost.

Dumping

Dumping, as defined by GATT, is the difference between the normal domestic price and the price at which the product leaves the exporting country. A discussion on dumping has been given fully in chapter four.

Devaluation and revaluation

Devaluation is the reduction and revaluation an increase in the value of one currency vis à vis other currencies. Under the floating exchange rate system devaluation and revaluation occur when currency values adjust in the exchange rate system in response to supply and demand. The idea behind devaluation is to make the domestic price more competitive and so more of the product can be bought for the same foreign currency. However, it can be negated by the higher price and costs induced by inboard goods and services which make up the export product. If the product is inelastic in demand, prices can be maintained if the competitive position is strong.

In revaluation, the revaluing country's prices are more expensive. These price increases may be passed on to the customers, absorbed or the domestic price may be reduced.

Inflation

Inflation is a worldwide phenomenon, and requires periodic price adjustments. Inflation accounting methods attempt to deal with the phenomenon. It is essential to retain gross and operating profit margins. Actions to maintain margins are subject to government controls (a typical African situation is where governments use price or selective price controls rather than rooting out the underlying causes of inflation or foreign exchange shortages), competitive behavior and the market itself. Price adjustments may affect the demand for products, and this is the ultimate arbiter of price alterations.

Transfer pricing

The concept of transfer pricing which was earlier limited to foreign multinational companies is, becoming increasingly significant for Indian companies as result of their increasing internalization. Indian firm's enter international markets by way of joint ventures, wholly owned subsidiaries etc., companies own distribution systems in international market, which makes transfer pricing crucial for formulating and international pricing strategy the price of an international transition between related parties is called transfer price. The objective of transfer pricing are as follows;

(i) Maximizing over all after tax profits

(ii) Reducing incident of custom duties payment

(iii) Circumventing the quota restriction on imports

(iv) Reducing exchange exposure ,circumventing exchange control and restricting repatriation so that transfer's firms are affiliates to the parent can be maximized

(v) Transferring of funds in location so as to suit corporate working capital policies

(vi) Window dressing operation to improve the apparent financial position of an affiliate so as to enhance its credit rating

The objective of transfer price apperatenly seems simple allocation of profits among the subsidiaries and the parent company, but the differences in the taxation pattern in various markets makes it's a complex phenomenon. Transfer prices come under the scrutiny of taxation authorities when it is different from the arm's length price to unrelated parties. Transfer pricing involves the following stake holder;

(i) Parent company

(ii) Foreign subsidiaries or joint venture or any other strategic alliance
(iii) Strategic alliance partner
(iv) Home countries and overseas manager
(v) Home countries governments
(vi) Host countries government

International transaction based on intra company transferred pricing involves; conflicting interests of various stake holder. Therefore, in view of divers interests of stake holder, a transfer pricing decision become a formidable tasks the factors influencing transfer pricing include;

(i) market condition in the foreign countries.
(ii) Competition in the foreign countries,
(iii) reasonable profit for the foreign affiliate
(iv) home country income taxes
(v) economic condition in the foreign countries
(vi) import restriction
(vii) customs duties
(viii) price control
(ix) Taxation in the host countries is eg. Withholding taxes
(x) exchange control

Types of transfer pricing

(i) Market-based
(ii) Non-market

(i) Market-based:- It is referred to as arm's length pricing, wherein the sales transactions occur between two unrelated arm's length parties. Transfer pricing comes under the scrutiny of tax authorities when it is different from the arm's length price to unrelated firms.
(ii) Non-Market pricing:- Pricing policies that deviate from market based arms' length pricing are known as non- marketing based pricing.
(iii) Pricing at direct manufacturing costs:- it refers to the intra-firm transactions that take place at the marketing cost.

The basic objective of such transfer pricing is to siphon profits away from high-tax parent company or its affiliate to low-tax affiliate and allocate funds to locations with strong currencies and virtually no exchange controls. With globalization companies are making use of differential rates of transfer pricing to optimize their profit in low – tax regimes at the expense of high-tax regimes. In India the detailed law on transfer pricing was introduced through the Finance Act,2001. The transfer pricing law encompasses all multinational companies which transfer goods and services across borders. This transfer pricing phenomenon deprives India of its share of tax on that income. The law requires companies to submit details of their own transactions with related parties along with comparable data of similar transactions by others to justify transfer pricing to tax authorities

Transfer pricing is more appropriate to those organizations with decentralized profit centers. Transfer pricing is used to motivate profit center managers, provide divisional flexibility and also further corporate profit goals. Across national boundaries the system gets complicated by taxes, joint ventures, attitudes of governments and so on. There are four basic approaches to transfer pricing.

- Transfer at cost: few practice this, which recognizes foreign affiliates contribute to profitability by operating domestic scale economies. Prices may be unrealistic so this method is seldom used.
- Transfer at direct cost plus overheads and margin. Similar to that in transfer at cost.
- Transfer at a price derived from end market prices: very useful strategy in which market based transfer prices and foreign sourcing are used as devices to enter markets too small for supporting local manufacturers. This gives a valuable foothold.
- Transfer at an "arm's length": this is the price that would have been reached by unrelated parties in a similar transaction. The problem is identifying a point "arm's length" price for all products other than commodities. Pricing at "arm's length" for differentiated products results not in a specific price but prices which fall in a predeterminable range.

Many governments see transfer pricing as a tax evasion policy and have, in recent years, looked more closely at company returns. Rates of duty encourage the size of the transfer price: the higher the duty rate the more desirable a lower transfer price. A low income tax creates a pressure to raise the transfer price to locate income in the low tax setting. Harmonization of tax rates worldwide may make the intricacies of transfer pricing obsolete.

Government controls, like cash deposits on importers, give an incentive to minimize the price of the imported item. Profit transfer rules may apply which restrict the amount of profit transferred out of the country. Other controls look at monopoly pricing like the case of the British Government against Hoffman-La Roche, forcing the price of its tranquilizers downwards.

Joint ventures

These present an incentive to transfer price goods at a higher rate than one that would have been used in transfer pricing goods to their own wholly owned affiliates because the company's share of the joint venture earnings is less than 100 percent. It is important, therefore, to work out an agreement in advance. The tax authorities' criteria of "arm's length" prices is probably the most appropriate for joint ventures.

Global pricing

There are three possible global pricing policies - extension (ethnocentric), adaptation (polycentric) and invention (geocentric).

Extension

The same global price. A very simple method but does not respond to market sensitivity.

Adaptation

Different prices in different markets. The only control is setting transfer prices within the corporate system. It prevents problems of arbitrage when the disparities in local market prices exceed the transportation and duty costs separating markets.

Innovation

A mix of a) and b). This takes cognizance of any unique market factor (s) like costs, competition, income levels and local marketing strategy. In addition it recognizes the fact that headquarters price coordination is necessary in dealing with international accounts and arbitrage and it systematically seeks to embrace national experience.

Financing of exports

Financing exports is a major decision area and one of some considerable complexity. Sources of funds can be both internal and external to the organization. Internal sources include subsidiaries and transfer within groups. External sources include the international money markets, factoring, leasing, hire purchase export credit guarantee schemes etc. A discussion on sources of funds is appropriate in a chapter on pricing as it is a "cost" which affects the end price and must be accounted for in selling prices.

Internal sources

The subsidiary: Self-funding obviates the need for currency transfers and avoids exchange rate fluctuations. It also lessens the burden on the parent company. The major problem may be the lack of sufficient funding which requires parent contribution.

Transfers within group: May take the form of loans, investment capital, material and/or licenses. Remittances back in interest, dividends, etc. will depend on tax liability operating in the host country (see previous sections). Whilst transfers are a greater risk than internal subsidiary funding they are more flexible in dates of payment, direction (one subsidiary to another) and type and scale.

External sources

Host country borrowing: Offers two advantages. Firstly it reduces the loss if expropriation occurs and secondly, interest payments raised locally can be paid out of revenues, leaving only excesses for exposure to transfer risk.

Export credit schemes and pre and post-shipment support facility: Zimbabwe does not have guarantee facility. Malawi is in the process of setting one up, so the schemes available are described in the following sections.

Export credit guarantee facility: The export credit guarantee (ECG) facility contributes to the growth and diversification of an export base by providing collateral support through guarantees to the banks extending pre- or post-shipment financing to enterprises for non-traditional export production and sales. The facility will help such exporters to secure financing and the facility will increase confidence among foreign buyers that exporters can fulfill their contractual commitments as reliable suppliers.

The facility is expected to be financially self-supporting in the long run, which means that the guarantee fee income will have to cover administration costs and claim payments. In order to fulfill its export development function, however, certain risks and guarantee losses will be inevitable and will have to be accepted. Malawi's facility (below) serves as an example of an ECG scheme.

The policies

Risk covered: The RBM credit guarantees will cover the risk of non-payment of exporters to the participating banks. The principal repayment source for a bank credit will be the export bill but it is the exporter's responsibility to repay the credit notwithstanding the foreign buyer's payment.

Pre-shipment credit guarantee: The pre-shipment credit guarantee is designed to provide collateral for bank credit of up to a maximum of 180 days, that is, granted in an amount of up to the domestic production /processing costs. The validity of the guarantee will always be in accordance with the production period, that is, from the purchase of inputs until the date of shipment and equal to the duration of the credit. Because the domestic costs may include refundable duties at shipment, 'it is possible that pre-shipment credit guarantee needs to be higher than the export price of the product.

Post-Shipment credit guarantee: The post-shipment credit guarantee is designed to provide collateral to a bank credit that is granted to refinance the supplier credit extended by the exporter to his foreign buyer. The maximum amount of credit to be guaranteed is the same as the supplier credit and the maximum guarantee period 180 days.

Packing/individual credit guarantee: Under the above categories of pre- and post-shipment credit guarantees, a guarantee limit is usually granted within which individual export transactions of the exporter are then financed and guaranteed (packing credit guarantee). A guarantee may also be provided without a pre-established limit against a specific export order to cover pre- and post-shipment advances to the exporter who occasionally sells abroad (Individual credit guarantee).

Spot marketing trading

Many market exchanges are done "on the spot". In such transactions, goods, services or money are transferred simultaneously between buyer and seller. Trade takes place on goods which have already been produced and the going price acts as the source of contracts, incentives and other relevant information. Spot market transactions can occur across several types of markets, including auctions, private treaty, etc. Auctions act is a "price discovery" mechanism. They are very useful for standard products - flowers, beef and so on and can give flexibility to the price mechanism where they may be updated on a regular basis. Auctions also have very low transaction costs.

Spot market trading has many advantages:

(i) It puts constraints on the individual - budgetary and purchasing.

(ii) Prices can be adjusted to market conditions almost on the spot, thus giving great flexibility.

(iii) The market price system gives incentives - the price automatically adjusts to productive effort or non-production. If the spot price is high and attractive, new producers may enter the market and be rewarded. If there are supply differences then the price adjusts upwards also. Of course, the converse happens with gluts.

(iv) It gives information to economies with market prices "summarizing" all, or most, of the information on transactions required to conduct trade.

Spot market trading is not just an agricultural commodity phenomenon, but can also be seen in industrials like oil and metals.

It is expected that a guarantee for pre-shipment finance will be more often used than post-shipment guarantees because the exporter is usually paid under a Letter of Credit. When this is the case the exporter will not need either post-shipment finance or guarantee coverage.

Eligibility

The primary objective of the facility is to increase production for export. Therefore, the facility will be available to all types of Malawi exporters of non-traditional products including not only industrial and agricultural producers but also export merchants and traders. However, to be eligible for the guarantee of the facility manufacturers have to show that their export products contain at least 30% local value added. Similarly, export traders have to prove that their products are locally manufactured with a value added as mentioned above.

Although the facility is designed to complement rather than substitute normal collateral, exports will not be classified in this regard in order to widen the risk of spreading of the guarantee portfolio so as to strengthen the self-sustaining nature of the facility.

Guarantee fee

Depending on the risk assessment, the guarantee fee may vary between 1 - 1.5% per annum for pre-shipment stage and 0.75 -1.24% for post-shipment. The fee is charged on the highest amount outstanding at any time during the month. In addition to risk assessment the size of the guarantee fee is also dependent on the operating cost of the facility.

Resource and assessment

RBM will not require any counter-guarantee or collateral from the exporters. However, foreign receivables will be usually transferred to the benefit of the bank or RBM. RBM reserves the right of recourse to the exporter to the extent that claims have been paid to a bank due to the default of the exporter. The aim of a recourse to the exporter is to discourage a solvent exporter escaping his repayment obligations to the bank just because the bank has secured a guarantee cover for the credit. It is expected that the bank would be inclined to seek guarantees to cover clients who, in their judgment, are potentially risky. It is therefore important that sufficient expertise be developed in RBM for its own risk assessment on exporters and their foreign transactions to minimize guarantee losses.

Foreign currency finance: Professional ·exporters understand how to use foreign currencies in their costing and negotiations. Foreign currency may be borrowed, or insurance taken out by covering forward. Exporters are not in the business of currency speculation per se.

Eurocurrency finance: Eurocurrencies are funds of major world currencies owned outside the relevant national boundaries. They can be borrowed in sizable amounts. Interest rates are often lower than the borrowing rate for the same domestic currency.

Currency swaps: Negotiations of outward collections and documentary letters of credit may be open to some but not all firms as they may not have an international credit rating. Currency swaps are a way to gain access to foreign capital at favorable rates. Swaps involve the exchange of debt from one currency to another. The process is as follows:

> "Swaps comprise contracts to exchange cash flows relating to the debt obligations of the two counterparties to the agreement. Although swaps are contracts between the two parties they do not alter the direct responsibilities that each party has for the debt obligation it has personally incurred. "Let us suppose a well respected Zimbabwe company wants to borrow Botswana pula but it is not well known in Botswana. If there is a company in Botswana wishing to borrow Zim dollars but is unknown in Zimbabwe, there is the possibility of a swap. If the Zimbabwe company borrowed in Botswana pula it would have to pay a relatively high interest rate reflecting its poor credit rating. Similarly the Botswana company would have to pay a relatively high interest rate on its borrowing in Zimbabwe. From an interest rate point of view it is better that the Botswana company borrows in Botswana pula and the Zimbabwe company borrows in Zim dollars. The two companies then swap currencies and the payments related thereto. The Zimbabwe company pays the interest and eventually repays the Botswana loan and vice versa.

"The simplest method of servicing the loans would be for the Zimbabwe company to pay the interest on the Botswana pula loan and for the Botswana company to pay the interest on the Zimbabwean dollar loan. In fact each counter party is paying interest on the other's loan as if it were the borrower. They are both in fact paying lower interest charges than if they themselves had borrowed the currencies they needed.

"The Botswana company has borrowed pula and the Zimbabwe company Zim dollars. They swap the currencies, the simplest basis being to do so at the spot price at the time of making the deal. When it comes to repayment, again the easiest method is for the currency to change hands at the spot rate. The Botswana company has to repay in Botswana pula; the Zimbabwe company makes the appropriate amount of Bots pula available to the Botswana company by selling Zimbabwe dollars at the spot rate.

"As can be seen.... a currency swap can be construed as a series of forward exchange contracts... The term (life) of currency swaps can vary. The swap document should clarify the rates of exchange that will be used. Normally one currency is recorded as the fixed principle amount, with an agreed rate of exchange for calculating the amounts in the second currency.

"One of the objectives of the currency swap is to take advantage of lower interest rates, another... is to restructure the currency base of a company's liabilities. If a UK based multinational found that nearly all its borrowings were in sterling, it would become worried if (sterling) was getting stronger against the currencies in which it was generating its earning. It might therefore attempt to swap some of it sterling debts into debts in other currencies. It would be attempting to reduce its risks due to exchange rate exposure. In restructuring the debts to balance its exchange rate exposure, the company could also take the opportunity to alter the structure of its interest rate liabilities. If many of its loans were at fixed interest rates and it was believed that interest rates would fall in the future, it could at the same time as swapping currencies move from fixed rate obligations to floating rate commitments."[1]

The problem is that, although the swap is covered by contract, each party remains responsible for the original loan (principle) it has incurred in its own currency. It is better, therefore, to get an idea what the balance on exchange might be at the outset and certainly to understand the counterpart.

Currency transactions

In every currency transaction there are risks which are the effects of currency exchange rate fluctuations on the realized value of such transfers. Shifts of rates up or down could lead to a bonus or a loss between sellers and buyers. The purpose of this section is to explore how the exposure to transaction risks affects prices and can be accounted for.

Risks can be tackled at two levels - policy and individual level.

Policy level

Risks can be reduced by raising in-country finance, by use of internal sources and by anticipating currency moves, hence allowing the organisation to devise a pricing policy which will balance out wins and losses. By holding price for a longer period and by balancing out the value of products marketed in foreign countries with imports or other cash obligations, net exposure is reduced. However, it is difficult to achieve in practice.

Individual transaction level

In currency movements there are risks to buyer and seller. As a supplier there are advantages in operating in your own currency, because the customer bears the risk. As a buyer, purchasing in exporter's currency you can accept the transaction risk by waiting to buy the necessary foreign currency at the time of settlement or alternatively you can try to reduce the risk by entering a forward exchange deal (known as "money market" cover). These are explained further below.

Pricing and the use of foreign currencies

An organisation which is prepared to quote prices and invoice in the buyer's currency can obtain many advantages. In the first place it has a marketing attraction because it simplifies the whole transaction for the buyer, telling him immediately what the cost is to him, and it demonstrates the exporter's efficiency. Secondly, because most sales are made on credit terms, there is a possible extra profit available by selling the expected currency receipts on the forward exchange market.

No operation in foreign currency need present any problems as the banks are fully equipped to provide all the information and facilities required. The London foreign exchange market is the most efficient and comprehensive in the world. Any foreign currency received in payment of exports can be readily sold through the exporter's bank.

Forward market: Where credit terms have been given and goods have been sold at a price expressed in foreign currency, the risk of changes in the exchange rate can be covered by selling the expected currency forward. All that is necessary is for the exporter to inform his bank that he expects to receive a certain sum in a foreign currency on such a date and establish with the bank a "forward" contract. The bank will quote NOW a rate at which it will buy the currency on that date. The exporter thus knows exactly how much of his own currency he will receive when the payment is made. The forward rates are quoted in the press daily for the principal currencies, usually for one, two, three and six months. For some of the major currencies it is possible to get quotations for up to two or three years and in the case of the US dollar a period of up to eight years has been arranged. The quotations are shown at a premium or discount to the spot rate.

Where the exporter cannot be certain as to the exact date when he will receive payment an "option forward" contract can be arranged. The "option" is not whether to proceed or not but merely as to the date of delivery of the currency. Say, for example, an exporter has sold on 90 day terms but expects a little slippage, he can sell the currency forward for three months fixed option one further month. He may then deliver the currency any time from the end of three months up to the end of the fourth month.

Exchange risk

London is by far the biggest money market in the world (480 authorized banks compared with 200 in the US and 100 in Frankfurt/Zurich). An exporter may see that a profitable deal at today's exchange rates would become unprofitable if there were a serious shift in the exchange rate before payment was received. Exporters are not in the business of exchange gambling, they have enough work making profits on exports anyway without running any additional risk by speculating in exchange. So how can the exporter eliminate the exchange risk?

(i) Invoice in domestic currency. This is the easy way out. Unfortunately all the exporter is doing is to transfer the exchange problem onto his customer. There may be occasions when it is better to invoice in sterling, however, and we need to be professional enough to identify these occasions.

(ii) Invoice in foreign currency, fixing exchange rate on the invoice. Here, obviously the exporter has to take a view on what will happen to the exchange rate. At least if he uses the forward rate being quoted by the bank he may be no worse off than if he had contracted forward with the bank. However the customer may well not like this method.

(iii) Borrow foreign currency from a bank, sell in dollars, and repay the loan with the proceeds of the sale. The cost of this may be less than it would cost the exporter to sell forward a currency which is going to a discount.

(iv) Offset imports in one currency with exports in the same currency so avoiding the need to change currencies and risk exchange loss.

Examples of forward rate calculations can be seen in the following case.

Arbitrage: Investments in forward currency are usually financed by borrowing. This means that the decision to buy forward or to hold foreign currency on deposit will face the organisation with additional cost in terms of interest charges. It would seek to reduce the risk and reduce the cost of borrowing. This can be done by involving three currencies, say:

BC = Buyer's currency

SC = Seller's currency

MC = Mediating currency (it is believed it will strengthen against SC in the period)

If buying for settlement in the exporter's currency in three months' time

(i) Borrow on BC

(ii) Convert at spot rate into MC if you expect MC to strengthen against SC

(iii) Invest MC to earn interest

(iv) On the appropriate date, cash the MC investment (original sum + interest)

(v) Convert this into SC - pay the vendor

(vi) Apply the residual to meet borrowing and transaction charges (this may necessitate converting the residual from SC into BC).

The dangers in this are the move into three currencies and the investment of MC. Currencies and investments may rise and fall.

Currency baskets

Organisations which have to trade in several currencies may seek to reduce transaction risk by adopting a portfolio or currency basket approach. There are two ways a) holding a basket of currencies or b) using a currency basket. For example, the UAPTA and the European ECU is a weighted average of member currencies and so fluctuates less than, say, between two currencies. Basket currencies sometimes reduce the accounting complexities faced when doing business in different currencies.

Spot marketing trading

Many market exchanges are done "on the spot". In such transactions, goods, services or money are transferred simultaneously between buyer and seller. Trade takes place on goods which have already been produced and the going price acts as the source of contracts, incentives and other relevant information. Spot market transactions can occur across several types of markets, including auctions, private treaty, etc. Auctions act is a "price discovery" mechanism. They are very useful for standard products - flowers, beef and so on and can give a flexibility to the price mechanism where they may be updated on a regular basis. Auctions also have very low transaction costs.

Spot market trading has many advantages:

(i) It puts constraints on the individual - budgetary and purchasing.

(ii) Prices can be adjusted to market conditions almost on the spot, thus giving great flexibility.

(iii) The market price system gives incentives - the price automatically adjusts to productive effort or non-production. If the spot price is high and attractive, new producers may enter the market and be rewarded. If there are supply differences then the price adjusts upwards also. Of course, the converse happens with gluts.

(iv) It gives information to economies with market prices "summarizing" all, or most, of the information on transactions required to conduct trade.

Spot market trading is not just an agricultural commodity phenomenon, but can also be seen in industrials like oil and metals.Factors Influencing Pricing Decision In International Markets

Cost

A large number of exporters in initial stages use cost-based pricing, which is hardly the best way to determine price in international markets. However, the cost is often a key determinant of the profitability of a firm in marketing the product. Firms located in difference countries do have significant variations in their cost of production and marketing but the price in international markets is determined by the market forces. Therefore, the profitability among international firms varies widely depending upon their costing.

Competitions

The competition is much higher in international markets compared to the domestic markets. The competitive intensity and its nature widely in international markets. In a large numbers of markets, the competition is from international firms while the local firms or local subsidies of multinationals compete only in a few markets. As local firms or local subsidies of multinationals compete only in a few markets.

Purchasing Power

Purchasing power of customers varies widely among the countries. A firm operating in international markets should take into consideration the buying power of the consumers while making pricing decision.

Grey Marketing

Grey marketing means import or export of goods and marketing them through unauthorized channel. Thus, the marketing channels for grey market involved un authorized market intermediaries .international brand with high price differential and low cost of arbitrage constitute typical grey market goods the arbitrage costs of grey market goods include transportation, customs tariff, taxes, and in a few cases cost towards product modification ex- the cost incurred on changing the language of instruction on the products. types grey marketing channels are:-

(i) Parallel importing
(ii) Re-importing
(iii) Lateral re-importing

(i) Parallel Importing:- This type of grey marketing takes place when a product is sold at a higher price to authorized imports in the overseas market than the price at which the product is available in the home market. This makes parallel importing directly through untorthorised marketing attractive as compared to buying from authorized importers or market intermediaries.

(ii) Re-importing- It becomes an attractive mean of grey marketing when a product is priced lower in international markets as compared to that in home market.Re-importing is particularly attractive when:

- the manufacturer's strategy is to sell into the foreign market at a substantially lower price than in the home market, due either to the market being poorer or there being dramatic exchange rate differences, and

- the foreign market is geograp hically close to the home market, thus minimizing return transport costs.

(iii) Lateral- re –importing:- Products are sold from one export market to another export market through parallel importing when price differences exists between different market which makes such grey marketing channel attractive. it is commonly reported that the price difference in automobile is substantial between the US and Canada as Canadian prices are relatively lower and there is hardly any customs tariff between the two countries, the Canadian distributors often engaged in selling to the US markets for which they are not authorized by the company.

Grey marketing channel adversely affect the established distribution channels of a firm besides, it also becomes difficult to spot counterfeit product in grey marketing. Products are sold by grey marketing channel at prices lower than that of legitimate importers and distributors.

The effects of parallel channels

There are a number of effects of all of this parallel importing activity. Here, the predicaments and opportunities created by these parallel distribution channels are discussed in more detail.

First, consumers may be prejudiced against buying products which have been parallel imported because sometimes they cannot be properly serviced or maintained. They also may be worried that the so-called technical requirements for certain products may not met by grey importers. It needs to be made clear that parallel imports are not counterfeits but genuine products that are often sold at a lower price to consumers than these distributed by regular channels (Ahmadi and Yang, 1995). However, these may not necessarily have a lower profit margin because they can free ride on the promo tonal efforts of authorized dealers. Consequently parallel imports may undermine authorized dealers' selling efforts. For example, by discouraging their investment in a sales-force or shelf-space.

In other words, parallel imports may have financial consequences for licensed distributors, if they do not derive sufficient revenue from the sale of these branded goods. In such instances they may not be able to continue with their advertising and promotional efforts. Parallel importing of trademarked goods may also create confusion for consumers. However, some authors argue that because parallel importers sell genuine trademarked goods there is no possibility of confusion about the origin or source of the goods. Although, modern trademark law does not support this view, involving an unauthorized channel or outlet increases the likelihood of consumer confusion about product source and quality. The "source function" of a trademark encompasses more than the geographic origin of goods. As a result of modern marketing and distribution techniques, consumers perceive a "genuine" article to be those from the wholesaler, retailer or servicing company they have been able to rely on in the past. The authorized distributor is in effect the "sponsor" of the trademarked good, providing many ancillary services. Consumer confusion is possible if the parallel importer does not disclose that they are not the authorized distributors or they do not offer the same warranty protection or services, which the consumer has come to expect. The "quality function" of the trademark does not replace the "source function" but stands alongside it as a "guarantee" of consistent quality. In the grey market, genuine trademarked goods possess identical product quality when shipped from the factory. Product quality, however, is not simply measured at the factory; it is also determined at the time of retail sale. Many trademark owners thus invest in their product by careful shipping, storage, inventory control, and quality management. This investment is a natural adjunct of their desire to build and protect the reputation of their product. In contrast, grey marketers may unknowingly or unknowingly sell inferior products because they provide less quality control and have less incentive to make these expenditures. Inferior products however, confuse and deceive consumers and may negatively impact genuine products and their image.

Manufacturer-distributor relations can also be strained by the appearance of parallel imports. Distributors feel frustrated by having them in their markets and look to the manufacturer to reduce or eliminate this unforeseen competition. Manufacturers profits also may decrease because of parallel imports. Sometimes they may be forced to buy back old stock from authorized distribute tutors because parallel importers create an oversupply in the market Despite the problems caused by parallel imports, there are also opportunities for consumers and for manufacturers as well.

- "There is some evidence to indicate that parallel import channels from the United States have been used to penetrate foreign markets.
- Some United States' manufacturers recognised that parallel channels could be used to increase overall foreign sales and market share" (Michael, 1998).
- Furthermore, when a final dec ision on an exclusive distributorship was pending, a parallel channel gives the manufacturer an opportunity to evaluate one distributor against another.
- Parallel channels may help overcome a weak distributor's performance at no additional costs to the manufacturer.
- Sales that go through parallel channels may expand a manufacturer's market coverage if the authorized distributor lacks the capacity for covering the whole market. This situation may be very common in

developing markets where distributors often lack the financial and marketing resources to effectively push and pull products through the distribution chain.

- "Parallel channels may also help to identify consumers in foreign markets whom the manufacturer may not be aware of" .
- However, by far the most interesting opportunity created by parallel imports is when manufacturers use it to circumvent trade restrictions. In other words "non-tariff trade barriers exist in the form of quotas or import licenses, the authorized importer has limited sales opportunities. The parallel exporter, who sells to a different importer under separate quota or license, provides the manufacturer with additional sales.

Future of parallel imports

The trend towards the globalization of markets, which is being facilitated by the development of a global communication system, envisages the end to domestic territoriality because of global competition. Because of the speed of new technologies and communication developments, parallel importation may be a short-term phenomenon. The impacts of globalization on parallel importation are two folds. First, as trade barriers between nations decrease, it will become more difficult to implement price discrimination policies based on country boundaries. Implicitly, parallel traders are therefore likely to gradually disappear, as there will be fewer opportunities for arbitrage. The issue of parallel importation may therefore become less significant as globalization continues. Secondly, traditionally, under international law, nations have asserted sovereignty based upon the territory that they legally control. Advances in electronic communications, including the Internet, however, have begun to change this. This development suggests that, rather than sovereignty based on territory, sovereignty will be based on information flows or economic spheres of influence will become the norm in cyberspace. This hypothesized shift will however, require a re-evaluation of present legal doctrines, which in turn may "re-establish parallel imports legality". Nevertheless, when the world economy becomes far more globally integrated, which is likely in a digitally based economy, it becomes necessary to harmonies the different transactional rules between nations. This means policy co-ordination among different.

Distribution Decisions

Distribution has two elements, the institutional and the physical. Whilst the modes of market entry were fully discussed in chapter seven, the actual institutions (for example retailers, agents and so on.) were not. These will be discussed briefly. Physical distribution aspects cover transport and warehousing, and again, these will be briefly touched on.

Whilst most agricultural exports from developing countries are either in a "primary" format (for example cotton, maize) or "finished" format (for example flowers, vegetables) increasing attention is being put on "processed" or "added value" formats. This means that, whereas in the former, exporters are in the hands of agents, merchants or other middlemen, in the latter much more needs to be understood of the channel itself. The more is known about the end user and the channel to reach him/her the better equipped will be the exporter to understand and meet the needs and also to perhaps gain more of the exported added value. It is a fact in flowers, for example, that these are sold on from the Dutch market to the Far East, where the price commanded is much more than the original exporter price. If the original exporter could participate in this channel, the greater would be the return.

The longer the channel, the more likely that producer profits will be indirectly reduced. This is because the end product's price may be too expensive to sell in volume, sufficient for the producer to cover costs. Yet cutting channel length may be impossible, as country infrastructure requirements may dictaA channel is an institution through which goods and services are marketed. Channels give place and time utilities to consumers. In order to provide these and other services, channels charge a margin. The longer the channel the more margins are added.

Channels are an integrative part of the marketer's activities and as such are very important. They also give a very vital information flow to the exporter. As seen in chapter seven, the degree of control one has over a channel depends on the channel type which is employed. Whilst for developing countries, as stated earlier, channels are almost given, this is not always the case, and as exporting becomes more and more necessary, it will not always be the case. In deciding on channel design the following have to be considered carefully:

- Market needs and preferences
- The cost of channel service provision
- Incentives for channel members and methods of payment
- The size of the end market to be served
- Product characteristics required, complexity of product, price, perishability, packaging
- Middlemen characteristics - whether they will push products or be passive
- Market and channel concentration and organisation
- Appropriate contractual agreements
- Degree of control.

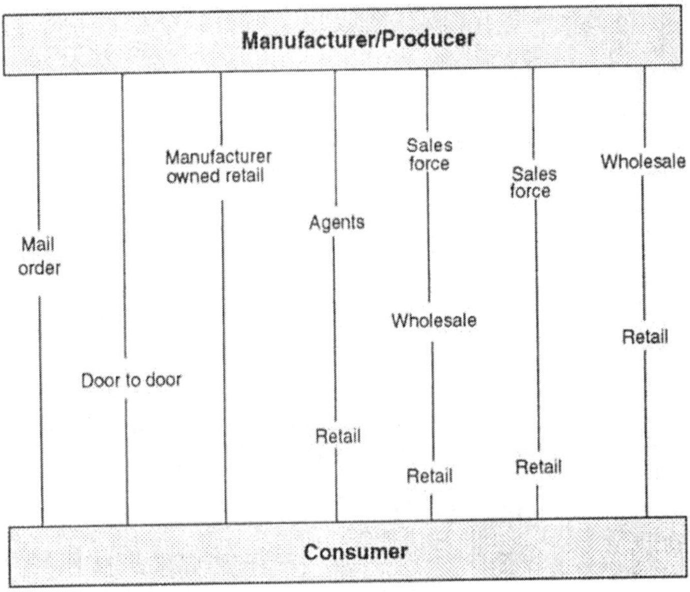

Figure 4.2 Consumer channel alternatives

Logistics & value chain

The objective of any business firm is to create value by way of performing a set of activities such as to conceptualized, design, manufacture, market, and service its market offerings. This set of inner-related activities is termed as value chain to gain competitive advantage over ist rivals ,a firm must provide comparable buyer value by performing activities more efficiently than its competitors or by performing activities in a unique way that create greater buyer value and command a premium price or accomplishes both.

Sclccting channel of International distribution

It is one of the most of crucial decisions a firm has to make while entering international markets. A firm may use the following criteria for the selection of channels of international distribution;

(i) International marketing objective of the firm
(ii) Financial resources
(iii) Organizational structure
(iv) Experience in international markets
(v) Firms marketing images
(vi) Existing marketing channel of the firm

(vii) Channel availability in the target market
(viii) Speed of market entry required
(ix) Legal implication
(x) Specific product need if any
(xi) Synergy with other element of marketing mix

Depending upon the firm objective and need, appropriate weights may be assign to each of the above criteria and final rating based on weightage may be arrived at for final selection of an appropriate international distribution channel. A firm has the following alternative channel strategy in term of market coverage.

Exclusive distribution:- The firms opts for a single or few market intermediaries.

Selective distribution:- The firm deals with as many numbers of intermediaries and outlets in the market as possible.

International Channel system

Where international marketing involved exporting two categories of marketing channel are involved viz channels between nation and channel within the foreign market. The international distribution system consist of two sub system, namely, the domestic system and the foreign system. The nature of the channel system is affected by, among other thing, by the method of exporting.

There are broadly two way of exporting namely, Direct exporting and Indirect exporting The indirect export involves home based independent middlemen who constitute the domestic sub system. No such independent middlemen is involved in direct export. When the export is direct, the producer makes direct sale to any one or more of the foreign customers. The important kind of foreign customer are importers distributors government department, sate buying organization, industrial buyers ,wholesaler, retailer, joint venture/ licensing and consumers. If any of these customer is not a final consumer he is a marketing middlemen or channel member between the producer and the final consumer. Fig 4.2.

Types of International Distribution channel

The international distribution channels may broadly divided into two categories, namely direct and indirect channel, as shown in below figure 4.2, a firm has goat the potion to make its product available in the international markets through either of the channel or a combination there.

Indirect channels

In this channel an international marketing firm deal with domestic agents or market intermediaries without any direct dealing with a foreign based firm as the firm is not required to deal directly in overseas markets, indirect market channel often the following benefits;

- since the firm has to deal with the market intermediaries in the domestic market it needs little investment and marketing experience.
- Indirect distribution channel provides low cost opportunity to test product in the international market however, indirect channel have certain limitation which are as follows;-
- As the firm has to heavenly depend upon domestic markets intermediary, it feed back from the ultimate customer is limited the firm has to part with relatibly highest share of its profits margins by way of commissions and other payment.
- The firm get little inside into the market even after operating for several year.
- The firm does not develop its own contact with the buyers and overseas market.

Direct Channels

As shown in fig 4.3 direct marketing channel involved selling of goods directly to a market intermediaries or the end user or customers in overseas markets. The major benefits of using direct channel are as follows:

(i) The firm develops a closer relationship with overseas buyer as it come in direct contact with them

(ii) The firm developed and insight into the market of operation which helps in restructuring its marketing strategies as per the market requirements.

(iii) The firms control over the export process is grater in direct marketing channel compared top indirect marketing channel.

Channel structure

Channel structure varies considerably according to whether the product is consumer or business to business oriented. The former tends to have a variety of formats, whereas the latter is less complicated. Figures 4.1 and 4.2 give a stylized channel alternative structure. The choice of which one is used depends on the requirements listed above.

In many countries there is a move to vertical or horizontal integration within channels, especially in developed countries where large chains dominate, as in the UK food retail trade. The converse is the scenario in many less developed countries. In East Africa, for example, small dukas (carrying less than 100 items and occupying no more than 506.75 square feet of space) operate widely on a margin of 12% as opposed to the developed countries' average of 24% margin. Also there can be very thriving parallel market systems, often

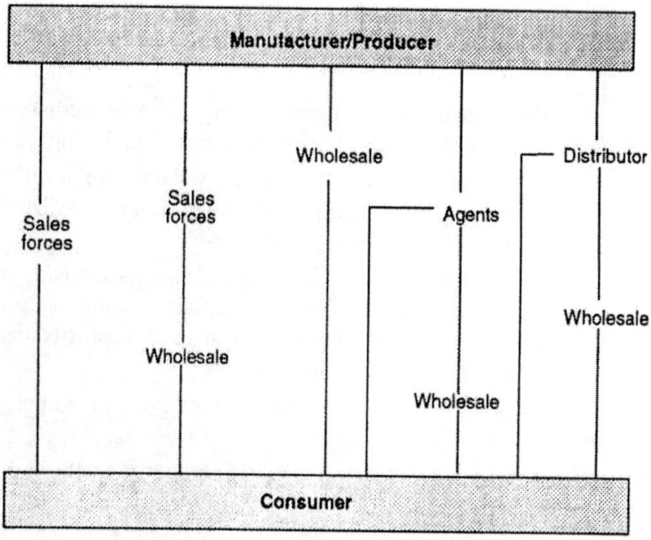

Figure 4.3 Business channel alternatives

difficult to track down. Decisions on what channels and entry strategy to adopt depend heavily on the risks, availability and costs of channels.

Most developing countries rely heavily on agents in distributing their products. Whilst criticism of being "ripped off" is often made, the loss caused by the shrinkage is less than that associated with more sophisticated channel forms.

We can now look in detail, at some important types of channel members relevant to agricultural marketing.

Brokers

Brokers do not take title to the goods traded but link suppliers and customers. They are commonly found in international markets and especially agricultural markets. Brokers have many advantages, not least of which is they can be less costly overall for suppliers and customers.

- They are better informed by buyers and or sellers.
- They are skilled socially to bargain and forge links between buyers and sellers.
- They bring the "personal touch" to parties who may not communicate with each other.
- They bring economies of scale by accumulating small suppliers and selling to many other parties.

- They stabilize market conditions for a supplier or buyer faced with many outlets and supply sources.

Personalized trading networks

Frequently, relationships may be built up between a buyer and a seller, in which over time as confidence grows, unwritten and informal understandings develop. These relationships reduce information, bargaining, monitoring and enforcement costs. Often, as relationships build, then trust develops which may become proxy for laws. Flexibility ensues which often means priorities or "favors" can be expedited. Trust and reciprocity can enable trade to develop in unstable economic circumstances, but both parties are aware the relationship can be undermined through opportunistic behavior. The Kenyan fresh vegetable industry is a classic example of personalized trading networks enabling international trade between Kenya suppliers and their familial (often Asian) buyers in the United Kingdom.

Associations, voluntary chains, cooperatives

Associations, voluntary chains and cooperatives can be made up of producers, wholesalers, retailers, exporters and processors who agree to act collectively to further their individual or joint interests. Members may have implicit or exclusive contracts, membership terms and standard operating procedures.

These forms of coordination have a number of advantages:

- They counter the "lumpy investment" phenomenon by spreading the cost of investment among members.
- They can reduce or pool members' risks by bulk buying, providing insurance and credits, pooling market prices and risk.
- They lower transaction costs of members through arbitration of disputes, provision of market information systems, been a first stop for output.
- They can reduce marketing costs through the provision of promotion, protection of qualities and monitoring members' standards.
- They can act as a countervailing power between buyers and producers. This is very important where supermarkets in the UK, for example, are now buying in such quantities that they are dictating terms to suppliers.

Developing countries do not have a history of good cooperative development, primarily because of poor management, financial ineptitude and over-reaching themselves. However, the Bombay Milk Scheme in India is working very well. The latter has been very successful in going into value added processing as well.

Contracting

Contracting represents an intermediate institutional arrangement between spot market trading and vertical integration. Marketing and production contracts allow a degree of continuity over a season, cycle or other period of time, without the "instantaneous" of spot trading.

The two main types of contract are:

(i) Forward Markets. These involve commitments by buyers and sellers to sell and purchase a particular commodity over a stated period of time. Specifications usually include weight, volumes, standards and values. Prices may be based on cost plus or negotiated. These contracts exist between farmers and first handlers and exporters and importers.

(ii) Forward resource/management contracts. These arrangements combine forward market sale and purchase commitments with stipulations regarding the transfer and use of specific resources and/or managerial functions. In such a contract the exchange of raw material or commodity is made on condition that it involves the use of certain inputs or methods, advised by the buyer, who may even take over the distribution function. This is a typical Marks and Spencer arrangement. Marks and Spencer is a very successful, high quality and price retail operation in the UK Such arrangements are found in many franchising, distributor or marketing/management agreements and help to internalize many future product transactions.

Both these forms of contract reduce the risks on both the buyers' and the sellers' side. By creating forward markets, the seller reduces market risk, and the buyer ensures that he receives commodities to certain specifications. Forward/resource management contracts also have the advantage of the provision of credit, market information and, perhaps, other "trade" secrets. Production contracts to farmers are also a source of credit collateral.

Integration

Integration vertically involves the combination of two or more separate marketing or production components under common ownership or management. It can involve investments "forward" or "backward" in existing activities or investments in interlinked activities. Integration horizontally means the linking of marketing or production separable at the same level in the system, for example, a group of retailers. Integration can bring a number of economies to food marketing systems, viz:

- Production/logistical economies: integration can bring economies of bulk, transport, and inventories.

- Transaction cost economies: integration brings cost economies because the firm may become the sole supplier of goods and services to itself; these include bargaining costs, information system streamlining and centralized decision making.
- Risk bearing advantages: vertical integration can overcome risk and uncertainty, i.e. by internalizing flows the organisation can eliminate the risk of variability in supplies, outlets, qualities and so on. More direct control over assets may enable the firm to invest in processing and marketing facilities which further enable the development of economies of scale. Typical examples include nuclear estates and out grower schemes.
- Market imperfections: these can be "absorbed" often by vertically integrated organisations. Taxes, prices and exchange controls and other regulations may be "absorbed" to give pecuniary gain. Also, integration enables the firm to increase its market share and leverage with suppliers and customers.

In agriculture, Lonrho and Anglo American provide excellent examples of vertically integrated organisations. Lonrho, with its estates in Kenya, is also in processing. Anglo American is also in agriculture and provides an interesting case of vertical integration giving advantages. If one takes the Anglo American operation in Zimbabwe, it owns, amongst other things, citrus estates. It not only grows, but processes and markets domestically and internationally. In addition, Anglo owns training facilities, transport facilities and gives credit and investment capabilities. Its international operation means it knows the Government tax, regulations, exchange controls and other measures very well, and so can "negotiate" around or within this legal/monetary framework.

Government

The Government can take a leading role in the distribution of goods and services via state-owned Marketing Boards. Government may provide an infrastructure which the private sector just cannot afford for example roads, utilities, training and extension. Government has the sovereign authority to provide the regulatory framework within which commodity or agricultural export systems can be developed. It can also define the rules for international trade and market entry. It can negotiate in either a bilateral or multilateral form, to facilitate a particular commodity transfer or arrange lower terms of access. Government also has other roles to play like cooperating or providing services in defined markets. It can provide credit or market information. It may stabilize prices with price controls like floor or ceiling prices, buffer stocks, quantity controls and so on. Government can regulate the competitive position of markets by passing regulations which protect or promote a market structure. It may force suppliers into Marketing Boards as the only outlet and so alter the whole competitive structure of industry. Both Marketing Boards and Marketing Orders can be used to control physical commodity flows, enforce market quality standards and pool market risk. Finally Government can "enable" suppliers through the introduction of export incentives, reduced taxes or export retention schemes. As an example of international channels decisions and management the following cotton example is given, adapted from the ITC training manual (1989)[1].

Cotton marketing

Customer requirements

In marketing cotton the basic question is, who is the customer? For cotton it may be an international merchant (large or small) or a local/regional merchant (large or small) or a spinning mill in the end user country. The customer has a number of clearly defined needs including the following:

- Availability - on time and in steady supply
- Quality - reliable, even running, free from foreign matter, no country damage and will pass the micro, PSI and GPT test values
- Shipment - on time, in a container, clearly marked and direct to customer
- Price - competitive at a given time. Its relative value must be competitive versus synthetics quality and against the Liverpool index.
- Terms - these must be simple - FOB, CFR etc. and be in tune with arrival/delivery schedules. Deferred terms and payment in home currency are advantageous
- Arbitration - a system for rejection, substitution and penalties must be agreed
- Information - advice on price developments, time to buy, who else buys and ranges of prices.

In addition, the producer and merchant have needs and objectives:

Producer:

- Maximum inflow - for goods and services (freight insurance)
- Maintain presence in key markets
- Image - quality, contract performance and administrative excellence

Merchant:

- Margin level
- Market share/key customers - either big, international or niche
- Image - cheapest, most aggressive, quality and customer service.

Channel structure

Figure 4.4 below gives a typical channel structure for cotton[1]. At each stage value is added. The typical value chain is seed merchants, farmers, country buyers/cooperatives, ginner, buyer, merchant, selling agent and end user.

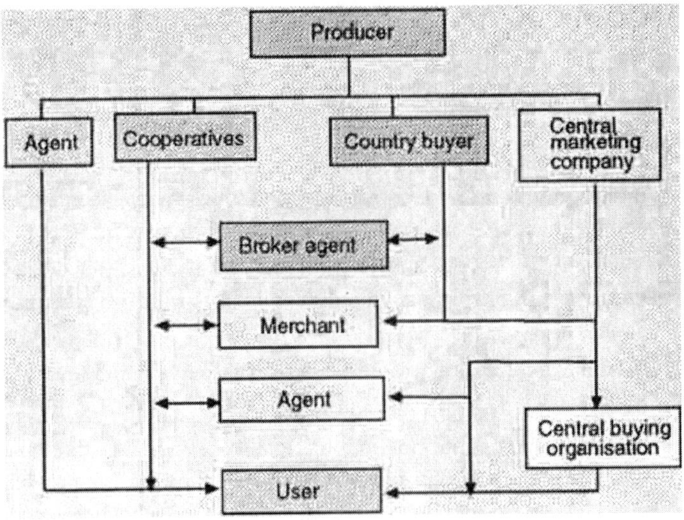

Figure 4.4 Cotton distribution

Channel alternatives

As can be seen from the above figure there are a possible number of alternatives for distributing cotton. Basically the choice comes down to two alternatives, the producer/seller selling direct or through an international merchant or agent.

International merchant/agent:

A good merchant is characterized by the following characteristics, in comparison to the producer/seller selling direct:

- Well informed
- Well disciplined
- Knows the detail of his business
- Thinks in terms of probabilities and absolute terms (risk/reward)
- Is concerned but not dogmatic - he can accept when he is wrong
- Reports to few and knowledgeable people

An international merchant acts as a bridge between producers and consumers. He performs the following functions:

- Language - conducts communications in suppliers' and consumers' preferred language
- Space utility - he prepares the logistics function including sea and/or land transportation arrangements, documentation preparation and arrangements for insurance coverage
- Time utility - financing through own/banking facilities
- Currency risks - buys and sells in currencies required by sellers and buyers, does currency conversions, provides financial information and technical assistance and offers a currency gap guarantee
- Market risks - takes a long or short market basis position, deals with hedging, options, off-take and supply deals and price guarantee contracts
- Terminal exchanges - provides a brokering service and fixations
- Countertrade - handles the cotton side of the deal
- Quality - gives information on quality available, give quality recommendations for consumers, handles quality option/basket contracts and shows quality alternatives and,
- Culture - handles and is a link between remote developing areas and highly advanced and sophisticated centers of the world.

As can be seen from this list the services offered are considerable. The services he can provide to a producer are as follows:

- Up-to-date market information
- Information on competitors and prices
- Financing (producer and end user)
- Buying of all exportable qualities
- Buying on local terms
- Prompt payment
- Buying when producer can/wants to sell
- Buying unfixed at seller's call and,
- Contract guarantee for proper fulfillment.

Despite all these benefits, the choice of a merchant and/or agent has to be taken after careful consideration of the following criteria:

- Knowledge - of local circumstances (political, business and general, and of textiles in particular);
- Professionalism - cotton know-how

- Market coverage - covers large segment of end users
- Finance - financially sound and not dependent on sales to poor customers
- Language ability - avoid misunderstandings
- Integrity - particularly on pricing and,
- Infrastructural sound, with good communications and administration.

Dangers to watch out for are:

- Representation - does agent handle other representations - cotton or non-cotton -, and how important and synergistic are they?
- Pricing integrity - does the agent ever try to change the price given by the principal?

Whilst most of these factors are producer oriented criteria, the trader himself has a predicament. Does he "think big" through looking at world supply/demand patterns, world economic conditions, the textile industry in general, fashion trends and currency movements, or does he "think small". Think small can be triggered by questions like will West Texas produce low microware cotton? Will XYZ Spinners go bankrupt? Will I find freight from Buenos Aires to Lagos? Will the price go up or down tomorrow? Whilst trying to find an answer to this dilemma, the trader may run out of time, money and courage and go broke. Risk and reward are ultimate advisers.

Producer/seller direct

In comparing the direct producer seller channel versus the merchant/agent channel, the question of control over distribution activities is the most telling argument as is the relationship which can be built up between producer and consumer. However, as can be seen from the previous section, the merchant/agent provides a number of services which are very powerful. Table 4.2 below summarizes the main points of comparison.

Table 4.2 Comparison of international merchant and producer/seller

Merchant	Producer/seller
Global presence	Local/single market growth
Can choose to do nothing	Forced to act
Flexible sourcing/selling	Always long
Can offer client alternatives	Limited assortment
Staffing flexibility	Local staff
Currency/market risks	Currency risks
Market information wide	Limited market information
Handles prompt payments	May have to wait for payment
Quality guarantees	May not guarantee same quality

Whilst experience with traders may lead to some unsatisfactory outcomes, in the main merchants/agents in the long run offer a more convenient form of channel of distribution than direct dealings.

Market strategy

In designing a marketing strategy, both external factors (macro-environmental) and internal factors (micro-environmental) have to be considered.

External factors

The principle factor to consider here is "government". In general the role of government has increased over the years with few truly free, purely supply/demand oriented producer countries.

Government has an effect on three areas - production, exports and imports.

- *Production* - Government has sought to promote its own cotton industry by certain measures. This has led to a competitive edge by certain countries. In Egypt, Sudan and Turkey, input subsidies on fertilizers, seeds and pesticides have been used. Colombia and Pakistan have obtained credit at favorable terms. Syria, the CIS and Egypt have had ginning realization. In most countries seed research has either been directly or indirectly funded by government.
- *Exports* - government influence here has been in minimum price legislation, special exchange rates, export credit facilities and export duties.
- *Imports* - Basically this has been free of influence for typical importing countries, but there are special ad hoc regulations for occasional imports. Because of the drought, Zimbabwe had to import lint in 1992/93 to keep its textile industry going. This, inevitably, was a special deal as Zimbabwe usually provides for its own needs from its own production.

As well as these forms of intervention, governments may pursue a specific policy for its cotton industry. The US cotton programme, for example, is to provide a stimulus to produce more or less and/or make US cotton competitive. This is done through loans, target price mechanisms, acreage reduction programmes, paid diversions, inventory reduction programmes and through the AWP (Average World Price).

Internal factors: A clearly defined strategy is required. Primarily the producer has to decide whether it will sell pre-season or when the crop comes in, and/or is it to be a one off or steady seller.

- Pricing - the producer has to decide on what pricing strategy to follow - average fixed, average on call, speculative or the use of options.

In theory the free market principle of supply and demand is applicable but in practice the question is whether the market is supply or demand driven. The demand for cotton depends on so many factors -elasticity, substitutes and the limits to cotton price elasticity, origin, shortages/disasters all affect price. Buffer stocks in cotton are not very relevant, as it would be difficult to make it work universally, hence limiting the price/supply option.

Added to the price equation is "basis" trading. A basis is defined as the difference to New York Futures, either on or off. Other definitions include "buying basis the country basis" or "basis Liverpool Index". Basis trading has become more prevalent for traders/exporters and mills for a number of reasons:

- the outright market position risk is too large (basis fluctuations are normally less than market hedging)
- in cases of default the trader's risk is basis difference which is often smaller than the market;
- many conserve cash for margins;
- a producer/exporter has the opportunity to obtain more US dollars (or less); and,
- a mill has the opportunity to obtain a lower (or higher) price.

A basis is established in the following way:

- Using US cotton as a common denominator. The US is a constant exporter, always in the market at any quality.
- Buying New York futures against a sale or selling New York futures against a purchase or directly quoting a basis.

The basic technical aspects include:

- choosing the correct month
- right to fix
- fixation deadlines
- before delivery
- after delivery (provision price)
- rolling forward or backward
- margin requirements in case of delayed fixation
- giving fixation orders.

Basis versus New York is inherent in any cotton price. New York futures are a legitimate way to hedge a market position for a merchant although one must realize that it is not often a perfect hedge. However, it is often the only way a trader can enter a far forward buying or selling commitment. For a producer or mill it is a risky attempt to maximize the dollar return for his product or lower the price of his purchase. It is also an indirect way to play with the futures market where a direct involvement for certain reasons is impossible. So on channels, a decision has to be made whether to sell direct, or through merchants, or use a combination or sell to any market or selected markets. Similarly, rotation in the choice of staff and staffing (traders, classes, administrators) - a decision has to be made on whether to use the same staff, international expertise through travel/congresses or low key and/ or train staff.

Marketing action

In order to make the cotton flow work the following must be observed:

- Marketing - know the markets, competition and customers; travel and meet people; document yourself; decide on a main focus (do not fragment); ensure feedback to producer, seed merchants and logistics providers
- Selling - select customers and agents carefully; look for standard terms with flexibility built in; stick to your agents and customers, lasting relationships build confidence, especially in times of difficulty; do not underestimate a first-class merchant's function; keep a customer file and be available at home
- Administrative - be efficient, have communication facilities and give prompt payment settlement
- Staffing - seek continuity of staff and provide training.

The cotton industry has a number of associations, which provide a variety of services. These include the International Cotton Advisory Committee (ICAC) which has government members and provides statistics and standards, ITMF which is user oriented, the Liverpool Cotton Exchange which does contracts and negotiation and the New York Cotton Exchange which deals in futures.

Physical distribution

As well as the institutional elements of distribution, channel management includes services and physical elements - transport, warehousing and inventory management. These are very specialized areas of distribution and include different modes of transport - land, sea, air, and services offered by freight forwarders, agents, insurance etc. The readings accompanying this chapter provide most of the detail, so here the modes of distribution are briefly covered.

As well as negotiating all the paperwork and the quota or tariff agreements described earlier in this section, the exporting company has to consider storage, documentation and transportation. The importance of these elements can be seen in the following case study of 1991 for the horticultural industry in Zimbabwe, Malawi, Tanzania and Zambia, reported by Collett (1991)[2].

East Africa horticulture marketing

In order to establish a successful horticultural export industry it is important that the producer, the importer and the government consider the venture as a genuine partnership, built on trust. The most important player in this partnership is undoubtedly the government which controls most aspects of production and marketing, in one way or another and will contribute to the success or failure of the industry. Most African countries face two main problems, namely, on the one hand unemployment and on the other, a shortage of foreign currency. Horticulture, being a major employer of labor and as a provider of export a significant earner of foreign currency, can contribute to easing both the employment and foreign currency situations.

World demand for high quality horticulture products, combined with the high cost of labor in the developed countries, has resulted in high prices and high returns for producers.

Partnership

In the partnership between grower, importer and government, each has different roles as follows:

Grower

- Horticulture is a high risk, high return industry requiring a very high standard of management
- Growers have to obtain, and employ if necessary, technical skills
- Transport options have to be considered
- Financial arrangements have to be made, particularly foreign currency and,
- At all times quality, quantity, and continuity has to be guaranteed.

Importer

- Importer has to create and maintain trust
- Provide information on demand, timing, price, and product
- Pay as soon as possible to ease cash flows
- Offer support to the exporter when prices drop
- Recommend new products and,
- Become a true partner to the grower.

Government

- Create the right climate to allow exports to expand
- Apply minimal regulatory requirements and ensure these are properly handled
- Ensure sufficient air freight capacity

- Maintain freight rates at acceptable levels for the industry as a whole
- Grant work permits for essential skills
- Make foreign currency available
- Waive duties and taxes to assist the industry
- Implement incentives
- Allow importation of new chemicals tested elsewhere and,
- Do everything possible to make the industry competitive in world markets.

Representative body

It is essential to form a body to look after all the requirements of the industry. Major representation must come from producers, who stand the major risk, but representation is essential from government and in particular, the Ministries of Finance, Agriculture and Transport. Officials serving on the body must be in a position to take decisions and act in the interest of the industry.

Selection of crops

Climatic conditions in each of the four countries varies from low lying hot to high altitude cool production areas capable of producing a very wide variety of crops. Final selection of crops to grow will depend on market demand, price and transport logistics. Long road and rail haul will determine which crops can be produced for export by air and when they will have to go by sea.

Production

Horticultural development already taking place is largely on commercial farms where capital, technical skills, irrigation and transport is on hand. Development in the small scale sector has been minimal due to the lack of capital etc., and the inability of the sector to raise credit without land title. It is highly probable that given the necessary training, capital etc., the small scale sector could produce very high quality, as is happening in Kenya.

The success of the commercial farming sector in producing export crops must be utilized to develop a parallel production system in the small scale sector. Initially, the sector must produce for the local market and change to export as skills are acquired.

Urgent development of the horticultural export sector in the region is necessary. The following figures indicate the relative importance of horticulture in countries in the region:

Kenya	50,000	tonnes
Zimbabwe	14,237	tonnes
Zambia	3,000	tonnes
Tanzania	1,000	tonnes
Malawi	200	tonnes
South Africa	+/-1 million	tonnes

Transport - air

International service (air): Export by air, weekly flights, freight rates, tonnes are given in table 4.3. Zimbabwe has 15 scheduled flights (passenger) per week to London, Frankfurt and Lisbon. It is hoped that by the end of 1991, Amsterdam, Paris and Geneva will be added to the list of available destinations. Cargo flights to Amsterdam, London and Cologne as well as Brussels by the national cargo carrier and the three charter flights are also available. Zambia is currently served by BA, Aero Zambia and UTA with flights to London and Frankfurt. In addition, the national carrier NAC flies twice weekly to London and Amsterdam. Tanzania has 18 scheduled flights to Europe and the Middle East through Dar es Salaam, some of which also stop at Kilimanjaro. As far as air services go, Tanzania is better served than any of the four countries visited.

Malawi has services to Amsterdam, London, and Paris with five flights per week. In addition, there is a weekly service by NAC offering 20 tonne capacity.

Table 4.3 International air service comparisons

	Malawi	*Tanzania*	*Zambia*	*Zimbabwe*
FLIGHTS				
Passenger	4	17	6	15
Cargo	1	1	2	6
TOTAL	5	18	8	21
FREIGHT RATES	> 500 kg	Unlimited	Per Palet	> 1000 kg
US$/kg	1.30-1.7	0.90-1.20	1.50 (winter 1.25)	1.20 - 2.30
TONNES	32	400 Est	2642	7937

Regional services: Regional trade at this stage is very limited air services are available significantly increase trade. Existing trade is limited to between Zimbabwe, South Africa, Angola and Mauritius and between Malawi and South Africa. In addition, Zambia has limited contact with Angola and Tanzania with Burundi.

Destinations: Traditional links between the four countries are all with the UK and it is not surprising the most of the cargo goes to this destination. Zambia and Zimbabwe, however, have built up significant flower trade with Holland and their requirements are largely met by cargo flights.

Statistics: Accuracy of statistics has to be questioned and most efforts to collect these be improved and linked to information available from the individual airlines. Major exports now taking place are from Zimbabwe and Zambia, both of whom have been in the business for only five years. Malawi and Tanzania export little air freighted cargo, but nevertheless have significant potential to export tropical, subtropical and temperate crops including fruit, vegetables and flowers.

Freight rates: Freight rates to international destinations vary considerably with Zimbabwe and Zambia the highest (see table 4.3). Rate structures in the region are considerably higher than in West Africa. These high costs have forced growers to concentrate on high value commodities such as flowers at the expense of lower value fruit and vegetables. Freight rate levels have to be set to give the airline a fair return while allowing the grower sufficient margin to be viable. A realistic return to the airline is essential to attract charters etc., to the region, without which growers could not export. The value per tonne of product produced for export must be high enough to meet the above criteria. Zimbabwe is currently receiving average prices of ZMD 8,000 per tonne CIF for produce and ZMD 11,000 for flowers. There is no doubt these values will improve as certain commodities are dropped and replaced.

Types of air services

Scheduled flights give preference to fruit and vegetables because of their heavy nature, while charter services prefer to uplift flowers at the higher freight rate. Charter operations prefer to load some heavy cargo as well, and a combination favored in Zimbabwe is 90% flowers with 10% fruit and vegetables. The developing trend is for scheduled flights to concentrate on fruit and vegetables into London and for charters and national cargo carriers to uplift flowers to Holland. Cargo to German destinations is increasing as exporters realize this market imports 70% of all flowers sold in Holland, and efforts are made to sell direct to the end user. Air transport into any country will depend on demand, including passengers as well as cargo, and as demand increases air links will provide the required services. It is very much a chicken and egg situation, and if existing air services have no available cargo space, growers will produce crops in the hope that space will be made available. Cargo operators also provide services where these are required. In general, there is more cargo coming into the central southern region of Africa than flies out, and coordination is required to make maximum use of empty return flights.

National cargo carrier

Each country is dependent on its own national airline and this service must be made full use of before resorting to outside service. Landing rights in all countries are granted by the authorities who sometimes limit these to airlines who are prepared to allocate them cargo space. Government has in its power to allow in as many flights as requested by international carriers, but it also has an obligation to its own airline, and where an open sky policy is not in the national interest, these requests are turned down.

Tourism: Tourism plays a major part in deciding how many flights to allow in, and the fate of this industry is closely linked to that of horticultural exporting, as both are dependent on available air services.

Freight forwarders: A very important sector of Zimbabwe's horticultural export industry is the freight forwarder, who in addition to chartering extra cargo flights also provides cold stores at the airport. This new development is in addition to their normal services which include booking space, documentation, phytosanitary certificates and applying to government for export incentives on behalf of exporters.

Penalties: Zimbabwe has instituted a strictly controlled penalty system for growers/exporters who book space and then do not show up. Allowance of 48 to 72 hours is given for notification of cancelled bookings, and anyone who does not do this is fined the full cost of his cargo space. This tough measure has brought a large degree of responsibility into the industry and firm plans and charter bookings can now be made with confidence.

Positive points starting to emerge in air transport include the following:

- Full use of scheduled cargo capacity
- 75 to 90% total capacity utilization of cargo flights
- Realization of the importance of cold chain and cold store facilities at airports
- The role played by freight forwarders
- Responsible approach by all sectors
- Full government support
- Growers building their own facilities inside airport perimeters.

Transport - sea

Sea freight offers growers the opportunity to export horticultural crops in large quantities at lower cost. Whilst fruit is the main sea-freighted crop, the list can be greatly extended if "controlled atmosphere containers" or the latest concept known as "modified atmosphere packaging" are utilized. Location of production areas and the distance from port will determine whether exporting by sea is viable or not. The availability of road and rail refrigerated transport is considered essential if quality is to be maintained. However, it is possible to transport citrus up to a week without refrigeration. Present routes through Mozambique are seriously affected by pilferage and theft, with extraordinary precautions having to be taken. Zimbabwe in 1990 suffered losses of USD 3.4 million due to theft of sugar while en route to Maputo, while Swaziland has re-routed its sugar exports through Richards Bay in South Africa for the same reason. Crops which are considered suitable for export by sea are citrus, deciduous fruit, sub-tropical fruit, pineapples and bananas, all of which are moved in considerable quantities. FOB prices for sea-freighted crops are in many instances the same as if the product was air-freighted, due to the longer time in transport. Pineapples ex Dar es Salaam give the same FOB price for both air freight and sea freight.

Handling

Horticultural exports from Africa to EC markets have to compete with high quality products from around the world, many of which are produced in developed countries under modern cultural methods and strict quality control. Quality depends on a combination of field management, post-harvest handling and an efficient transport system from field to market. Quality coming out of the field cannot be improved on, but only maintained, and it is essential in the first instance to produce high quality products.

Field production of high quality products is dependent on the correct selection of seed and variety, spacing, fertilization, insect and disease control and time of harvest. Post-harvest handling involves reaping under correct conditions, including cutting correctly from the plant, placing into containers that will not damage the product, reaping when temperatures are low and reaping two or three times a day to ensure the product is harvested at the ideal stage. Having reaped correctly, products have to enter the cold chain - be refrigerated as soon as possible and remain so until they are bought by the customer in the retail outlet. To ensure the most efficient cold chain conditions, products must be reduced in temperature to the ideal for the product as soon as possible. Every farm must have its own cold store complex, and so must the airport where the produce is delivered before export. Some cold chains are more complicated than others. The most sophisticated should have separate intake and dispatch cold stores, with the central grading and packing area also having refrigeration or being subjected to lower temperatures. Time taken for grading and packing must be kept at a minimum to prevent products increasing in temperature during this process. The more sophisticated grading sheds allow for the product to be packed into the airline containers in the dispatch cold store, and the containers being transported to the airport. This process reduces handling considerably and allows the exporter to pack carefully with minimal damage and discolouration to the boxes. A wide variation from the ideal handling system is found in different countries. Whilst Zimbabwe makes the most use of cold stores and suitable transport, one exporter in Tanzania does not have a cold store on the farm, and the first refrigeration takes place at the airport. The importance of refrigeration is widely known. Cold stores are available at all the main airports, apart from Lusaka where the growers are building their own facility. Zimbabwe has the most sophisticated cold stores with several being available, both at the airport and in Harare itself. Plans are developed in Zimbabwe to construct a very modern large cargo terminal which will provide the most modern facilities for horticulture. In Zimbabwe, freight forwarders play a very significant role in handling exports and maintaining storage under ideal conditions until loading. Several have their own cold stores and handling complexes. In addition, freight forwarders charter flights and compete on freight rates with the national carrier. Handling of crops for the local market is a major feature of marketing in Zimbabwe. Apples, pears and citrus are stored on farm and by wholesalers, to maintain prices. These crops are stored for three to four months and sold during high price periods. Onions are also stored for up to 5 months for the same reason, but this is only done by the larger producers. The very significant awareness of quality, and particularly post-harvest handling in Zimbabwe, is due to regular seminars being held with international speakers from USA, Europe and South Africa addressing these meetings. Zimbabwe growers also travel regularly investigating the markets and discussing requirements with their importers. Regular contact cannot be over-stressed.

The high cost of transport in some producing countries can significantly affect the viability of a horticultural export industry. In order for a new industry to survive and develop, very careful consideration must be given to product selection and presentation. Products requiring high capital investment and specialized technical skills are normally in short supply and at high prices, while others which can be produced more easily tend to be over supplied and low priced. High prices can also be achieved by pre-packing and semi-processing at source. Demand is increasingly swinging towards well presented pre-packed products. Attention must be paid to semi-processed products such as vegetables and fruit salads pre-packed at source. These developments, in addition to realizing higher prices, can significantly reduce air transport costs by making better use of available air space.

Maximizing pre-packing in farm pack-houses. The value per tonne of exports from Zimbabwe of both fruit and vegetables and flowers has increased considerably by selecting the high value lines and varieties and excluding others. In addition, more importance is being placed on value added by

Mangetout prices can be increased by up to one pound sterling by pre-packing instead of selling in 2.5 kg boxes. Likewise, a switch from summer flowers to roses has increased the value per tonne considerably. Indications are that Zambia in particular is following this trend, while recent developments in Malawi could lead to export of pre-packed products to supermarkets.

Importers

Following recent bankruptcies of importers in Europe, as a result of which exporters lost a lot of money, it is now more essential than ever for exporters to know who they are dealing with. Records and reputations of importers are well known in the industry and exporters must make enquiries before entering into firm commitments worth hundreds and thousands of dollars. Payment terms are important in that some imports take 3 to 4 months to pay while others make part payments immediately on shipping with the balance paid 2 to 4 weeks later, after sale. Recent trends between importers and exporters is towards establishing long term partnerships or understandings for the benefit of both parties. Importers require high quality products on a continuous basis and are prepared to assist growers to achieve this. On the other hand, growers want reliable outlets who will supply all the necessary market information, etc. This example concludes this section on distribution. Along with price, distribution forms a major element in international marketing and the detail is essential if success is to be guaranteed.

International Retailing

Organized retailing is gaining significant across the world and, therefore, has emerged as a powerful marketing channel that need to be carefully studied as consider by the firms from developing countries . The global trend indicates the declines in the number of retail outlet but an increased in their average size. As the size of retail outlet increases, the emphasis shifts to market expansion and efficient management of international distribution large retailers start their operation in international market and evolve supply chain systems in an internationally integrated manner so as to achieved efficency.the global retail sales where estimated to be US $ 8 trillion in 2002 . The top 200 retailers have captured 29% of the world wide market. The largest of the large retailer have continued to increase their market share. In 2002, the total sales for top 200 global retailer reached US$ 2.2 trillion, which was an increase of 4 % over 2001.

Types of foreign intermediaries

A brief account of the foreign intermediaries are;-

(i) Importers

(ii) Distributors

(iii) wholesalers .

(iv) retailers.

(i) Importer:- Although all the foreign customer who buy directly from the exporters are technically importers, here the term importer refer to one who import the product in large quantity either as an agent for foreign buyer or for re-sale. Such importer include among others, large import houses and trading houses .The importer who buy on their own account may sale the product to the distributors, industrial and other institutional customer wholesaler etc.

(ii) Distributor:- A distributor who buys directly from the exporters and holds large stocks of s product has an exclusive right to sell the product in particular area or to a particular type of customer.

The distributor may re sale the product to the wholesalers, retailers or consumers.

(iii) Wholesaler:- Wholesalers often buy from the importer or distributor, there are also wholesaler who buy directly from the exporter.

(iv) Retailer:- Large retailers may buy directly from the exports. department store, supermarket other types of chain stores among the most important direct retail buyers . Other retailers may depend on distributors or wholesalers.

Multiple channels

In some cases, an exporters may use multiple channel i.e more then one channel for a product . for ex- an exporter may sell directly to the wholesaler, large retailer and institutional consumer, even while having distributors.

Government Deptt

In some country government deptt by large quantity of certain goods often on a long term basis these are generally essential goods of mass consumption or for use in government deptt.

State buying organization

In some country the import of goods are done by the government organization like a state trading organization .this was the case until recently in the centrally planned economies. in India import of several commodities are channelized i.e only designated government agencies can import these goods.

Joint venture

A very important export marketing channel i.e growing in popularity is collaborated arrangement between exporter and foreign firm.

Joint venture i.e . enterprises in which both ownership and management are shared by firms from two or more countries, are very common between firms developed and developing countries .firms from developed countries may supply technologies and participate in the equity in joint venture in developing countries. The collaboration with the developed country firm become very helpful in marketing the product in the foreign countries. Such joint venture are very common in several industries including food processing industries.

Another type of international collaboration is licensing or franchising.

Factor infusing channel selection

The important factors influencing the choice of channels are the following;

(i) product characteristic- Product characteristic like unit value, perishability ,bulk degree of product standardization, complexity and service requirement, determine to some extend the way the product should be distributed.

(ii) Market and customer characteristics:- The size and location of the market, the number and geographical dispersal of the customer, the frequency of purchase and the typical size of the purchase, customer's buying habits and susceptibility to different selling methods are important factors to be consider in the choice of channel selection.

(iii) Middlemen Characteristic:- Middlemen differ in their ability and willingness to carried promotional activities and to push the product. The margin for the middlemen is another important issue the type of products dealt with by a particular intermediary should also be an important consideration further, the marketer particular may be restricted in his choice of channel by the non availability of particular middlemen.

(iv) Company characteristics and objectives:- The choice of the channel is also influence by such factors as the company's size, financial strength, product mix, past channel, experiences, overall marketing policies and channels objectives.

(v) Competitor's Characteristics:- Like any other marketing decision the channel decision is influence by the nature of the competitor . some time, it may be appropriate to adopt a channel policy similar to that of the competitors, but some time it may be more profitable to design a quite a different channel policy.

(vi) Environmental Characteristic:- The channel design is also influence by such environmental factors as the economic situation, social and cultural factors, the physical environment and govt policies and regulation.

Promotion Decisions

Marketing promotion plays a very important role in marketing, both domestic and International. Effective promotion is crucial to firm's success in international markets. The marketing communication or promotion mix involves advertising, sales promotion, public relation, personal selling, and direct and interactive marketing as shown in fig 4.5

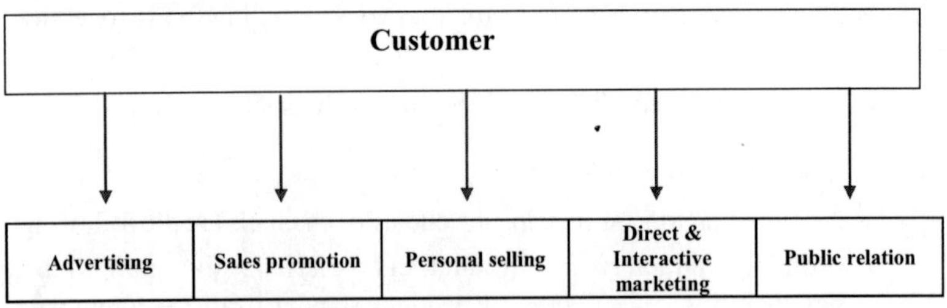

International Marketing Promotion Mix Fig- 4.5

A firm generally uses a mix of all these promotion tools after considering the firm's strategy and marketing requirements. Ads is a paid form of promotion carried out through magazines, radio, TVs, news papers and etc. Besides, it is also a non –personal form of promotion. Sales promotion comprises short term marketing measures which stimulate quick buyers' action and result in immediate sale of the product. It includes rebates and price discounts, firm's catalogues and brochures, samples, coupons, and gifts. Direct marketing is also an effective marketing promotion tool where in a firm has direct interaction with customer. Personal selling involves direct selling by firm's sales force and is considered to be a two way method of marketing promotion. Which helps in building strong customer relationship.

Products or services will not sell unless people are told about them. It is true that few companies from developing countries are global in operation, so much of the promotion process is limited to either third party advertising (for example the Dutch advertising Kenya grown flowers) or taking part in international exhibitions (for example the Zimbabwe International Trade Fair in Bulawayo). As many primary products of developing countries become the end products of developed countries, most promotion is limited to mentions of origin in developed country promotion.

Nonetheless, the rules still apply for effective promotion, whether it is of limited or more extensive nature.

Most basic marketing textbooks cover the "ground" rules for effective advertising and promotion and so the reader is referred to these rather than repeat these again here. It is usual to distinguish between "advertising " and "promotion". Advertising is defined as:

"Any form of communication in the paid media".

Promotion, on the other hand, is defined as:

"An incentive, usually at the point of sale, intended to enhance the intrinsic value of a product or service".

Other expressions in common use are "above the line" and "below the line", the line being an imaginary one, defining the boundary between promotion from the retailer to consumer and the other from manufacturer to retailer.

Process of International Marketing Promotion

It aims at conveying firm's message as effectively and accurately as possible. The basic process of marketing promotion, as shown in fig-4.6.

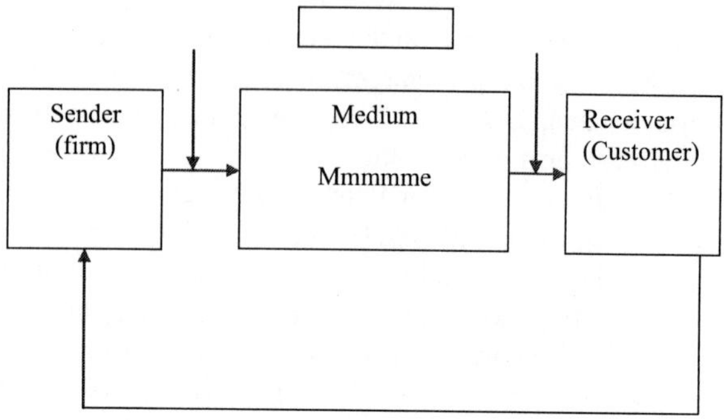

Sender

It refers to the marketing firm which is conveying the message

Encoding

Before a message can be send, it has to be encoded . putting thoughts, ideas, information in to a symbolic firm is termed as encoding. encoding ensures the correct interpretation of message by the receiver, who is often the ultimate customer. The use of words, signs, or symbol should be such that they become familiar to the target customer. Firms often use symbols for encoding message that has universal meaning. Language and cultural issues need to be taken care of while encoding the message .

Message

A message may be verbal or non- verbal, oral, written, or symbolic. A msg contain all the information or meaning that a sender aim to convey. A message is put in to transmittable form depending upon the channels of promotion.

Medium

The channel used to convey the encoded massage to the intend receiver is term as medium . The medium can be categories in the following manners.

Personal, it involves direct interpersonal contact with the target group. Sales people serves as the channel of promotion as they delivered the sales message to the target customers. Friend, peers, neighbors, and family members constitute social channel.

Non- Personal

These are channels which convey message without any interpersonal contact between the sender and the receiver. Since the message is communicated to many persons at a time, these channels are also referred to as mass media or mass promotion channels. The non- personal channels of promotion may further be broadly classified as follows-

(i) Print Media- News papers, magazines, direct mail, etc.

(ii) Electronic media- Radio & TVs

Decoding

It is the process of transforming the senders message back in to thought . decoding is highly influenced by the self reference criteria which is unintended reference to one's own culture.

Receiver

It is the target customer who receive the message by way of hearing, reading or seeing. A number of factors influenced how the message is received these include the clarity of message ,the interest generated, the translation, the sound of words, and the visuals used in the message .

Noise

The unplanned distortions or interferes of the message is termed as noise . a message is subjected to a variety of external factors that distortion or interfere its reception.

Feedback

In order to assess the effectiveness of marketing communication process. Feedback from the customers is crucial . The time needed to assess the communication impact depends upon the type of promotion used .ex- an immediate feedback can be obtain by personal selling where as it takes much longer time to assess the communication effectiveness in case of ads.

An international markets, a firms has to communicate with the customers and the channels intermediaries locate in overseas markets that have considerably different marketing environment characteristic the differences in cultural environment, economic development of the market regulatory frame work language, and media availability make their task of international marketing communication much more complex compared to domestic markets.

Promotion strategy

On the basis of promotional focus on market intermediaries in the distribution system or the end customers, a firm has the following two option in marketing communication strategy ,

Push strategy – in this strategy the promotional program me is priminarly directed at the market intermediaries in their distribution systems. It aims to motivate the market intermediaries to stock, promote, and sale the product to the ultimate customer. As shown in below fig 6.3

The market intermediaries, such as the distributors, wholesalers and retailers, are offered a variety of incentives to push the product in the market. Generally, in push strategy the distributors are motivated to promote the product to the wholesalers, who intern, promote the product to the retailers who finally push the product to the consumers.

The tools used in these strategy include personal selling and sales promotion, contest for salesperson, and trade shows .Push strategy is usually found to be more effective under these situation-

(i) lack of product differentiation.

(ii) Weak brand identity

(iii) Low brand loyalty

(iv) Difficulty in appreciating products benefits

(v) Industrial Products

(vi) Institutional sales

(vii) Lack of access advertising media

(viii) Low promotional budgets

(ix) Shorts and Direct marketing channel

(x) Low wages(i.e., cost of employing salesperson is lower than advertising cost).

Firms with low promotional budgets often adopt push strategy to move their product through the distribution channels . Besides commoditization of brands has made it difficult for the customers to differentiate between the competiting brand, making push strategy more effective.

The biggest drawback of push strategy is that hardly any brand loyalty is created even after spending huge sums of money. Besides, the channel intermediaries become more demanding and ask for increase in their margin to support the product. In case the demand for a product is low a marketers has to exceed to the demand of channel intermediaries. These triggers and un healthy competition among the marketers to often more and more margins, which furthers squeezes their promotion budgets advertising. In developing countries the size of the retail outlet is small and a majority of them are managed by one or two person only. Therefore, the customer come in direct contact with the sellers and often and their seek their opinion about the product. The margin of the seller on a particular product often determine his opinion under such situation, push strategy serves as an effective promotional tool.

Pull Strategy

The process of motivating y the customer to buy the product from the retailers through promotional programs as shown in below fig 6.4 is referred to as pull strategy, a retailers ask for a product from a wholesalers and the wholesalers ask for the product from a distributor who gets the product from the firm. pull strategy is more effective in following situation,

(i) Perceived product differentiation
(ii) Strong brand identifies
(iii) High brand loyalty.
(iv) High involvement product categories
(v) High promotional budgets
(vi) Self service in retail system (i.e. supermarket culture)

The promotional techniques used for pull strategy includes, Ads, sales promotion, campaigns directed as consumers ,such as discounts ,gift voucher, samples ,etc in retail outlets where self service is predominant ,pull strategy is more effective .Besides, pull strategy also facilitate long term brand loyalty among the customers.

However, In view of market condition and factors mentioned above ,a firm may used a judicial mix of pull and push strategy for market promotion.

The nature of global promotion

Generally advertising is used primarily for low cost, mass volume consumer products. Products like fertilizers, canned and fresh produce and tobacco - all products which are used by end consumers - are the subject of heavy promotion. In intermediate products like timber, leather and cotton the advertising may be more limited in nature due to the fewer end purchasers of the raw material. Until recently, per capita GNP and advertising were directly correlated, due to the more widespread availability of media and higher incomes, giving a larger potential market for products. This is no longer the case. Optimal levels of advertising occur where the advertising/sales overseas effect is equal to the marginal advertising expenditure. The problem is in estimating the levels of each.

Global expenditure on advertising is believed to be more than US$ 200 billion, with the US the largest spender and Japan next. Individual companies like General Motors and IBM are each spending billions on advertising per annum. Worldwide, although less in Africa, the average advertising expenditure as a percentage of GNP is around 1.4% The major expenditure is on the television medic, the USA spending over US$ 30 billion on this medium. In many African countries radio is widely used, especially where television is not available, as in Malawi. Global programmes like CNN news and MNet television have dramatically increased the global advertising and direct selling possibilities via satellite. Print advertising continues to be a major medium in Africa.

Global promotion

When organisations advertise across international boundaries a number of important factors have to be taken into consideration. Whilst the process is ostensibly straightforward, (that is someone (seller) says something (message) to someone (buyer) through a medium) the process is compounded by certain factors. These are illustrated in figure 4.5.

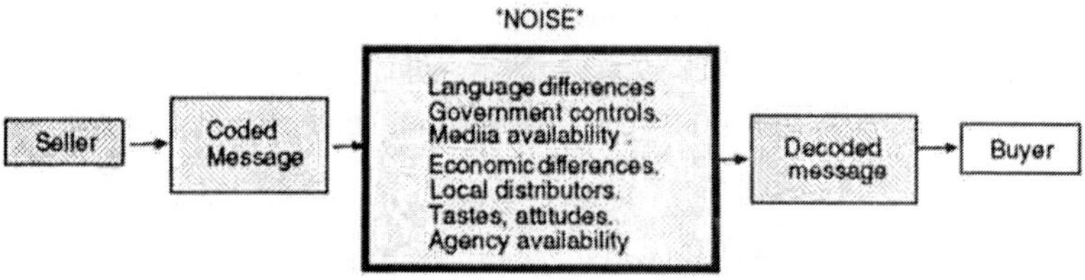

Figure 4.5 The advertising paradigm

These mitigating factors can be called "noise" and have an effect on the decision to "extend", "adapt" or "create" new messages.

Language differences may mean that straight translation is not enough when it comes to message design. Advertising may also play different roles within developed, between developed and underdeveloped and within underdeveloped countries. In developing countries "education" and "information" may be paramount objectives. In developed countries, the objectives may be more persuasive.

Cultural differences may account for the greatest challenge. However, many, notably Elinder (1961)[1] challenged the need to adapt messages and images, as he argued that consumer differences between countries are diminishing. Changes may be needed only in translation. However, this is only one point of view, as there is no doubt that cultural differences do exist across the world. For example, it would be quite unacceptable to have swimsuited ladies advertising sun care products in Moslem countries.

Three major difficulties occur in attempting to communicate internationally: the message may not get through to the intended recipient, due to a lack of media knowledge; the message may get through but not be understood, due to lack of audience understanding and: the message may get through, be understood but not provoke action. This may be due to lack of cultural understanding.

Media availability is a mitigating factor. Take for example, television. Whilst in Africa a number of countries do have it, the extent of its use and time available may be limited. Media use and availability, coupled with the type of message which may or may not be used, is tied to government control. Government may ban types of advertising, as is the case of cigarettes on British television. Intending advertisers should refer to the appropriate codes of advertising practice available in each country.

Campaign design

Before embarking on a promotion campaign, the following questions, among many others, must be answered. What can be said about the product? Which audience is being reached? What resources does the organisation have? Can someone do it better, say an agency? The basic steps in designing a campaign are set out in figure 4.6.

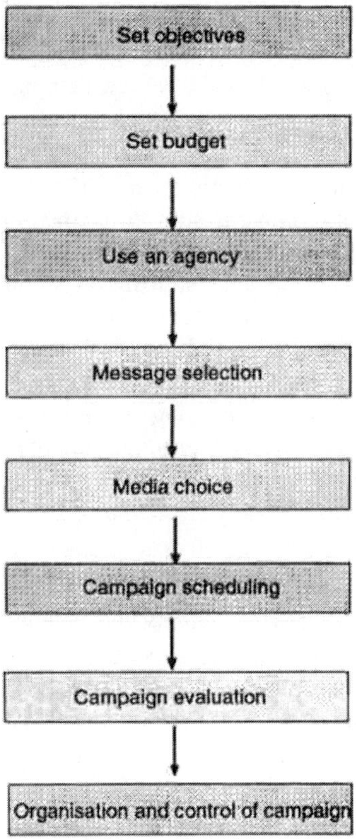

Objectives

Advertising must only be undertaken for a specific purpose(s) and this purpose must be translated into objectives. Whilst difficult to directly attribute to advertising, persuasive advertising's ultimate objective is to obtain sales. Other objectives include building a favorable image, information giving, stimulating distributors or building confidence in a product. Whatever objective(s) are pursued, these must be related to the product life cycle and the stage the product is in.

Budgets

Budgets can be set in a variety of ways. Many budgets use a percentage of past or future sales, objective and task methods, or rule of thumb. "Scientific" methods include sales response methods and linear programming.

Agency

Agencies can be used or not depending on the organization's own abilities, confidence in the market and market coverage. Many organisations, like Lintas and Interpublic, are worldwide and offer a wide range of expertise.

Message selection

Message selection is probably where the most care has to be taken. Decisions hinge on the standardization or adaptation of message decision, language nuances and the development of global segments and customers. Message design has three elements, illustration, layout and copy. Advertising appeals should be consistent with tastes, wants and attitudes in the market. Coke and Pepsi have found universal appeal. With the "postmodern age" now affecting marketing, message design is becoming particularly crucial. It is not just a question of selling, but of crafting images. It is often the image, not the product, which is commercialized. Products do not project images, products fill the images which the communication campaign projects. Coke's "Life" theme is a classic in this regard.

Media selection

There is a great difference in variety and availability of media across the world. The choice of media depends on its cost, coverage, availability, character (national or local or international) and its "atmosphere", for example in Zimbabwe posters versus adverts in the Financial Gazette.

In advertising the choice is television, radio, press, magazines, cinema, posters, direct mail, transport and video promotion. In promotion the choice is wide between money-off offers, discounts, extra quantities, and so on. Other forms of promotion include exhibitions, trade missions, public relations, selling, packaging, branding and sponsored events. Governments can be a very powerful promotion source, both by providing organisations like Horticultural Promotion Councils and by giving information and finance. GATT/UNCTAD Geneva provides a promotional service, giving information about products to interested parties. Trade Fairs are popular both as a "flag flyer", and as a product display and competitive information gathering facility. There are over 600 trade fairs worldwide; These include the Hanover Fair, Germany, the Royal

Agricultural Show, UK for machinery and the Zimbabwe International Trade Fair for agricultural produce and other things in general. The criterion for participating in fairs is always cost versus effectiveness.

Campaign scheduling

Scheduling international campaigns is difficult, especially if handled alone rather than with an agency or third party. Scheduling decisions involve decisions on when to break the campaign, the use of media solely or in combination, and the specific dates and times for advertisements to appear in the media.

Evaluation

Advertising campaign evaluation is not very easy at the best of times. Whilst it would be nice to say that "X" sales had resulted from "Y" advertising inputs, too many intervening factors make the simple tie-up difficult. Evaluation takes place at two levels - the effectiveness of the message and the effectiveness of the media. Few African developing countries, except Kenya, have any sophisticated methods for campaign evaluation. Measures include message recall tests, diary completion, and brand recall.

Organisation and control

Whilst companies like Nestle may have centrally organized and controlled advertising campaigns, many are devolved to local subsidiaries or agencies. The degree of autonomy afforded to local subsidiaries depends on the philosophy of the organisation and the relative knowledge of the local market by the principal.

Whilst truly global advertising, or even regional advertising, is a phenomenon not normally associated with African countries, as time goes by it may be. Unfortunately few countries see or use the overseas media to advantage. For developing countries, trade missions can be very useful for promotion. This is a relatively cheap but effective medium. Few countries activate their overseas embassies sufficiently to generate possible trade. If, however, it is done, the foregoing sections have to be considered carefully in order that possible mistakes are avoided.

Marketing

Marketing agricultural produce is different from marketing every other product. Agricultural produce is alive and sensitive. Its quantity, quality and price are almost totally dependent on natural conditions. They literally change with the weather. Moreover, unlike the other products, agricultural stock simply cannot be kept. This means that, unlike other producers, the farmer has no way of regulating the price his goods will fetch on the market. He cannot even assure himself a definite price when he ships them for export.

To deal with these limitations, Agrexco has created an extensive and flexible marketing system which balances, reliable and efficient consumer service with optimal prices for its farmers. Most of its sales are made through a panel of local importers working with the overseas Agrexco branches; some sales are made directly from Israel. In other case, most products are sold on a "regulated consignment" basis. How does it work? Taking into account the short-term supply, forecast and other pertinent market information, Agrexco sets minimum prices for about a week in advance- this to obtain at least a certain stability. But then if anything should change, if a product doesn't sell at the suggested price, for example, or if a bad weather results in an unexpected shortage of something else, prices are readjusted - this for the sale of flexibility.

Sales promotion and market research

To find out what its customers want, Agrexco conducts extensive market research into buying habits and consumer preferences. It searches opportunities for new products and for improving its tried and true standbys. It evaluates the success of its marketing, advertising and promotional campaigns, and its follows up to the introduction of new products into the market. All of this prepares the ground work for penetrating new markets and keeps existing ones healthy and growing.

Advertising and promotion let our customers know what Agrexco has to offer and how they can enjoy its many products. Overall planning is directed form the Agrexco office in Israel, while the branches, which are in touch with local media are buying patterns are directly responsible for the advertising, public relations, in-store demonstrations and special sales campaigns in each of their countries.

Transport

Every year about 500,000 pallets of Carmel products, totaling over 350,000 tons, leave Israel by sea or air.

During the main export season, Agrexco has four refrigerator ships, two of them bearing the Carmel name, in constant operation, as well as a support service of ventilated liners. Agrexco products set sail from Haifa and Ashdod- at the latter, the Carmel Kor (an Agrexco subsidiary) terminal handles 200,000 tons of fresh produce a year. About 80% of the produce is sent to the allocation and distribution center in Marseilles: the rest is shipped directly to ports in the U.K. and Northern Europe. Especially sensitive products, such as flowers, goose liver and strawberries, are sent exclusively by air. Approximately 70,000 tons of fresh agricultural produce leave Ben Gurion Airport every year. Seventy percent of it is flown during the winter season, carried at the rate of about 2500 tons a week, on 20-25 weekly jumbo jet cargo flights, as well as on additional regular flights when necessary. About 45% of the air cargo lands at the allocation and distribution centre in Cologne, Germany; the rest is sent to its various destinations directly.

The Agrexco terminal at Ben Gurion is able to store a large range of produce in quantities that amount to the capacity of four 747 jumbo jets. Boasting an expert staff, the terminal has been equipped with the latest in sophisticated refrigeration, conveyor and computer system to ensure that the fresh produce reaches its destination in the shortest time and best possible condition.

Indeed, the need to transport perishable goods and to keep them in peak condition over very long distances has made transportation Agrexco's largest single expense, far larger than for any of its competitors. Agrexco's leased refrigerator ships, for example, have been especially adapted to transport products requiring different storage conditions and a carefully regulated range of temperatures. Only constant efforts to cut costs through improved organization and technology have enabled Agrexco to stay in the running. Among any other efforts in this direction, Agrexco is cooperation with shipping experts to create a vessel that will meet its own strict specifications for both efficiency and economy. It invests funds, technological expertise and engineering vision to design today the ship that will be right in the future.

Quality control

Carmel products are under constant quality control, from planting through picking, packing and delivery. All along the way, the products are repeatedly and meticulously inspected for export suitability according to international criteria.

The supervisory process begins with the preparations of the fields and the planting and growing of the crops. Special Agrexco teams dispersed all over Israel provide extension services, which keep the Tel Aviv office informed of what's happening on the farm and assists the growers with needed advice. More than once, disaster has been averted by disqualifying produce while it was still in the ground or by having district supervisors offer on-the-spot counseling.

The product itself is first inspected at the transit and packing stations. Here the Phytosanitary Administration of the Ministry of Agriculture determines whether each and every item does or does not meet internationally agreed upon export standards. Those that do not, are disqualified and channeled to the domestic market or slated for destruction.

The final inspection takes place at the branches abroad. Quality inspectors working alongside the branch managers report to Israel on the quality and conditions of the shipments, follow up consumer complaints, re-sort and re-package produce that has been damaged en route, and provide feedback on new crops and varieties.

Packaging for every product

Carmel products travel a long hard road from the field to supermarkets shelves in European cities. The average route was calculated at 3,000 km. So that every one of hundreds of products reaches its destinations fresh and undamaged, each must be properly packed, in keeping with its particular characteristics and sensitivities. In charge of this task is the packing department, which handles the planning, specifications, purchase and distributions of the packaging. The unit utilizes a large variety of materials and technologies, including paper and plastic, cardboard and metal, wood and fiber, rubber and resins, and a range of receptacles, from bulk crates, cardboard containers, wooden pallets, punnets, bags, and sleeves through to wrapping papers and plastic bags. The annual packaging budget amounts to approximately $15 million.

The packing department is highly respected at home and abroad. It has been honored with the Kaplan prize for "developing effective packaging which results in significant savings.

Keeping cool

Israel is a natural greenhouse. But along with many advantages of its hot sunny climate are a host of difficulties that begin as soon as the fruit or vegetable is detached from the plant and end only when it arrives at market. To stay fresh and crisp over the thousands of kilometers it travels, the produce has to be kept at the right temperature along the entire route, in an unbroken cooling chain. It is picked and packed in the cool early morning hours, promptly loaded onto refrigerator trucks, and kept under refrigeration in the warehouses, ships, planes and trains as well.

Global Marketing, Logistics - Access And Documentation:-

Exporting and importing are two sides of the same coin; both supply customers with products manufactured outside the country. Exports now account for over 15% of global GNP and are growing at an annual compound rate in excess of 10%. Export marketing requires a knowledge of the target market, a marketing mix decision, planning, organisation and control and information systems. Exporting is often an incremental process, from unsolicited order filling to deliberate export planning. No doubt few firms will export unless profit and growth opportunities are expected. Theories of trade stress the basis as "comparative advantage", but in practice this is of little use. The most significant factors affecting trade are "firm" not "product" characteristics. McGuiness and Little (1981)[1] found two firm characteristics "restrained from exporting" and "high technology" as opposed to product characteristics had an overwhelming influence on the decision.

Whilst exporting and importing are, this is not the way governments look at it when making policy. Simply, policy can be construed as two-faced. Often, every effort is made to improve and encourage exports whilst every effort is made to curb imports. The combination of policy measures can have an offsetting effect. Government, however, seeks to support export activities in three ways: by applying lower rates of tax to earnings from exporting or refunds; outright subsidies or assistance like information giving. Many African countries have incentives like export retention schemes and revolving schemes to aid potential exporters.

Complexity

Exporting and importing requires an enormous amount of thought and attention to detail, especially documentation. If documents are missing or wrongly filled out then the transaction will be void. Consider the following example of the exportation of horticultural produce from Kenya.

Terms of access

Terms of access refer to the conditions that apply to the importation of goods manufactured in a foreign country. The major instruments covered by this include import duties, import restrictions or quotas, foreign exchange regulations and preference arrangements.

Tariff systems

Tariff systems provide either a single rate of duty for each item applicable to all countries, or two or more rates, applicable to different countries or groups of countries. Tariffs are usually grouped into two classifications:

Single column tariff: A simple schedule of duties in which the rate applies to imports from all countries on the same basis.

Two column tariff: The initial single column of duties is supplemented by a second column of "conventional" duties, which shows reduced rates agreed through tariff negotiations with other countries. The second column is supplied to all countries enjoying "most favored nation" status within the framework of GATT. Signatories to GATT, with some exceptions, apply the most favorable tariff to products.

Preferential tariff: A reduced tariff rate applied to imports from certain countries. GATT prohibits preferential tariffs except historical preference schemes like the Commonwealth, those part of a formal economic integration treaty like a free trade area and preference to companies of a developing country importing into a developed country.

Types of Duties: Customs duties are of two different types - ad valorem or specific amounts per unit, or a combination of these.

(i) Ad valorem - This duty is expressed as a percentage of the value of goods. As definitions of customs value vary from country to country it is best to secure valuation policy information first.

A uniform basis for the valuation of goods for customs purposes was elaborated by the Customs Cooperation Council in Brussels and was adopted in 1953 (the Brussels Nomenclature came out of this). In this case the customs value is landed GIF cost at the port of entry. This cost should reflect the arm's length price of the goods at the time the duty becomes payable.

(ii) Specific duties - Expressed as a specific amount of currency per unit of weight, volume, length, or number of other units of measurement, e.g. 25 cents per kg. Usually specific duties are expressed in the currency of the importing country.

(iii) Alternative duties - In this case both ad valorem and specific duties are set out in the customs tariff for a given product. Normally, the applicable rate is the one that yields the higher amount of duty, although there are cases where the lower is specified.

(iv) Compound or mixed duties - These duties provide for specific plus ad valorem rates to be levied on the same articles.

(v) Antidumping duties - Applied if injury occurs to domestic producers. These are special additional import charges designed to cover the difference between the export price and the "normal" price, which usually refers to the price paid by customers in the exporting countries.

(vi) Countervailing duties - Additional duties levied to offset subsidies granted in the exporting country.

Other import charges: These include variable import charges, temporary import surcharges and compensatory import taxes

(i) Variable import charges - Can be used to raise imported product prices to the domestic price level.

(ii) Temporary import surcharges - Used as a local industry protection measure and in response to balance of payments deficits.

(iii) Compensating import taxes - In theory these taxes correspond with various internal taxes, such as value added taxes and sales taxes.

According to GATT such "border tax adjustments must not amount to additional protection for domestic producers or to a subsidy for exports". This can lead to great inequities.

Non tariff barriers

Non tariff barriers are measures, public or private, that cause internationally traded goods and services to be allocated in such a way as to reduce potential real world income (the attainable level when resources are allocated in the most economically efficient manner). They virtually prevent sales in a foreign market.

(i) Quotas and trade control - Specific limits and controls, and once the quota is filled the price mechanism is not allowed to operate. Some countries, for example Zimbabwe, operate state trading.

(ii) Discriminatory government and private procurement policies - "Buy British" policies aimed at restricting foreign supply.

(iii) Selective monetary,controls and discriminatory exchange rate policies - Act distortively on import duties and export subsidies. Some countries require an import deposit, thus in effect raising the price of foreign goods.

(iv) Restrictive administrative and technical regulations - Include antidumping, size regulations, safety and health. The EU, for example has very strict hygiene measures for imports of horticultural products.

Tariff classification

Before World War II specific duties were widely used and the tariffs of many countries were very complex. Tariff administration has been made more simple by the Brussels Nomenclature (BTN), worked out by an international committee of experts under the sponsorship of the Customs Cooperation Council, which in 1955 produced a convention that entered into force in 1959. These rules now apply to most GATT countries.

The BTN groups articles mainly according to the materials from which they are made. With many new products appearing the task of classifying becomes more difficult. Exporters should seek the most favorable classification for their products to minimize the duty levied. Sometimes products can be reclassified to get an advantageous rate. Difficulties of classification raise serious questions about the accuracy of data in international trade patterns. In using data on trade, the numbers may often reflect hasty and arbitrary classification which distorts the true picture of the trade flows. This often explains the discrepancies in import and export figures of the same commodity between two countries.

International trade

The export transaction is founded on a contract of international sale of goods with the special characteristic that it is entwined with other contracts, a thing that differentiates the international sale from the local sale. These connected contracts are the contract of carriage by sea or air under which goods are exported and the contract of insurance by which the goods are insured. In many export transactions, delivery of the shipping documents amounts to performance of the contract of sale. These shipping documents consist normally of the bill of lading, the marine insurance policy and the invoice. The position becomes more involved when payment is made under a banker's documentary credit because this common method of payment requires the addition of two other contracts to the export transaction viz: the contract of the bank with the buyer and seller respectively.

Export contracts

A contract is a general agreement between a seller making an offer and a buyer making an acceptance. The acceptance should be unqualified and any variation is regarded as a repudiation of the contract.

The export contract should be very explicit regarding goods and specifications, price, mode of payment, storage, packing, delivery schedule and so on. Normally the contract is sent with a pro forma invoice by airmail.

Although contracts may be oral or partly in writing and partly by word of mouth, it is always safer for the exporter to produce his terms of selling in writing and obtain the signatures of his buyer or authorized representative.

The essential elements of a contract of sale should include the following:

(a) Names and addresses of the parties
(b) Product, standards (quality) and specifications
(c) Inspection of products
(d) Packaging, labeling and marking requirements
(e) Marine insurance
(f) Port of shipment, destination and delivery schedule
(g) Method of payment
(h) Price FOB, CIF, C & F etc. in international currency or currency asked for by the buyer and,
(i) Settlement of disputes including arbitration clause.

If the buyer is satisfied with the terms set out in the contract and the pro forma, the exporter can then get an order with duplicate copy of the contract, detailing payment arrangement and other details and an indication that a letter of credit (LC) has been opened in favor of the exporter. Details of documents required will also be indicated in the export order. The following must happen:

(a) Acknowledgment - exporter must acknowledge receipt of the order indicating that confirmation follows

(b) Scrutiny - contents of the order in respect of product, sizes, specifications etc. as per quotation must be examined in terms of elements of contract conveyed by the exporter to his buyer. Qualities/ volume should be examined and ascertained in respect of capability to supply within the stipulated time.

Delivery schedule: All efforts should be made to ensure adherence to delivery schedule as this would affect the requirements of the LC. The export order should indicate whether part shipment is permissible or not.

Terms of payment

This is very important: If payment is to be by LC the following should be borne in mind when examining the LC:

(a) confirmation of the LC

(b) documents stipulated in the LC will be submitted by the exporter's bank

(c) draft to be drawn against the LC is for the period set out in terms of the contract, "sight draft" is payment by the recipient or "usance draft" if credit has been allowed in the contract

(d) the credit validity period allowed in the LC

(e) payment against the LC is permissible according to requirements of foreign exchange control regulations.

Documents

Since the LC indicates the documents required along with the bill of exchange, the exporters should look for availability of the documents called for by the importer and particularly:

(a) Commercial customs consular/legalized invoice. The Buyer should endeavour to send a special form of invoice required by him.

(b) Kind of Bill of Lading (usually "clean on board") and the number of copies required by him along with the bill of exchange and non-negotiable copies to be sent to the buyer.

(c) Certificate of origin

(d) Packing list - number of copies required

(e) Marine Insurance Policy whether in FOB or CIF contract is to be effected by the exporter on behalf of the importer. The name of the company from which the insurance contract is to be obtained should also be mentioned.

Pre-shipment inspection

To be carried out by an appointed body or any other agency.

Packing, labeling and marking requirements

Special or usual activities for example, color contents, language, packing etc.

Confirmation

If the exporter is satisfied with all of the above, then he must send his confirmation of the export order to the buyer. No special form of confirmation is needed as any letter giving details of order and indicating clearly terms and conditions would be sufficient.

If dissatisfied, the exporter should write to the importer to seek for clarification and necessary corrections, If the export transaction presents itself to the businessman as a natural and indivisible whole and he is apt to pay little attention to its constituent parts, like the motorist who thinks of the components of his car only when he notices a fault in them.

Special trade terms in export sales

Export transactions based on the contract of sale usually have terms which are not customary in the local trade. The most common are the FOB and CIF clauses. Other clauses are ex-works, or ex-warehouse or ex-store, the FOR, FOT, the COF, ex-ship, ex-quay and arrival.

Ex-works or ex-warehouse or ex-store (where the goods are situated)

This is an arrangement which is most favorable to the seller who desires to conduct export trade as closely as possible on the lines of a home market sale. The clause means that the overseas buyer or his agent must collect the goods at the place where the seller works or where his factory, warehouse or store is situated. The seller must provide goods of the contract description and place them at the agreed collection point. Notice should be given to the buyer that the goods are ready for collection.

Free on rail or free on truck (FOR/FOT)

Here, the seller has little to do with the actual exportation of the goods and many overseas risks. But unlike the above, the goods are not collected at the seller's doorstep but have to be delivered by him into the custody of the railway or transport authority at the agreed point.

The seller, under an FOR or FOT contract, has normally to procure the railway wagon or other means of transport. The seller should give immediate notice to the buyer of the loading or delivery to enable him to make a claim on the carrier within the time prescribed, in the event of loss.

Free alongside ship (FAS)

This involves certain elements which are absent in a sale on the home market. The seller will have performed his obligations when the goods are carried alongside the ship so that they can be placed on board. The actual loading of the goods is the responsibility of the buyer.

Under the FAS contract, the duty to nominate an effective ship falls on the buyer.

Once the seller has placed the goods alongside a ship in the customary way and at the agreed time, all subsequent expenses and costs are to be met by the buyer.

Free on board; named port of shipment (FOB)

Here, the seller assumes further responsibilities. He undertakes to place the goods on board a named ship at a named port and berthing place. All charges to, and including the delivery of the goods over the ship's rail, have to be borne by the seller while the buyer has to pay all subsequent charges such as the stowage of the goods on board ship, freight, marine insurance as well as unloading charges, import duties, consular fees and other incidental charges due on the arrival of the consignment in the port of destination.

This transaction differs markedly from an ordinary sale in the home market where no dealings in a port have to be carried out and yet it does not display the complexion which is a true mark of the export transaction. There are two types of FOB contract, the strict or classical type and the one with additional services. Under the strict FOB contract the arrangements for shipment and, if he so wishes, for insurance are made by the buyer direct. Under an FOB contract the duty to name an effective ship falls on the buyer. Failure to name such a ship will make the buyer liable to an action for damages for non-acceptance. This is shown in the following case:

In an FOB contract with additional services, the parties agree that the arrangements for the carriage by sea and insurance shall be made by the seller but for, and on behalf of, the buyer. In both types of FOB contract the cost of putting the goods on board ship is borne by the seller. Delivery is complete when the goods are put on board ship. The risk of accidental loss under the Sale of Goods Act passes to the buyer when the seller has placed the goods safely on board ship. The seller must give notice of shipment to the buyer so as to enable him to insure. If the seller omits to do this, the goods shall be at his risk. This can be seen in the following case:

Cost Insurance Freight (CIF) (named port of destination)

This is the most common export clause. A CIF contract is not a sale of the goods themselves but a sale of the documents of title. Thus, a buyer is under an obligation to pay against the shipping documents even if the goods do not arrive. The right of the buyer where the goods have not arrived is to sue the contract of carriage or insurance which is assigned to him by the seller under the contract of sale. However, if the goods are lost from a peril not covered by the ordinary policy of insurance current in the trade, the buyer must nevertheless pay the full price on delivery of the documents. This can be seen in the following case:

The property under a CIF contract passes when the documents are taken up by the buyer but what the buyer obtains, when the title under the document is given to him, is the property in the goods, subject to the condition the goods reverts if upon examination he finds them not to be in accordance with the contract. If, however, the goods are not ascertained at the time the documents are taken up, no property in the goods will pass until the goods are ascertained. An example of this can be seen in the above case.

The duties of the seller under CIF contract are: to ship at the port of shipment goods of the description contained in the contract; to procure a contract of carriage by sea, under which the goods will be delivered at the destination contemplated by the contract; to arrange a contract of insurance on the terms current in the trade for the benefit of the buyer; to make out an invoice for the goods and to tender within a reasonable time after shipment the bill of lading, the policy of certificate of insurance and the invoice to the buyer so that the buyer may obtain delivery of the goods, if they arrive, or recover for their loss if they are lost on the voyage. The bill of lading tendered must correctly state the date of shipment otherwise the buyer can reject the goods. Under a CIF contract the buyer has the right to reject the documents and also a right to reject the goods. These two rights are quite distinct. This distinction can be seen in the following case:

Contracts Expressed to be CIF but not True CIF Contracts

The strict rules discussed above do not apply to other contracts, in particular arrival contracts and other contracts which are not true CIF contracts, though they may be described as CIF contracts by the parties. Thus, the terminology used by the parties is not conclusive evidence as to the nature of the export contract. The following case evidences this.

Apart from the above situation where a bill of lading is replaced by a delivery order, a contract expressed to be a CIF one will not be truly such also where delivery of the goods is expressed to constitute performance of the contract.

Accepted variants of the CIF contract

The following are some of the variants of the CIF contract which are reconcilable with the legal nature of a true CIF contract.

CIF and C; CIF and E; CIF and C and I: CIF AND C STANDS FOR COST, insurance, freight and commission, E stands for exchange and I for interest. The commission is the export merchant's commission which he charges when acting as buying agent for the overseas buyer. The expression "exchange" is ambiguous; it is sometimes said to refer to the banker's commission or charge, while sometimes it refers to exchange fluctuations. In the former case it denotes that the banker's charges are included in the calculation, whereas in the latter it means that the purchase price is not affected by the subsequent rise or fall of the stipulated currency of payment against another currency. It is thought that the former interpretation is more common as currency fluctuation arrangements are most explicitly made. The clause CIF and C and I is used when goods are exported to distant places where some time elapses before the bill drawn on the buyer abroad is settled. When the seller negotiates the bill to his bank the latter charges him commission and interest until payment has been received on the draft in the seller's country, and the seller by adding in his contract of export the letter "I" to the clause indicates to the buyer that the quoted price includes the bank's interest and commission.

Date of arrival of goods is mere determinate for payment of price: The parties sometimes agree on CIF terms adding "payment on arrival of goods" or "payment 'x' days after arrival of goods". This clause is ambiguous and its meaning can be ascertained from the intention of the parties. As a general rule, these words refer to the time at which payment has to be made. If the goods do not arrive, payment shall be made on tender of the documents at the time at which the goods would normally have arrived.

C and F (Named Port of Destination)

This stands for cost and freight. The seller is responsible for procuring the contract of carriage of goods but not the contract of insurance which is to be effected by the buyer. However, the seller must promptly inform the buyer of the shipping of the goods to enable him to insure the goods. The C and F clause is not frequently used by export merchants except in the case of some countries, which for political reasons, or due to lack of foreign exchange, require their importers to insure at home rather than buy CIF.

Arrival of ex-ship (Named Ship and Named Port of Arrival): Where this clause is used, the goods must arrive at the place of destination. It is not sufficient that documents evidencing shipment of the goods to that destination are made available to the buyer. When examining whether a particular contract is a CIF contract or an arrival contract, attention must be paid to the situation of the parties; the terms used by the parties are not conclusive. (See previous case 12.8 Comptoir d'Achat vs Luis de Ridder).

Export documentation

In internal/inland trade, the commercial parties to a sales contract agree on a price based on the buyer taking over the goods at the seller's or supplier's warehouse, or on delivery by the seller to the buyer's warehouse, or delivery by the seller to a specified rail or road carrier. This is because it is simple for either buyer or seller to arrange to pay for all formalities involving the movement and insurance of the goods from one place to another in the same country.

In international trade, the position is a little complicated. There are likely to be three separate contracts of carriage of the goods, i.e. from the seller's or supplier's warehouse to a place within the seller's country, from which there will be an international movement of the goods to a place of arrival within the buyer's country, with a possible internal carriage within the buyer's country to his warehouse.

Basic export documents

Below is a list of basic documents used in export trade. These have been covered in detail in other sectors of this text.

(a) Invitation to quote
(b) Quote
(c) Pro forma Invoice
(d) Order confirmation/acknowledgement
(e) Bill of lading/short form bill of lading
(f) Airway bill
(g) Marine (other) insurance policy
(h) Commercial invoice
(i) Consular invoice
(j) Certified invoice
(k) Certificate of origin
(l) Packing list/weight note
(m) Specification sheet
(n) Manufacturer's analysis certificate
(o) Health, sanitary, phytosanitary, veterinary certificates
(p) Quality inspection certificate/certificate of value
(q) Independent third party inspection certificate
(r) Dispatch advice note

(s) Dangerous goods declaration
(t) Shipping or export consignment notes
(u) Documentary credit of payment drafts
(v) Export licenses
(w) Import licenses
(x) Exporter's commission advice to agent
(y) Customs and Excise export entry forms
(z) EU Movement documents EUR 1 Form
(a_1) Other specifically requested documents

Not all of these will be relevant depending on whether the exporter is from a developed or less developed country.

Note:

A great number of exporters find it more convenient to control the volume and variety of paper work and related matters by designing a file folder that has printed on the covers the entire control procedure covering documentation, production of goods, payment, shipping instructions and so on. Each separate transaction is then allocated to a numbered filed folder.

The documents are either required by the importer to satisfy the country's trade control authorities or to enable a documentary credit transaction to be implemented. Trade control authorities want to ensure that each document controls the import of a good/commodity for sanitary/veterinary reasons, or to ensure no plant disease likely to affect the local seeds is imported from another country. The importer also wants to ensure that the exporter fulfills these requirements under documentary letter of credit operations in order for payment to be effected.

Commercial documents

Of the documents described earlier, this section will single out some and describe them in detail.

Pro forma invoice

This is a form of quotation by the seller to a potential buyer. It is the same as Commercial Invoice except for the words "Pro forma Invoice" which appear on it. It may be an invitation to the buyer to place a firm order and is often required by him so that the authorities of the importer's country will grant him an import license and/or foreign exchange permit. The pro forma invoice normally shows the terms of trade and price so that once the buyer has accepted the order there is a firm contract to be settled as stipulated in the pro forma. Details from the accepted pro forma must be transposed identically to the commercial invoice that goods are in accordance with the pro forma invoice. No pro forma invoices are used in settlements:

- in advance
- on consignment
- subject to tender
- after an invitation to tender has been accepted by the seller.

Commercial invoice

The following details must appear on a commercial invoice used in international trade:

- Names and addresses of buyer and seller and date
- Complete description of goods. If payment is to be obtained by means of documentary letter of credit, this description of goods must exactly match the details in the documentary credit
- Unit prices where applicable and final price against shipping terms
- Terms of settlement e.g. under documentary credit or 30 days sight Documents against Acceptance
- Shipping marks and numbers
- Weight and quantity of goods
- Name of vessel if known or applicable.

Sometimes it is necessary to show to the customs authorities in the buyer's country:

Seller's signature

- Origin of goods
- Ports of loading and discharge or places of taking in charge and delivery
- Details of freight and insurance charges specified separately where applicable.

Certified invoice

A certified invoice may be an ordinary signed commercial invoice specially certifying:

(a) That the goods are in accordance with a specific contract or proforma

(b) That the goods are, or are not, of a specific country of origin

(c) Any statement required by the buyer from the seller.

There are also formal certified invoices which when submitted to the importing authorities will provide them with the necessary evidence to pass the goods through customs with a lower import duty or none at all. Combined certificates of value and origin (CVO) are used between members of the Commonwealth and special invoices for the other major trade areas such as the EU. All certified invoices must be signed and in case of combined certificates of value and origin they should be signed by a witness as well.

Weight note

This certificate may be issued by the seller or often by a third party - it indicates weight of goods, which should tally with that shown on all the other documents. Weighbridge tickets are sometimes produced for road or rail shipments. Banks will accept superimposed declaration of weight on shipping documents, unless credit calls for a separate or independent document.

Packing list and specification

These documents set out details of the packing of the goods. These are required by the customs authorities to enable them to make spot checks or more thorough checks on the contents of any particularly package. The packing list has no details of cost/price of the goods; the specification does have these details.

Manufacturers analysis certificate

The certificate states the ingredients and proportions revealed by an analysis of chemicals, drugs etc.

Third party certificate of inspection

This is a certificate declaring the result of an examination of the goods by a recognised independent inspection body. In order to protect himself from paying when substandard or worthless goods have been shipped an importer can call for an independent check or examination of goods before they are dispatched.

This is important for the buyer as banks' liabilities and responsibilities under documentary credit are limited to documents and not goods represented by the documents. The usual independent body which serves buyers/sellers is the Society General de Surveillance.

Official documents

These are legion. This section looks at the following few official documents only for example purposes,

(a) EURI form

(b) TzL form

(c) Consular invoice
(d) Legalized invoice
(e) Combined invoice and Certificate of Origin
(f) Chamber of Commerce Certificate of Origin
(g) Blacklist Certificate
(h) Veterinary Certificate.

EC documents EURI and TzL

EURI form is used in respect of preferential exports from an EU country to a non EU country. The TzL is used for trade between EU member states, where the goods are being transported directly between member states and without passing through the territory of a non member country.

Consular invoice

Importing authorities of several countries require consular invoices to be produced before goods may be cleared through customs. These invoices are normally obtained by the exporter from the Embassy of the importing country and are submitted to the Embassy for stamping at a charge. Sometimes a Chamber of Commerce is required to certify on the Consular Invoice that the origin of the goods is as stated. This mainly happens in the South American countries. The selling price is mainly examined in the light of current market price to ensure that there is no "dumping" or that importers are not siphoning money overseas or that the correct basis for levying import duty can be determined by the Customs Authorities.

Legalized invoice

Some countries require that commercial invoices should be legalized by their own embassy or consulate in the seller's country. Sellers produce their own invoices and have them stamped (visaed) by the buyer's embassy. This is normally required in the Middle East countries.

Certificates of origin

These constitute signed documents evidencing origin of the goods and are normally used by the importer's country to determine the tariff rates. They should contain the description of goods and signature and seal of the Chamber of Commerce.

Blacklist certificate

Countries at war or with badly strained political relations may require evidence that:

(a) The origin of the goods is not that of a particular country

(b) That the parties involved (manufacturer, bank, insurance company, shipping line etc.) are not blacklisted or,

(c) That the ship or aircraft will not call at ports in such a country unless forced to do so.

Health, veterinary and sanitary certificates

Sometimes these are required for official purposes in the purchase of foodstuffs, hides and skins, livestock and in the use of packing materials.

Insurance documents

The following are insurance documents required in international trade:

(a) Letter of insurance

(b) Insurance company's open cover certificate

(c) Lloyds' open cover insurance

(d) Insurance policy.

Letter of insurance

It is normally issued by a broker to provide notice that an insurance has been placed pending the production of a policy or a certificate. Sometimes this takes the form of a cover note. The above documents do not contain details of the insurance being effected and therefore are not considered satisfactory by banks which normally require evidence of an insurance contract in documents required under a documentary credit.

Broker's certificates, and cover notes are issued by a third party and not the insurer so that in the event of any claim, it would be made against the broker.

Insurance certificates

These are issued by insurance companies to embrace either open covers or floating policies. The systems of open cover and floating policies are similar in that:

(a) Once the system has been arranged, the insured party is covered for all his shipments on the terms and for the risks agreed. The insured will declare to the insurance company the value and details of each shipment and will receive a pre-printed insurance certificate made valid and the document will show the risks covered and be presigned by the insurer.

(b) Under English Law, no action will be obtained on a contract of insurance evidenced solely by an insurance certificate. So, any action to be taken against insurers can only be on production of a policy to be sued on.

Transport documents

Airway bill

The IATA airway bill (sometimes called an air consignment note or air freight note) is often issued in a set of 12 of which 3 are commercially important, the remainder being copies for airline purposes. The three important documents are:

(a) for the issuing carrier

(b) for the consignee

(c) for the shipper.

The waybill is a receipt only and not a document of title, and the goods are delivered to the named consignee without further formality once customs clearance has been obtained. If the third original document is in the hands of the shipper this can be surrendered to the airline before delivery is made to the consignee.

There might be an arrangement for payment whereby the bank might wish to have a lien over the goods until payment is effected by the importer. The goods will, therefore, be consigned to a correspondent bank (provided that the correspondent bank is agreeable to this) and in such a case the bank will release the goods or documents as instructed. The document should bear the airline stamp with date of dispatch and flight number, and be signed on behalf of the airline.

Combined transport bill of lading

As a natural sequel to unitization of cargo it has become increasingly customary for the "unit load", especially where the cargo has been packed in a container of 20 feet in length, to be shipped on one contract of carriage from a "place of taking in charge" to a "place of delivery". This is known as a "combined" or "multi-modal" transport, and is a substitute for the traditional port-to-port bill of lading. Its name is combined bill of lading "combined transport bill of lading" is used. When such a document is required under a documentary credit it does not make sense for such credit to specify ports of loading and discharge, or to prohibit transshipment as the essentials are the places of taking in charge and delivery.

House bill of lading

These documents are issued by freight forwarders for their own services. This exhibit is the form recommended by The Institute of Freight Forwarders Limited for trading members of the Institute and bears the IFF Standard Trading Conditions.

Under the Carriage of Goods by Sea Act 1971, any sea waybills, data freight receipts, house bills, forwarding agents' receipts or similar non-negotiable documents, not being bills of lading or title documents, are nonetheless, subject to the Hague Rules relating to bills of lading where the non-negotiable documents provide evidence that they relate to contracts of carriage of goods by sea.

Rail consignment note

With the growth of freight liner traffic the volume of goods being exported by rail through to final continental destination is increasing. Consequently, the carrier's receipt, or duplicate copy, frequently accompanies the other documents. Goods will be released to the consignee, upon application and normal proof of identify, by the rail authorities at destination or by delivery direct. Control over the goods would be arranged in the same way as for an air consignment. The rail consignment note should bear the stamp of the station of departure and the date of departure.

Road waybill (CMR)

The CMR (Convention Merchandises Routiers) consignment note is an internationally approved and recognised non-negotiable transport document used when goods are travelling by road through or to countries which are parties to the CMR. The contracting countries are Austria, Belgium, Bulgaria, Czechoslovakia, Denmark, Finland, France (including overseas territories), Federal German Republic, German Democratic Republic, Gibraltar, Greece, Hungary, Italy, Luxembourg, Netherlands, Norway, Poland, Portugal, Romania, Spain, Sweden, Switzerland, United Kingdom (including Northern Ireland) and Yugoslavia.

As well as its function as a receipt and delivery document, the note provides written evidence that goods are being carried under the terms of the CMR.

Bills of lading

This document is the receipt given by the shipping company to the shipper for goods accepted for carriage by sea. If in negotiable form it also conveys title to the goods and the goods will only be released by the shipping company at destination against surrender of a signed original of the bill of lading. Finally, the bill of lading evidences a contract of carriage.

Short form bills of lading

One of the three functions of a bill of lading is to provide evidence of the underlying contract of carriage by sea which comes into being with the reservation of space on board a ship. The shipping company's terms are usually given in full on the reverse, but with the short form bill this is not the case.

The essence of the "short form" is the complete removal from the reverse of the bill of lading of the "small print" which gives details of the contract of carriage. Article 19(b) (ii) of the Uniform Customs and Practice for Documentary Credits, defines such short form bills of lading as "bills of lading issued by shipping companies or their agents which indicate some or all of the conditions of carriage by reference to a source or document other than the bill of lading". In a number of countries, including the UK, the use is being encouraged of a short form bill of lading common to a number of different shipping companies. This is not pre-printed with the name of the shipping company, so the "name of the carrier" has to be typed in with the other data relating to the specific shipment. This type of document is known as the "common short form bill of lading". Banks will accept such bills of lading when presented under documentary credits unless the credit specifies otherwise.

Bills of lading (Liner)

These are issued by shipping companies in respect of goods carried on regular line vessels with scheduled runs and reserved berths at destination. Such means of transport has possible advantages over tramp vessels which do not necessarily adhere to a very strict schedule and may make unscheduled calls at various ports on the way to the ultimate destination. Shipping lines serving the same routes or destinations may form a conference, within which agreements are made over such matters as the terms and conditions of bills of lading, freight rates, and sometimes of sailing and use of berthing facilities.

Non-negotiable sea waybills

The processing of bills of lading is slow since they may have to pass through several hands. Therefore, these documents may not be received by the consignee before arrival of the vessel. The non-negotiable sea waybill was developed to avoid delay in handling of goods at destination, and has been adopted by a number of shipping lines as an alternative to bills of lading. It resembles the air waybill, as the goods are delivered to the named consignee without any need to hand over the waybill.

Mate's receipts

Rarely seen in trade circles, and rightly so, for this is merely a receipt for goods shipped abroad. Not being a document of title, it should be exchanged for the set of bills of lading by the shipper at the offices of the shipping company.

Financial and financing documents

The financial documents, bills of exchange and promissory notes are listed below. A short description then follows:

(a) Bill of exchange drawn in foreign currency and payable at sight

(b) Bill of exchange drawn in sterling and payable at sight
(c) Bill of exchange accepted payable at 30 days' sight
(d) Promissory note
(e) Inspection and sampling order
(f) Delivery order
(g) Warehouse receipt
(h) Trust receipt.

Bills of exchange

The legal definition (Bills of Exchange Act 1882, Section 3) of a bill of exchange is an unconditional order in writing, addressed by one person (drawer) to another (drawee), signed by the person giving it (drawer), requiring the person to whom it is addressed (drawee) to pay on demand, or at a fixed or determinable future time, a certain sum in money to, or to the order of, a specified person (payee), or to bearer. The words in brackets do not appear in the Act, but have been inserted for clarity.

Bills of exchange are widely used in international trade, partly since they are convenient vehicles for collecting payment from traders abroad. Finance may be arranged in a number of ways using bills of exchange, both for the buyer (drawee) and for the seller (drawer). Bills of exchange which have been dishonored may be used in their own right as the basis for legal action. After payment, the discharged bill of exchange is retained by the drawee as evidence of payment, in other words it becomes a receipt for the money. It is the practice in some European countries for banks to avail bills of exchange by adding the bank's name to the bill; this raises the status of the document as the availing bank has guaranteed payment at maturity.

Promissory notes

Whilst not bills of exchange, these are largely subject to the same rules and are used for a somewhat similar purpose, the settlement of indebtedness. Instead of being drawn like a bill of exchange by the person expecting to be paid, they are made by the person who owes the money, in favor of the beneficiary. A simple way of looking at a promissory note is to consider it an IOU. When due, it is presented for payment by the holder, who may be the payee or someone to whom the promissory note has been negotiated.

Inspection and sampling order

When banks are protecting consignment stocks for foreign exporters to, say, the UK, or if they are lending to a UK importer against a pledge of goods, the goods are usually warehoused in the bank's name pending sale to buyers. Prospective buyers frequently need to inspect and sometimes sample the goods before buying them, and it is necessary to be able to authorize a warehouse to permit this to take place. Assuming that the overseas seller or UK importer authorizes sampling and/or inspection, a bank may issue such an order on a warehouse and hand it to the prospective buyer.

Delivery order

This is an order on a warehouse instructing it to deliver goods to the bearer or a party named in the order. Banks issue such orders when goods stored in their name are to be delivered to a buyer or are to be reshipped and have to leave a warehouse.

Warehouse receipt

This is a receipt for goods issued by a warehouse. The document is not negotiable and no rights in the goods can be transferred under it. Delivery orders may be issued against the receipt for the goods which relate to it.

Trust receipt

When a bank wishes to release documents of title, or the goods themselves, to a customer of undoubted integrity, whilst still retaining its security rights in those goods and/or the proceeds of their sale, it may obtain a completed trust receipt from its customer to whom a loan has been made. This is an acknowledgement of the pledge of the goods to the bank and an undertaking of the customer to take the documents as trustees for the bank and to:

(a) arrange for goods to be warehoused in the bank's name, or

(b) arrange for processing of the goods and their return to the warehouse in the bank's name, or

(c) arrange for sale of the goods and to pay all sale proceeds without deduction to the bank immediately on receipt or within a short, stated period of time.

Export financing

There are various methods used in the international sale of goods to pay the purchase price. These are as follows:

Drafts covering exports

These may be on sight basis for immediate payment or drawn to be accepted for payment 30, 60 or 90 days after sight. Drafts directed to a bank for collection are accompanied by shipping documents consisting of a full set of bills of lading in negotiable form, airway bills of lading, or parcel post receipt, together with insurance certificates, commercial invoices, consular invoices and any other documents that may be required in the country of destination.

Sales against cost advances

These are used where credit is doubtful, exchange restrictions difficult, or unusual delays may be accepted. They are very little used today.

Sales on a consignment basis

No tangible obligation is created by consignment sales. In countries with free port or free trade zones, it can be arranged to have consigned merchandise placed under bonded warehouse control in the name of a foreign bank. Sales can then be arranged by the selling agent and arrangements made to release partial lots out of the consigned stock against regular payment terms. The merchandise is not cleared through customs until after the sale has been completed.

The two most common methods are payment under a collection agreement and payment under a letter of credit, also called a documentary credit. In both cases, banks are used as intermediaries and the shipping documents are used as collateral security for the banks.

In the case of a collection agreement the bank in the buyer's country is squarely responsible for effecting payment, whereas in the case of a letter of credit this responsibility falls on the bank in the country of the seller.

Usually, in international sales, the seller draws a bill of exchange either on the buyer or on a bank. This bill is usually payable a certain number of days after sight, e.g. 90 days after sight.

Collection arrangements

Where a collection arrangement is organized the seller hands the shipping documents including the bill of lading to his own bank, the remitting bank, which passes them on to a bank at the buyer's place, the collecting bank. The collecting bank then presents the bill of exchange to the buyer and requests him to pay or to accept the bill. When the buyer has complied, the collecting bank releases the shipping documents to the buyer, who is then able to receive the original bill of lading that enables him to obtain the goods from the carrier on arrival of the ship. The collecting bank is liable to the seller if it releases the shipping documents to the buyer without having received finance from him.

Letters of credit

These are of particular importance. A letter of credit arrangement will be agreed upon in the contract of sale. The buyer instructs a bank in his own country (the issuing bank) to open a credit with a bank in the seller's country (the advising bank) in favor of the seller, specifying the documents which the seller has to deliver to the bank for him to receive payment.

If the correct documents are tendered by the seller during the currency of the letter of credit arrangement, the advising bank pays him the purchase price or accepts his bill of exchange drawn on it, or negotiates his bill of exchange, which is drawn on the buyer. Whichever method used is pre-arranged between the seller and the buyer.

Types of letters of credit

Letters of credit can be revocable or irrevocable, confirmed or unconfirmed. Whether the credit is revocable or irrevocable depends on the commitment of the issuing bank. Whether it is confirmed or unconfirmed depends on the commitment of the advising bank. These commitments are undertaken to the seller, who is the beneficiary under the credit.

There are four main types of letters of credit, namely, the revocable and unconfirmed letter of credit, the irrevocable and unconfirmed letter of credit, the irrevocable and confirmed letter of credit, and the transferable letter of credit.

The revocable and unconfirmed letter of credit: Neither the issuing nor the advising bank is committed to the seller and as such the credit can be revoked at any time. This type of credit affords little security to the seller that he will receive the purchase price through a bank.

The irrevocable and unconfirmed letter of credit: In this case, the authority that the buyer gives to the issuing bank is not revocable and the issuing bank is obliged to pay the seller provided that he has tendered the correct document before the expiry of the credit. If the issuing bank defaults, the seller can sue them in the country where the bank has a seat. In some circumstances, the seller can sue the issuing bank in his own country if there is a branch office. From the point of view of the seller this type of letter of credit is a more valuable method of payment than a revocable and unconfirmed letter of credit.

The irrevocable and confirmed letter of credit: In this type of credit, the advising bank adds its own confirmation of the credit to the seller. Thus, the seller has the certainty that a bank in his own country will provide him the finance if the correct documents are tendered within the time stipulated. The confirmation constitutes a conditional debt of the banker, i.e. a debt subject to the condition precedent that the seller tenders the specified documents. A confirmed credit that has been notified cannot be cancelled by the bank on the buyer's instructions. See the following case:

Transferable:

The parties to a contract of sale may agree that the credit is transferable.

The seller can use such credit to finance the supply transaction. The buyer opens the credit in favor of the seller and the seller (who in the supply transaction is the buyer) transfers the same credit to the supplier (who in the supply transaction is the seller). This type of credit is used when a person buys goods for immediate resale and wishes to use the proceeds of resale to pay the original seller.

The doctrine of strict compliance

Under this doctrine, the seller, to obtain payment, must tender documents which strictly comply with specifications by the buyer, otherwise the correspondent bank will refuse to honor the credit. The banks which operate the documentary credit act as agents for the buyer, who is the principal, and as such they should not pay against documents that are different from those specified. Lord Summer emphasized the importance of this requirement in Equitable Trust Co. of New York vs Dawson Partners Ltd. (1926).

Fraud in letter of credit transactions

Letters of credit have been described by an English judge as "the life-blood of commerce" and as such the defense of the bank that it will not honors the credit because fraud has occurred is accepted rarely and with reluctance. Such a fraud may occur if the shipment of the goods is fraudulent or if the bills of lading tendered under the credit are falsified or forged. Where there is a mere suspicion by the bank that fraud has occurred, refusal to honors the credit is not accepted. Such refusal will only be accepted if it is proved to the satisfaction of the bank that the documents tendered are fraudulent and the seller is a party to the fraud or knew of it. The following case sets this out:

Conflict of law

Where a sale of goods transaction is made on the home market, little difficulty arises as problems that crop up are easily resolved by looking at the rules in The Sale of Goods Act (where the parties have not agreed otherwise). However, international sales pose the problem of conflict of law. The laws of the seller's country and those of the buyer's country may be different in some areas and the question arises as to where to sue and which law to apply.

In the absence of treaty provisions, rules of Private International Law are used to resolve these problems. It is normally advisable to sue in the country where the defaulting party resides or is incorporated and has an office and property, in the case of a company. This is so because the defendant can be more easily compelled to go to court and answer the case than when he is out of the jurisdiction of the court. On the type of law to apply, the proper law of the contract, i.e., the law of the contract country having the closest connection with the contract, is applied. Several factors are weighed in order to arrive at a conclusion as to which is the proper law of the contract, viz: the lex focii lex loci solutions, lex situs, lex loci contracts, the law of the country whose language, currency or flag (flying on the ship carrying the goods) is used.

Lex Focii

This means the law of the country in which the case is tried.

Lex Locii Solutions

This means the law of the country where the contract is performed.

Lex Situs

This means the law of the place where the property is situated.

Lex Loci Contracts

This means the law of the country where the contract is made.

Various treaties have been signed in order to unify the law relating to international sales, thereby avoiding the difficult task of weighing various factors in deciding on what law to apply. The two Hague conventions signed in 1964 are perhaps the most important of such international agreements. These are the Uniform Law on the formation of contracts for the International Sale of Goods, and the Uniform Law on the International Sale of Goods.

The uniform law on the formation of contracts for the international sale of goods

The provisions of the convention relate to offer and acceptance. An offer is generally revocable until the offered has dispatched his acceptance. However, under the convention an offer is not revocable if it either states a fixed time for acceptance, or that it is irrevocable. This is different from the common law position where such a standing offer would be revocable if not supported by consideration.

At common law, an acceptance which varies the terms of the offer is not valid. However, under the convention, the acceptance will only be invalid if the qualification consists of an additional or different term which materially alter the terms of the offer unless the offer or promptly objects to the discrepancy. The convention rules also deal with the case of late acceptances which will be good unless the offer or notifies to the contrary.

The uniform law on the international sale of goods

This agreement consists of provisions dealing with the obligations of the seller and the buyer as to the time and place of delivery, the insurance and carriage of goods, the conformity of goods with the contract and the giving of goods title. Other rules deal with the passing of risk and the buyer's obligations as to payment and the taking delivery of the goods. These rules are in several respects different from the rules under the Sale of Goods Act. In particular, the uniform laws do not recognize the concept of the "condition" which exists under common law for the breach of which the buyer can reject the goods even though the breach causes him no loss. The uniform laws instead introduce a concept of "fundamental breach". Thus, in order to determine whether the buyer has a right to reject, one must examine the breach that has occurred together with its consequences. Rejection will be possible only if the breach is "fundamental", i.e. if a reasonable person in the position of the buyer "would not have entered into the contract if he had foreseen the breach and its effects".

The two conventions have been given statutory effect in UK by the Uniform Law on International Sales Act 1967. Malawi, for example, has not passed any enactment to give legal recognition to the Hague conventions and as such the rules under it do not have legal effect here unless a seller and buyer expressly agree that these rules shall govern their contract.

On April 11th 1980, another important convention - The United Nations Convention on contracts for the International Sale of Goods - was signed in Vienna. The intention of the convention was to supersede the Hague Conventions.

The contract of international sale of goods reflects a complexity which is absent in the home market sale. This is so because this contract is entwined with other contracts, specifically the contract of carriage of goods, the contract of insurance and the letter of credit arrangement.

These different transactions are often looked at as one entire activity unless something goes wrong somewhere, when the fault is isolated, thereby requiring separate analysis of the contract in question. Trade terms which have evolved over the years from the custom of merchants are used. These serve to outline the rights and duties of the seller and buyer. The most common of such trade terms are the FOB and CIF clauses. Although the meaning of these trade terms may vary slightly from one country to another, uniformity is obtained when the parties adopt the International Chamber of Commerce meaning of trade terms.

The international sale also involves another complexity; the problem of jurisdiction and choice of law where rules as to obligations of the seller and the buyer are different in their respective countries. Although Private International Law rules help in dealing with this problem, there is need for the signing of treaties to try and provide ready rules on international sales which are uniform. This happened at the Hague in 1964. The United Nations Commission on International Trade Law is also busy promoting the convention of 1980. However, these efforts are wasted if countries do not pass national laws to give effect to the conventions as is the position in, for example, Malawi, with regard to the Hague conventions.

Organizing, Planning And Controlling Global Marketing Operations:-

The key to good organizing, planning and controlling in global marketing is to create a flexible structure or framework which enables organisations to respond to relevant differences in the markets in which they operate, but, at the same time, delineates relationships clearly between parts and personnel of the company. There are no prescriptive solutions to the questions of what is the most appropriate organizational structure, planning framework and form of agricultural control. One thing is clear though -organisations can only work effectively if structure is defined, standards of performance are designed and communicated, and the control framework is fair, clear to all and agreeable. This is not to say that once the structure is defined, it cannot be changed. In fact, modern marketing thought is that formal structure is just not the order of the day. Many informal structures develop within formal frameworks. Many organisations make the mistake of setting a structure first, long before they have decided on a strategy. This is a recipe for disaster as it forces organisations to fit the strategy to the structure, with all the inherent dangers of such rigidity.

Agricultural systems: organisation, coordination and performance overview

As constantly stated in this text, production and marketing systems, whether they be food commodities, inputs or whatever, are interdependent. As such the activities and economic entities within the network of exchange relationships and any other coordinating mechanisms are complex. Because of this, analysts usually look at the activities of organisation, coordination and performance evaluation within a subsystem or single commodity. But this approach has drawbacks because the distinctions between traditional commodity systems are breaking down. Take for example the manufacturer of ready -to -eat meals. Not only does the manufacturer draw from meat, vegetables and many other raw material suppliers but substitute technologies may begin to "stray" into the traditional raw material supply system, for example, artificial flavorings.

Most agricultural products and commodity systems exhibit widely different organizational characteristics between countries. Different governments have different programmes, horizontal and vertical structural elements can vary, as can terms of access, competitive conditions, parallel marketing channels and the types of contractual and ownership integration.

Coordination in international marketing is complex and vital. For Israeli fresh produce to arrive on a UK's family table within 48 hours or less is quite remarkable, but a complex operation. Vertical coordination, harmonizing all the vested production, marketing, exchange interfaces and value added stages is a challenge. In order to make the process flow smoothly, information is vital as well as an understanding of all definitions and permissible behaviors of the participants. Most failures to vertically coordinate will probably reveal themselves in resource misallocations, technical inefficiencies and other risks. An over-supply of tomatoes, for example, may incur storage costs or waste. One good example of an almost perfectly coordinated system is that of Geest bananas. Not only do the bananas ripen on the voyage over to the UK from the West Indies, but they are specially treated so that they ripen at the exact time when required. In evaluating agricultural performance a large number of indicators and norms are utilized. This-so called "structure, conduct and performance" paradigm is well documented (see Helmberger et al 1981)[1]. Most work has centered around operational and locative efficiencies as well as longer term development patterns and the environmental and the economic impact of commodity systems. But the analysis cannot stop there, as agricultural marketing involves marketing, so the quality of marketing sources should also be assessed, and put into quantitative forms.

Transaction costs should also be included. These primarily relate to costs associated with buying, selling and transferring ownership of goods and services, and are very wide ranging. These costs include information, negotiating contracts, the actual costs of transferring goods, services, money and ownership rights, costs of monitoring trade conditions and enforcing trading terms and conditions. Transaction costs tend to get less attention than other costs. Table 1 gives a summary of performance criteria useful in agricultural marketing.

The form of appropriate organisation depends on a number of factors including company goals, size of business, the number of markets operated in, the level of involvement in the market, international experience, the nature of the product, the width and range of the product line, the nature of the marketing task and the risk involved. Many organizational forms in developing countries are relatively unsophisticated. Many are "domestic" based, that is, they may have a small export division within the domestic based operation. Most organisations deal through agents or other merchanting houses which have their own organisation. Flowers and vegetables, exported from Eastern and Southern Africa, are generally sold through agents, auction systems or distributors in the country of destination. Because of this relative lack of sophistication this chapter will concentrate only briefly on the various forms of organisation.

Depending on the factors described above organizational development usually starts with dependence on outsiders, for example horticultural produce is usually handled by overseas agents who have their own exporting organisation or by a local network of services like cool store owners, freight forwarders and so on. As the organisation grows it usually has an overseas subsidiary which reports to it. This is exemplified by Oserian and Sulmac flowers of Kenya, who in turn are part of multinationals. Eventually, the organisation grows in complexity and extent of operations, which then gives rise to an International Division structure, with its own personnel. The next stage of evolution is the development of regional headquarters or regional management centers. Differences between regions are a pressure to create the regional centers. Regional centers can be costly, so they must be developed with care.

Table 4.4 Performance criteria useful in global marketing activities

Operational activity	*Allocative efficiency*	*Long term development/economic*	*Marketing service*	*Transaction costs*
Production Extraction yields Capacity Utilization Unit costs Input/output ratios	Opportunity costs Costs of storage, transport Prices versus consumer preferences	Profitability Rates of return Rates of growth and volume and value Levels of raw materials, commodity wastage. Quality Variety Employment rates Innovation Technological development Risk analysis Income distribution Market access, Structure.	Transport delivery rates Order Grading Labelling Supply adjustments Uniformity to standards Mix of products Supply regulating Timing Information provision	Personal time, Travel, Communications Advertising Promotion Market research Inspection Services Property guards Recovery Reporting of stolen property Distribution Legal Consultancy Advocacy Advertising Insurance Transport Storage Financial Credit rating checks Delayed payment procurement.

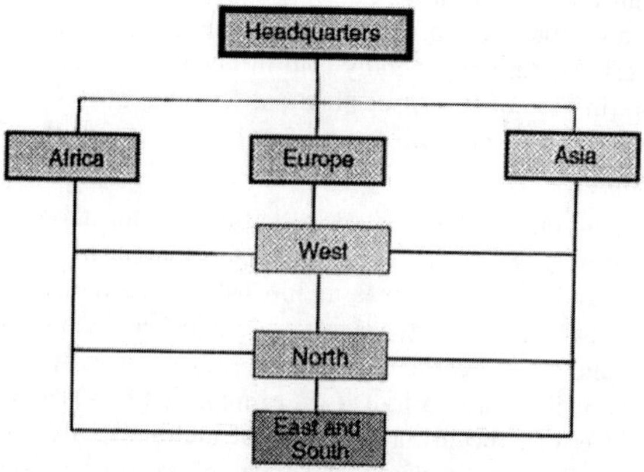

Figure 4.7 Area organizational structure

As the organisation continues to evolve, the international division may be replaced by a variety of structures like a geographical, product, function or strategic business unit approach. The area organizational form is used by highly orientated organisations with stable products. See figure 4.7.

The advantages and disadvantages of this form are as follows.

Advantages

- growth of regional groupings
- expertise grouping
- ease of communications
- knowledge of areas

Disadvantages

- suboptimal product and functional expertise allocation
- duplication
- lack of coordination.

A second organizational form is the product organization structure. These product groups have global marketing responsibility See figure 4.8.

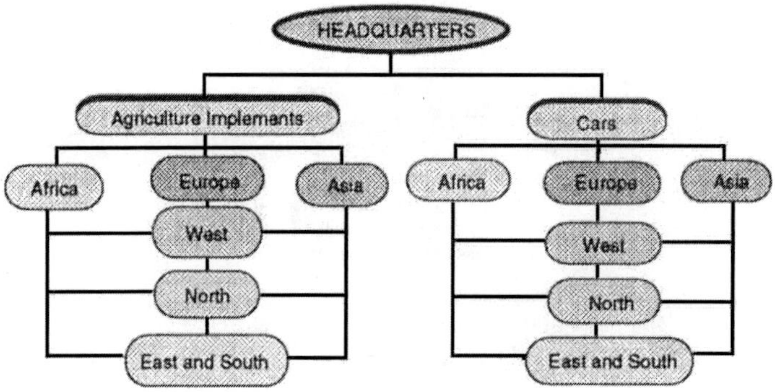

Figure 4.8 Product organizational structure

The advantages and disadvantages of this form are as follows:

Advantages

Disadvantages

- flexibility
- shortage of area knowledge
- can miss marketing opportunities
- difficult to coordinate.

A third organizational form is the functional organizational structure. Here executives on functional areas have global responsibility. See figure 4.9.

The advantages and disadvantages of this form are as follows:

Advantages

- good for firms with narrow, homogeneous product line,
- good where regional variations are not too great

Disadvantages

- may miss market opportunities because of narrow focus.

Strategic Business Units (SBU)

SBUs are defined as a group of products or technologies that serve an identified market and compete with identified competitors. In many ways an SBU is not part of a formal structure but represents a process or system overlay for the purpose of developing a business strategy.

The final organizational form is that called a Matrix organizational structure. See figure 4.10. Matrix organisations are the most sophisticated form of organisation and bring together four competencies -geographic knowledge, product knowledge and know-how, functional competence in such fields as finance, production and marketing, and a knowledge of the customer

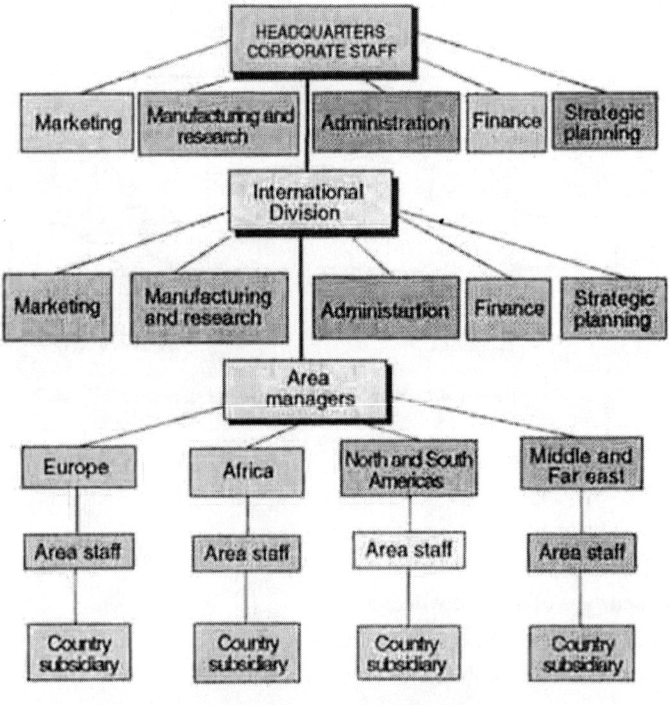

Figure 4.9 Functional organizational structure

(figure 4.10) industry and its needs. Management's task in a matrix organisation is to bring together all the above perspectives and skills to achieve particular objective(s). Matrix structures require a fundamental change in management behavior, organizational culture and technical systems. One of the important things to remember is that structure must always follow strategy. Too often structures are developed long before a strategy is worked out. This can cause "straitjacketing" and lead to an inflexibility which is both unnecessary and stifling.

It is likely to be quite a while before less developed countries have developed a number of the organizational forms described above. The important thing is to keep an arrangement which allows the company to grow, control and manage its destiny.

Global marketing planning

Planning involves where the organisation would like to be and how to get there, which involves goal setting and strategy determination. Planning involves three main activities:

(a) Situation analysis - where are we now?

(b) Objectives - where do we want to be?

(c) Strategy and tactics - how can we best reach our goals?

Planning gives a number of advantages:

- Gives rise to systematic thinking

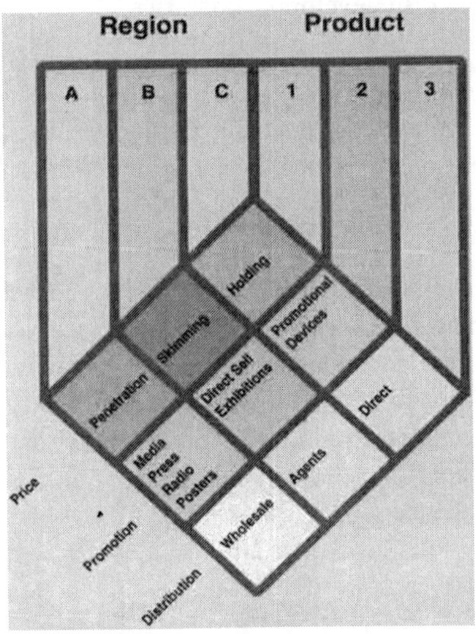

Figure 4.10 Matrix organizational structure

- Helps coordinate activities
- Helps prepare for exigencies
- Gives activity continuity
- Integrates functions and activities
- Helps in a continuous review of operations.

The planning task depends on the level of involvement in a country. Exporting and licensing give minimum country involvement but joint ventures involve more in-country activity and give a greater degree of integration and control. Wholly owned subsidiaries give the organisation almost total control. Because of the "external uncontrollable" international planning is rather more difficult than domestic planning (see table 4.5). Planning can be standardized, decentralized or interactive.

Standardized plans

These offer a number of advantages:

- Cost savings on limited product range and economies of scale both in production and marketing, for example fertilizers.
- Uniformity of consumer choice across the world.

There are disadvantages:

- Different market characteristics make uniform products inappropriate, for example, fresh milk products.

Environmental obstacles disallow standardization; for example lack of refrigerated transport in developing countries.

Decentralized plans

Decentralized plans take into account the subtleties of local conditions; however they are usually very costly and resource consuming.

Interactive plans

In this approach headquarters devises branch policy and a strategic framework, and subsidiaries interpret these under local conditions, for example Nestle. Headquarters coordinates and rationalizes advertising, pricing and distribution. Within any of the above approaches plans can be either long or short term. Increasingly planning is becoming fairly routine. Most companies operate "annual operating plans" although these are often "rolled forward" to cover a few years hence.

Table 4.5 Domestic vs. international planning

	Domestic Planning		*International Planning*
1.	Single language and nationality	1.	Multilingual/multinational/multicultural factors
2.	Relatively homogeneous market	2.	Fragmented and diverse markets
3.	Data available, usually accurate and collection easy	3.	Data collection a large task requiring significantly higher budgets and personnel allocation
4.	Political factors relatively unimportant	4.	Political factors frequently vital
5.	Relative freedom from government interference	5.	Involvement in national economic plans; government influences business decisions
6.	Individual corporation has little effect on environment	6.	"Gravitational" distortion by large companies
7.	Chauvinism helps	7.	Chauvinism hinders
8.	Relatively stable business environment	8.	Multiple environments, many of which are highly unstable (but may be highly profitable)
9.	Uniform financial climate	9.	Variety of financial climates ranging from over-conservative to wildly inflationary
10	Single currency	10.	Currencies differing in stability and real value
11	Business "rules of the game" mature and understood	11.	Rules diverse, changeable and unclear
12	Management generally accustomed to sharing responsibilities and using financial controls	12.	Management frequently unautonomous and unfamiliar with budgets and controls

Planning concepts

In order to operate any type of plan, three types of information are essential:

(a) Knowledge of the market - customers, competitors and government

(b) Knowledge of the product - the formal product, its technology and its core benefit

(c) Knowledge of the marketing functions.

In many cases LDCs have found it difficult to make real international inroads often because they lack the information required. “Country grouping” is an effective way to plan. Hence countries are grouped according to a number of criteria and treated alike. Such criteria include market size, market accessibility (market or commercial economies), stage of market development, prospects for growth, and promise for future growth and development. Zimbabwe may be a “promising” country for investment, but Somalia may not be “promising”. Other concepts for planning are “competence centers”. The mission of a competence centre is to formulate a global business strategy for a new business. Competence centers are not those developed through “leadership” ability but involve a number of factors like strategic location and skills.

In marketing planning, ultimately, the decision on the type of plan rests entirely on the size of the task, type of task and competence to achieve the task. In exporting flowers, say, to Europe, Zimbabwe would be well advised, with the small quantities involved, to leave the task to those experts in Holland and Germany whose knowledge and competence is far superior. The downside is that some market opportunities may be overlooked.

Global marketing control

Factors like distance, culture, language and practices create barriers to effective control. Yet without control over international operations, the degree to which they have or have not been successful cannot be judged.

Plans are the prerequisite to control, yet these are developed in the midst of uncertain forces both internal and external to the firm. Basically control involves the establishment of standards of performance, measuring performance against standards and correcting deviations from standards and plans. In international marketing the ability to control is disturbed by the distance, culture, political and other factors. Figure 4.12 illustrates a typical plan/control cycle.

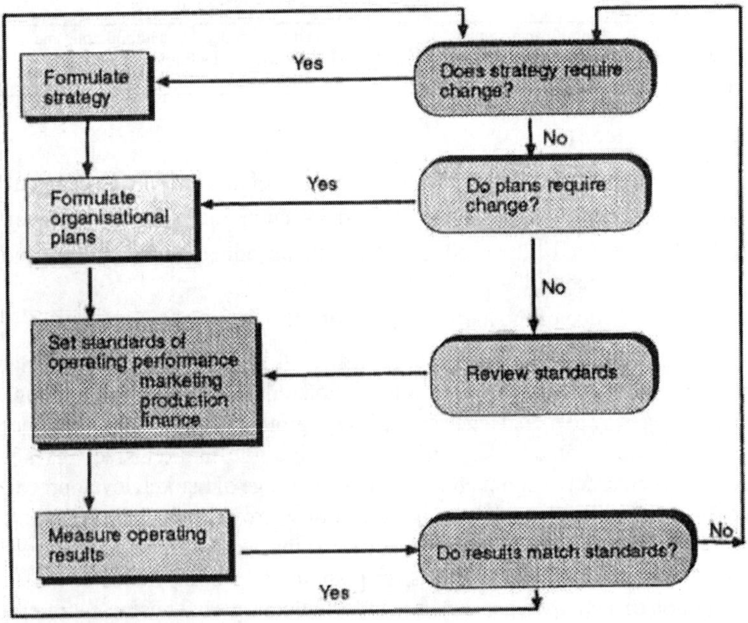

Figure 4.12 The planning and control cycle.

In well developed international operations headquarters may seek to achieve control over subsidiaries by three types of mechanism - data management mechanisms, merge mechanisms, which shift emphasis from subsidiary to global performance, and conflict resolution mechanisms that resolve conflicts triggered by necessary trade-offs.

The method of export control in many less developed countries takes the form of direct organisation by government. The appendix note at the end of this section describes the types of control imposed.

Formal control methods

Planning and budgeting

Planning and budgeting are the main formal control methods. The budget spells out the objectives and necessary expenditures to achieve these objectives. Control consists of measuring actual sales against expenditures. If there is tolerable variance then no action is usually taken.

Evaluating performance

Performance is evaluated by measuring actual against planned performance. The problem is setting a performance standard. Usually it is based on historical performance with some kind of industry average. Problems of international comparison inevitably occur like how does one plan in an environment where exchange rates fluctuate quite often during the budget period.

Influences on marketing budgets

In preparing a budget or plan, the following factors are important:

(a) Market potential - how large, can it be tested?

(b) Competition - what is the competitive level?

(c) Impact of substitute products - packaging can be substituted in many ways

(d) Process - headquarters may impose an "indicative planning" method or guidance.

Other performance measures

Other measures of performance include share of market, image, position or corporate acceptance. Often these are difficult to obtain where data or data collection is difficult.

Informal control method

When staff are transferred from market to market, they often take their standards of performance with them and these can be assessed. Other methods include face-to-face contact and evaluation.

Variables influencing control

A number of factors may influence the control methods. These include:

(a) Domestic practices and values of standardization - these may not be appropriate

(b) Communication systems - have a heavy influence on control mechanisms - electronic control measures may not always be available

(c) Distance - the greater the distance, the bigger the physical and psychological differences

(d) The product - the more technological the product the easier it is to implement uniform standards

(e) Environmental differences - the greater the environmental differences the greater the delegation of responsibility and the more limited the control process

(f) Environmental stability - the greater the instability in a country the less relevance a standardized measure of performance has

(g) Subsidiary performance - the more a subsidiary does, or reports, a non variance, the less likely is there to be headquarters interference

(h) Size of international operators - the bigger and greater the specialization of headquarters staff the more likely will extensive control be applied.

Obviously the ability to control any international operation, whether it be very sophisticated or relatively unsophisticated, the process will break down without adequate face-to-face and/or electronic communications.

Operations globally can be evaluated and improved by a global marketing audit. Audits have a wide focus, are independently carried out, are systematic and conducted periodically. To be successful audits have to have objectives, data, sources of data and a time span and reporting format. Audits can cover the environment, strategy, organisation, system, productivity and functions. Unfortunately, as in any attempt to gather global data, all the pitfalls of politics, culture, and language differences arise.

Much of the preceding discussion covers more sophisticated forms of international control, except budgeting which is applicable to all types of exporting or global marketing. As stated earlier, many less developed countries have export controls imposed by governments.

Problems in International Marketing Communication

Development of appropriate International marketing communication is a difficult task because of several complexities and intricacies important problems or factors which make the development of International marketing communication difficult are the following:-

(a) Differences in regulation- regulation governing promotion very widely between countries. And exporters has to understand these regulation thoroughly and ensure that the promotion programme are conformity which such regulation of each country concern. A communication strategy or approach that permitted in one country could be illegal in another countries.

(b) Social/Cultural Differences- Cultural factors have at most consideration in designing the advertisement strategy, particularly the message design. The cultural factors, however, are very complex and difficult to understand.

(c) Media factors- The effectiveness of media, the availability of media, the cost of media etc differ between countries and these may call for different promotional media strategy in different countries.

(d) Infrastructure- besides the availability and efficiency of the promotional media, there are several other infrastructure factors which affect marketing communication like the availability and equality of advertising agency marketing research firm etc.

(e) Cost Factors- The cost of promotion particularly advertising in advanced countries is often prohibitively costly for Indian exporters who, in general are of small mean the advertisement out lay should normally be very large if it should have any impact.

(f) Language factors- There are many examples of language causing problems in International marketing communication.

(g) Home country regulation- There may also be home country regulation which affect promotion. Ex, Indian exporters are confronted with certain government of India regulation regarding promotion abroad like the restriction on expenditure abroad for promotion.

Regulation

Most countries impose some regulation on advertising. The purpose behind these regulation is two fault (i) To protect the consumer against misleading advertising and their won gullibility and(ii) to protect smaller business from the completive threats of large corporation. It is interesting to note that adverting regulation is more common in developed society than in developing countries. This difference may be explain by the fact that the advertising industry is still in its infancy in most developing countries and therefore is ignored as yet. Besides not all developing country have the administrative machinery to enforce regulation. regulations affecting advertising in various region of world have grown both in number and stringency over the year some example of ads regulation includes-

(i) china, the world's largest and potentially most lucrative cigarette market .has banned tobacco.

(ii) India announced and upper limit of 10000 $ for advertising expenses for all companies doing business in India expenditure over that limit where to be taxed at the rate of 50% wide spread cancellation of advertising in reaction to this low, however caused withdrawal of these tax, as the government was concerned with effects that the cancellation of advertising might have on employment.

(iii) In Costarica, a low provides for the national majority ownership of the media and the agency.

(iv) In Germany television advertising on the commercial station is restricted to 20 minutes per day in block of 5 to 10 minutes between 5 p.m and 8 p.m with no advertising on Sunday and holidays. In the Netherland television commercial must be confined to 5 minutes blocks in the evening.

(v) Turkey- the state owned commercial television station carries 12 minutes of non commissionable advertising each evening in 3 minute blocks.

(vi) Denmark, Germany and Italy medical product advertising must be supervised as to content .

Tool for international marketing communication

An international marketing communication strategy may use a variety of marketing tools, such as advertising, direct marketing, sales promotion, personal selling, Public relation, trade fair and Exhibitions.

(1) Advertisement- Any paid form of non personal communication by and identified sponsored is termed as advertising. it can be for a product, service, and idea, or organization. The non personal means such an news paper magazine, TV, or radio can transmit the message to large number of individuals often at the same time. Advertising is most widely used form of promotion, specially for mass marketing. Media advertising communicates information to a large number of recipients, paid for by a sponsor. It has three main aims:

1. To impart information
2. To develop attitudes
3. To induce action beneficial to the advertiser (generally the purchase of a product or service).

An advertisement for washing powder is paid for by the manufacturer to achieve greater sales; a party political broadcast aims to increase votes.

sIt must be remembered that advertising is only one element of the communications mix, but it does perform certain parts of the communicating task faster and with greater economy and volume than other means.

How large a part advertising plays depends on the nature of the product and its frequency of purchase. It contributes the greatest part when:

1. Buyer awareness of the product is low
2. Industry sales are rising rather than remaining stable or declining
3. The product has features which are not obvious to the buyer
4. The opportunities for product differentiation are strong
5. Discretionary incomes are high
6. A new product or new service idea is being introduced.

Advertising models

These have been drawn from several sources, particularly psychology, and from advertising practitioners in order to explain how advertising works.

1.1 The stimulus/response formula

This was used at first, later models taking into consideration the environment in which the decision to buy is made. Daniel Starch said in 1925 'for an advertisement to be successful it must be seen, must be read, must be believed, must be remembered and must be acted upon'. This model assumed that the advertisement is the main influence on the state of mind of the consumer in respect of the product and makes no allowance for combined or multiple effects of advertisements.

1.2 The DAGMAR philosophy

Colley's DAGMAR model in 1961 (Defining Advertising Goals for Measured Advertising Results) allows for the cumulative impact of advertisements and also maps out the states of mind consumers pass through:

1. From unawareness to awareness;
2. to comprehension;
3. to conviction;
4. to action.

This is described as the marketing communications spectrum. Advertising, along with promotion, personal selling, publicity, price, packaging and distribution, move the consumer through the various levels of the spectrum as follows:

Unawareness/awareness The advertisement tries to make potential customers aware of the product's existence.

Comprehension The customer recognizes the brand name and trademark and also knows what the product is and what it does; knowledge gained from the advertisement or from an information search prompted by it.

Conviction The customer has a firm attitude, preferring a particular brand over all others. Preferences may have an emotional rather than rational basis.

Action Some move is made towards purchase, thus the advertisement has been acted upon.

This illustrates the concept that the purpose of advertising is to cause a change of mind leading toward purchase, but it is rare for a single advertisement to have the power to move a prospect from complete unawareness to action. Effectiveness is judged by how far an advertisement moves people along the spectrum.

1.3 The Lavidge and Steiner model

This consists of a hierarchical sequence of events on six levels:

1. Awareness
2. Knowledge
3. Liking
4. Preference
5. Conviction
6. Purchase

These steps divide behaviour into three dimensions: cognitive (the first two), affective (the second two) and motivational (the third two). Although this differs from the 'DAGMAR' model in the number and nature of stages, there is agreement that purchase is the result of the persuasion elements, making the assumption between changes in knowledge and attitude towards a product and changes in buying behaviour there is a predictable outcome.

Dissonance theory, however, illustrates a two-way relationship, with behaviour influencing attitudes as well as attitudes influencing behaviour. After making a decision to purchase, the prospect will be involved in cognitive dissonance and will actively seek information to reinforce the decision, focusing on attractive features and 'filtering out' unfavourable data. The major implication of this is that advertising for existing brands in the repeat purchase market should be aimed at existing users to reassure them in the continuation of the buying habit at the expense of the competition.

1.4 The Unique Selling Proposition

This was developed by Rosser Reeves (1961) who reported the principles his agency had adopted for 30 years. This states that the consumer remembers one key element of an advertisement - a strong claim or concept. This proposition must be one that the competition does not offer, which will be recalled by the consumer and will result in purchase at the appropriate time.

1.5 The 'brand-image' school

This was led by advertising practitioner David Ogilvy who focused on non-verbal methods of communication to invest a brand with agreeable connotations aside from its actual properties in use, such as prestige and quality.

It must be remembered that an advertisement is the channel through which the sponsor communicates their message. The encoded message reaches recipients, through advertising or salespeople, who then decode and absorb it either fully or partly. The quality of the transmission can be distorted by 'noise' occurring because the receiver does not interpret the message in the way the source intended (due perhaps to differences in cultural backgrounds of the two parties). It may however be because of cognitive dissonance which occurs when peoples' receipt of the message does not agree with what they previously believed.

Dissonance may cause a number of different reactions by the receiver:

1. Rejecting the message
2. Ignoring the message
3. Altering the previous opinion
4. Searching for justifications

The first two reactions are of course negative, and from this feedback the source may change the message or stop communicating altogether with a particular receiver who is not receptive to the source's ideas. It can, therefore, be seen that advertising does not always convert people into users of a particular product. It can, however, have a positive effect in preventing loss of users, and increasing their loyalty.

1.6 Advertising by objectives

Advertising situations are so varied and unique that it is not possible to generalize about how advertising works. Any potential advertiser should therefore adopt an advertising-by-objectives approach that will make clear what they are trying to achieve, how they will achieve it and how they are going to measure its effects.

Few companies give any detailed scientific thought to exactly what they are trying to achieve through advertising. Clear objectives are needed to aid operational decisions, which include:

- The amount to be spent on a particular campaign
- The content and presentation of the advertisement
- The most appropriate media

- The frequency of display of advertisements or campaigns
- Any special geographical weighting of effort
- The best methods of evaluating the effects of the advertising.

Corkindale and Kennedy (1976) found that systematically setting and evaluating objectives provided the following benefits.

1. Marketing management has to consider and define in advance what each element in the programme is expected to accomplish.
2. An information system can be set up to monitor ongoing performance, with the nature of information required clearly defined.
3. Marketing management will learn about the system it is operating from accumulated experience of success (and failure) and can use this knowledge to improve future performance.

Majaro's (1970) major study on objective setting revealed that most managers saw increasing sales or market share as their main advertising objective. In fact, this is a total marketing objective and it is unreasonable to expect to achieve this objective through advertising alone (unless it was the only element of the marketing mix used, as in direct mail and mail order businesses). Majaro's study also revealed that methods of evaluation used by most companies were not relevant, and that clear, precise advertising objectives, known to all involved, would rectify this situation. The following advantages of the advertising-by-objectives approach became clear.

1. It helps to integrate the advertising effort with other ingredients of the marketing mix, thus setting a consistent and logical marketing plan.
2. It facilitates the task of the advertising agency in preparing and evaluating creative work and recommending the most suitable media.
3. It assists in determining advertising budgets.
4. It enables marketing executives and top management to appraise the advertising plan realistically.
5. It permits meaningful measurement of advertising results.

When setting objectives, all personnel in a company who have an interest in, and influence on, advertising decisions have different ideas of the purpose of advertising. The Chairman may be concerned with corporate image, whilst the Advertising Manager may see it as an investment direct toward building a brand image and increasing market share. Marketing objectives have to be separated from advertising objectives. Overall marketing objectives should be defined, and the next step is to determine the contribution that advertising can efficiently make to each of these. An advertising objective is one that advertising alone is expected to achieve.

Advertising objectives should be set with the following points in mind.

1. They should fit in with broader corporate objectives.
2. They should be realistic, taking into account internal resources and external opportunities, threats and constraints.
3. They should be universally known within the company, so that everyone can relate them to his or her own work and to the broader corporate objectives.
4. They need to be flexible, since all business decisions have to be made in conditions of partial ignorance.
5. They should be reviewed and adapted from time to time to take account of changing conditions.

Setting advertising objectives should not be undertaken until all relevant information on the product, the market and the consumer is available. Consumer behaviour and motivation must be thoroughly assessed, particularly that of the company's target group of customers. The statement of an advertising objective should then make clear what basic message is intended to be delivered, to what audience, with what intended effects and the specific criteria to be used to measure success.

(2) Direct mail and direct marketing

Direct mailing is the use of the postal service to distribute promotional material directly to a particular person, household or firm. It is often confused with the following related activities, which all fall under the general heading of 'direct marketing'.

1. **Direct advertising** One of the oldest methods of reaching the consumer, with printed matter being sent directly to the prospect by the advertiser, often by mail, but sometimes by through the letter box personal delivery, handing out to passers-by or left under the screen wiper of a car.
2. **Mail order** Mail order advertising aims to persuade recipients to purchase a product or service by post, with deliveries being made through the mail or other carrier or through a local agent. Thus it is a special form of direct mail, seeking to complete the sale entirely by mail and being a complete plan in itself. Mail order is a type of direct mail, but not all direct mail is mail order.
3. **Direct response advertising** This is a strategy of using specially designed advertisements, usually in magazines or newspapers, to invoke a direct response, such as the coupon-response press ad, which the reader uses to order the advertised product or request further information. Other variants offer money-off coupons and incentives to visit the retail outlet.

The usage and acceptance of direct mail is increasing rapidly, and one reason for this is that the media has become increasingly fragmented, with many commercial TV channels and the rapid growth of 'free sheets' and special interest magazines. This means that advertisers have to either spend more money to reach their audience, or spread the same amount over a wider range of media. Improvements in the quality of large mail shots have attracted an increasing number of large advertisers. Direct mail, with increasing sophistication of computerisation, now enables advertisers to segment and target their markets with greater flexibility, selectivity and personal contact.

Direct mail can be used to sell a wide range of products or services, and its uses are also varied. To help define direct mail more fully, it is appropriate to deal with direct mail to consumers and businesses separately.

2.1 Consumer direct mail

Some of the most common uses of consumer-targeted direct mail are:

1. **Selling direct** Direct mail is a good medium for selling a product directly to the customer by a company that has a convincing sales message. It provides a facility for describing the product or service fully and for an order to be sent straight back, cutting out the 'middlemen'.
2. **Sales lead generation** Some products/services require a meeting between the customer and a specialized salesperson, and direct mail can be used to acquire 'qualified' leads. A mailshot that has been well thought through can reveal the best prospects and rank other leads in terms of 'potential', enabling some responses to be followed up by a salesperson. An invitation can be made for the customer to view the product in a retail outlet, showroom or exhibition. Such 'cordial-contact' mailings can create a receptive atmosphere for salespeople by building on the reputation of the company and creating a good impression, which can be converted into buying action later.
3. **Sales promotion** Promotional messages such as special offers will reach specific targets through direct mail and in the same way prospects can be encouraged to visit showrooms or exhibitions.
4. **Clubs** The most popular users of direct mail here are book clubs and companies marketing 'collectibles'.
5. **Mail order** Direct selling and recruitment of new customers and agents are possible through direct mail.
6. **Fundraising** It is easy through direct mail to communicate personally with an individual, and therefore it is an excellent method of raising money for charitable organizations. Large amounts of information can be included to induce the recipient to make a donation.

7. **Dealer mailings** Dealers or agents can use direct mail to reach the prospects in their own area.
8. **Follow-up mailings** These help to keep the company's name before the customer following a sale, for example checking that the customer is satisfied with a purchase. New developments, products and services can also be communicated or invitations issued, thus maintaining contact and increasing repeat sales.

2.2 Business direct mail

For business, this is more effective than mass advertising for identifying different market sectors and communicating to each an appropriate message. Some of the more common uses are:

1. **Product launch** Direct mail is able to target the small but significant number of people who influence buying decisions.
2. **Sales lead generation** Direct mail provides qualified sales leads, as well as doing some initial selling.
3. **Dealer support** Dealers, retail outlets, franchise holders etc. can be kept fully informed of marketing promotions and plans.
4. **Conferences** Potential delegates in specific business sections can be issued with invitations through direct mail.
5. **Follow-up mailing using customer base** Mailing existing customers regularly encourages repeat sales.
6. **Market research/product testing** Market research (especially amongst existing customers) can be very effective where it is possible to do this through direct mail, using questionnaires as part of a regular communication programme. Small-scale test mailings can give an accurate picture of market reaction, with low risk, and a successful product can later be mailed to the full list.

2.3 Direct mail as part of the promotional mix

When direct mail is added to, say, a television or press campaign, the effectiveness of the overall campaign can be significantly raised. The media reaches a broad audience and can raise general awareness of the company and its products, while the direct mail campaign is targeted specifically at the groups of people or companies most likely to buy. Mailing lists of respondents to couponed press advertisements or television or radio commercials with a 'phone-in' number can be used for direct mail approaches.

(3) Exhibitions

Exhibitions are another form of below the line promotional activity.

As with many other below-the-line methods they are growing in use and popularity. They come in three basic forms.

1. those aimed at the consumer,
2. those aimed solely at the trade,
3. those aimed at and open to both.

The third category has become the most common. Most exhibitions start off as trade exhibitions and then after the first week or so when all of the 'trade' business has been conducted they are usually opened to the public. The public usually pays an entry fee that brings in revenue for the exhibition organiser and helps to pay for the costs of actually staging the exhibition. The general public may have an actual interest in the products and services being exhibited for example Clothes Shows, Motor Shows and Home Exhibitions. Sometimes the products and services are of little direct interest to the general public. That is, they are highly unlikely to buy any of the products on show, but nevertheless attendance at the exhibition can be a 'good day out' (e.g. an agricultural show or an air show) and the public is prepared to pay for this privilege.

Exhibitions tend to attract a high quality audience and company directors will often attend an important trade exhibition. Such trade exhibitions offer the marketing firm the opportunity to come in personal contact with high status decision making unit (DMU) members.

(4) Public Relations and Publicity

Public relations is an organization's communications that seek to build good relationships with an organization's publics, including consumers, stockholders, and legislators. It includes obtaining favorable publicity, building up a good "corporate image," and handling or heading off unfavorable rumors, stories, and events. **Publicity** is unpaid communication about an organization that appears in the mass media. Public relations may consist of writing press releases, holding special events, conducting and publishing consumer surveys about a product or the company, and efforts to put a positive spin on negative company news. Unlike sales promotions, public relations activities do not usually seek a short-term increase in sales. Instead, they try to craft a long-term positive image for the product or the organization. Compared with personal selling, advertising, and sales promotions, expenditures for public relations are usually low in most organizations. Since companies do not pay for publicity, they have less control over the publication of good or bad company news. But this often means that consumers find this type of news source more believable than if the information were disseminated directly by the company.

Marketing and Non-marketing Public Relations

The basic rule of public relations is to do something good and then talk about it. Public relations is crucial to an organization's ability to establish and maintain a favorable image.**Non-marketing public relations** refers to a company's messages about general management issues. When a company makes a decision that affects any of its publics, input from public relations specialists can help to smooth its dealings with those publics. A company, for example, that decides to close a plant would need advice on how to deal with the local community. Other examples include a company's attempts to gain favorable public opinion during a long strike or an open letter to Congress published in a newspaper during congressional debates on a bill that would affect a particular industry. **Marketing public relations** refers to narrowly focused public relations activities that directly support marketing goals. Marketing public relations involves an organization's relationships with consumers or other groups about marketing concerns and can be either *proactive* or *reactive*. With *proactive marketing public relations*, the marketer takes the initiative and seeks out opportunities for promoting the firm's products, often including distribution of press releases and feature articles. It is a powerful marketing tool since it adds news coverage that reinforces direct promotion activities. Although some publicity happens naturally, more typically a "buzz" needs to be created by a firm's publicists. *Reactive marketing public relations* responds to an external situation that has potential negative consequences for the organization. The goal in this case is to manage the flow of information to address concerns so that consumers don't panic and distributors don't abandon the product. The Internet has expanded the capabilities of the traditional public relations function. Corporate websites post testimonials from customers, make new product announcements, and respond quickly to important events. News releases posted on the company website may double as sales vehicles. The Internet can also be very effective in handling company crises. With a host of Internet news sites, companies can respond to a crisis online in far less time than other forms of communication such as press releases or conferences.

4.2 Public Relations Objectives

Public relations specialists need to operate at many levels to ensure that various publics of a company receive coordinated, positive messages about the firm. These groups include customers, suppliers, employees, the media, stockholders, and government regulators.

Companies that practice integrated marketing communication strategies know that public relations strategies are best used in concert with advertising, sales promotion, and personal selling in order to send a consistent message to customers and other stakeholders. As part of the total IMC plan, public relations departments may perform any or all of the following functions to achieve communications objectives:

- *Public Affairs* – Building and maintaining national or local community relations.
- *Lobbying* – Building and maintaining relations with legislators and government officials to influence legislation and regulation.
- *Investor Relations* – Maintaining relationships with shareholders and others in the financial community.
- *Development* – Public relations with donors or members of nonprofit organizations to gain financial or volunteer support.
- *Location PR* – Enhancing the image of a city, region, or country.
- *Press Relations* – Creating and placing newsworthy information in the news media to attract attention to a person or product.
- *Product Publicity* – Publicizing specific products to consumers as well as other organizations.

4.3 Public Relations Tools

Public relations tools. They are:

- *News*,
- *Speeches*,
- *Special Events*,
- *Mobile Marketing*,
- *Written Materials*,
- *Audiovisual Materials*,
- *Corporate Identity Materials*, and
- *Public Service Activities*.

One of the major tools is *news*. PR professionals find or create favorable news about the organization and its products or people. *Speeches* can also create product and company publicity. Increasingly, company executives must field questions from the media or give talks at trade associations or sales meetings. Another common PR tool is *special events*, ranging from news conferences, press tours, grand openings, and fireworks displays to laser shows, hot air balloon releases, multimedia presentations and star-studded spectaculars, and educational programs designed to reach and interest target publics. Recently, *mobile marketing*—traveling promotional tours that bring the brand to consumers—has emerged as an effective way to build one-to-one relationships with targeted consumers. Public relations people also prepare *written materials* to reach and influence their target markets. These materials include annual reports, brochures, articles, and company newsletters and magazines. *Audiovisual materials*, such as films, slide-and-sound programs, and video- and audiocassettes, are being used increasingly as communication tools. *Corporate identity materials* can also help create a corporate identity that the public immediately recognizes. Logos, stationery, brochures, signs, business forms, business cards, buildings, uniforms, and company cars and trucks—all become marketing tools when they are attractive, distinctive, and memorable. Finally, companies can improve public goodwill by contributing money and time to *public service activities*.

4.4 Planning a Public Relations Campaign

A public relations campaign is a coordinated effort to communicate with one or more of the organization's publics. This is a three-step process of:

1. Developing Objectives,
2. Executing, and
3. Evaluating.

The organization must first develop clear objectives for the PR program that define the message it wants people to hear. The PR specialists must develop a campaign strategy that includes:

- a statement of objectives;
- a situation analysis;
- specification of target publics, messages to be communicated, and specific program elements to be used;
- a timetable and budget; and
- a discussion of how the program will be evaluated.

Execution of the campaign means deciding precisely how the message should be communicated to the targeted publics and implementing the decisions. An organization can use a variety of public relations tools: news conferences, special events, written materials, etc.

One of the barriers to greater reliance on public relations campaigns is the difficulty encountered when trying to gauge their effectiveness. It is possible to tell if a PR campaign is getting media exposure, though it's more difficult to gauge bottom-line impact. In-house assessments, awareness and preference research studies, and the measurement of print and broadcast coverage generated by PR activities as well as impression counts can be used in the PR campaign evaluation.

(5) Sales Promotion

Sales Promotion is the use of short-term incentives to encourage the purchase or sale of a product. Sales promotions are programs such as contests, coupons, displays, trade shows, samples, premiums, product demonstrations, or other incentives that marketers design to build interest in or encourage purchase of a product during a specified time period. Sales promotions are intended to stimulate immediate action, often in the form of a purchase, rather than to build long-term loyalty. Whereas advertising and personal selling offer reasons to buy a product, sales promotion offers reasons to buy *now*. Sales promotion geared to marketing intermediaries is called **trade promotion**. Companies actually spend about as much on trade promotion as on advertising and consumer-oriented sales promotion combined. Trade promotion strategies include offering free merchandise, buyback allowances, and merchandise allowances along with sponsorship of sales contests to encourage wholesalers and retailers to sell more of certain products or product lines.

Sales promotion tools are used by most organizations, including manufacturers, distributors, retailers, trade associations, and not-for-profit institutions. They are targeted toward final buyers, retailers and wholesalers, business customers, and members of the sales force. Several factors have contributed to the rapid growth of sales promotion, particularly in consumer markets. First, inside the company, product managers face greater pressures to increase their current sales; and sales promotion is viewed as an effective short-run sales tool. Second, externally, the company faces more competition; and competing brands are less differentiated. Increasingly, competitors are using sales promotion to help differentiate their offers. Third, advertising efficiency has declined because of rising costs, media clutter, and legal constraints. Finally, consumers have become more deal oriented, and ever-larger retailers are demanding more deals from manufacturers. The growing use of sales promotion has resulted in promotion clutter, similar to advertising clutter, however. Consumers are increasingly tuning out sales promotions, weakening their ability to trigger immediate purchase. Manufacturers are now searching for ways to rise above the clutter, such as offering larger coupon values or creating more dramatic point-of purchase displays.

5.1 Sales Promotion Objectives

Sales promotion objectives differ widely:

- Increase Short-Term Sales (consumer promotion)
- Build Long-Term Market Share (consumer promotion)
- Encourage Retailers to Carry New Items and Additional Inventory (trade promotion)
- Encourage Retailers to Advertise and Provide More Shelf Space (trade promotion)
- Encourage Retailers to Buy Ahead (trade promotion)
- Increase Sales Force Support (sales force promotion)
- Increase Number of New Accounts (sales force promotion)

Sellers may use *consumer promotions* to increase short-term sales or to help build long-term market share. Objectives for *trade promotions* include getting retailers to carry new items and more inventory, getting them to advertise the product and give it more shelf space, and getting them to buy ahead. *Sales force promotion* objectives include getting more sales force support for current or new products or getting salespeople to sign up new accounts.

Sales promotions are usually used together with advertising, personal selling, or other promotion mix tools. Consumer promotions must usually be advertised and can add excitement and pulling power to ads. Trade and sales force promotions support the firm's personal selling process.

In general, rather than creating only short-term sales or temporary brand switching, sales promotions should help to reinforce the product's position and build long-term customer relationships. Increasingly, marketers are avoiding "quick fix," price-only promotions in favor of promotions designed to build brand equity.

5.2 Consumer-Oriented Sales Promotion

The main consumer promotion tools include samples, coupons, cash refunds, price packs, premiums, advertising specialties, patronage rewards, point-of-purchase displays and demonstrations, and contests, sweepstakes, and games. Consumer-oriented sales promotions can be classified as either price-based or attention-getting consumer promotion.

Price-Based Consumer Promotion: Price-based consumer promotions emphasize short-term price reductions or refunds, encouraging consumers to choose a brand while the deal is on. If used too frequently, however, consumers become conditioned to purchase the product only at the lower promotional price.

Coupons

A **coupon** is a certificate that gives buyers a saving when they purchase a specified product. Coupons can stimulate sales of a mature brand or promote early trial of a new brand. Redemption rates have been declining in recent years, however, as a result of coupon clutter. Most major consumer goods companies are issuing fewer coupons and targeting them more carefully. They are also cultivating new outlets for distributing coupons, such as supermarket shelf dispensers, electronic point-of-sale coupon printers, or "paperless coupon systems."

Cash Rebate Offers

A **cash rebate** is an offer to refund part of the purchase price of a product to consumers who send a "proof of purchase" to the manufacturer.

Price Packs

A **price pack** is a reduced price that is marked by the producer directly on the label or package. Price packs can be single packages sold at a reduced price, or two related products banded together. Price packs are very effective—even more so than coupons—in stimulating short-term sales.

Patronage Rewards

A **patronage reward** is cash or other award for the regular use of a certain company's products.

Special Packs

A **special pack** is a package that gives the shopper more product instead of lowering its price. A special pack also can be a separate product given away along with another product.

Attention-Getting Consumer Promotion: Attention-getting consumer promotions stimulate interest in and publicity for a company's products.

Samples

A **sample** is a small amount of a product offered to consumers for trial. Sampling is the most effective—but most expensive—way to introduce a new product. About 84 percent of consumer packaged-goods marketers use sampling as a part of their promotion strategy. Some samples are free; for others, companies charge a small amount to offset its cost. The sample might be delivered door-to-door, sent by mail, handed out in a store, attached to another product, or featured in an ad. Samples can also come with the morning newspaper, in a sample pack, or via the Internet.

Premiums

A **premium** is a good offered either free or at low cost as an incentive to buy a product. A premium is not the product being promoted. It is used as an incentive to encourage purchase of the featured product. A premium may come inside or outside the package, or through the mail.

Advertising Specialities

An **advertising specialty** is a useful article imprinted with an advertiser's name, given as a gift to consumers. Typical items include pens, calendars, key rings, matches, shopping bags, T-shirts, caps, nail files, and coffee mugs. In a recent study, 63 percent of all consumers surveyed were either carrying or wearing an ad specialty item. More than three-quarters of those who had an item could recall the advertiser's name or message before showing the item to the interviewer.

Point-of-Purchase (POP) Promotions

A **point-of-purchase promotion** is a display or demonstration that takes place at the point of purchase or sale. Unfortunately, many retailers do not like to handle the hundreds of displays, signs, and posters they receive from manufacturers each year. Manufacturers have responded by offering better POP materials, tying them in with television or print messages, and offering to set them up.

Contests, Sweepstakes, and Games

Contests, **sweepstakes**, and **games** are promotional events that give consumers the chance to win something—such as cash, trips, or goods—by luck or through extra effort. A contest calls for consumers to submit an entry—a jingle, guess, or suggestion—to be judged by a panel that will select the best entries. A sweepstakes calls for consumers to submit their names for a drawing. A game presents consumers with something—bingo numbers, missing letters—every time they buy, which may or may not help them win a prize.

5.5 Trade-Oriented Promotion

Manufacturers direct more sales promotion dollars toward retailers and wholesalers (78 percent) than to consumers (22 percent). Trade promotion can persuade resellers to carry a brand, give it shelf space, promote it in advertising, and push it to consumers. Shelf space is so scarce these days that manufacturers often have to offer discounts, allowances, buy-back guarantees, or free goods to retailers and wholesalers to get products on the shelf and, once there, to stay on it. Manufacturers use several trade promotion tools. Many of the tools used for consumer promotions—contests, premiums, displays—can also be used as trade promotions.

Discounts

A **discount** is a straight reduction in price on purchases during a stated period of time. This is also called *price-off*, *off-invoice*, or *off-list*. The discount could be based on the volume of the product ordered

Market Entry of Indian Firm

India economic integration with the rest of the world was very limited because of the restrictive economic policies followed until 1991. Indian firms confined themselves, by and large, to the home market. Foreign investment by Indian firms was very insignificant.

With the new economic policy ushered in 1991, there has, however, been a change. Globalization has in fact become a buzz-word with Indian firms now and many are expanding their overseas business by different strategies. Indian industry can move towards globalization by different strategies such as developing exports foreign investments including joint ventures and acquisitions, strategic alliance, licensing and franchising etc.

Exporting: Exporting is, by far, the most important entry route employed by Indian firms. Because of the inward looking economic policy pursued until 1991, the progress made on the export front was not in general something commendable. With the economic liberalization, an environment for globalization of Indian exports, however, is slowly emerging. In a truly globalize environment, the exports will also be very much global: the sourcing of finance, materials and managerial inputs will be global, based on purely business considerations.

Several Indian companies have entered foreign markets targeting their exports at the ethnic population. West Asia, with a large expatriate Indian population, naturally is the first target in many of these cases.

The Mumbai based American Dry Fruits (ADF) which began selling a range of packaged foods like chutneys, spices, canned vegetables, ready-to-eat pulses etc under different brand names later moved to other countries with large Indian population.

As foreign firms, generally, have neither the expertise nor interest in the ethnic products, Indian firms do not have to face competition from them, making market entry and growth fairly easy.

A firm which makes the ethnic segment of the market its entry point may, in due course, after gaining experience in doing business and establishing a foothold in the foreign market, take up marketing of non-ethnic products and to non-ethnic consumers.

Food products are not only category being targeted at ethnic population. Raymond's and Birla-VXL, for example have a number of showrooms in West Asia top sell their range of textiles items. Shaw Wallace launched a beer brand called Lal Toofan in UK through Shaw Wallace Overseas; the target consumers of this brand sold at the up market Indian restaurants are Indians.

India has potential for significantly increasing the exports of many products if appropriate measures are taken. As a matter of fact, in case of number of products several other developing countries which started their exports later than India have gone much ahead of India while India€™s progress has been slow. With the right policy and procedural reforms and institutional support, with technological up-gradation and modernization and enlargement of production facilities, with thrust on quality and value added products, with improvements in infrastructural facilities and with right marketing strategy great strides could be made in the export of a number of products. Broadly there are three strategies to increase the export earnings, viz.,

(i) Increase the average unit value realization.

(ii) Increase the quantity of exports.

(iii) Export new products.

One of the most important considerations in exports should be to achieve maximum unit value realization. Value added exports are a much needed graduation for India to enhance the foreign exchange earnings. A very disquieting fact is that India€™s agricultural exports still are mostly commodity exports, i.e. they are exported mostly in bulk form and the progress achieved in value added exports is not anything significant.

Value added exports assume greater significance particularly in view of the stagnation or fall in the exportable surplus of several commodities like pepper, cardamom, Tea, coffee etc.

The major part of India€™s manufactured exports end up in the low-price segments of the foreign markets. Quality up-gradation and marketing efforts are needed to reach the upper segments and to achieve enhanced value realization. Technology imports or foreign collaborations are required for this in many cases.

In many cases, what come in the way of increasing exports are the supply constraints. This is true of a number of manufactured products as well as agricultural commodities. Given the constraints for area expansion, increase in agricultural production should come mostly from increase in productivity which is very low in India. In respect of many industrial products, the production capacity is very low and highly fragmented so that there are a large number of cases of Indian firms not being able to accept from abroad for purchase of large quantities of the products which are far beyond the capacity of these firms to supply.

Managing Image in the International Marketplace.

Every exporter has to contend with three levels at which Image works – Country Image, Corporate Image and finally, for branded products, the Brand Image.

Most of our exporters suffer due to the poor image that buyers have of India as a country, and of Indian companies. India is perceived as backward, and Indian companies have a non-professional image in terms of almost any parameter known to affect successful marketing. Our quality is perceived as shoddy, packaging is not up to international standards, delivery is unreliable and export procedures unfathomable. There are, of course, some bright exceptions to the generally lackadaisical export performance. But there is still an image problem for India's goods abroad. Issues like child labor, lack of environmental safeguards, and cruelty to animals have also had a negative image contribution to various Indian exports such as carpets, garments and leather goods.

The international image of Japan, South Korea, Taiwan or Singapore, on the other hand, is one of an industrialized, highly reliable, quality conscious country, and this now rubs off on all the individual suppliers from those countries. It is however, a point to be noted that this image was not built up easily. It came after years of innovative product design, manufacturing control and automation and of course, marketing. Some of the incremental innovations may have been due to the participatory work culture followed in some of these countries. In other words, these countries have been following good management practices in all the functional areas. Companies like Canon, Toyota, Minolta, Nissan and Honda have all contributed to the powerful image that Japan now has in the world. With the possible exception of biotechnology, pharmaceuticals and computer hardware & software (Microsoft, Intel and IBM) where US companies still hold a better image, almost all other high technology business areas seem to be in the firm grip of Japan today.

Can India do the same? Possibly it can; and to do it, one of the things we must do is mend our image - project ourselves as people who are industrious, who keep promises, who guarantee their products without questions, and consistently maintain a high quality. It is necessary to work backwards from there and keep the marketing strategy tuned to the needs of customers.

Adding Value

The second major lacuna our country suffers from in the area of international business is the continuing emphasis on export of raw materials and semi-finished goods. Value- addition is now almost passé in other regions of the world. And yet, we refuse to look at the writing on the wall. There are some obvious areas like food processing, and branded agricultural commodities or spices that we have not yet exploited to their potential. In some of these like the leather goods industry, we have at least moved in the right direction, recognizing the need for value addition. But in most manufactured goods, we continue to cut a sorry figure in international trade. Our country possesses the potential to manufacture and export almost everything from hairpins to defense equipment. Yet our exports of manufactured goods are insignificant by world standards.

Unless we adopt as our strategy the production of quality manufactured goods, both for domestic and export markets, and work on it, little will change. In a small way, Maruti and a few other car manufacturers have started exporting cars. But why is it that we cannot leapfrog into the forefront of any manufactured goods and be number 1, 2 or 3 in the world. It is not entirely beyond the realm of possibility, as some companies like Moser Baer in hi-tech electronics have shown, for Indian companies to be cost-competitive and hi-tech at the same time. Moser Baer is an Indian company, the eighth largest manufacturer of floppy disks in the world. It is also one of the least cost producers of disks, and supplies disks as an original equipment supplier to Sony, BASF, in addition to selling them under its own brand name Xydan (source: various reports in the Economic Times, and the company's website).

The only area where our country seems to have progressed considerably is in some select services. For example, RelQ is a provider of verification and validation services to software developers and is doing well in a niche market (the Economic Times, 2001).

A Two–Pronged International Marketing Strategy

Thus, a fresh approach by individual companies is required for international marketing strategy. At its core must be the two factors - value-added, preferably branded products or services, and the cultivation of a high quality image. Then, and only then, can Indian companies hope to achieve the kind of success that their East Asian counterparts have achieved.

Value Addition

The prescription for adding value to goods is comparatively easy to follow, because the crux of it lies in identification of the "correct" (in terms of the strategy) goods. After this, the product design and development has to follow the demand patterns from customers. Good rapport with potential buyers is necessary for achieving this, such as keeping track of changing fashions in readymade jeans. One way of providing added value from the perspective of an Indian firm could be to provide unique tastes, flavors, or "experiences" to global audiences who are bored with the monotony and sameness of their products or "experiences". Ger (1999) expounds this thesis with a lot of examples from Turkey, speculating how "local" products or services can be successfully marketed globally. Some recent successes of Indian films like Taal, Lagaan etc. in global markets seem to indicate that this is a possible route to success. But care should be taken that such products/experiences do not remain a part of "exotica", but develop stable and sustainable markets. In the case of services, India is not doing too badly, but care should be taken to keep adding value to our software and other services, to prevent getting stuck in the low-cost services sector. At best, low-cost services can be an entry point into developed-world markets. But we must leverage the entry to graduate to high value service offerings. Lovelock and Yip (1996) have classified services into three types - People processing, Possession-processing, and Information-based. Among the three categories, India is doing well in the information-based services in the global arena, but can graduate to service "products" eventually.

A good place to begin in the goods arena is the finished goods (unbranded) sector and graduate slowly to the branded goods, one level higher. For example, India produces engineering goods, castings, forgings etc. in large quantities. If these products can be initially sold to leading global buyers to be marketed by them, Indian companies can gain valuable experience of the designs, and price-quality equations in global markets. These can then be used to sell abroad using Indian brand names. Technological, marketing or strategic alliances such as the one between HMT and Guildemeister of Germany, cited by Bajaj (1991), or Kirloskar Brothers and SPP, could be used to graduate to the next level. Some Indian pharmaceutical companies like Ranbaxy and Dr. Reddy's Labs already have a marketing tie-up with multinational companies to market their products in the American market. Just as multinationals use joint ventures or strategic alliances as entry strategies, Indian companies must learn to do the same. Of course, those who can manage entry single-handed without an alliance can take the leap themselves, and reap richer rewards if successful.

Image Building

On the other hand, it may not be so easy to start building an image abroad. A variety of factors contribute to the image a company has overseas. Some of these are within the company's control, and some are not. Of the factors which the company cannot entirely control, are the media coverage of a country by the world press and television, the occurrence of extraordinary events such as the unification of East and West Germany, or the breakup of Yugoslavia etc. which may affect international perceptions. Also, tourists from other countries may carry impressions of a country from their personal experience. In the case of India, for example, recent successes of Indian women in beauty pageants have contributed positively to a good image.

Considering these factors, the international marketer must give top priority to those image factors which he can control. For instance, if he participates at a trade show, he must have complete details of the products he sells, indicative price lists, photographs or actual products where feasible, and possibly keep a person handy who knows two or three major foreign languages during the trade show, to translate for prospective customers who do not know his language. An order which is received must be treated with utmost care and treated as if his life depends on it in terms of product quality and service. Especially important are the first few orders he receives from a new country. Word of mouth publicity may play both a negative and positive role in international markets.

You do not have to be manufacturer of Toyota cars, to have a high quality image in world markets. It could be that you manufacture beer cans (which incidentally, India has the potential to supply the entire western world with) but the image of a top quality beer can manufacturer ultimately helps other suppliers from the country to gain a foothold in the market, and it can have a chain reaction. After all Japanese products have lived with the experience of being known as 'cheap' and 'third rate'. But today their image is enough to sell almost any Japanese product. So much so that someone in the U.S. even prescribed a simple solution for the poor image that U.S. made products now have in their own country - rename the country 'Japan'.

References

Bajaj, C. (1991), "Foreign Collaborations: An Innovative Option", IIMB Management Review, Vol. 6, No. 1&2, pp.142-145.

Das, N., Quelch, J. and Swartz, G. (2000), "Prepare Your Company for Global Pricing", Sloan Mangement Review, Fall, Vol. 42, No. 1, pp. 61-70.

Ger, G. (1999), "Localizing in the Global Village: Local Firm Competing in Global Markets", California Management Review, (Summer), Vol. 41, No. 4, pp. 64 – 83.

Hastings, D.F (1999), "Lincoln Electric's Harsh Lessons from International Expansion", Harvard Business Review, May-June, pp. 162 – 178.

Krugman, P.R. (1996), Rethinking International Trade, Cambridge, MA: MIT Press.

Helmberger P., Campbell C and Patson W. "Organisation and Performance of Agricultural Markets in A Survey of Agricultural Economies Literature".

Cain, W. W. "International Planning: Mission Impossible? *"Columbian Journal of World Business"*. No. 58, July-August 1970.

Mkandawire, G. M. "Controlling Export Operations". In Carter S. (ed), "Export Procedures", Network and Centre for Agriculture Marketing Training in Eastern and Southern Africa, FAO, August 1991, pp. 129-132.

Dixie G.B.R. "An Overview of the International markets for Horticultural Produce", in S. Carter (ed) "Horticultural Marketing Training in Eastern and Southern Africa", 1991 ch. 8, pp. 72-92

Considering these factors, the international marketer must Axtell R. E. (1989) "The Do's and Taboos of International Trade". John Wiley and Sons,

Bradley F. (1991) "International Marketing Strategy", Prentice Hall

Paliwoda S. (1993) "International Marketing Strategy "2 Edition Heinemann

Philip C, Lowe R. and Doole I. (1994) "International Marketing Strategy; Analysis", Butterworth Heinemann.

Terptsra V. and Sarathy R. "International Marketing", 6th Edition, Dryden Press, 1994

"International Marketing Review" MCB Publications, UK.

Malnight, T. W. "G localisation of an Ethnocentric Firm: *An Evolutionary Perspective Strategic Management Journal.* Vol. 16 No. 2 Feb 1995 pp. 119-141.

Sandelands E. "Europe and International Business" Vol. 28 No. 6 1994 pp. 5-14 *European Journal of Marketing,* Special Issue, Section 1 Marketing

Das M. "Successful and Unsuccessful Exporters from Developing Countries". "Some Preliminary findings". European *Journal of Marketing* Vol 28 No. 12 1994 pp. 19-33.

Jaffee S. (1992) "Exporting High Value Food Commodities". World Bank Discussion Paper 198 World Bank.

Keegan, W. J. (1989) "Global Marketing Management", 4th ed. Prentice Hall International Editions.

Terpstra, V.(1987) "International Marketing", 4th ed. Dryden Press.

Elinder, E., "How International Can European Advertising Be?" *Journal of Marketing,* April 1965, pp. 7-11.

Carter, S. (1989) "Lecture Notes". University of Leeds, U.K.

Cunningham, M.T. "Strategies for International Industrial Marketing". In D.W. Turnbull and J.P. Valla (eds.) Croom Helm 1986, p. 9.

Pavord and Bogart. "Quoted in The Export Marketing Decision" S.A. Hara in S. Carter (Ed) "Export Procedures", Network and Centre for Agricultural Marketing Training in Eastern and Southern Africa 1991.

Piercy, N. "Company Internationalisation: Active and Reactive Exporting". *European Journal of Marketing,* Vol. 15, No. 3, 1982, pp. 26-40.

Collett, W.E. "International Transport and Handling of Horticultural Produce" in S. Carter (ed.) "Horticultural Marketing". Network and Centre for Agricultural Marketing Training in Eastern and Southern Africa, 1991.

Korey, G. "Multilateral Perspectives in International Marketing Dynamics". *European Journal of Marketing,* Vol. 20, No. 7, 1986, pp. 34-42.

Khoury, S.J "Countertrade: Forms, Motives, Pitfalls and Negotiation Requisites". *Journal of Business Research,* Vol. 12, 1984, pp. 257-270.

Shipley, D.D. and Neale, C.W. "Successful Countertrading. Management Decision", Vol. 26, No. 1, pp. 49-52.

Anderson, E. and Coughlan, A.T. "International Market Entry and Expansion via Independent or Integrated Channels of Distribution". *Journal of Marketing,* Vol. 51. January 1987, pp. 71-82.

Keegan, W.J. "Global Marketing Management", 4th ed. Prentice Hall International Editions, 1989.

Khoromana, A.P. "The Experience and Problems in Exporting Spices". In S. Carter (ed.) Export Procedures Network and Centre for Agricultural Marketing Training in Eastern and Southern Africa, August 1991.

Basche, J.R. Jr. "Export Marketing Services and Costs". New York: The Conference Board, 1971, p. 4.

Bheenich, R. and Shapiro, M.O. Mauritius: "A Case Study of the Export Processing Zone. In Successful African Development", EDI Development Policy Case Series, No. 1, 1989, pp. 97-127.

Jaffee S. "Exporting High Value Food Commodities". "World Bank Discussion Paper" pp. 198, 1993.

Chalanda, M.S. "Export Financing". In S. Carter (ed.) "Export Procedures" Network and Centre for Agricultural Marketing Training in Eastern and Southern Africa, August, 1991, pp. 113-117.

International Institute for Cotton, Liverpool. "Futures and Hedging Trading in Cotton". In Manual on Cotton Trading Operations. International Trade Centre UNCTAD/GATT, Geneva, 1989, pp. 117-130.

Keegan, W. "Global Marketing Management", 4th ed. Prentice Hall, 1989.

Osborn, I. "Sources of Export Finance". In Manual on *Cotton Trading Operations.* International Trade Centre UNCTAD/GATT, Geneva, 1989, pp. 170-180.

Smith, P. "International Marketing", MBA notes, Hull University, 1990.

Straub, W. A "Short Introduction to Exchange Traded Options". In Manual on Cotton Trading Operations. International Trade Centre UNCTAD/GATT, Geneva, 1989, pp. 131-146.

Locher, W." Marketing and Sales". In Training Manual on Cotton Trading Operations. International Trade Centre UNCTAD/GATT, Geneva, 1989, pp. 79-112.

Collett W. E. "International Transport and Handling of Horticultural Produce". In S. Carter (Ed) Horticultural Marketing. Proceedings of Second Regional Workshop on Horticultural Marketing - Network and Centre for Agricultural Marketing Training in Eastern and Southern Africa, 1991 pp. 268-288.

Keegan, W.J. "Global Marketing Management", 4th ed. Prentice Hall International Editions, 1989.

McGuiness, N.W. and Little, B. "The Influence of Product Characteristics on the Export Performance of New Industrial Products", *Journal of Marketing,* Spring 1981, pp. 110-122.

Kwelepeta, S.L, "Legal Aspects of Foreign Trade", S. Carter (ed.), "Export Procedures" Network and Centre for Agricultural Marketing Training in Eastern and Southern Africa, August 1991, pp. 78 - 85.

Kimweli P.K. "Exporting of Horticultural Produce in Kenya". In S Carter, ed. "Marketing Management in the Horticultural Industry". Network and Centre for Agricultural Marketing in Eastern and Southern Africa, FAO, November 1991, pp. 131 -151

Keegan, W.J. 1989, "Global Marketing Management", 4th ed., Prentice Hall International Edition.

Kwelepeta, S.L., "Export Documentation", op. cit. pp. 89-98.

Chapter - Five

International Marketing and Technology

Technology and Competitive Advantage

Technology is one of the eight factors considered by the World Economic Forum to evaluate the global competitiveness of nations. The 1999 *Global Competitiveness Report* of the Forum, which continued to increase its focus on information technology as a new source of competitiveness, observes that there are at least three aspects to this. First, e-mail has greatly expanded the possibilities for interpersonal, inter- firm and international communication. Second, the Internet has allowed for much more extensive and rapid dissemination of information. Third, the emerging area 0commerce f e-offers a potentially huge increase in the customer base for companies and huge savings in marketing costs and search costs in finding low-cost suppliers Competitiveness in all of these areas is closely linked with the competitiveness of the local telephone infrastructure and with the penetration of the computer culture in the local economy. The Report also observes that for a successful internet culture the population needs to have computers, telephones need to work, and the country's telecommunications hardware needs to support high bandwidth for Internet traffic.

Innovation is a very important factor that provides competitive advantage and consequently, determines success.

Joseph Schumpeter, "a well known economist, has given a lot of importance to innovation in economic development. According to him significant advances in the economy occur by disharmonious leaps and spurts as entirely new investment horizons are exploited. The entrepreneur, who is the innovator is the central figure in the Schumpeterian analysis. Innovation may take any of the following forms: The introduction of a new product; the use of a new method of production; the opening of a new market; the conquest of a new source of raw material supply; the reorientation of an industry. Our concern here is technological innovation; some of the above, obviously do not represent technological innovation.

In the business context, innovation may be defined as "the technical, industrial and commercial steps which lead to the marketing of new manufactured products and to commercial use of new technical processes and equipment."

Betz classifies innovations in to the following types or what is called scales. This is based on how big an impact does a technology change make on the applications.

1. *Radical Innovation* - a basic technological innovation that establishes a new functionality (e.g. steam engine or steam boat).
2. *Incremental Innovation* - a change in an existing technology system that does not alter functionality but incrementally improves "performance, features, safety or quality or lowers cost (e.g. governor on a steam engine).
3. *Next-generation Technology Innovation* - a change in an existing technology system that does not alter functionality but dramatically improves performance, features safety, or quality or lowers cost *and* opens up new applications (e.g. substitution of jet propulsion for propellers on airplanes).

Innovations may help companies to increase market share, capture new markets create new market segments or even to create entirely new industries and markets. Although, innovation is expected to give a company a competitive advantage or success in the market, it is not uncommon that some other company or substitute, product steals away the show from the innovator. For example, in the US the steel tin plate manufacturers developed the market for cans for soft drinks and the like. However, it was later taken away by the aluminum industry.

Innovation is a very important factor that can contribute to success in international business.

All innovations need not be commercially successful. For example, many new products fail commercially due to a variety of reasons. A combination of factors is often required for the success of a' new product - the product itself, R&D support, allocation of required finance and effective marketing. Deficiencies in respect of any of these can cause failure.

Stage of negotiation

A negotiation normally involves the following five stages.

1. Preparation. This stage involves background research, collection and analysis of data and preparation of the plan and strategy for presentation and negotiation. Understanding the cultural nauces of the negotiating party and the dynamics and other characteristics of the negotiating team or individual is also an essential part of this

stage. It is observed that the best negotiators are the Japanese because they will spend days trying to get to know their opponents. The worst are Americans because they think everything works in foreign countries as it does in the USA"

2. Non-task Sounding. This refers to the time at the beginning of the negotiation meeting devoted to introduction and getting acquainted. In other words, it is the time spent on interpersonal relationship building by talking subjects other than the task or business, such as personal and family matters and general subjects of common interests. The nature of non-task sounding may be influenced by cultural differences. For example, the non task time is normally short in respect of the Americans who would like to get into the business straight away quickly, but people of several cultures would like to have long informal time.

   Non-task sounding is very useful. It helps one to understand the characteristics of the persons with whom to negotiate. "Learning about a client's background and interests also provides important cues about appropriate communication styles... There is a definite purpose to these preliminary non-task discussions. Although most people are often unaware of it, such time almost always is used to size up one's clients. Depending on the results of this process, proposals and arguments are formed using different jargons and analogies. Or it may be decided not to discuss business at all if clients are distracted by other personal matters or if the other person seems untrustworthy. "

3. Task-Related Information Exchange. Task related information exchange starts after establishing a good personal relationship. This stage involves exchanging information in an effort to provide the background, establish common facts, and set the contexts of negotiations. This stage is expected to provide both the parties by each other with all the information required in sufficient detail and clearly. However, cultural differences often create problems. All the required information may not be divulged, deliberately or otherwise, the language and expression may create problems o understanding sometimes even feeding misunderstanding.

4. **Persuasion**. This stage is characterized by attempts to make the other party accept the counterparts desired set of exchanges. Both the parties normally try this with each other. "This step of negotiations is considered by many to be the most important. No side wants to give away more than it has to, but each knows that without giving some concessions, it is unlikely to reach a final agreement. The success of the persuasion step often depends on: (1) how well the parties understand each other's position; (2) the ability of each to

identify areas of similarity and differences' (3) the ability to create new options; and (4) the willingness to work toward a solution that allows all parties to walk away feeling they have achieved their objectives."

There may not be a clear separation between the third and forth stages as the task-related information exchange stage may be characterized by each side definition and refining the needs and preferences.

Persuasion requires a lot of tact based on a clear understanding of the organizational cultural and personal characteristics of the negotiators.

5. Agreement. The negotiation Is finally concluded if a mutually acceptable exchange is agreed upon. As indicated in the four Cs of negotiation, conflicts interests would be resolved by trade offs or compromise leading to the agreement

Prerequisites for Effective Negotiation

Cateora and Graham suggest four steps which can lead to more efficient and effective international business negotiations. They are:

1. Selection of the appropriate negotiation team.
2. Management of preliminaries, including training, preparations, and manipulation of negotiation settings.
3. Management of the process of negotiations, that is, what happens at the negotiation table.
4. Appropriate. follow-up procedures and practices.

Cultural Problems in International Negotiations

Important problems in international negotiations caused by cultural differences include those pertaining to the following:

1. Language and non-verbal behaviors
2. Values
3. Thinking and decision making processes.

Some problems may arise when negotiators are not able to properly communicate common language. Even when the same language is used, problems may arise o different meanings for the same word in different cultures or because of different connotations when used in different contexts

Negotiating with Regulators

In many instances government is a party in international business negotiations. There are several governmental factors which are difficult to change and therefore will have to be taken as given. However, the relative bargaining powers can influence terms. Governmental versus company strength in negotiations, therefore, is an important factor.

There are two view points of the governmental authority, viz., the hierarchical view and the bargaining view.

Hierarchical View

In a hierarchical view of governmental authority, companies accept international business regulations as "givens," in which case they comply with, circumvent, or avoid operating because of the regulations. Companies will comply when the regulations d'on't unduly constrain their desired mode of operations, when benefits are sufficiently attractive in spite of regulations, and when they cannot practically alter the regulations o their benefit. Companies will circumvent regulations they find unacceptable through loopholes, legal or illegal. Avoidance is simply the reverse of compliance as a company decides not to operate in a given locale because of its regulations."

Bargaining View

The bargaining school theory holds that the negotiated terms for a foreign investor' operations depend on how much the investor and host country need each other' assets.'? If either a company or a country has assets that the other strongly desires and if there are few (or no) alternatives for acquiring them) negotiated concessions may be very one-sided.

The bargaining relationship between companies and governments depends v much on whether the parties see agreements as zero-sum (one party's gain equals the other party's loss) or positive-sum (both parties have net benefits) gains. In former, relationships may conflict because the parties think they lose by making any concessions. In the latter the relationship may be seen as a partnership of co-operation and interdependence."

Determinants of Bargaining Power

Negotiation is defined as "the process of bargaining with one or more partics to arrive at a solution that is acceptable to all" .13 The relative bargaining strength would, therefore, influence the terms and conditions of the agreement.

The important factors which determine the relative bargaining power are following:

1. Relative Importance of the Project. If the project negotiated is very important for one party and not very important for the other, the relative bargaining power the former would be week. It may be noted that the importance may depend only on the intrinsic value of the project negotiated, but also on other factors such as the strategic importance of it. For example, a project that gives an entry country may have a lot of strategic importance.

2. Alternatives. The number of alternatives available to each party is an important factor that determines the relative bargaining power. If one party has s options (for example, several other parties are keenly interested in the project negotiation) and the other party does not have this advantage, the former would have a stronger bargaining power.
3. Urgency. The time available for taking up and executing the project is another influencing factor. If the time left for this is very short, this is likely to weaken the bargaining power of the project sponsor/ owner. Longer lime would facilitate exploring more alternatives and better evaluations.
4. Strengths. The strengths, including reputation, is another factor that influences the bargaining power. For example, a company which is very resourceful and reputed would have greater bargaining power than one which is weak on these.

Company Strengths include factors such as financial soundness, technological capabilities, previous experiences, particularly in the project area considered track records, business diversity (for example a host country government may prefer company in diverse businesses, other things being equal, because of the possibility of several businesses getting benefited in different ways), marketing expertise, ability to export the products from foreign investment and of others, etc.

The Country Bargaining Power depends on factors such as political stability, level of economic development and size of the national market, economic policies and business friendliness of the nation, the ability to act as a regional or global hub etc.

The computer, by capturing, storing, and combing bits of information about who we are. Where we live, what we like, what we need, what we buy, is making countless niches in the marketplace identifiable and accessible-creating what economist Robert J. Samuelson has dubbed computer 'communities' today the number of existing computer communities or niche markets where people with common characteristics of interest can be found or assembled is mind boggling.

Indeed, "the trend towards individualize marketing is not an isolated commercial phenomenon. It is part of a board societal shift in our times.

Individualized marketing has been strengthened by the development of customer relationship management (CRM). "The Internet has opened up immense new possibilities for creating a relationship with global customers, potential customers, supplier and channel members. The end of segmentation means that markets can focus on delivering value to the individual customer.

Database Marketing is an essential ingredient of CRM. A customer database is an organized collection of comprehensive information about individual customers or prospects that is current, accessible, actionable for such marketing purpose as lead generation, lead qualification sale of product or services or maintenance of customer relationships. A business databases ideally would contain past purchases of business customers, past volumes, prices and profits, buyers team member names (and their ages birthday, hobbies and favorite foods), status of current contracts an estimate of the supplier's share of the customers business competitive suppliers.

Technology is a powerful driving force of globalization. Several barriers to globalization have been removed or reduced by Technological advances.

In international marketing, the marketer is faced with a dilemma of having too much data and too little information. There is plenty of global data from sources like the World Bank, but often a lack of specific information on countries and markets. In helping to reduce uncertainty around decision making, precise information is the key, getting it is quite another thing. Whilst searching for opportunities globally, uncertainties will arise due to four main factors: lack of knowledge of the existence of possible new market alternatives, the conditions internal and external to the firm which will determine the consequences of a new alternative, what consequences these conditions when known may have for the firm, and how these consequences may be expressed in relevant terms of goal fulfilment. Uncertainty arises due to the time lapse between the decision and the outcome of the action decided on. Carlson (1975)[1] also believes that uncertainty increases with the degree of "foreignness" of the place of outcome, the cost of information and the learning effect, that is, when entering a foreign market knowledge of it builds slowly, usually by experience and its attendant uncertainty.

When marketing domestically the system is fairly easy to learn. When crossing global boundaries the whole process is exaggerated by necessary paperwork, exchange rates, cash flows and transportation problems to name but a few. This uncertainty gives rise to the need for information.

Table 5.1 Specific information

Marketing decision	*Marketing intelligence*
Go international or remain domestic	Assessment of global market and firm's potential share in it, in view of local and international competition, compared to domestic opportunities.
Which markets to enter	A ranking of world markets according to market potential, local competition and the political situation.
How to enter target markets	Size of markets, international trade barriers, transport costs, local competition, government requirements and political stability.
How to market in target markets	For each market, buyer behaviour, competitive practice, distribution channels, media, company experience

Elements of the information system

The following constitute the elements of the global information system. Data may be specific or general or both and used for decisions on whether to enter markets or not, in what degree and what emphasis in terms of the marketing mix. General information includes data on the following:

(i) Economic - rate of growth of GNP, level of inflation, incomes
(ii) Social - people, demographics, culture, subculture
(iii) Political - risk, instability, attitudes to "foreigners"
(iv) Technology - current, rate of change, infrastructure
(v) Resources - money, manpower, materials, acquisitions, joint ventures
(vi) Fiscal - taxes, exchange rates
(vii) Institutions - money markets
(viii) Managerial - funds

Specific information may include the following (see table 5.1)[1]:

Table 5.2 Categories for a global intelligence system

1. Market information	
Market statistics and potential	Consumer attitudes and behaviour, spending power, per capita income
Physical features - infrastructure, communications, money markets, banks etc.	Channels of distribution - type, availability, effectiveness
Media - availability, effectiveness and cost	Information sources - quality, availability and cost
Resources - money, human, materials (availability, cost, quality, development)	
2. Environmental factors **Economic factors**	
Economic - rate of growth, structure, conduct, capital, economic blocs, (SADC), GNP, GDP, NI	Social - customs, culture, attitudes, preferences
Political/Legal - laws, regulations, investment, "climate", government ideology, stability.	Technology - state, trends development
Competition - type, structure, operations, strategy plans, programmes, acquisitions, mergers	Trading partner(s)
Management capability	Foreign embassies, NGOs and other developmental thrust
3. Financial/Exchange **Balance of payments**	
Terms of access - quotas, tariffs, duties etc	Inflation rates
Monetary and fiscal policy	Expectations - economists, bankers, business people
Commodity exchanges	Currency alterations and movements, controls and regulations
International competitors	Taxes - inflation, incentives, dividends tax rules, earnings, repatriation of profits
Spot, forward market	Intervention by outside bodies e.g. IMF or World Bank and their effect on policy

The information required could be put into a subject agenda list with specific data requirements (see table 5.2)

Scanning modes: surveillance and search

Once the agenda has been set, data collection or scanning can be done by two methods: surveillance or search. In surveillance the scanner is geared to collect relevant information which crosses his/her scanning attention field, in search the scanner is deliberately seeking information either informally or formally. Most organisations collect information through surveillance, primarily due to time restraints.

Because detailed market scanning can be expensive, many writers suggest the process be split into two stages, a preliminary screen to assess basic alternatives, then, once through this test, more detailed treatment. Hibbert (1985)[2] calls the first phase an assessment of market ecology giving general data about a country - its political and demographic stance for example. This may lead to the avoidance of costly mistakes. A micro assessment, for example, of Zimbabwe may reveal an opportunity for imported South African wines, but the scope may be limited when one looks at the big picture of population and disposable income. Albaum et al[3] (1989) describe an approach to the preliminary screening of foreign markets - the "expansive" and "contractible" methods.

The first gives a gradual expansion from those markets which approximate in cultural and geographic terms to one's own market. "Contractible" methods are more extensive in scope. This approach scans all markets, then narrows them down through applying various criteria. The most attractive are then subject to detailed analysis. Criteria can be self developed or using the methods like the Business Environment Risk Index (Haner, 1972)[4]. This assesses over forty countries on dimensions like political stability, monetary inflation, legal system etc. on a scale of 0 (unacceptable) to 4 (superior conditions).

Contractible scanning methods are superior to expansive methods as they are less likely to overlook market opportunities and to employ standard evaluation instruments. They are, however, very resource intensive and a compromise may be worked out between the two methods. Expansive methods have the advantage of flexibility, the burden of market acceptability rating and are less risky. However, their main disadvantages are "complacency" and missed opportunities to competitors.

Whichever method of data collection is employed, it will affect the global strategy adopted, for example, "contractible" methods favour global strategies. The outcome of the first phase (market screening) will serve to eliminate the two risk markets, then those which are selected after screening will be subjected to a product/market screening phase. This will entail more detailed research on market size, trends, prices etc. Wind and Douglas (1981)[5] suggest that market attractiveness should be assessed at two levels - on a stand alone basis and in the light of other elements of the company's activities. A "portfolio" approach would be useful here. Also the company should assess its own strengths and weaknesses and the risk/returns decisions should transcend the focus on absolute costs and look at opportunity costs of servicing this product market rather than other product markets. (Attention is drawn to the reference section where general surveillance data is exemplified and specific information on products markets is given in an agricultural context).

Sources of global information

Sources of information include documented sources, human resources or perceived sources.

Documented sources

In recent years there has been an information explosion, especially in the documented, or "secondary" source area. (Primary data collection will be dealt with later). Various sources of documented data are available including:

(i) Governments
- Central office of information (UK)
- Central Statistical Office (Zimbabwe)
- EU documentation centres
- Boards of trade, or Ministry of Commerce

(ii) International bodies
- the UN Statistical Yearbook
- World Bank - general statistics
- OECD - general statistics
- ITC - Geneva (information service)

(iii) Business, trade, professional
- Chambers of Commerce
- Institute of Marketing
- American Management Association
- The Market Research Society

(iv) Foreign embassies, trade missions
- Commercial newspapers
- Financial agencies - Price Waterhouse
- Kompass Register of companies
- Economist Intelligence Unit (UK)

(v) Other
- Libraries, universities, colleges.

There are excellent sources of overseas data, in the horticultural industry, giving information on markets, prices and produce required for those wishing to sell into Europe. An example of these are given below:

- International Trade Centre (ITC) Geneva
- COLEACP, Paris
- Natural Resource Institute (NRI) UK
- GTZ, Germany
- CBI, Netherlands
- IMPOD, Sweden
- Chambers of commerce
- Food and Agriculture Organization of the United Nations

Secondary data from such sources are relatively cheap to obtain and readily available. However the disadvantages are legion.

- The data may have been collected and manipulated for a specific use, therefore it may be incomplete, ambiguous or out of context.
- Data may be compiled in different ways in different countries making comparability difficult., For example, in Germany consumer expenditures are estimated largely on the basis of turnover tax receipts, in the UK they are measured on tax receipts plus household surveys and production sources. Similarly with GNP measures, it only reflects average health per head of population and not how it is dispersed. As seen earlier, bimodalities are normal, thus introducing bias. GNP may be understated for political reasons and may not reflect education (i.e. wealth based on minerals). Also infrastructure may reflect channelled funds, say for tourism, rather than society as a whole - typical of many African countries.
- Data may be corrupted by methodological and interpretive problems, for example, definitional error, sampling error, section error, non response error, language, social organisations, trained workers, etc.
- Data may be nonexistent, unreliable or incomplete thus making inter country comparisons very difficult
- Data may be inflated or deflated for political purposes

Data from documented sources must, therefore, be treated with care and caution.

Human sources

These include executives based abroad, specific "look see" missions which are very important, and sales people, customers, suppliers, distributors, and government officials. This information is "internal" to the firm as opposed to documentary sources which are generally external. Most of the information is gathered on a face to face basis.

Perception sources

These are "sensory" sources of information, for example, if one heard of the construction of a new cold store at an airport, it could mean that the industry which produces products for airport store is planning to export in quantity. This could give rise to a market opportunity for another potential exporter of the same produce. Direct perception could be achieved by in country visits, where it would be possible to exercise all the sensory receptors sight, taste, touch, intuition, hearing and smell. Often there is no substitute to "feeling out" a situation. Participation in exhibitions, discussions with importing organisations and participation in Government working parties can all be useful sources of data.

E-Marketing

Marketing has pretty much been around forever **in one form or another**. Since the day when humans first started trading whatever it was that they first traded, marketing was there. Marketing was the stories they used to convince other humans to trade. Humans have come a long way since then, (Well, we like to think we have) and **marketing has too**. Advances in information technology are revolutionalising the modus operation of marketing and the business system. Technology experts are anticipating that the internet and world web wide would become the centre of commercial universe. Electronic market will eliminate the need for intermediaries and that direct contact between manufacturer and customer will bring down the cost of transaction and the cost of final product. The internal has the potential to evolve into an interconnected electronic market place. Bringing buyers and sellers to unit together to facilitate commercial exchanges. The internet is fast becoming an important new channel for commerce in a range of business much faster than anyone who would have predicted in the past. The opportunities presented by this new channel seem to be radily apparent Revolution changes in information technology have been business sweeping across the global business. Development in telec-ommunications and information technologies have reduced the barriers to time and place in doing business. It is now possible for customer, suppliers to transact business at any time any part of the globe, without having to come together physically, thanks to the development in optical fiber technology, videophone and teleconferencing facilities. The net has changed face and pace of business to business marketing and retailing. Very simply put, **e-Marketing** or electronic marketing refers to the application of marketing principles and techniques **via electronic media** and more specifically the Internet. The terms **eMarketing**, **Internet marketing** and **online**

marketing, are frequently interchanged, and can often be considered synonymous. eMarketing is the process of **marketing a brand using the Internet**. It includes both direct response marketing and indirect marketing elements and uses a range of technologies to help connect businesses to their customers.

By such a definition, eMarketing encompasses all the activities a business **conducts via the worldwide web** with the aim of attracting new business, retaining current business and developing its brand identity.

Benefits of internet business

When implemented correctly, the **return on investment** (ROI) from eMarketing can far exceed that of traditional marketing strategies. Whether you're a "bricks and mortar" business or a concern operating purely online, the Internet is a force that cannot be ignored. It can be a means to reach literally millions of people every year. It's **at the forefront of a redefinition** of way businesses interact with their customers. The internet have the following important The Internet is a powerful tool that can make your business more productive and profitable. Business Link states that when the Internet and email are used effectively, they help streamline business activities, communicate more efficiently with customers and even generate new customers or clients—all while helping to reduce business expenses.

Reduced Mailing Expenses

Using Internet resources for business can reduce or eliminate the need for traditional postal mailing and all of the costs associated with that contact method. The Internet makes it easy to stay in contact with customers via email and online networking tools such as discussion boards, chat rooms, and social networking sites like Facebook. Using Internet communication tools effectively, you can keep up a continuous dialogue with customers and prospects. The Small Business Association (SBA) explains that even small mom-and-pop shops can generate additional business with a no-frills website and by posting in newsgroups. You can send special offers and announcements to existing customers via email, send links to your online catalog when a new product is released, or post virtual coupons via social networking sites.

Improved Efficiency

The SBA explains that Internet Application Service Providers (ASPs) provide a variety of ready-made applications to help run day-to-day operations in your business. These Internet services help with finance management, inventory control and human resources, allowing you to lower costs while also reducing the time and labor force needed to run the business. ASPs help with streamlining customer support requests as well. Providing online product documentation and frequently asked questions, for example, enables your customers to get support 24 hours a day without engaging a customer service representative. When an employee's help is needed, Internet tools can help route the service request to the appropriate department and log the progress of resolved or unresolved issues for future reference.

Increased Business

According to the SBA, "Setting up your business on the Internet can be a lucrative way to attract customers, expand market and increase sales." Even local coffee shops and dry cleaning operations can create inexpensive online advertisements to target local audiences. These advertisements can announce special events your company is sponsoring, contests, and special sales or discounts. In some online advertisement areas, you can even promote goodwill with potential customers by having a "Happy Birthday" advertisement display to them on their birthday.

Global Reach:- Internet provides a firm global reach and thereby expands its marketing communication horizon and marketing potential.

Improved Operational efficiency:- The internet can help improve operational inefficiency of companies. Many organizations have implemented virtual teams for customer service, sales and product development.

Small Businesses

- One of the benefits of the Internet for small businesses is that the Internet creates a competitive marketplace in which small businesses have the opportunity to grow as much as larger companies.

Marketing and Advertising

- Creating a website benefits businesses because people can market their products and services without using traditional marketing techniques such as fliers, mailings and newspaper ads. Online marketing saves the company money that would otherwise be spent on traditional means of advertising.

Larger Customer Base

- A key benefit of the Internet for business is the potential for customer growth. A small business without a website may be able to compete only with other local businesses. However, people conducting business on the Internet have the potential to gain customers from around the world because Internet companies are open 24 hours a day.

Networking

- Another benefit of the Internet for business includes the availability to network with other businesspeople and organizations. Many Internet businesspeople have created organizations with others in their field in which they can talk about the challenges and rewards of Internet business. This interchange of encouragement often helps new businesses experience growth.

Saves Money on Office Supplies

- Businesses that use the Internet for transactions save money on paper and other office supplies. Instead of mailing or faxing multiple letters to clients and other businesses, they can correspond via email or set up paperless eFax accounts (see Resources).

Affiliate Programs

- Internet businesses that participate in affiliate programs gain extra income by marketing the products and services of other companies on their websites. Many companies that regularly do business with certain companies join these programs, which help both companies gain more customers and revenue.

Global Electronic Supply chain

The concept of supply chain embraces the following points.

(i) The supply chain identifies the complete process of providing goods and services to the final user.

(ii) The supply chain extends across organizational boundaries.

(iii) The scope of the supply chain includes procurement, production and distribution operation.

(iv) Objectives of individual supply chain member are achieved through the performance of the chain as a whole

Managing the supply chain is also managing the value chain. A firm's value chain is an important determinant of competitive advantage.

Context Suppliers

Context suppliers, also called portals, support the use of the electronic channel both for customers and suppliers. Their key functions are to offer access to the channel and reduce the complexity of the electronic environment.

Sales Agents

Sales Agent are those who support suppliers primarily through offering shopper quality address bank of potential customers, often with a wealth of information about customer preferences, demographics, and other data.

Purchase Agents

On the customers 'side electronic purchase agents help the internet shopper to find desired goods, or services.

Market makers

Market makes are mediators that bring together buyers and sellers and increase market efficiency like the auction sites.

Payment and Logistic Specialist

These are firms which facilitate payment for products ordered on-line and the delivery of such product to the buyer. Development of digital payment system will be a conducive factor for the growth of e-marketing.

Targeting the individual customer

Market segmentation and targeting was developed as a strategy to overcome some of the limitations of mass marketing. This strategy too has its limitations because segmentation amounts to aggregation of customers on the basis of homogeneity, ignoring some of the factors of heterogeneity. The exciting development in the way data can be gathered, analysed ,stored, retrived disseminated and used, made possible by the advances in the information technology have added new dimensions to marketing strategies and practices.

Chapter - Six

Building brands in International Markets

Brands play a critical role in a firm's international expansion. A coherent international brand architecture is a key component of the firm's overall international marketing strategy as it provides a structure to leverage strong brands into other markets, assimilate acquired brands, and rationalize the firm's international branding strategy. This article looks at how firms have developed an international brand architecture and the drivers that shape that architecture. Branding decisions are generally based on the basic marketing principle of identifying and satisfying the needs and wants of consumers that differ widely. Under the strategic framework for international product promotion, the product function needs satisfied, and conditions of use of a product differ among various market segments and need to be responded tpo by different marketing strategies. Product extension communication adaptation strategy is used In situations where the conditions of product use remain the same but the need satisfied differs. Since consumers do not behave in a rational manner for their purchase decisions, marketers have to identify the emotional aspects of their decision-making process and develop a framework for brand building. The basic concept of brand building is based on the rational and emotional aspects of the product.

In starting a new business or seeking to increase growth at your current business by expanding into international markets, establishing and building a brand identity becomes essential.

Branding involves what people think about your business and your products.. "Building a reputation in any new market, including overseas, involves a first impression, which comes from the initial interactions someone has with your company, products, and services."

Businesses can attempt to shape or form the branding of their company or products in many ways, including advertising, media, word-of-mouth, and contact with your products or services. A lot of thought and effort goes into branding, including naming products, designing logos, and ensuring that service is uniform throughout the business. Through continued exposure over time, your brand — or your reputation — is formed with potential and existing customers. "A brand is essentially a short cut, it is a way for a customer to get an instant recognition on what the promise is of a product or service and how that will benefit them," Roth says.

The reason businesses spent time and money developing brand recognition is so that they can charge a premium for a product or service. People will pay more for a brand name product or service if it is recognized as a leader and a trusted brand and they know what they will get. Apple, for example, can charge more for its computers than some other companies because of its brand reputation for offering innovative design and quality electronics. The same can be said about Honda City or BMW automobiles.

Need to Expand brand

When businesses try to expand their brand globally, those goals don't change. But there are several steps you should take to make sure that your products or services will have a market overseas, that you can maintain quality in delivering and/or distributing your goods or services, and that your business or product branding meets cultural expectations — and doesn't insult anyone — in different parts of the world.The following steps may help you in building an international brand:

- **Make sure you have a market.** "Proven success with current target audience doesn't automatically mean that new target will connect in the same way with your products or services. First and most important, want to determine if a market exists for product. If so, make sure the want or need isn't already being well met by someone else. If there are existing competitors, what makes you remarkably different? If there is a market and there are no competitors, make sure and find out why — are there laws against distributing products or can consumers buy them through other means.
- **Make sure you can deliver.** Make sure you can get your product to, or manufactured within, the new market. "Import and manufacturing laws vary from country to country. Ensure you can make products reliably and consistently available to new target markets." Investigate the local laws. You need to make sure products meet the local standards for construction of components, use of chemicals, disposal of goods, proper labeling of products, etc.
- **Re-examine your business and/or product names.** In choosing a name for your business or product, need to be culturally sensitive if intend to sell in foreign markets. Make sure product names make sense to customers in your new markets, both in English and in the local translation. Sales of the drink increased dramatically when Starbucks began using the German word for gingerbread and rebranded the drink, the Lebkuchen Latte. If you are considering

translating names, don't rely on computer translation. "You don't want what you think is an effective name to mean something opposite or offend potential customers," Williams says. "Work with someone locally who can help make sure you communicate what you intend."

- **Give your logo another look.** Similarly, review your logo to make sure that you don't use any wording or symbols that would offend in a foreign market. "Ensure that any logos or symbols you use make sense and don't offend," Williams says. "Do an international search to make sure your logo isn't similar to that of another international company." For example, if you are selling products in some Middle Eastern markets, a logo featuring the face of a woman might not be appropriate. The best way to understand these cultural sensitivities is to consult a branding or design firm — either a local one or an international firm that can research cultural sensitivities.
- **Understand packaging requirements.** If you're selling a product, you need to consider the laws and customs and packaging requirements in your new markets before deciding on packaging for your products. Your packaging may use a clear plastic shell that hangs from a rod, but your competition may package their product in a box that can go on a shelf, Williams says. This may put you at a disadvantage. "If you're selling a packaged product around the world there are incredible hurdles," Roth adds. Shipping food across borders may require you to provide more nutritional information on packaging, in more languages, and there may be laws prohibiting the use of certain products in some markets .

General Brand Strategies

Brand strategy is aimed at influencing people.s perception of a brand in such a way that they are persuaded to act in a certain manner, e.g. buy and use the products and services offered by the brand, purchase these at higher price points, donate to a cause. In addition, most brand strategies aim to persuade people to buy, use, and donate again by offering them some form of gratifying experience. As branding is typically an activity that is undertaken in a competitive environment, the aim is also to persuade people to prefer the brand to competition. A global brand needs to provide relevant meaning and experience to people across multiple societies. To do so, the brand strategy needs to be devised that takes account of the brand.s own capabilities and competencies, the strategies of competing brands, and the outlook of There are four broad brand strategy areas that can be employed.

(1) Brand Domain

Brand domain - specialists are experts in one or more of the brand domain aspects (products/services, media, distribution, solutions). A brand domain specialist tries to pre-empt or even dictate particular domain developments. This requires an intimate knowledge, not only of the technologies shaping the brand domain, but also of pertinent consumer behaviour and needs. The lifeblood of a brand domain specialist is *innovation* and *creative* use of its resources. A brand domain specialist is like a cheetah in the Serengeti preying on impala and gazelle. The cheetah is a specialist hunter with superior speed to chase, and the claws and teeth to kill these animals. The cheetah is also very familiar with the habits of its prey. It finds ways of approaching, singling out and capturing its prey. The cheetah is one of the most accomplished of hunters within the wild cat species; it catches up to 70% of prey that it hunts.

(2) Brand Reputation

Brand reputation -specialists use or develop specific traits of their brands to support their authenticity, credibility or reliability over and above competitors. A brand reputation specialist needs to have some kind of *history, legacy or mythology*. It also needs to be able to *narrate* these in a convincing manner, and be able to live up to the resulting reputation. A brand reputation specialist has to have a very good understanding of which stories will convince consumers that the brand is in some way superior. A brand reputation specialist is like a horse. It can be pure-bred, have a certain nobility and bearing, and exhibit qualities that can be traced back to these (e.g. grace, speed, temperament, looks). Like a horse, the brand reputation specialist can also thrive on association with celebrities.

(3) Brand Affinity

Brand affinity-specialists bond with consumers based on one or more of a range of affinity aspects. A brand affinity specialist needs to *outperform* competition in terms of *building relationships* with consumers.

This means that a brand affinity specialist needs to have a distinct appeal to consumers, be able to communicate with them affectively, and provide an experience that reinforces the bonding process. A brand affinity specialist is like a pet dog. A dog is generally considered to be man's best friend, due to its affection, its obedience, its loyalty, the status and the protection it provides to its owners. Different kinds of dogs will command a different form of affection.

(4) Brand Recognition

Brand recognition -specialists distinguish themselves from competition by raising their profiles among consumers. The brand recognition specialist either convinces consumers that it is somehow *different from competition*, as is the case for niche brands, or *rises above the melee* by becoming more wellknown among consumers than competition. The latter is particularly important in categories where brands have few distinguishing features in the minds of consumers. In some cases, a brand recognition specialist needs to be able to outspend competition to gain unbeatable levels of awareness. In other cases, a brand recognition specialist needs to convince a loyal following of consumers that it is unique. A recognition specialist is like a peacock. Most of us will know little about birds, but we can recognise a peacock from a large distance. We may not know its precise qualities, but if we were to choose between birds we are more likely to plump for a peacock than for a more ordinary specimen, because of its beauty and presence. To continue the analogy, animals that are transplanted from their original habits, face particular difficulties. Their specialist skills, particular traits or specific qualities may no longer be to their advantage and they may need to develop new ones. The cheetah may fare fine in other parts of the world where there are grassy plains with sufficient game. However, if the cheetah moves from the plains to the jungle it will need to develop an appetite for different prey (e.g. monkey), change the way it hunts (e.g. climb trees) and compete with new predators (e.g. snakes).

Although horses are widely considered noble animals, the way they are viewed does differ between societies. In some, the horse is mainly considered as a mode of transport and competes with cars and trucks. In another, the horse is mainly seen as an opportunity for gambling and there it competes with casinos and dog races. Yet in others, the horse is hardly used and seen as symbolising independence and pioneering spirit. Each of these roles requires different traits from the same animal. Similarly, a dog is not considered a loveable or desirable animal in all societies. The relationship with a dog can be functional in some societies (e.g. sleigh dogs), affective in others (e.g. pet dogs), and ambitious (e.g. fighting dogs) in yet other societies. Thus, a dog may need to build a totally different kind of relationship depending on its new owner.s background.

A peacock may be highly recognisable all over the world, but it symbolises something different depending on local culture. In Bengal, the peacock symbolizes prosperity, while in Bali it represents the power of knowledge, and in China it symbolises beauty and dignity. As in the animal kingdom, there is also a place for generalists who mix and match strategies to their advantage. For instance,. Brands also use complementary strategies. In the case of Nokia, it has been developing its brand affinity through Club Nokia and the Nokia Game.The following section deals with factors that influence brands. strategies when operating in societies other than their original habitats.

The Brand Environment

A brand operates in a space that is defined by its own company or organisation, its competitors, and the societies where it operates. There are both internal and external factors that influence how a brand is finally perceived and experienced by consumers.

(i) Internal Factors

Factors that are internal to a brand.s company or organisation can be categorised as being strategy-related, performance-related and stemming from the brand.s past. The *strategy-related factors* are those that derive from the business strategy and the marketing strategy. There is a strategy hierarchy, whereby business strategy takes the lead, guiding brand strategy. Brand strategy in its turn guides marketing strategy.

The business strategy is aimed at achieving particular consumer behaviour. Only if consumers actually purchase, use (more often), pay a higher price or donate (more) will objectives of a business strategy be met. These objectives may include a larger market share, increased returns, higher margins and increased shareholder value. Brands are designed to persuade consumers to exhibit the behaviour that will make these objectives come true for the organisation. Thus the influence of business strategy upon brand strategy is direct and compelling.

The marketing strategy aims to translate the brand strategy into actual products or services, with a specific price, to be sold at specific outlets, to be promoted through specific communications activities and channels, and to be supported by specific service. The influence of the marketing strategy is thus indirect in that the correct translation of the brand into the marketing mix determines whether consumers get the correct impression of the brand. The *performance-related factors* are dependent upon the marketing implementation, i.e. the actual production and delivery of the products and services,their accompanying messages to consumers, and the actual product or service experience. The implementation eventually determines whether consumers experience what the brand strategy set out to provide. The marketing implementation may make or break a brand at the moment that is of most importance to consumers: e.g. when they actually experience the brand through advertising, promotions, purchase, usage, and after-sales service.

The *factors that stem from the brand.s past*are the brand.s internal legacy and its internal conventions. The brand.s internal legacy is about who have developed it, who have managed it over the years, and what the role of the brand has become for the organisation. This influences how management, staff, partners, distributors and shareholders view the brand and its future potential. It may prove difficult to change such perceptions once a brand has been slotted into a specific position. The internal conventions of an organisation are such issues as how things are typically done, support systems, what the culture is like, who has the power to decide, who has the power to frustrate decisions, the structure of the organisation, its policies, and its (other) activities. For a global brand, such influencing factors exist at *central* as well as at *local* levels. More often than not, there are tensions between central and local as specific factors work in opposite directions, and people within the organisation have different agendas for the brand.

(ii) External Factors

External influences upon a brand strategy come mainly from three quarters: competition, consumers and media. These external influences will vary between the markets and societies where a brand operates. Therefore, these influences need to be determined locally. When a brand is introduced into a foreign society, it will encounter particular brand strategies that are being practiced by competitive brands. Unless competitors are very complacent, head-on confrontations with them are generally not the best way of winning the hearts and minds of consumers. It is, therefore, important to determine competitors. brand strategies and to find ways of flanking established competition by choosing an alternative strategy. *Category conventions* are the unwritten rules that govern the way in which products or services are designed, advertised, distributed, serviced, priced, experienced, etc. Challenging such conventions may provide a brand with a competitive advantage. It is imperative that such a challenge has value to consumers and that they are willing to go along with the challenge. *Needs conventions* determine the forms in which consumers. needs are manifested .Human needs are not universal and neither is the importance placed upon each need. However, the major differences lie in the manner in which a need is articulated or the form of a solution that is provided to a need. For example, although there is a general need for nutrition, there are considerable differences between societies with regard to which foodstuffs are acceptable for specific meals. Not to mention foods that are totally unacceptable to specific societies, as witnessed by the controversy over the consumption of dog meat during the upcoming world cup soccer finals in Korea. The media can seriously affect a brand strategy in a positive or a negative manner. In some developing countries foreign brands are promoted by the media as examples of modernity, while in others these same brands may be portrayed as the vanguards of a foreign domination. Particularly, bad news about brands can spread like wild fire across boarders, as Coke found out in Belgium, where the outsides of some bottles were ontaminated with a fungicide, causing a health scare.

Impact on Brand Strategies

The factors discussed above each have their own specific impact on the four general brand strategies and their strategy sub-types. Due to the limitations of its format, this paper focuses on factors that influence the four general strategies only.

Domain Specialists

Domain specialists generally require economies of scale to be able to sustain their investments in constant innovation. Brand proposition standardisation or harmonisation is part of this drive towards economies of scale. Domain specialists tend to centralise brand management, which leaves little room for local adaptation. Domain specialists, therefore, need to either establish new conventions themselves (through a successful challenge) or not enter the market at all. Information and communications technology (ICT) companies have had the advantage of establishing conventions without having to challenge existing category conventions. They have had the opportunity to shape their category. This is why many ICT companies have been able to establish highly standardised global brands. Among the world.s ten most valuable brands in 2001 (compiled by Interbrand) are four such ICT domain specialists, namely Microsoft, IBM, Intel and Nokia. Shaping a category does involve having indepth knowledge not only of technology, but also of consumers. Iridium, the mobile satellite phone operator, did not have this knowledge and failed miserably when it introduced a service that few felt a need for. Most people already had excellent alternatives to the expensive and unwieldy system. Domain specialists are particularly susceptible to *category conventions*, as these largely govern the brand domain aspects. Renault, which introduced a fair number of innovative car designs during the past decade (e.g. Twingo, Nano,,Espace), has little or no position outside Europe. While the brand has successfully challenged automotive design conventions in Europe, it fails to persuade consumers across the Atlantic. Other European car brands, many less innovative than Renault, have been successful in the USA. Domain specialists can also be prone to *cultural conventions*, especially beliefs and customs directly related to the products or services involved. For instance, there is a traditional belief in Chinese culture about the efficacy of certain herbs. Proctor & Gamble tapped into such beliefs by adding Showu root extract to its popular Rejoice shampoo, claiming it makes black hair shinier. This adaptation provided Rejoice with a competitive response to local competition such as the Olive brand, which had earlier staked its claim of providing lustre to black hair. Domain specialists. brand building activities consist mainly of introducing global brand extensions to reinforce the perception of the brand.s innovativeness.Without constant and consistent extensions, the brands would quickly lose their relevance to consumers.

(iii) Reputation Specialists

Reputation specialists are a diverse bunch, some of whom rely heavily upon their pedigrees while others leverage their connections to celebrities, and yet others build on a promise that they have demonstrably been able to keep. Reputation specialists are often good at tweaking their brands to ensure relevance to consumers in specific societies. This means that brand and marketing management need to be largely localised, with a largely a guiding task for global management. It also means that competencies such as consumer understanding and narration need to be available locally. Reputation specialists are particularly susceptible to *cultural and needs conventions*. Brands that leverage their country-of-origin make use of beliefs (sometimes stereotypes) about those countries. However, the significance and essence of such beliefs can vary widely across societies. Reputation specialists often make use of people.s senses of insecurity and their needs for belonging. A toothpaste brand that is endorsed by dentists may meet security needs in one society, while the relevant security need in another country is whiteness. A particular celebrity endorsement may work wonders in one country, but the same person may not mean a thing in another country.

For example NikeAmerican football and baseball star Bo Jackson for advertising in the USA, but substituted him for local sports celebrities in other countries. Reputation specialists often have a limited scope for challenging category conventions. However, they also have less of a need for doing so. Volkswagen, which builds on a reputation for the excellent quality and resale value of its cars, does not feel the need for constant innovation. Unlike Renault, Volkswagen.s sales do not dry up when it doesn.t introduce innovative designs every few years. Reputation specialists. main brand building activities are narration to and education of consumers about their brand, as well as an experience that is consistent with the brands. reputations.

(iv) Affinity Specialists

Affinity specialists are able to pluck the heartstrings of consumers. They way they do so differs markedly between brands, but the common result is unrivalled brand loyalty. Some affinity specialists are able to standardise their brands across societies by using themes that are common across various societies. For instance, Mercedes is a brand that many (successful) people around the world wish to be associated with. However, most affinity specialists need local brand management in order to be able to build a worthwhile rapport with consumers. Affinity specialists need to get close to consumers to be able to connect with them. This closeness requires affinity specialists to understand exactly which conventions can and cannot be challenged. This also means that the brand.s organisation must encourage local brand management initiatives. Affinity specialists are particularly susceptible to *cultural and needs conventions*. For instance, a financial services brand that connects to it customers by employing empathy utilises a society.s prevailing values and esteem needs. In a collectivist society, the brand's empathy is likely to be expressed through showing deference to customers. In an individualist society, the empathy is likely to be expressed through personal recognition and advice pertaining to the customers. specific financial situations. Affinity specialists also make use of people. sense of belonging. Many youth brands seek ways of appealing to consumers in such a manner that they wish to be associated with the brand. This entails constant cool hunting and staying closely in tune with teens and young adults. Tommy Hilfiger was the epitome of teen cool, but when the brand got stuck in the same rut for a season it instantly became obsolete. Affinity specialists have the greatest scope for *challenging category, needs and cultural conventions*. Due to their general closeness to consumers, affinity specialists are in-tune with their consumers and can sense when conventions are shifting. The Body Shop challenged packaging conventions by using simple plastic refill bottles, thereby reinforcing the social conscience of the brand, which resonated with likeminded consumers affinity specialists is *relationship building*.

It differs considerably between the types of affinity brands how this is achieved, whether that is through events (e.g. Harley Davidson), through service experience(e.g. Starbucks), a loyalty programme (e.g. Shell), an Internet information site (e.g. Pampers), through demonstrating an understanding of target consumers (e.g. MTV), extolling principles relevant to target consumers (e.g. Greenpeace), or by demonstrating coolness and hipness at relevant occasions (e.g. Burton). The particular connection with consumer needs to be constantly reaffirmed by the brand through behaviour, advertising, publicity, direct communications, brand extensions, etc. Brand extensions generally aim at reinforcing that bond by offering products or services that bring consumers into closer or more frequent contact with the brand (e.g. Harley Davidson aftershave).

(v) Recognition Specialists

Recognition specialists succeed by using two aspects, namely consumers. *Inability to discriminate* between a multitude of brands in a category and their *inability to know* more than a few brands in a category. In some categories it is difficult for consumers to understand the differences between brands. Subsequently consumers will opt for those brands that they know, the ones they hear of often. These will usually be the big players in a market. For instance, most people are not able to fathom the differences in the propositions offered by various banks. What they are aware of are the well-known banks. This awareness breeds confidence and leads most people to choose one of these. A more extreme case is the mass wine category, which is teeming with unfamiliar brands. By raising its profile, the Ernest &Julio Gallo brand provides a safe-haven for consumers. It is a brand that they can trust to provide a consistent quality at an agreeable price. In some categories, consumers actively know only one or two brands. Apparently,there is an inability or a reluctance to know more brands. This may be due to the fact that competition is weak at raising its profile or the category is a low-interest one. Such brands become the points of reference in their category. For instance, people will generally be actively aware of only one or two toilet paper brands. These brands will usually have very distinct propositions, e.g. one is soft and the other is decorative. Distributors. own brands will usually occupy the value positions. The recognition specialists keep their advertising expenditure at high levels to preserve this situation. These high levels of advertising expenditure necessitate recognition specialists to find economies of scale in this area. Developing regional or global campaigns is a logical consequence. Recognition specialists, therefore, tend to centralise brand management, which leaves little room for local initiatives. Recognition specialists often have a limited scope of adapting to local conventions. However, recognition specialists are susceptible to category conventions and needs conventions. For example, Citibank presents its credit cards as *.dependable.* in the USA and as having *.distinction.* in Hong Kong. Citibank thus adapts to the prevailing conventions of representation in both markets. Obviously, the main brand building activity of recognition specialists is (mass) advertising. A high general awareness among consumers forms a formidable barrier to competition. A recognition specialist, therefore, requires advertising skills as one of its core competencies.

International Brand Architecture

With the globalization of markets and the growth of competition on a global scale, companies are increasingly expanding the geographic scope of their operations, setting up or acquiring companies in other countries, or entering into alliances across national boundaries. At the same time, with the spread of global and regional media, the development of international retailing, and the movement of people, goods, and organizations across national borders, markets are becoming more integrated. As a result, firms need to pay greater attention to coordinating and integrating their marketing strategy across markets.An important element of a firm's international marketing strategy is its branding policy. Strong brands help to establish the firm's identity in the market place, and develop a solid customer franchise (Aaker 1996, Keller 1998, Kapferer 1997) as well as providing a weapon to counter growing retailer power (Barwise and Robertson 1992). They can also provide the basis for brand extensions, which further strengthen the firm's position and enhance value (Aaker and Keller 1990). In international markets, an important issue for the firm is whether to use the same brand name in different countries, leveraging brand strength across boundaries, or whether to maintain local brands responding to local customer preferences. A related issue is what level of branding to emphasize, i.e. corporate/house or product-level brands or some combination of both.

The central role of branding in defining the firm's identity and its position in international markets means that it is critical to develop an explicit international brand architecture. This implies identifying the different levels of branding within the firm, the number of brands at each level as well as their geographic and product market scope. The most critical element in this structure is the number of levels, i.e. corporate, house/product business and product and how these are used in conjunction with each other. Related to the development of this architecture, is the question of how to manage brands that span different geographic markets and product lines. Who should have custody of international brands, and be responsible for coordinating their positioning in different national or regional markets, as well as making decisions about use of a given brand name on other products or services. The significance of the various issues depends to a substantial degree on how a firm has expanded internationally, and how its international operations are organized. Some firms, such as P&G and Coca-Cola, have expanded through leveraging their domestic "power" brands in international markets. Consequently, as they seek to expand further, they have to consider whether to develop brands geared to specific regional or national preferences. Others such as Nestlé and Unilever have traditionally adopted country-centered strategies, building or acquiring a mix of national and international brands. Such companies have to decide how far to move towards greater harmonization of brands and integration of their brand architecture across countries, and if so, how to do so.

A global brand should have a minimum level of geographical spread and turnover in various global markets. However, in the fields of information and communication technology, a lot of leapfrogging has taken place and a number of IT companies from India have aimed at global market with little presence domestically. Quelch identifies the following six traits for a brand to be global:

- Dominates the domestic market which generates cash flow to enter new markets.
- Meets a universal consumer needs
- Demonstrates balanced country market coverage
- Reflects a consistent positioning worldwide
- Benefits from positive country of origin effect
- Focus is on the product category.

Life Cycle Concept and Product Categorise

Markets are at different stages of evolution at any given time for a product category as shown in fig 6.1. The stages of development of product categories are summarised below"

Embryonic

The product category at this stage is not developed and the customers are almost unaware. Products produced locally are marketed with no imports. The local manufacturers and sellers are highly fragmented. When De Beers entered India in 1992. diamonds as part of the jewellery product category were not developed. So De. Beers emphasized on developing diamonds as a

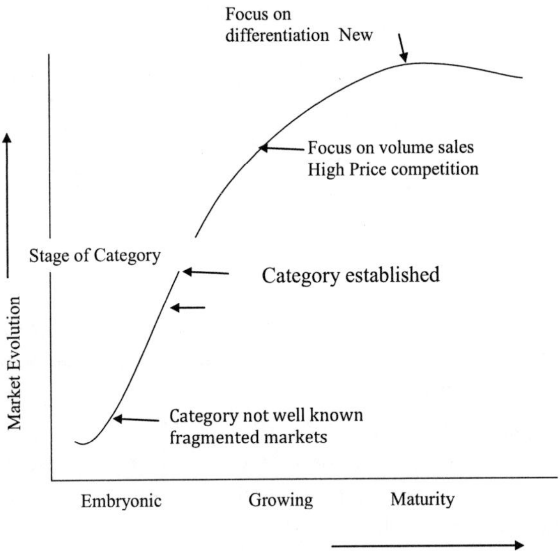

Fig 6.1 Category Development in International marketing.

category. He identified the concerns pf Indian customers to gift jewellery to their daughters or daughters-in-law, to be passed on from one generation to another. Consequently, De Beers' market promotion stressed that a Diamond is for ever, which allowed the company to make inroads into the Indian market, thus far dominated by gold jewellery.

Growth

Once customer expectations are identified and addressed, there is a gradual shift in customers' preferences as the product category gets established in the market. Subsequently, the customer segment evolves in the product category.

Maturity

As the category becomes well established in the target market, sales volumes rise. This attracts many other competitors in the market as the category is expected to provide volume sales and good margins. Since the number of competitors increases, the focus shifts to intensive price competition and achieving higher turnover.

Decline

The increasing number of market players competing fiercely on price and volume exert pressure on the firm's margins. The marketers look for new segments in the target market and customer sophistication. This appears to be a case in India's mobile phone market in 2004 with fierce competition on consumers price and sales volume. Mobile phone companies are now looking towards creating new market segments by providing sophisticated services so as to use a differentiated marketing strategy by different segments. This also gives rise to many new market segments and proliferation of competing brands in the market.

Life Cycle Concept and Brand

Similar to product categoies, a brand can also be at different stages (Fig 6.2) of its life cycle in various markets. The major development stages of a brand may be summarized as follows"

(i) Embryonic:- New markets, where the brand is not presently introduced, are termed as markets at the embryonic stage. The primary strategy of a firm in such markets is to create brand awarenss and test the markets fo their suitability to the brand launch.

(ii) Growth:- Once the markets are identifieds and targeted for the launch of a brand, the company attempts to penetrate them with heavy marketing communication. There is heavy promotion to entice non-users and attract them to the brand users category. However, the firm may choose either penetration or skimming pricing strategy depending upon other marketing factors.

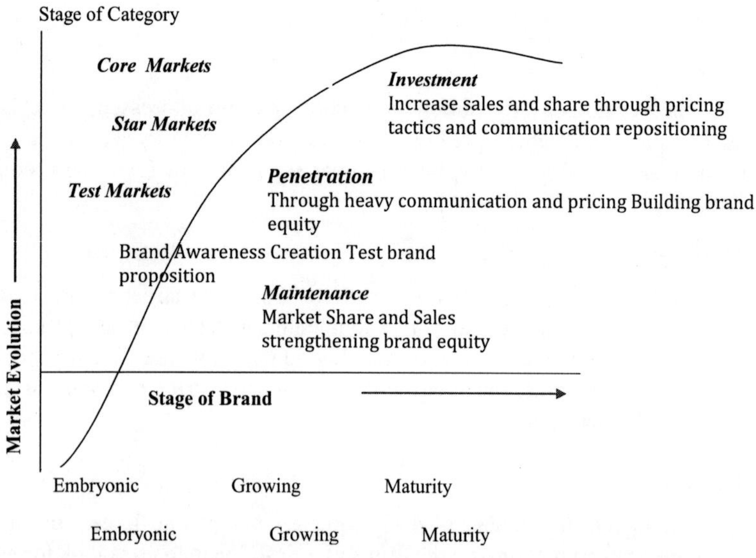

Fig 6.2 Brand Development in international Markets.

(iii) Maturity:- In mature markets with high sales volumes and large market share of the brand, firms attempt to maintain their volume and market share. The marketing strategy is focused on strengthening brand equity using various tools to reinforce customer loyalty and increase frequency of consumption. The firms often attempt to reposition the brand and extend the brand to other product categories.

(iv) Decline:- As a result of increased competitive intensity and proliferation of brands, firms find it difficult to maintain their sales volume and market share. The key strategy in this phase is to compete on price and strive to increase sales volume. The consumption pattern of the target market needs to be carefully examined and the market segments with high growth potential are identified so as to customize promotional efforts to achieve sales volume and retain market share.

International Branding Strategy

Based on the above life cycle stages of theproduct category and brand, a firm has to make an assessment of the development of the category and the brand in the market. Category development index (CDI) and Brand development index (BDI) are the most widely applied tools for determining international branding strategy. These can be computed as follows:

$$\text{CDI for country A} = \frac{\text{Per capita sales of the category in country A}}{\text{Per capita sales of the category in the world}}$$

$$\text{BDI for country A} = \frac{\text{Per capita sales of the brand in country A}}{\text{Per capita sales of the brand in the world}}$$

These indices facilitate the assessment of markets in terms of development of the brand and the category. The findings may be transformed in the form of a matrix, as given below:

High	Build category	Maintain leadership
Low	Secure	Build market share

On the basis of this analysis, the markets may be divided into four categories that need different marketing strategies.

Markets where the category is not developed and the brand is not in use fall under the low CDI—low bDI markets. The focus has to be on establishing 'roots' and creating customer awareness about the product.

Low CDI—High BDI Markets

In countries with high intensity of brand use but low intensity of category prevalence, emphasis has to be laid on developing the category so that the brand automatically gets the largest share. As De Beers controls about 80% of the world's total diamond business, it emphasizes the development of dimonds as a category. In India too, De Beers attempted to develop diamonds as a product category as a part of jewellery and replace gold jewellery sales with sales of diamond studded jewellery. Similarly, platinum had never been used earlier in India for making jewellery. Therefore, the strategy to develop the platinum jewellery market in India was adopted by firms in an attempt to develop platinum as a category before emphasizing on their particular brands.

Perspectives on International Branding

Most discussion and research on branding, whether domestic or international, focuses on the equity or value associated with a brand name and the factors which create or are the underlying source of value (Aaker 1996, Kapferer 1997, Keller 1998). Considerable attention has, for example, been devoted to examining how the value embodied in a brand and its equity can be extended to other products without resulting in dilution of value (Aaker and Keller 1990). This interest has been stimulated in part by the increasing market power and value associated with a strong brand and in part by the prohibitive costs of launching a successful new brand.While this focus is appropriate for a relatively few high profile brands such as Nike or Coca-Cola, it ignores the issues faced by the vast majority of multinational firms who own a variety of local and international brands that differ in their strength, target market and their association. Such firms have to determine how to develop a cohesive and effective brand structure, which brands to emphasize and build, whether to use the same brands across product groups and across countries, and how different brands at different levels of the organization should be interrelated so as to maximize their market impact and efficiency.

As the firm expands in international market, issues relating to brand architecture or brand structure become even more complex. In addition to considering the number of levels in the hierarchy, another dimension, namely the degree of brand coordination or standardization across countries, needs to be determined. Especially if the company expands through acquisition or strategic alliances, the question of whether and how brand architectures of different firms are merged, arises. Irrespective of the expansion process, companies have to determine an appropriate brand architecture that transcends national boundaries and how far branding is integrated or standardized across countries.

Development of International Branding Structures

Corporate-dominant architecture tended to be most common among firms with a relatively limited range of products or product divisions, or with a clearly defined target market, e.g. Shell, Kelloggs, Nike, Benneton, etc. Product dominant architecture, on the other hand, was typically found among firms such as Akzo Nobel with multiple national or local brands, or firms such as P&G or Mars that had expanded internationally by leveraging "power" brands. The most common were hybrid or mixed structures, consisting of a mix of global corporate, regional and national product-level brands, or corporate endorsement of product brands or different structures for different product divisions.Both corporate and product dominant structures were evolving towards hybrid structures. Firms with corporate dominant structures were adding brands at other levels, for example, the house or product level, to differentiate between different product divisions. Product-dominant structures, on the other hand, especially where these emphasized multiple local (national) brands were moving toward greater integration or co-ordination across markets through corporate endorsement of local products. These companies also varied in the extent to which they had a clearly articulated international brand architecture to guide this evolution. Some, for example, laid out the different levels at which brands were to be used, the interrelation between brands at different levels, the geographic scope of each brand and the product lines on which a brand was to be used, while others had few or no guidelines concerning international branding.

Corporate dominant branding

A few of the companies studied had a very simple brand structure based on the corporate name, as for example, Shell, Philips, Apple, Nike, etc. In general, these were business-to-business organizations with a heavy emphasis on corporate branding, or a relatively narrow and coherent product line. Other cases included consumer goods companies focused on a global target segment such as Nike or Benneton. Their prime objective was to establish a strong global identity for the brand rather than respond to local market conditions. In some instances, the corporate logo and visual identification (Apple and Nike) played a major role in identifying the brand and defining brand image worldwide.

Product-dominant branding

Other companies as, for example, P&G, or Best Foods used a product dominant strategy. This strategy was common among U.S. firms who had expanded internationally by leveraging "power" brands, as, for example, P&G with brands such as Camay, or Pampers. Firms with domestic product dominant structures, that had expanded by acquiring national companies often acquired a substantial number of national and local product brands, in addition to their own global and regional product brands. Best Foods, for example, has several international product brands such as Hellmans, Knorr, etc., as well as national product brands such as uncle chips, parle, amul.

A few international companies, though this seemed to be rare, had structures consisting almost exclusively of national product brands. Often these were well-established traditional brand names known for their quality and reliability. For example, Akzo Nobel owns brands such as Diamond Salt in the US and Sikkens' paint brand in Europe. Products were tailored to local preferences and product innovation was relatively low. Since customer preferences were highly localized with few links across national boundaries, management saw few potential synergies from harmonizing brands across borders.

Hybrid branding strategies

A number of companies had hybrid brand structures with a combination of corporate and product brands. Coca-Cola, for example uses the Coca-Cola name on its cola brand worldwide, with product variants such as Cherry Coke, Coke Lite or Diet Coke or caffeine free Coke in some, but not all countries. In addition, Coca-Cola has a number of local or regional soft drink brands, such as Lilt in various fruit flavors in the U.K., TabXtra, a sugar-free cola drink in Scandinavia, and Cappy, a fruit drink in East Europe and Turkey.

In other cases, companies used the corporate name for some product businesses, but not on others. Mars, for example, used the Mars name on its ice-cream, soft drink and confectionery lines, but used the Pedigree house brand for pet food. This was intended to create separate and distinct images for the confectionery and pet food businesses. Similarly, Danone used the Dannon/Danone name on yogurt worldwide, on bottled water in the US and on cookies in Eastern Europe. Danone also owns the Lu and Jacob brands which are used on biscuits in Europe and the US, and three other bottled water brands, Evian, sold worldwide, Volvic and Badoit only sold in France, as well as Kronenbourg and Kanterbrau beers, and Vivagel and Marie frozen foods in Europe.

Other companies had different brand architecture for different product divisions. For example, Unilever has a global brand architecture in its personal products division. The yellow fats division consists mostly of local brands with some harmonization in positioning or brand name across countries, while the ice-cream division had a combination of local and global product brands such as Magnum, Cornetto and Solero. These are endorsed by a country or regional house brands such as Walls and Algida, and all shared a common logo worldwide.

Drivers of International Branding Strategy

Brand architecture is essentially fashioned by three major factors: firm-based characteristics, product market characteristics and underlying market dynamics. While the firm's history shapes its brand architecture, market dynamics and the growth of economic and political integration as well as rising media costs create pressures to harmonize branding across country markets to achieve economies of scale and scope. As a result, brand architecture, like any living organism, is continually changing, both shaped by and evolving in response to these drivers.

The brand architecture of an organization at any given point in time is in large measure a legacy of past management decisions as well as the competitive realities it faces in the marketplace. The firm's history creates 'brand baggage'. This includes strong brands with rich traditions (like Louis Vuitton) as well as the burden of weak brands with strong traditions (Samsonite). Management inertia and vested interests within the firm often create barriers to the pruning of weak brands or their absorption into strong brand categories. Brand architecture also reflects product market characteristics. Where products are strongly culturally embedded, local or national brands are likely to proliferate, catering to specific local preferences. On the other hand, where customer preferences and desired product attributes are relatively homogeneous worldwide, and products share common functions, there are greater opportunities for global or international brands at the corporate or product divisional level.

Firm-based drivers

Brand architecture inevitably reflects the imprimatur of previous generations of management directives. In the first place, the firm's administrative heritage and in particular, its organizational structure, establish the template for its brand architecture. Secondly, the firm's international expansion strategy and notably the mode of expansion, i.e. via acquisition or organic growth affect how brand structure evolves over time. Entry into strategic alliances in order to broaden the geographic scope of the firm's operations will result in a need to meld the branding strategies of the partners. The importance of corporate identity and the diversity of the firm's product lines and product divisions will also impact the range and number of brands.

Administrative heritage: The firm's administrative heritage is central to understanding its branding strategy (Bartlett and Ghoshal 1989). A firm that has historically operated on a highly decentralized basis where country managers have substantial autonomy and control over strategy as well as day-to-day operations is likely to have a substantial number of local brands. In some cases, the same product may be sold under different brand names in different countries, e.g. Unilever's yellow fat brands, Promise and Flora. In other cases, a product may be sold under the same brand name but have a different positioning or formulation in certain countries e.g. Haagen-Daz.

Firms with a centralized organizational structure and global product divisions, such as Sony or Siemens, are more likely to have global brands. Both Siemens and Sony adopt a corporate branding strategy emphasizing the quality and reliability of their products. Product lines are typically standardized worldwide, with minor variations in styling and features for local country markets.

Expansion strategy: Closely related to the firm's administrative heritage is its international expansion strategy. Here of particular importance in determining the number and composition of the brands owned by the firm is its mode of expansion, i.e., whether it has expanded through organic or greenfield growth or through acquisitions and strategic alliances.

Firms that expand internationally by acquiring local companies, even where the primary goal is to gain access to distribution channels, will typically also acquire local brands. Where these brands have high local recognition or a strong customer or distributor franchise, the company will normally retain the brand. This is particularly likely if the brand does not occupy a similar positioning to that of another brand currently owned by the firm. Best Foods typically expands internationally through acquisitions and has, for example, acquired Pfanni, a German company selling mashed potatoes and dumplings, Telna, a soup company in Israel and a sauce company in Chile. These companies are then used as a platform to distribute Best's other brands.

Sometimes, a company expands by acquiring companies in the same or related product businesses. For example, when Kimberley Clark acquired Scott Paper, it also acquired a number of paper product companies in Europe, some of whom had strong local brands. Kimberley Clark decided to adopt a transition strategy, gradually changing local brands to the Kleenex brand. For example, Kimberley Clark acquired Page, the leading Dutch brand of tissues, toilet paper and paper towels, and placed the Kleenex brand on all Page products. The Kleenex name and little dog logo was also used in all promotional campaigns. Over time it is expected that the local brand will become smaller and possibly eventually be phased out.

Other companies have expanded and diversified at the same time through a strategy of acquisition. Nestlé, for example, has expanded by acquiring companies in a range of different product markets, mostly food and beverage. These range from well known global brands in mineral water such as Perrier and San Pellegrino, confectionery companies such as Rowntree and Perugina, to pet food companies and brands such as Spillers and Alpo and grocery companies such as Buitoni, Crosse and Blackwell and Herta. The proliferation of brands obtained through this acquisition from 1960-1990 generated a need to consolidate and integrate company branding structures. Consequently, the

Nestlé branding tree was established . This consists of ten worldwide corporate brands, such as Nestlé, Carnation and Buitoni; 45 worldwide strategic product brands such as KitKat, Polo and After Eight (these are always endorsed by a corporate level brand); 25 regional corporate brands; 100 regional product brands, such as Contadina and Stouffer; 700 local strategic brands, and approximately 7,000 local brands (Parsons 1996).

Firms that have expanded predominantly by extending strong domestic brands into international markets tend to have a product-level brand strategy. For example, Procter & Gamble has rolled out a number of its personal products brands such as Camay, and Pampers, into international markets. This strategy appears most effective, where customer interests and desired product attributes are similar worldwide and where brand image is an important cue for the consumer.

Importance of corporate identity: The relative importance placed by the firm on its corporate identity, also influences brand structure. Companies such as IBM and Apple, place considerable emphasis on corporate identity (Schmitt and Simenson 1997). In the case of IBM, "Big Blue" is associated with a solid corporate reputation and reflects the company's desire to project an image of a large reliable computer company, providing products and services worldwide. The IBM logo is featured on products and advertising worldwide in order to convey this image. Equally, Apple used its colored apple logo to project the image of a vibrant challenger in the personal computer market.

Japanese companies also frequently emphasize corporate identity as a means of reassuring customers and distributors that the company is reliable and stands behind its products. As a result, even companies with highly diverse product lines such as Kao with detergents, personal care products and computer floppy disks and records, rely on the corporate brand name (and its logo) to project an image of reliability.

Product diversity: A fourth issue concerns the diversity or conversely, the interrelatedness of the product businesses in which the firm is involved. Firms that are involved in closely related product lines or businesses that share a common technology or rely on similar core competencies, often emphasize corporate brands. GE, for example, is involved in a range of product businesses worldwide from aerospace and electric generators to medical equipment. All rely heavily on engineering skills. Use of the GE name provides reassurance and reinforces the firm's reputation for engineering competency and reliable products worldwide.

Conversely, when firms are involved in a range of diverse product businesses that target different customer segments, and have different associations, they sometimes opt to develop separate identities and associations for individual product businesses or products. For example, Unilever has no corporate brand and emphasizes either product or house brands, thus establishing separate identities for its businesses such as food, personal care, and detergents. It was considered particularly desirable to avoid association between the (now sold) chemicals business and foods products. Similarly, Procter and Gamble has emphasized product brands in its detergents business in order to target distinct market segments, and avoid creating an impression of market dominance.

Product market structure

The nature of the product market(s) in which the firm is involved also influences its brand architecture. Three factors play an important role in brand architecture: the nature and scope of the target market, the degree of market integration, and the cultural embeddedness of the product.

(i) Target market: Global branding is frequently an effective means of reaching target markets with relatively homogeneous needs and interests and similar sociodemographic profiles and media habits worldwide (Hassan and Katsanis 1996). Luxury brands such as Godiva, Moet and Chandon, Louis Vuitton and Aveda as well as brands such as Bodyshop or Benneton are all targeted to the same market segment worldwide, and benefit from the cachet provided by their appeal to a global consumer group.

(ii) Market integration: Another factor impacting the firm's brand architecture is the degree of product market integration. This can be viewed not only in terms of whether the same customers are present in different country markets or regions and have similar purchase needs and interests worldwide, but also whether the same competitors are present in these markets (Douglas and Craig 1996). Where markets are fully integrated and the same competitors compete in these markets worldwide, as in aerospace, use of global brands help to provide competitive differentiation on a global basis. Where the same competitors compete in all or most markets, but local competitors are also present, use of a multi-tier branding structure, including global corporate or product brands as well as local brands is desirable. Coca-Cola, for example, not only has its global brand of colas, but also numerous local and regional brands catering to specific market tastes.

(iii) Cultural embeddedness: A final, and in many cases, critical factor influencing brand architecture is the degree of cultural embeddedness of a product. As noted earlier, markets where demand is relatively homogeneous worldwide are likely to be prime candidates for global branding at either the corporate or product level. Products which are deeply culturally embedded, as for example, food or in some cases, household products are on the other hand, more likely to thrive as local brands. In some cases, they may be products which cater to specific local tastes, such as food products. Particularly, where these are traditional products and market tastes have evolved little over time, a well-established local brand name may have substantial value. In some instances, where the product is associated with local cultural habits and tastes, use of a local sounding brand name may be preferable.

Market dynamics

While the firm's history and the product markets in which it operates, shape the firm's brand structure, market drivers create and continually change the context in which this brand architecture evolves. In the first place, removal of political and economic barriers between markets together with regulatory change create opportunities to harmonize branding across countries resulting in fewer brands. The integration of markets and in particular, the growth of regional and global media also encourage a move towards international brands in order to obtain cost efficiencies and reinforce brand strength. Advances in global communication technology and the internationalization of retailing further facilitate the growth of international branding and stimulate a shift towards international brands (de Mooij 1997). Increased consumer mobility enhances the value of establishing a global identity and potential synergies from establishing a global presence.

Political and economic integration: Increasing political and economic integration in many parts of the world has been a key factor stimulating the growth of international branding. As governments remove tariff and non-tariff barriers to business transactions and trade with other countries, and people and information move easily across borders, the climate has become more favorable to the marketing of international brands. Firms no longer need to modify products to meet local requirements, and develop specific variants for local markets, but can market standardized products with the same brand name in multiple country markets. In many instances, harmonization of product regulation across borders has further facilitated this trend.

Infrastructure: The growth of a global market infrastructure has acted as a major catalyst to the spread of international brands. Global and regional media provide an economical and effective vehicle for advertising international brands, particularly where these brands are targeted to focused global and regional market segments, as for example, upscale and more affluent consumers, teenagers, etc. (Hassan and Katsanis 1996). At the same time, global media play an active role in laying the groundwork for consumer acceptance of and interest in international brands by developing awareness of these brands and the life-styles with which they are associated in other countries. In many instances, this stimulates a desire for the brands consumers perceive as symbolic of a coveted life-style.

The internationalization of retailing has further facilitated and stimulated the development of international manufacturer brands. As retailers move across international borders they provide an effective channel for international brands, but at the same time, their power increases. Consequently, manufacturers need to develop strong brands with high market share in multiple countries in order to obtain adequate retail space for these brands and minimize slotting allowances (Barwise and Robertson 1992). Strong international brands can also be extended to provide manufacturers with an effective negotiating tool and to ensure the placement of new products.

(iv) 'Consumer mobility: A final factor underlying the power of international brands is increased consumer mobility. While global media provide passive exposure to brands, increasing international travel and movement of customers across national boundaries provides active exposure to brands in different countries (Alden, Steenkamp and Batra 1999). Awareness of the availability and high visibility of an international brand in multiple countries enhances its value to consumers, and provides reassurance of its strength and reliability. Increased exposure to and familiarity with new and diverse products, and the life-styles and cultures in which they are embedded also generates greater receptivity to products of foreign origin or those perceived as "international" rather than domestic (Featherstone 1990). All these factors help to create a climate more favorable to international brands.

In brief, while, on the one hand, firm-based drivers, often responding to product market structure, influence the formation of international brand architecture, market drivers provide a continually changing environmental context to which this architecture must be adapted in order to be effective. At the same time, the image and strength of the firm's brands in the marketplace changes, as the firm enters new countries or markets, acquired brands are integrated into the architecture, new brand extensions or product lines are added, or a positioning is modified or radically changed. As a result, brand architecture is continually evolving both in terms of structure and scope.

Dynamics of International Brand Architecture

Corporate endorsement and brand extension

As a result of rising media and promotional costs as well as the trend towards globalization, brand architecture is increasingly subject to pressures at both the corporate and product level. Increasingly complex brand structures are beginning to emerge, characterized on the one hand, by corporate endorsement of product brands, and on the other, by extension of strong brands across countries and product businesses.

Corporate endorsement: At the one end of the spectrum, international expansion and consumer needs for reassurance about product quality and reliability is resulting in a shift toward corporate endorsement of product brands. This helps to forge a global corporate identity for the firm and gathers its products under a global umbrella, thus generating potential cost savings through promotion of the global corporate brand, rather than multiple independent product brands. At the same time, endorsement by the corporate brand provides reassurance for the customer of a reliable corporate image and enhances visibility.

Corporate endorsement of product level brands is increasingly used as a mechanism to integrate brand structure across country markets, providing a unifying element across product offerings. For example, Cadbury uses the Cadbury name on all its confectionery products, in conjunction with product brands such as Dairy Milk, Whispers, etc. Equally, a house brand is sometimes used on a product business worldwide. For example, Akzo Nobel places the Sikkens name on all its paint products. The relative size of the corporate or house name and the brand name varies from one company to another. In some cases, e.g. Cadbury or Nestlé, the corporate brand has equal prominence to the product name. In other cases, it is smaller and used primarily as an endorsement rather than an identifier.

In some cases, the prominence and role of the corporate brand or logo varies from country to country. For example, Douwe Egbert uses the Friesen lady logo on its coffee in all countries, but the size of the lady and also the positioning statement vary from country to country. In Spain, for example, the positioning emphasizes the richness of the coffee and the master brewer, while in the UK, its continental taste, and in Holland, the association with family and comfort are featured.

Brand extension: At the other end of the spectrum, rising media costs, coupled with the importance of building high visibility and the need to obtain cost economies, create pressures to extend strong brands across product lines and country borders. Increasingly, new products and variants are launched under existing brand names to take advantage of their strength and consumer awareness. Mars, for example, has launched an ice-cream line as well as a soft drink under the Mars brand name. Cadbury's Milk Tray brand has been extended to desserts, leveraging the brand's association with creaminess. Strong international brands often have high visibility and are prime candidates for brand extensions, especially for entry into new and emerging markets such as Eastern Europe or China. In some cases, a well-known brand name is used on a product line which is marketed under another brand name elsewhere. For example, Danone uses the Danone name to market biscuits in Eastern Europe, in order to leverage customer familiarity with the name. Similarly, Nestlé's Maggi brand, used on sauces and seasonings, had high recognition in Eastern Europe and so was extended to frozen foods rather than the Findus brand used elsewhere in Europe.

The key international brands

The growing prevalence of corporate endorsement and brand extensions, coupled with a focus on building a limited number of strong brands in international markets, has led firms to develop procedures to manage and monitor key strategic brands. A key objective is to maintain their identity and value in international markets. Two important aspects need to be considered; first, the consistency of brand positioning in different countries and across product lines, and secondly, the value and/or risks of brand extensions in international markets. Widely different approaches have been adopted for managing strategic brands in international markets and assigning custody for them. Typically these vary depending on the organizational structure of the firm and the desired degree of control, and range from having no explicit custody strategy to highly centralized tight control by corporate headquarters.

Limited or negotiated custody: Firms with strong country management, operating in product markets where brands are not important purchase cues may have no explicit custody strategy. Attention is centered around trademark issues and their infringement in different markets. In cases where product markets are becoming more integrated and there is concern to improve brand harmonization across countries, specific brand positionings may be negotiated between corporate headquarters and country managers. This approach may, however, be somewhat cumbersome where there are multiple brands to manage.

Brand champion: An approach that appears to be becoming increasingly popular is to appoint a brand champion. The brand champion is typically given responsibility for building and managing the brand worldwide. This includes monitoring the consistency of the brand positioning in international markets, as well as authorizing use of the brand on other products or other product businesses. The brand champion can either be a senior manager at corporate headquarters or a country manager or product development group. For example, a lead country or one with major market share for the brand can be given responsibility for the brand.

In examining consistency in brand positioning across countries, often there is recognition that some adjustment to local market conditions will be needed, especially for mature brands. Typically, however, it is considered desirable that the core positioning should be maintained, though execution may vary. The extent to which some deviation is permitted typically varies considerably from company to company, and from one product business to another. For example, Nike strictly controls positioning centrally while Douwe-Egbert permits substantial adaptation.

The brand custodian is also often responsible for authorizing or providing an opinion on brand extensions. An important issue with brand extensions is to avoid over-extension or stretching of the brand and dilution of its equity and image. Criteria for sanctioning brand extensions vary considerably depending largely on the firm's organizational structure, the diversity of its product lines and businesses and management philosophy. Often, however, a proposed extension has to be consistent with the core brand's positioning and reinforce or sustain the existing brand concept. For example, extension of a confectionery brand to ice-cream or dessert should emphasize the same core attributes. In many cases, proposed extensions of strategic brands are also required to have international market potential. Procedures for resolving conflicts in relation to brand extensions also vary considerably depending on custody management principles and the firm's organizational structure.

Centralized custody and brand manual

Some companies centralize control of brands within the product division. This typically occurs with relatively new products or brands, where there is greater consistency in market characteristics across countries, and limited history of strong country management. In this case, brand manuals are often used as mechanisms for ensuring consistency of brand positioning and identification across countries. The brand manual is typically developed at corporate headquarters and details the specific positioning and visual appearance of an international brand packaging, logo, etc. Country managers are normally required to stick closely to these guidelines. Brand manuals are, for example, used by Unilever's ice-cream division, by Beiersdorf for their Nivea brand and Sara Lee's tobacco division.

Managerial Implications

International markets continue to change rapidly (Craig and Douglas 1996).As markets evolve, firms need to consider how to modify their brand architecture and look for opportunities to reduce the number of brands and improve efficiency as well as to harmonize brand strategy across product lines and country markets. Focus on a limited number of strategic brands in international markets enables the firm to consolidate and strengthen its position and enhance brand power. Effective management of international brand architecture in the light of changing market conditions and the firm's market expansion, is, however, crucial to maintaining its position and strengthening key strategic brands in international markets.

Designing international brand architecture

First, management needs to design an efficient harmonious brand architecture that spans operations in different countries and product lines. This establishes the framework for decisions relating to the firm's brands in international markets. It should clearly define the importance and role of each level of branding, as, for example, at the corporate, product division or product brand level, as well as the interrelation or overlap of branding at each level. It should also determine the appropriate geographic scope for each level relative to the firm's current organizational structure.

The design of this architecture should satisfy a number of key principles:

1. **Parsimony**: The brand architecture should incorporate all of the firm's existing brands, whether developed internally or acquired. It should provide a framework for consolidation in order to reduce the number of brands and strengthen the role of individual brands. Brands that are acquired need to be melded into the existing structure, especially where these brands occupy similar market positions to those of existing brands. Equally, when the same or similar products are sold under different brand names or have different positionings in each country, ways to harmonize these should be examined.
2. **Consistency**: Another important element of brand architecture is its consistency relative to the number and diversity of products and product lines within the company. A balance needs to be struck between the extent to which brand names serve to differentiate product lines, or alternatively, establish a common identity across different products. Establishment of strong and distinctive brand images for different product lines helps to establish their separate identities and diversify risk of negative associations (for example between food and chemicals). Conversely, use of a common brand name consolidates effort and can produce synergies.
3. **Endorsement**: The value of corporate brand endorsement across different products and product lines, and at lower levels of the brand hierarchy also needs to be assessed. Use of corporate brand endorsement either as a name identifier or logo identifies the product with the company, and provides reassurance for the customer. In international markets, corporate brand endorsement acts an integrative force unifying different brand identities across national boundaries. At the same time, corporate endorsement of a highly diverse range of product lines can result in dilution of image. Equally, negative effects or associations can harm and have long-lasting effects across multiple product lines. Thus, both aspects need to be weighed in determining the role of corporate brand endorsement in brand architecture.

Managing international brand architecture

Where brand architecture includes multiple brands at different levels of the hierarchy (as opposed to a single corporate brand), management should identify the key strategic international brands, that will provide the lynchpin of the firm's global strategy. These provide the focus for building the firm's position in international markets, and the basis for international growth and expansion. The pivotal role of these brands in global markets implies that it is critical for management to set up procedures to manage them to ensure that they retain their integrity, visibility and value. This entails assigning custody for the brand and establishing procedures for sanctioning brand extensions and monitoring brand positioning.

(i) **Assigning custody:** Custody for a brand should be assigned to a senior manager within the organization, or to a key organizational unit. It is critical that the brand custodian report directly to top management and have clear authority to sanction/and or refuse brand extensions to other product lines and product businesses, so as to maintain the integrity of the brand and avoid brand dilution. This should have top priority in establishing brand management responsibilities.

(ii) **Monitoring consistency of brand usage:** Procedures or tools to monitor consistency of brand use and positioning in different countries/geographic area or by different product businesses also need to be established. Here the degree of centralization and standardization in brand positioning and use of brand identifiers such as logos, packaging, etc., will depend on the firm's strategy in international markets as well its administrative heritage and organizational structure. In general, however, the newer the business, and the more it is targeted to a specific global market segment, the more feasible it is likely to be to exercise a high degree of centralized control.

Auditing brand architecture

Brand architecture is not a static framework, but one that needs to be monitored and modified continually. The mechanisms established for brand custody help insure that an individual brand is managed in a consistent fashion across multiple countries. However, given the dynamic nature of international markets and the changing competitive realties, the structure must be reviewed, at least annually. An international brand architecture audit should be performed to insure compliance with established procedures and to determine whether the structure of the architecture should be changed. This needs to take place on two levels. First, the degree to which individual strategic brands have adhered to established guidelines needs to be assessed. Second, the entire portfolio of brands has to be examined in terms of whether the overall brand architecture requires modification.

Compliance audit: A bottoms-up audit of the individual brands allows an assessment of how well each functions as part of the overall brand architecture of the firm. The key steps of this phase are: (a) collection of information that establishes how the brand has been used in each country that it is marketed in, (b) assessment of deviations from its established position in the structure and reasons, and (c) evaluation of the brand's performance.

Deviations are particularly diagnostic. They may suggest poor management of the brand globally or, more importantly, fundamental changes in the underlying market dynamics. If the underlying market dynamics or product market structure has changed, then the brand's position in the overall architecture needs to be modified accordingly. With these preliminaries conducted, the audit should culminate in a face-to-face meeting of key participants, including the brand custodian, to establish guidelines for the coming year.

Strategic audit: The second phase is a strategic, top down audit, conducted on multiple levels. First, logical groupings of strategic brands need to be assessed in terms of their compliance with established guidelines. Once this has been accomplished, senior management needs to evaluate the overall structure of international brand architecture to determine the fit at different levels across multiple countries. Again, a key factor here is how the underlying drivers of brand architecture have changed. In addition to market dynamics and the product market structure, an important consideration is how the firm itself has evolved, particularly with respect to acquisitions or market expansion initiatives. If the end-result of the strategic audit is that the firm's brand architecture no longer fits underlying drivers, steps should be taken to revise the firm's architecture so that it reflects the new realities of the marketplace.

The central role of branding in establishing the firm's identity and building its position in the global marketplace among customers, retailers and other market participants, makes it increasingly imperative for firms to establish a clear-cut international branding strategy. A key element of success is the framing of a harmonious and consistent brand architecture across countries and product lines, defining the number of levels and brands at each level. Of particular importance is the relative emphasis placed on corporate brands as opposed to product level brands and the degree of integration across markets. Escalating media costs, increasing communication and linkages across markets, together with the internationalization of retailing, create pressures for parsimony in the number of the firm's brands and consolidation of architecture across country markets. Focus on a limited number of international strategic brands generates cost economies and potential synergies for the firm's efforts in international markets. At the same time, procedures for managing the custody of these brands have to be established. These should be clearly understood and shared throughout all level of the organization, leading to a culture/ mentality that promotes the growth of strong international brands without diluting their strength by over-use or inconsistencies.

For a brand to be global it should have minimum level of market penetration in diverse markets, dominate the domestic market so as to generate cash flow to enter new markets meet a universal consumer needs, reflect a consistent market positioning world wide and focus on the product categories.

However, in categories like information and communication technology, the leapfroggying effect plays an important role in brands going global. This is highly significant in Indian context where brands have attained leadership in global markets in a number of information technology related off –shore services.

Life cycle concept for product categories and individual brands exhibit different stages of market development in different markets that required separate branding strategies .

References

Aaker, David (1996), Building Strong Brands, New York: The Free Press.

Aaker, David and Kevin Keller (1990), "Consumer Evaluations of Brand Extensions," Journal of Marketing, 54, 1, 27-33.

Alden, Dana, Jan-Benedick E.M. Steenkamp, and Rajeev Batra (1999), "Brand Positioning Through Advertising in Asia, North America and Europe: The Role of Global Consumer Culture," Journal of Marketing, 63, 75-87.

Bartlett, Christopher A. and Sumantra Ghoshal (1989), Managing Across Borders. Boston, MA: Harvard Business School Press.

Barwise, Patrick and Thomas Robertson (1992), "Brand Portfolios," European Management Journal, 10, 3 (September), 277-285.

Caller, Linda (ed.) (1996), Researching Brands, Amsterdam: ESOMAR.

Court, David C., Anthony Freeling, Mark C. Lerter and Andrew J. Parsons (1997), "If Nike Can 'Just Do It' Why Can't We," McKinsey Quarterly, No. 3, 25-34.

Craig, C. Samuel and Susan P. Douglas (1996), "Responding to the Challenges of Global Markets: Change; Complexity, Competition and Conscience," Columbia Journal of World Business, 31, 6-18.

De Mooij, Marieke (1997), Global Marketing and Advertising, Understanding Cultural Paradoxes, Thousand Oaks, CA: Sage Publications.

Douglas, Susan P. and C. Samuel Craig (1996), "Global Portfolio Planning and Market Interconnectedness," Journal of International Marketing, 4, 93-110.

Featherstone, Mike (1990), "Global Culture: An Introduction," Global Culture: Nationalism, Globalization and Modernism, in Mike Featherstone (ed.), London: Sage Publications.

Hassan, Salah S. and Lea Katsanis (1994), "Global Market Segmentation Strategies and Trends," in Globalization of Consumer Markets: Structures and Strategies, Salah S. Hassan and Erdner Kaynak (eds.), New York: International Business Press, 47-62.

Kapferer, Jean-Noel (1997), Strategic Brand Management, second edition, London: Kogan Page.

Keller, Kevin (1998), Strategic Brand Management, New Jersey: Prentice Hall.

Laforêt, Sylvie and John Saunders (1994), "Managing Brand Portfolios: How the Leaders Do It," Journal of Advertising Research, September/October, 64-76.

Olins, W. (1989), Corporate Identity, London: Thames and Hudson.

Parsons, Andrew (1996), "Nestlé: The Visions of Local Managers," McKinsey Quarterly, no. 2, 5-29.

Schmitt, Bernd H. and Alex Simenson (1997), Marketing Aesthetics: The Strategic Management of Brands, Identity and Image. New York: The Free Press.

Aaker, David (1996), Building Strong Brands, New York: The Free Press.

Aaker, David and Kevin Keller (1990), "Consumer Evaluations of Brand Extensions," Journal of Marketing, 54, 1, 27-33.

Alden, Dana, Jan-Benedick E.M. Steenkamp, and Rajeev Batra (1999), "Brand Positioning Through Advertising in Asia, North America and Europe: The Role of Global Consumer Culture," Journal of Marketing, 63, 75-87.

Bartlett, Christopher A. and Sumantra Ghoshal (1989), Managing Across Borders. Boston, MA: Harvard Business School Press.

Barwise, Patrick and Thomas Robertson (1992), "Brand Portfolios," European Management Journal, 10, 3 (September), 277-285.

Caller, Linda (ed.) (1996), Researching Brands, Amsterdam: ESOMAR.

Court, David C., Anthony Freeling, Mark C. Lerter and Andrew J. Parsons (1997), "If Nike Can 'Just Do It' Why Can't We," McKinsey Quarterly, No. 3, 25-34.

Craig, C. Samuel and Susan P. Douglas (1996), "Responding to the Challenges of Global Markets: Change, Complexity, Competition and Conscience," Columbia Journal of World Business, 31, 6-18.

De Mooij, Marieke (1997), Global Marketing and Advertising, Understanding Cultural Paradoxes, Thousand Oaks, CA: Sage Publications.

Douglas, Susan P. and C. Samuel Craig (1996), "Global Portfolio Planning and Market Interconnectedness," Journal of International Marketing, 4, 93-110.

Featherstone, Mike (1990), "Global Culture: An Introduction," Global Culture: Nationalism, Globalization and Modernism, in Mike Featherstone (ed.), London: Sage Publications.

Hassan, Salah S. and Lea Katsanis (1994), "Global Market Segmentation Strategies and Trends," in Globalization of Consumer Markets: Structures and Strategies, Salah S. Hassan and Erdner Kaynak (eds.), New York: International Business Press, 47-62.

Kapferer, Jean-Noel (1997), Strategic Brand Management, second edition, London: Kogan Page.

Keller, Kevin (1998), Strategic Brand Management, New Jersey: Prentice Hall.

Laforêt, Sylvie and John Saunders (1994), "Managing Brand Portfolios: How the Leaders Do It," Journal of Advertising Research, September/October, 64-76.

Olins, W. (1989), Corporate Identity, London: Thames and Hudson.

Parsons, Andrew (1996), "Nestlé: The Visions of Local Managers," McKinsey Quarterly, no. 2, 5-29.

Schmitt, Bernd H. and Alex Simenson (1997), Marketing Aesthetics: The Strategic Management of Brands, Identity and Image. New York: The Free Press.

Chapter - Seven

International Marketing Research

International Marketing Research (IMR) can be defined as *market research* conducted either simultaneously or sequentially to facilitate marketing decisions in more *than one country*. The process calls for studying the various market characteristics for facilitating marketing decisions that can be taken across countries. The studies deal with tracing the various components that are responsible for the marketing the product. In simple terms, international marketing research is a study conducted to assist decision. Making more than one country market research is the function that links an organization to its markets through information collection and analysis it involves the systematic gathering, recording, and analyzing of data about problems related to marketing of goods and services.

International marketing research can be defined as research that crosses national borders and involves respondents and researchers from different countries and cultures. It may be conducted simultaneously in multiple countries or sequentially over a period of time. The major objective of International marketing Research are:-

(a) To carry out country screening and selection

(b) To evaluate a country's market potential

(c) To identify problems that would not require a country's listing for further consideration.

(d) To identify aspects of company's environment that needs further study.

(e) To evaluate the components of marketing mix for possible adoption.

(f) To facilitate in developing a strategic marketing plan.

Marketing research

Should secondary data be insufficient to meet all needs (it seldom is!!) then it may be necessary to conduct marketing research (the "search" scanning mode). There are three modes of search:

- Investigation - short term, specific data search

- Research - formally organized effort to acquire specific information
- Continuous - formally gathering longitudinal data on a continuous basis using panels of respondents

Whilst there are differences in approach, which will be discussed shortly, as in domestic research one has to be clear on the following:

(a) Objectives - why is the data being gathered, for what purpose and what are the proposed sources
(b) Development of ideas or hunches on the procedure
(c) Hypothesis development
(d) Research designs, experiments, observations, simulations, descriptive research
(e) Questionnaire design
(f) Data collection method - mail, telephone, interview, observations
(g) Sample size and selection
(h) Data collection methodology and supervision
(i) Analysis and report writing

We have already seen some of the difficulties associated with the comparability of data. There is also the problem of assessing demand. Market demand can be existing - served by existing supplies, latent -demand which would be expressed if a product was offered to customers at an acceptable price, or incipient - demand which will emerge if present trends continue. The skill is in assessing which demand type is current or about to break.

Assessing market opportunity requires a measure of both the overall size of a market and the competitive conditions in the market. In assessing existing demand it is a question of finding out a differential advantage for your product and marketing that differential. In the latent demand situation it is a question of identifying opportunity and launching products rather than competitiveness. In incipient demand situations it is a question of looking at the market and matching products to potential. This could be the case in say exotic fruit marketing to developed countries. It is on seeing the product that the market reacts.

The research process

The research process has been covered comprehensively in the text on "marketing management" in this series, and, therefore it is not necessary to repeat the detail here. However, in international marketing research the following should be borne in mind.

(a) **Basic rules:** Before beginning research ask some basic questions like what information is needed, where can it be obtained, when, why and at what cost? Start with desk research, identifying the type of overseas sources, know where to look and do not assume that the information is comparable or accurate if secondary in nature.

(b) **Primary surveys:** In carrying out primary surveys it is essential to be familiar with the process involved. Of paramount importance are the time and cost elements. It may be very desirable to obtain data to the n'th degree, but in doing so, it is all too easy to run up a large bill, especially in international research.

Attention has to be paid to:

The research design: The design can be descriptive, experimental, observational or simulation. international research is of a descriptive nature or observational. The ability to conduct simulations or experiments depends on the sophistication of the market and the research facilities available.

Questionnaire design: Whilst in domestic research, questionnaires can be "closed" or "open ended". Unless trained staff can be found, and the nuances of translation can be mastered, "closed" questionnaires are mainly the norm in international research. The form of data gathered by "closed" questionnaire is mainly of a behavioural or quantitative nature. The form of data gatherered by "open ended" research is qualitative.

Attention has to be paid to length, translation, ease of response and method of questionnaire return. The rate of return in international research is often as low as 6% as it is very difficult to give incentives to the respondent. Covering letters should be succinct and written in the language and idiom of the country of destination. Marketers can often use clever devices to increase the response rates, for example in France, a red dot on the envelope denotes an "official" letter.

Questionnaires may contain ranking and rating questions (scaled questionnaires) and these can only be used if the respondent is fully aware of what is being asked. Often, in translation, the nuances and differences of interpretation may make scaling techniques difficult to utilise.

Data collection method: Data collection can be done in a variety of ways including personal interview, mail, telephone and observation (either mechanical or human.) Each method has its own merits and demerits. Personal interview allows the building of a relationship between interviewer and interviewee, and allows the "explanation" and "showing".

This is particularly important when conducting group discussions or carrying out in depth-research rather than one to one personal interviews. The gathering of "motivational" or "qualitative" data by group discussions will depend to a large extent on the availability of trained interviewees in the researched country.

Mail methods allow a longer questionnaire with considered response, but suffers from non response and interpretive problems. The telephone is quick but expensive and in many countries getting to the respondent may be difficult due to lack of a telephone infrastructure. Observation may not be always possible due to cultural blockages. In the end, time and cost elements often dictate the method, but generally mail and personal methods are the most widely used.

Sample size and selection: Samples can either be probabilistic or non probabilistic (random and non-random). Random samples can either be simple non-random or multi-random (stratified). Non random samples include quotas, selective or judgemental methods. With probabilistic samples it is possible to be more sophisticated in the analysis by using parametric methods of analysis or project results with greater statistical reliability. With non random sampling techniques, descriptive statistics are more appropriate. In agricultural marketing, rapid rural surveys are a well used method, which are basically a mix of the two sampling techniques. In international research random sampling can be very expensive.

Another important decision is the size of sample. Again, the larger the sample size and more difficult it is to obtain (if randomly chosen) the higher the cost will be. Whilst quota sampling may be cheaper there is the possibility that bias may exist in the sample because of inaccurate prior assumptions concerning population or because the field workers select the respondents, unwittingly, in a biased way.

A quota sample is chosen by taking known characteristics of a universe and including in the sample respondents as they proportionately occur in the known universe. For example if the quota was on a male/female age basis, it is possible to stratify and select the quota as follows: -

Population 20,000													
Male 45% (9000)							*Female 55% (11000)*						
	15%	**10%**	**10%**	**15%**	**10%**	**40%**		**15%**	**10%**	**10%**	**15%**	**10%**	**40%**
Age	0-16	16-24	25-34	35-44	45-54	55+	Age	0-16	16-24	25-34	35-44	45-54	55+
Number	1350	900	900	1350	900	3600	Number	1650	1100	1100	1650	1100	4400

The sample would firstly include 45% male and 55% female. The male and female split will then be in proportion to the age groupings, according to the actual population percentages. So the final quota sample will be according to sex and age.

Suppose a seller of tractors wishes to measure a population with respect to the percentage. It wishes the sample to be accurate to within 5% points and to be 95% confident of this accuracy.

It must first consider the standard error of a percentage given by the following formula

$$SE(p) = \sqrt{\frac{(p)(q)}{n}}$$

It assumes on guessing, that the likely percentage of ownership is 30%.

Then,

$$SE(p) = 2\sqrt{\frac{(30)(71)}{n}}$$

But, (SE(p) must equal 5% (the level of accuracy required)

$$i.e.\ \ 5\% = 2\sqrt{\frac{(30)(70)}{n}}$$

$$25\% = \frac{4[(30)(70)]}{n}$$

$$n = \frac{4[(30)(70)]}{25}$$

$$\frac{8400}{25} = 336$$

The firm requires to take a sample of, say, 340 (rounding up). Generally, then, for percentages, the sample size may be calculated using:

$$n = \frac{4(p)(q)}{(SE)^2}$$

for accuracy at the 95% level.

Analytical techniques for researching international market: Besides the usual descriptive data analysis methods, there are a number of other techniques which can be used in analysing market potential. "Usual" methods include univariate methods (mean, median, mode, standard deviation), bivariate methods (regression, correlation, cross tabulations), and multi variate methods (including multiple regression, cluster analysis, multiple factor indices and multidimensional scaling).

(a) Industrial growth patterns: may give an insight into market demand. Statistics can be obtained from in country sources.

(b) Income elasticity measurements: Describe the relationship between demand for goods and changes in income. This could, for example, show what could happen to the demand for basic agricultural products, if income rises. In theory, it should decline.

(c) Regional lead-lag analysis predicts what could happen to the pattern of demand in a considered country based on the pattern of demand in a leading country. If Zimbabwe, for example, introduces a new form of tobacco drying, it is likely the other tobacco producing countries around it will do the same.

(d) When it is difficult to obtain data, resourceful ways are needed to estimate demand. One of these methods is analogy. There are two ways of using this technique, one is by cross sectional comparison, the other by time series analysis. Cross sectional analysis assumes that a factor which correlates with demand in country A could be translated to country B. Time analysis is a similar technique but adds the time dimension, very similar to the estimate of the stage in the international life cycle. One USA chemical company found that soup consumption was the only reliable index forecasting sales in Asia. There are limitations to the analysis. These include whether the two countries can really be compared, whether technical or social developments have led to a leapfrogging of the product under consideration, and whether the difference between potential and actual demand (which could depend on other factors like price, adaptability etc.) may subsume analogy.

(e) Comparative analysis: Comparative analysis, say between countries on intracompany, intercompany, national - subnational markets can be useful for estimating potential demand. It is not unreasonable, say, to compare Zambia and Tanzania.

(f) Cluster analysis: Computer packages exist to cluster similarities and differences between countries which may show factors which could be common and therefore potential markets. Such packages include multidimensional or clustering techniques.

(g) Multiple Factor Indices: MFIs indirectly measure potential demand, using variables that either intuition or statistical analysis suggest can be closely correlated with the potential demand for the product under review. Variables should be restricted to those which relate to product demand and these may be GNP, net national income or total population. In assessing the demand for coffee appliances, for example, an index which includes coffee drinkers and type of coffee consumed would be useful.

(h) Regression analysis: A very useful and powerful tool. The procedure selects the independent variable that accounts for the most variance in the dependent variable, then the variable that accounts for the remaining variance etc. Often multiple regression is needed as a single variable will not do. Predictions are often made on market demand for products based on what would happen if GNP were increased. As seen earlier, an increase in GNP could be good for luxury or durable goods but not basic commodities. However, high GNP per capita, may be a good predictor of, say, exotic high value horticultural produce, out of season produce or technological advanced agricultural machinery.

Different from Domestic Marketing

The process of international marketing research though involves the same disciplines as domestic research, has some differences compared to its domestic version.

The major differences are • The national differences between countries arising out of political, legal, economic,

social and cultural differences and, • The comparability of research results due to these differences.

National Differences

The main factors that affect the way in which people from different cultures behave are:

(a) ***Cultural Differences:*** Culture refers to widely shared norms or patterns of behavior of a large group of people. It is defined as the values, attitudes, beliefs, artifacts and other meaningful symbols represented in the pattern of life adopted by people that help them interpret, evaluate and communicate as members of society. The need for greater cross cultural awareness is heightened in our global economies. Cross cultural differences in matters such as language, etiquette, non-verbal communication, norms and values can lead to cross cultural blunders.the following marketing mix:

(i) ***Product***: A soft drink was introduced into Arab countries with an attractive label that had six-pointed stars on it. The Arabs interpreted this as pro-Israeli and refused to buy it. Another label was printed in ten languages, one of which was in Hebrewagain the Arabs did not buy it .

(ii) ***Price***: An American firm was trying to get an acceptable price for their product from a Japanese buyer. The Americans presented a very detailed presentation and offered what they felt was a reasonable price. After a few moments of silence, the Americans thought the Japanese were going to reject the offer so they lowered the price. There was more silence by the Japanese. The

Americans then said they would lower their price one last time and that this was the lowest they could go. The Japanese accepted this offer after a brief silence. The Japanese later said the first price was within an acceptable range, but it was their custom to consider the proposal *silently* before giving their decision. The Americans lost a lot of profit by jumping the gun and believing that Japanese respond just like the Americans do.

***(iii) Promotion*:** When Pepsico advertised Pepsi in Taiwan with the ad "Come Alive With Pepsi" they had no idea that it would be translated into Chinese as "Pepsi brings your ancestors back from the dead."

(b) ***Racial Differences*:** This would refer to the differences in physical features of people in different countries. For example, the types of hair care and cosmetic products needed in U.S would differ from those needed in South East Asia.

(c) ***Climatic Differences*:** This would include the meteorological conditions like degree of rain and temperature range in the targeted foreign market. For instance, Bosch- iemens had to alter their washing machines with a minimum spin cycle of 1,000 rpm and a maximum of 1,600 rpm in Scandinavia, owing to irregular sunshine. In Italy and Spain, on the other hand, it is sufficient to have a spin cycle of 500 rpm as there is abundant sunshine (Stevens & Davis, 1997).

(d) ***Economic Differences*:** The level of economic development in a market can affect the desired properties of a product and in this way can inspire a company to adapt its products in order to meet the needs of the local market. The level of economic progress in a market can be assessed by a series of indications:

The level of revenue and buying power of local consumers: This will have an influence on the technical conception and marketing of exported products. In richer countries where the state of economic progress is more advanced, consumers generally having a higher purchasing power and tend to prefer purchase of more sophisticated products with advanced functions, while people in poorer markets would be interested in a simplified version of the product.*the state of infrastructure in the market*: The general level of the quality of infrastructure in the country consisting of elements such as transport, energy communication systems, etc. can affect how the product is constituted as it can bring about different conditions of use. For instance when car manufacturer Suzuki entered India, it had to reinforce the suspension or the "road clearance level" of the cars as the state of the roads were poor.

(e) ***Religious Differences***: Religion has many impacts on products, more particularly on the ingredients, that constitute them. For example, in Islamic countries, companies, exporting grocery products based on beef have to furnish a certificate declaring that the animals have been slaughtered respecting "Halal" methods. Alcoholic drinks are equally banned in Middle Eastern countries. Religious restrictions can therefore require product adaptation.

(f) ***Historical Differences*****:** Historical differences help explain facts such as the playing of cricket in England, as opposed to game of boules in France. These differences have slowly evolved over time but have a profound effect on consumer behavior. For example, drinking Scotch whiskey is considered prestigious and trendy in Italy, but old-fashioned and almost boring in Scotland.

(g) ***Language Differences*****:** Language is an important aspect of international marketing research. Inappropriate use of language could result in loss of market apart from turning out to be a cross cultural gaffe. For instance, U.S. and British negotiators found themselves at a standstill when the American company proposed that they "table" particular key points. In the U.S. "Tabling a motion" means to not discuss it, while the same phrase in Great Britain means to "bring it to the table for discussion." (Ricks, 1999).

(h) ***Differences in Actual and Potential Target Groups*****:** In countries like England and Germany it is possible to do national samples. Small towns and villages can be included because distances are not great. In Spain, interviews can be conducted only in cities with populations of over 100,000 people, as the cost of interviewing people in small towns and villages is prohibitively high . In addition, the international marketing researcher may also have to deal with other factors such as differences in the way that products or services are used, differences in the criteria for assessing products or services across various markets and differences in market research facilities and capabilities.

Process of International marketing Research

It is a planned, systematic, and comprehensive approach to carry out international market research. As shown in fig 7.1, it involves problem identification, research methodology decision, identification of data sources, collection and compilation of primary and secondary information, and analyzing and interpretation of data.

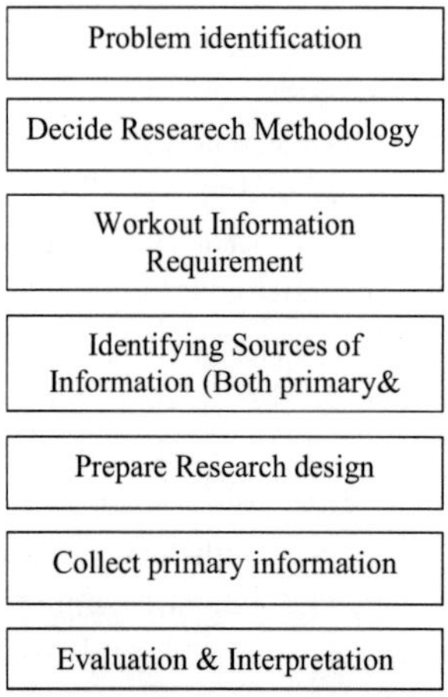

9.1 Process of International marketing Research

Problem of identification

It is the first of the international marketing research process and is very crucial. It has to be as precise as possible. It may include one of the following:-

(a) Whether to remain in domestic market or enter into international markets.
(b) Product identification for international markets
(c) Deciding international market entry
(d) Deciding upon mode of entry into international markets
(e) Decision related to international marketing mix
(f) Decision for implementing and controlling the strategic international marketing.

however, the problem identification in international markets is influenced by marketer's self reference criteria. Which is an unconscious reference to one's own culture values.

Deciding research Methodology

Different marketing decisions require different kind of marketing research likes Marketing mix Decision:- Product Policy, Pricing distribution, Distribution, Ads, Ads post –testing, sales force, sales promotion .

Working out information Requirement

Once the problem is identified and the methodology is decided for the market research detailed information requirement needed to be worked out. It helps in identifying information sources and compilation. The basic information requirements for international marketing research are as follows:

(a) decision regarding whether to operate in domestic market or enter international markets.

- Analysing basic trade statistics related to the firm's products
- Assessment of international market demand
- Competitiveness of the firm's product in domestic and international market.

(b) Estimating market size

- Total sales in the market last three year growth rate as well as the projected sales growth.
- Total imports of the product into the country last three year growth rate as well as the projected rate of growth (both in value and volume terms)
- Sources of import by country, shares of each country change in shares in last three years(Special focus on whether and how much import from India).
- Domestic production last three year growth rate as well as the projected production growth.
- Balance of payment- Last three year

(c) Assessing market assess-

- Import policies- control mechanisms
- Import licencing- band, restricted open
- Tariff regim: ad valorem, specific,mixed-MFN, Preferential, tariff quata
- Basis for duty valuation
- Exchange rate,convertible, non convertible
- Foreign exchange control, foreign exhange authorizes

(d) Market selection- privatization international market on the basis of market size

- tariff barieer
- non tariff barrier
- Political risk and relationship with India

(e) Internation marketing mix decision- competition analysis

- consumer behaviour
- Pricing strategy and exchange rate
- Marketing channel
- Promotional and advertising decision

(f) Decision for implementing and controlling the strategic international marketing plan
- turn over and profit analysis
- market share and profit growth analysis
- analysis of marketing expenses

Identifying sources of information

Secondary information play important role in international market research. Since carrying out oversease field surveys involves considerable cost and time,the secondary information results into a considierable saving in cost and time,. Besides there may be situation when conducting field survey is either difficult or infeasible due to the resource constraints of a firm. A researcher in such a case ,has to heavily rely upon secondary data.at times the secondary data related to market estimation,competitors turn over, an profit etc., may be more reliable than the date collected through independent market research.

Limitation of secondary data

Avilability- This type of secondary data may not always be available in international markets.Generally, availability of detaied secondary data is directly proportionl to the state of market development in a particular country.for example in countries like japan, Uk,Singapore,and some of the European countries comprehensive data are available on wholesellers,retailers, manufacturers and traders, which is hardly available in many developing and less develop countries, however, the general data on demographic profile compile by national governments and the UN organization are readily available.

Comparability:- data collected from secondary sources by various agency across the country may not be comparable due to a different methodology used for data collection in each country.for ex- there is a wide variation in trade statistics collected by various agencies such as by the directrate general

Secondary Data Collection

Issues in international research problem formulation:

- A major problem is the unfamiliarity with the foreign environment - lack of familiarity may lead to false assumptions, poorly-defined research problems, and, ultimately misleading conclusions about the foreign market
- To reduce part of the uncertainty, some exploratory research at the early stage of the research process is often fruitful
- A useful vehicle for such preliminary research is an omnibus survey - conducted by research agencies at regular intervals

Framework for international marketing research:

Determine research design:

Exploratory (informal, unstructured) - *to gain background information, to define terms, to clarify problems & hypothesis and to establish research priorities.*

- secondary data
- experience survey
- case analysis
- focus groups
- projecting techniques (asking participants to act in controlled/ simulated conditions)

Descriptive research - *to describe and measure marketing phenomena at a point in time.*

- provides answers to questions such as;
  – who customer, competitor
  – what product, brand, design, size
  – where places of purchase, wholesale
  – when time & frequency of purchase
- one point in time - *cross-sectional surveys, sample surveys.*
- longitudinal - *repeat measurements on the same sample over a period of time.*

Causal research - *to determine causality, to make "if then" statement.*

Identify alternative information sources:

– internet
– international publications
– country research reports
– trade / production statistics
– trade / diplomatic offices
– local chamber of commerce

Secondary data information sources

Secondary data may be readily available and may also be cheaper than primary research. International marketers, however, need to very carefully evaluate the relevance, objectiveness and timeliness of the secondary data. Following aspects about the secondary data need to be evaluated for use in any international marketing research;

Secondary data

- *what was the purpose of study?*

- *who collected the information?*
- *what information was collected?*
- *how was the information obtained?*
- *how consistent is the information with other information?*

Data quality

- *timeliness, accuracy, relevance*

Issues with secondary research

- Accuracy of data may vary due to variation in definitions of various variables
- Quality and reliability of information may also be compromised by the mechanisms that were used to collect them
- International trade statistics do not cover cross-border & undocumented activities
- Comparability of data across countries is constrained as different resources on a given item produce contradictory information
- One way to reconcile these differences is to triangulate - obtain information on the same item from at least three different sources and speculate on possible reasons behind these differences
- Comparability of data may also be hindered by the lack of functional or conceptual equivalence - functional equivalence refers to the degree to which similar activities or products in different countries fulfill similar functions - conceptual equivalence reflects the degree to which a given concept has the same meaning in different environments
- Finally, in many developing nations, secondary data are very scarce. Information on retail and Primary Data Collection

Primary data:

- **Data collection**
  - sample must be representative of the population
  - questions must be appropriate to various cultural and social backgrounds of the respondents
  - data collection process must be feasible in every international market
- **Execution**
  - controls need to be decided and implemented so that the data collection may be correctly implemented
  - cross-check information from various sources for relevance & accuracy

Issues with primary global research:

- Sampling problems arise out of biased respondents, difficulties in reaching to the respondents, nonavailability of accurate telephone and street directories
- Different languages and cultural variations cause translation and meaning problems
- Even if the interviewee is successfully reached, there is no guarantee that he or she will cooperate and furnish the desired information. There are also different reasons for nonresponse - may be due to culture, govt. control, attitude towards privacy, inexperienced researcher etc.
- A focus group is a loosely structured free-flowing discussion among a small group of target customers facilitated by a professional moderator - moderators need to be culturally sensitive and familiar with the local language and social interaction patterns
- Questionnaires need to fulfill the criteria of conceptual, functional, translation and scalar equivalence
- Two procedures often used in practice to avoid sloppy translations are back-translation and paralleltranslation
- Sampling plan has added complexity in international research - there may be absence of sampling frames and various cultural hurdles - desired sample sizes and criteria of target population also varies
- Viable contact methods also vary due to prevailing cultural norms in different countries
- Collection of information is affected by courtesy, social desirability and other biases

Analysis, interpretation & report presentation

Marketers / researchers should ensure that the following aspects are addressed in the research analysis report;

- data source must be identified
- data projection must be explained
- identify those interviewed
- highlight alternative courses of action
- for translation of questionnaires and the international marketing research analysis report the following should be observed;
    - equivalence of language
    - method of translation *(different cultural & linguistic backgrounds lead to different ways of perceiving the world)*
    - measurement & instrumentation

Problems in international marketing research

- **Problems of numerous markets:**
  - definition error caused by the way problem is defined
  - instrument error which arises from questionnaire and the interviewer
  - frame error - occurs when sampling frames are available from different sources in different countries – selection error which results from the way actual sample is selected from the frames
  - non-response error - which results when different cultural patterns of non-response are obtained
- **Problems with data:**
  - secondary data - comparing several markets
  - primary data
- language
- social organization
- obtaining responses
- infrastructure constraints
- convergence / divergence of consumer behavior across cultures

  (source; International Trade centre,export market research)

Research techniques for analyzing international data

- **Demand Pattern Analysis**
  - Industrial growth patterns provide an insight into market demand. Because they generally reveal consumption patterns, production patterns and are helpful in assessing market opportunities. Additionally, trends in manufacturing production indicate potential markets for companies that supply manufacturing inputs. At the early stages of growth in a country, when per capita incomes are low, manufacturing centers on such necessities as food and beverages, textiles, and other forms of light industry. As incomes rise, the relative importance of these industries declines as heavy industry begins to develop. Countries at different levels of per capita income, thus, have diverse patterns of consumption & production. Such data can be gathered on macro levels for most countries. This simple technique, known as multiple-factor index approach, allows insights into consumption-production profiles of many countries. Though relatively crude, it gives a clue both to a country's present position and the direction it is going. This in turn helps the firm identify possibilities for export or local production in that market.

- **Multiple-Factor Indexes**
  - A multiple-factor index measures market potential indirectly, using as proxies a number of variables that intuition or statistical analysis reveal to be closely correlated with the potential for the product in question. A model for forecasting the demand for television sets in international markets could be a function of the market size for TV and consumer's capacity to by TV. Market size can be indicated by the proxy variables of number of households, percent of literacy, percent of urbanization etc. Capacity to buy can be indicated by per capita income, index of standard of living, price per unit, and price per unit relative to per capita income etc.
- **Income Elasticity Measurements**
  - Income elasticity describes the relationship between demand for a good and changes in income. Studies have shown that basic necessities such as food and clothing are characterized by inelastic demand. Stated differently, expenditures on products in these categories increase but at a slower percentage rate than do increase in income. Demand for durable consumer goods such a furniture and appliances tends to be income elastic, increasing relatively faster than increase in incomes.
- **Market Estimation by Analogy**
  - For countries with limited data, estimating market potential can be a precarious exercise. Given the absence of hard data, one technique - estimation by analogy - can be useful in getting better feel for market potential in such countries. This estimation is done in two ways:
  - **The cross-section comparison approach** involves taking the known market size of a product in one country and relating it to some economic indication, such as disposable personal income, to derive a ratio. This ratio (of product consumption to disposable personal income in above illustration) is then applied to another country where disposable personal income is known in order to derive the market potential for the product in that country.
  - **The time-series approach** estimates the demand in the second country by assuming that it has the same level of consumption that the first country had at the same level of development (or per capita income) at a different point in time.
- **Comparative Analysis**
  - One of the unique opportunities in global marketing analysis is to conduct comparisons of market potential and market performance in different country markets at the same point in

time. – Gap analysis analyzes the difference "gap" between estimated total market potential and a company's sales. The gap can be divided into four categories: *Usage gap, Competitive gap, Product-line gap, Distribution gap*

- **Cluster Analysis**
  - The objective of cluster analysis is to group variables into clusters that maximize within-group similarities and between-group differences. Cluster analysis using macroeconomic and consumption data is a favored technique for identifying similar markets. The goal here is to ensure that the countries with the greatest potential make it to the short list for further investigation.
  - Countries can also be clustered based on product diffusion patterns - the rate at which new products are adopted in a market. If such segments can be derived, managers could use information from the **lead market**, about variables such as growth in market size, when sales reach a peak, to make inferences on the same variables for **lagging markets**.

Comparability of Tasks

The concept of comparability refers to the problem faced by a researcher in comparing the results and interpreting the implications when dealing with two or more countries, is referred to as the comparability of tasks. This is absolutely essential to any research that has been set up to provide as basis for an international marketing decision. As firms push the geographic frontiers of their operations to take advantage of growing opportunities, they need to collect information from a broader and more diverse range of markets. Increasingly, this entails conducting research in unfamiliar and distant markets in the Far East, the Middle East, Latin America and Africa. This in turn poses a number of challenges, not only in collecting accurate and reliable information on behavior patterns in an expeditious and cost-effective fashion, but also in predicting response to new and unfamiliar stimuli, and interpreting the implications thereof for marketing strategy.

About the IMR Industry

For many years, estimates have been provided of the size of national research markets. These estimates have been based on data collected by national market research trade associations and national research societies, along with the work of a few individuals and earlier ESOMAR studies. It has been estimated that in terms of research expenditure, the top three countries are the United States, the United Kingdom and Germany (Kobayashi & Draper, 1990). Research in Europe is primarily conducted in Germany, the United Kingdom, France, Italy and Spain (Demby, 1990). The top 25 global research organizations earned $11.6 billion in revenue in 2003, up by 1.4 percent over

2002 (Table 30.2). Of the top 25 global firms, 12 are based in the United States and 67.3 percent of the revenue came from international operations Honomichl, 2004). The worldwide marketing and opinion research industry now accounts for about $17 billion of revenue and employs more than 650,000 people. About 1000 top clients' countries are accountable for about 80% of the global turnover; 65% of their MR budgets goes to 25 research providers.

Internationalization of Business Operations

More companies are taking to operations on a global or regional scale than a national scale. The complexity and sophistication of the operations changes as the company steps into international markets. The guidelines to these issues can be found in the EPRG framework (Wind, Douglas, & Perlmutter, 1973). This framework identifies four types of orientations towards internationalization as the company expands into international markets. They are:

(a) Ethnocentrism – orientation towards home country
(b) Polycentrism – orientation towards host country
(c) Regiocentrism – regional orientation and,
(d) Geocentrism – world orientation

These attitudes reflect the goals and philosophies of the company and help in developing management strategies and planning procedures with regard to its international operations.In the ethnocentric stage, the top management views domestic techniques and personnel as superior to foreign and as the most effective in overseas markets.

The company sees its domestic business as its priority and views foreign sales as a profitable extension of its domestic sales. A company with this domestic market extension concept typically identifies markets where demand is similar to the home market and where its domestic product will be acceptable. Meter-Man Inc. could be said to follow this orientation. A polycentric attitude emerges once the company begins to recognize the importance of the inherent differences in offshore markets. A company guided by this concept is of the view that country markets are vastly different and that, market requires an almost independent program for each country. The company also believes in using local personnel and techniques to suit the local market conditions. The company with such a multi-domestic market concept adapts its products without coordination with other country markets; its advertising campaigns, pricing and distribution decisions being localized. Fedder, according to its plans, fits this orientation. In the regiocentric and geocentric stages, the company recognizes the regional commonalities and undertakes regional strategies by considering the region or the entire world as a potential market, ignoring national boundaries. The firm develops policies and organizes activities on a regional or worldwide basis. Firms using this global marketing concept design product lines, pricing decisions, promotions and the channels of distribution for regional or worldwide markets. Coca-Cola, Ford Motor Company, General Motors and several other companies follow this orientation and can be described as global companies.

Specialists or Generalists

A company can be a global company if it achieves efficiencies of scale by developing a standardized product of dependable quality, and sells it in the global market at a reasonable price throughout the world. The global marketing concept is about viewing an entire set of country markets as one unit, identifying groups of prospective buyers and developing a marketing plan through cost standardization.When evaluating foreign markets, several other factors need to be considered for standardizing the products across markets. These factors can be grouped into foreign uncontrollables which includes economics forces, cultural issues, political/legal forces and level of technology among others. So, while the marketing plan can be standardized, a researcher will have to take into consideration the uncontrollable factors that will have an effect on business in the respective foreign market. This process of considering theuncontrollable factors particular to a market into the overall marketing plan is known as the specialist approach in international marketing research. While the generalists consider the world markets as a whole, specialists take in all the country and region specific factors that would govern the marketability of the product in those markets. The effect of uncontrollables on a product can be seen in the case of Nike. The logo on a new line of shoes represented flames or heat rising off a blacktop.Unfortunately, the logo inadvertently resembled the Arabic script for the word “Allah”,the Arabic word for God. After receiving complaints from Muslim leaders regarding the use of this word on the shoes, Nike recalled the offending shoes (Associated Press, 1997). This case shows how easy it is to offend when the uncontrollables are not properly accounted for, as in the case of religion as explained here. Hence global research calls for specialists and not generalists, since it is important to address the country specific issues in the marketing process while researching new markets.

Centralized vs. Decentralized Research

Centralized research is done when the researcher conducts research in two or more countries from the headquarters. Centralization of the project can add to the complexity of problems with hierarchy and authority since such a study can involve staff at the headquarters, staff at foreign offices of the company, foreign survey conductors and possibly an overall survey coordinator. This can result in dispute, delay and inefficiency. Decentralized research is done when the researcher has the company office in each country conduct the research based on the guidelines from the headquarters. In a decentralized research, the researcher in the foreign country should be able to conduct research in the language specified by the headquarters or should be able to translate the information gathered correctly into the language at the headquarters. Consider the example of Parker Pens. They had a decentralized marketing department with ad agencies in more than 40 countries developing ads for them. A new team of executives were hired and all their marketing decisions were centralized in the company's headquarters in Janesville, Wisconsin. They wanted to standardize the promotion, packaging, pricing, promotional materials, and advertising. They believed the difference in the cultures were less important than the similarities. They wanted to use one ad agency to develop one ad to be used around the world. Subsidiaries complained that the pens may be similar, but the markets were not. When the same ad was used in all countries, the ads tried to say something to everyone but ended up saying nothing to anyone. The company's campaign floundered following which the CEO was forced to resign and the rest of the team either quit or were fired. The company then returned to a decentralized marketing system. Thus, from the above example it is clear that due to a centralized research approach, Parker Pens ended up with a centralized marketing strategy overlooking crosscultural values and norms. This marketing research blunder could have been avoided had there been a decentralized research which would have recognized the various country specific issues that determined the way of functioning of each market.

Research Across Countries

International Marketing Research includes a range from Single country research to the more elaborate Multi-country research. A brief description of each mode is discussed below.

Single-country Research

This type of research is done when there arises a need for organizations to conduct research in a single foreign country market. Typically, this need arises when a researcher based in country A wants to know whether the marketing strategies that work well in its domestic environment can be translated to a country market B. The single country research is useful in bringing out the unique characteristics of the foreign market that would require adapting the product to serve the needs of the local consumers better.

Multi-country Research

Multi-country research, as the name indicates, involves research conducted in more than one country market. Multi-country research can be further classified into three broad categories:

(a) Independent Multi-country Research: This is perhaps, the most common form of international marketing research that can be seen in the industry today. Independent multi-country research studies occur when subsidiaries of the companies independently conduct research on the same products in a number of countries. Examples of this type of research are brand awareness/perception of international products or test marketing of new products. The major disadvantages of this type of research are that it often leads to duplication of effort (such as questionnaires, etc.) and since such studies are conducted in isolation, comparisons of results across countries are made difficult.

(b) Sequential Multi-country Research: Sequential Multi-country Research is a way to research a range of geographical markets. It is attractive as the lessons can be learned in the first one or two markets to be researched and then can be applied to the other countries subsequently involved in the research program. The sequential approach is typically used when a product or service is the subject of rolling launch across countries.

(c) Simultaneous Multi-country Research: This type of research involves conducting marketing research in multiple country markets simultaneously, and is, perhaps, the 'purest' form of international marketing research. It is a test for the researcher capabilities and also creates in its most acute form, the question of comparability.

Cross Cultural Response Bias

Cross-cultural researchers conducting studies across different cultural groups need to consider whether the scores obtained are comparable. In order to achieve meaningful cross-cultural comparisons, the issues of equivalence and response bias has to be addressed. Response bias is the systematic tendency to distort responses to rating scales so that observed scores are unrelated to the true score of the individual by either selecting extreme or modest answers (extreme or modesty response bias) or a shifting of responses to either end of the scale (acquiescence response bias) (Byrne & Campbell, 1999; Cheung & Rensvold, 2000). The cultural tendencies belonging to different cultural groups, are likely to change the responses of participants and make them incomparable across cultural groups and therefore resulting in a bias (Fischer, 2004). Hofstede (1980) was among the first to advocate the use of standardization as an adjustment of raw scores in cross-cultural research to correct for such response tendencies.Techniques such as Structural Equation Modeling (Cheung & Rensvold, 2000; Little, 1997, 2000) and Item Response Theory (Butcher, Lim, & Nezami, 1998; Huang,Church, & Katigbak, 1997) can be used to identify whether different response strategies were used by participants in different samples. Researchers can then decide whether they want to standardize their data or not. There are four major groups of standardization procedures. These four groups are:-

(a) adjustment of means,

(b) adjustment for dispersion (e.g., using standard deviation),

(c) adjustments using means and dispersions, and

(d) covariate analysis. These groups can be classified into within-subject, within-group, and within-culture categories, based on the statistical information they use for standardization.

The within-subject standardization procedure refers to the adjustments of scores for each individual using the mean for that individual across all variables (Hofstede,1980). The average of a subset or all variables for that particular individual is subtracted from each individual's raw score. Hence, the resulting score is the relative position of the individual on a variable in relation to the other scores. The mean across variables for this individual will average to zero. This procedure is also called Ipsatization (Hicks, 1970).The within-subject standardization procedure has several variants. The most common form is the computation of *z* scores whereby the group mean is subtracted from the variable raw score and then divided by the standard deviation (Howell, 1997). Hence,the resulting score is the relative position of one specific individual on one variable relative to the position of other individuals in that group.

The mean across individuals is zero and, assuming a normal distribution of responses, the resulting standard deviation will be 1. An adjustment procedure, commonly referred to as Centering (Aiken &West, 1991) is also available wherein, only the mean across individuals is used.In the within-culture standardization (Bond, 1988; Leung & Bond, 1989), instead of using the group mean across one item (as done in *z* transformation), the mean across all items and all individuals (the grand mean) is used. It is possible to adjust this deviation score by dividing it by the standard deviation across items and individuals.A combination of within-subject and within-culture, called Double Standardization can also be used (Leung & Bond, 1989). Initially, the scores are adjusted within the individual (within-subject standardization), and then the resulting scores are adjusted within the group (within-culture standardization). Thus, the means for each individual across variables and the mean for each variable across individuals will be zero.Assuming normality of the raw data, the adjustment using the standard deviation should yield standard deviations of 1 for both individuals across variables and variables across individuals.

It is important to note that these standard procedures can be done both at item level and at construct level. One may standardize individual items using the relevant mean across either items or individuals or one may standardize the mean for one specific construct using the relevant mean across either items, constructs, or individuals.

Idiosyncrasies of Collecting Data in International Settings

Personal Interviews tend to be the dominant mode of data collection outside the United States and Canada (Monk, 1987). Lower wage costs imply that personal procedures are cheaper than in the United States. In Latin countries, and particularly in the Middle East, interviewers are regarded with considerable suspicion. In Latin countries, where tax evasion is more prevalent, interviewers are often suspected of being tax inspectors. In the Middle East, where interviewers are invariably male, interviews with housewives often have to be conducted in the evenings when husbands are at home.

Mall Intercept Surveys are very popular in the United States and Canada, though not commonly used either in the European countries or in developing countries.

Telephone Interviews are not as advantageous in international marketing research as low levels of telephone ownership and poor communications in certain countries limit the coverage provided by telephone surveys. In countries such as India, which is predominantly rural, the telephone penetration is only 1 percent, and hence telephone surveys may not be the ideal method to adopt Sopariwala, 1987).Even in relatively affluent societies such as Great Britain, telephone penetration is only 80 percent, and telephone interviewing is not widely used because many practitioners are still skeptical about it. In Britain and France, there are substantial declines in telephone response rates in large cities. The Eastern European countries and countries in the newly formed Commonwealth of Independent States have a poor telecommunication system. In such countries, conducting telephone surveys may not be a good idea. However, with the decline of international telephone costs, multi-country studies can be conducted from a single location. This significantly reduces the time and costs associated with negotiating and organizing a research project in each country, establishing quality controls, and so on. Although the additional costs of making international telephone calls are incurred, these may not be highly significant when a centralized location is used. International calls also obtain a higher response rate. Results obtained using this technique has been found to be highly stable. Interviewer and client control is considerably greater.

Mail Surveys in international settings can have limitations because of the absence of mailing lists, poor mail services, and high levels of illiteracy. For example, mail surveys are ineffective in countries such as Brazil, where it has been reckoned that 30 % of the domestic mail is never delivered; or Nicaragua, where all the mail has to be delivered to the post office. Even in countries where literacy levels and mail services make the use of mail surveys feasible, a tendency to regard surveys as an invasion of privacy may limit their effectiveness. Thus, while mail surveys may be used effectively in industrial marketing research, in consumer research they may be appropriate only in industrialized countries where levels of literacy are high and mailing lists are generally available.

Focus Groups in the international setting, can be effective as long as it is realized that it is important for the moderators to be conversant with the language and also the patterns of social interaction and the nonverbal cues used by people in that part of the world.

The Need to Adjust for Cultural Effects

Companies with a worldwide presence must conduct research across all their global markets, present a combined corporate view, and contrast these markets to identify hot spots for special initiatives or new ventures. They need methods to minimize cultural effects and adjust results to differentiate response pattern differences due to language or cultural norms affecting surveys from real differences in performance or perceptions due to products, services, or market conditions. Hence, it becomes essential on the part of the researchers to address cross-culture calibration of measurements. In this context, harmonizing languages as part of questionnaire design and implementing the challenges that data collection poses, poses a challenge to the researchers (Devlin & Nicholas, 2004). So how does one get good translations? Though there are online translation resources available, it may not be sufficient considering the cultural, regional and language disparities within the foreign market. It is always advisable to take professional help as it is critical to relate to the native speakers and the online resources may not be adequate in that regard. To illustrate the need for a professional help, here is an example of how incorrect translation would lead to a product failure. A U.S. toothpaste manufacturer promised its customers that they would be more "interesting" if they used the firm's toothpaste. What the advertising coordinators did not realize, however, was that in Latin American Countries "interesting" is another euphemism for "pregnant". To find a trustworthy and reliable translation service would be the next step. In the age of electronic communications, the researcher need not be limited to a local search. Translations can be easily delivered by e-mail, and under most circumstances, the project details can be discussed over phone. However for other logistical reasons, the researcher may find it more convenient to work with a provider in the home country.

The following factors may be considered while appointing a translation service:

(a) *Native Speakers*: It is important to find out if the provider works with translators who are native speakers of the languages. This is so because only native speakers have a perfect feel for their language.

Working with native speakers will ensure that the translations sound natural to the audiences of various countries, and not like a translation from a foreigner. For example, a blonde woman is called a rubia by Cubans, a güera by Mexicans and a mona by Colombians.

(b) *Specialist Knowledge*: It may not be enough to just speak the language. The people who translate the material must know the industry and the market in particular.

(c) *Location*: The best translators are those who work from their native countries. As they are up-to-date with current developments and changes in the languages, it would be very helpful as the translations will be linguistically and culturally appropriate.

(d) *File Formats*: To avoid extra work and costs, the researcher can choose a translation firm that can work with the same file formats as the researcher would use. Once the translation provider has been decided upon, the researcher can work together with them closely in order to maximize the quality of the translations. While the researcher must allow sufficient time for the translation, it should also be made sure that the source material is written well. Providing as much background material as possible would help the translators understand the product-specific needs and hence result in a much closer translation.

The Biases in Qualitative Methods

Much empirical research involves comparison of two or more groups and the determination of differences between these groups with regard to a single factor of interest. The results of a study undergo statistical analysis based on the assumption that the groups are representative of the defined population and that the measurements taken on the sample were true reflections on what the researcher was actually trying to measure. open to bias from many sources, including errors in statistical analysis. Most errors related to statistical analysis relate to failure to use appropriate statistical methods. Some examples would be failure to distinguish between independent and dependent observations, failure to adjust for confounding variables, or failure to appreciate the assumptions of normality and equality of variance underlying parametric significance tests. Avoiding biases in international marketing research requires a lot of effort from the researcher. The first step would be to try and understand the research problem from the perspective of the foreign country. This is easier said than done because the root of the problem may be the researcher's lack of sensitivity and understanding to such cultural nuances. A feasible alternative would be to include researchers from different cultural backgrounds in the research team so that the team as a whole can consider all of the different facets of the research problem. At every stage of the research process, the researcher who is familiar with the specific culture takes the lead in conducting the study and the results are then compared across countries.As with quantitative research, much of the potential for bias can be minimized through rigorous study design and the employment of various techniques. These include recognition by researchers that observers are also research instruments; "disciplined subjectivity"; explicit incorporation of the subjective aspects of interaction between researcher and participant into the study design; and 'triangulation', whereby information obtained is considered tentative until corroboration by information collected by other means.

Design Scales in Cross-National Research

Douglas & Craig (1983) suggest that designing scales for international marketing research calls for a great deal of adaptation on the researcher's part. It has to be decided whether a single scale can be used in all of the countries or whether it should be customized to suit each country. Americans use a five-point or seven-point scale; however, people in countries such as France, are familiar with a 20-point scale.

Semantics play an important role in the accuracy with which a scale measures any given attribute. Some cultures tend to overstate their feelings, while many others are modest. The word 'excellent' may connote different levels of perfection to Japanese and Italians. The scales used in domestic marketing will not be helpful to the researcher in analyzing the international market. This may be due to low educational or literacy levels and cultural biases that exist in various markets.It has been observed that verbal rating scales work the best in international context. All respondents are accustomed to verbally express their feelings, irrespective of the country or the culture to which they belong. There could, however, be a problem with these scales. In some countries, 1 would be rated as the best while in other countries it would be the least preferred choice. The researcher should clarify this before asking respondents to rate attributes. Research has been conducted to find out whether there is a pan-cultural scale. The semantic differential scale seems to be the closest to being a true pan-cultural scale. It consistently gives similar results in terms of concepts or dimensions that are used to evaluate stimuli, and also accounts for a major portion of the variation in response when it is administered in different countries. An alternative approach that has been attempted is to apply techniques that use a base referent, a self-defined cultural norm. This type of approach is likely to be useful in evaluating attitudinal positions where evidence exists to suggest that these are defined by the dominant cultural norm.

The Equivalence Issues in Primary Data Collection

When crossing cultural borders, the very meaning of a scale may change and classical quality indicators such as reliability and validity may be strongly influenced by cultural factors. Consequently, international marketing research calls for appropriate equivalence and comparability checks. It is important for the researcher to be able to compare data across countries and hence, it is essential to examine the various aspects of data collection process and establish their equivalence. This is illustrated by the following example of a survey conducted in Europe (Min-Han et al., 1994). While initial data suggested that the percentage of Belgian women taking baths was far higher than any other nationality; a closer look at the data revealed that the time period was not comparable.. In all other countries the question had been, "Have you had a bath in the last three days?" The types of equivalence are briefly explained . Construct equivalence deals with the function of the product or service that is being researched and not the method used in collecting the information. Different countries that are being must have the same perception or use for the product that is being researched. If this is not the case, comparison of data becomes meaningless. For example, if the bicycle market is being studied, it should be understood that it comes under the category of recreational sports in the United States and as a basic means of transportation in countries like India and China. Measurement equivalence relates to establishing equivalence in terms of procedures used to measure concepts or attitudes.

Three aspects will have to be considered to establish measurement equivalence

(a) *Calibration Equivalence* – Equivalence has to be established with regard to the calibration system used in measurement (Kumar, 2000). This would include monetary units, measures of weight, distance and volume and perceptual cues like color, shape or form. Various countries around the world follow different units of weights and measures. Americans are used to weighing things by the pound or ton while the British and most of the commonwealth countries use the gram and kilogram. If the wrong terminology is used, responses will not be accurate. This is true for currencies also. For instance, one billion in the United States may not mean the same amount in the United Kingdom. Researchers should also take care to establish equivalence in terms of interpretation of perceptual cues. Colors also mean different things to different cultures. White, for example, is considered a symbol of purity and peace in the Western world but, a color of mourning for the Japanese (Jacobs et al., 1991). In the People's Republic of China, notes written using red ink suggest that the writer will die soon and the number four should be avoided at all costs as this too signifies death.

(b) *Translation Equivalence* – The research instrument has to be translated such that respondents in all countries involved in the study understand it. The instrument should also contain equivalent meaning in each research context. This becomes more complicated when the researcher has to interpret and translate nonverbal clues. It may not be possible to translate a questionnaire verbatim into another language because of lack of equivalent words in the foreign language. For instance, there is no equivalent term for "husband" in Japanese. The researcher should focus on conveying the intent of the question to the respondent and obtain an answer that can be comparable across countries.

(c) *Metric Equivalence* – Metric equivalence is the scoring or scalar equivalence of the measure used. The researcher has to ensure equivalence of the scaling or scoring procedure used to establish the measure. Care should also be taken to establish equivalence in terms of the responses to a given measure in different countries. The scales used in different countries may vary depending on the culture and education level of the respondents. As mentioned earlier, in the United States researchers typically use a five or seven point scale; however, there are countries where scales can have as many as 20 categories. When the sample consists predominantly of people incapable of reading, pictorial scales are used. The specific country also determines whether the scale should be unipolar or bipolar and whether there should be a neutral point on the scale. For instance, researchers studying the Japanese market design scales with no neutral point, as the Japanese tend to remain neutral if given a choice. The researcher should also ensure equivalence of the response to a given measure in different countries.Lack of metric equivalence in the complete set of measures may occur due to cross-national differences in response styles (Baumgartner & Steenkamp, 2001). The term response style refers to a person's tendency to systematically respond to questionnaire items on some other criterion that what the items were supposed to measure (Paulhus, 1991). Baumgartner and Steenkamp (2001) described a procedure to clean observed scores from stylistic responding by regressing the raw summated scale scores on response bias indices. Sampling equivalence is concerned with the decision making process. For instance, if the purchasing behavior regarding toys is being studied, researchers need tounderstand that while in the United States children get to select their toys in other countries parents may make the purchase decisions. Hence while collecting information, children in United States need to be interviewed and parents in other countries. Analysis equivalence deals with addressing the various biases that might exist in different cultures. Different countries differ in their assessment of situations and problems. For instance, Japanese tend to take a neutral point, so it is wise to avoid a scale with a neutral point in order to obtain useful information. Likewise, Latin Americans and Italians tend to exaggerate their response and Americans do not typically go into details with open-ended question. Factors such as this should be kept in mind while designing the scales for measurement. Thus, establishing equivalence for an international marketing research study is an important task and requires judgmental decisions on the part of the researcher. The researcher will have to decide on the methodology that will work in the respective country.

Market Research with a Small Sample Size

When conducting cross-country marketing research, researchers may deal with a smaller sample size, thereby putting a check on the research exercise. This may also affect the subsequent analyses that follow the sampling stage. In such a scenario, it is advisable to go in for country pooling technique. That is, *similar* countries can be pooled to get a sufficiently large sample to carry on with a 'normal' research process. The key here, is to identify similar countries that can be pooled together for, the otherwise may lead to highly skewed and unusable research results. The pooling can be done according to three factors. They are:

(a) Economic status – Countries can be clubbed on the basis of economic conditions.This type of similar pooling would give the researcher a larger sample to work with,apart from keeping the research results from being skewed. Factors such as economic wealth, market potential index, Gross National Product (GNP), population, inflation, price levels, unemployment rate and interest rates are some of the factors can be considered for pooling countries according to economic similarity. This type of pooling would be suited for studies involving effects of prices on sales and marketing mix models.

(b) *Cultural setting* – The cultural setting is probably the most challenging among the three factors to international marketers. The cultural factors that can be considered for pooling are measure of high/low context culture, attitudes of people, differences in lifestyle, religion, language, literacy, values, work ethics, role of family and gender roles among others. For this type of pooling, Hofstede's classification of countries on the basis of Individualism Vs. Collectivism, Power Distance, Uncertainty Avoidance, 30 Masculinity Vs. Femininity and Strategic Orientation (short term vs. long term) may be utilized. The challenging part of getting this pooling right is that, the marketer must be aware of the frame of reference used in their decision to pool any set of countries. Once a frame of reference is established, it becomes an important factor in determining or modifying a marketer's reaction to situation, especially if experience or knowledge of accustomed behavior is lacking. Consider Belgium, which is neatly divided neatly in half, between Flanders in the north and Wallonia in the south (Sager, 1997). While the Flemish people use margarine, Walloons use butter. Thus, cultures could vary within a single country and this factor should be considered while adopting a culture pooling technique. This type of pooling would be suited for product positioning and product acceptance studies.

(c) ***Geographical proximity***– Under this type of pooling, countries within close proximity can be considered. Factors that can be considered for this type of pooling can be size of the country, its close neighbors, common climatic conditions and demographic indicators among others. This type of pooling would be helpful for segmentation studies. However, caution must be exercised while pooling countries that are geographically closer. For instance, even though Canadian market may feel similar to the United States market due to their geographical proximity, both countries should be addressed as two distinct cultures. Thus clubbing of countries into similar pools would help researcher in solving the small sample size problem. The key here is to, consider the nature of the study and then use appropriate pooling technique to achieve significant research results that can be better used for developing effective strategies.

Interpretation of Data from one Country to Another

Interpretation of data is a major aspect in qualitative and observational techniques and it is entirely dependent on the researcher. This is where the Self-Reference Criterion (SRC) comes into play. The researcher may have problems attributing the right reasons for a purchase behavior. If for instance, in a developing country, a consumer were to choose a product that has been packaged in aluminum container instead of a plastic carton, the reason could simply be that the consumer plans to use this container for storage purposes after the contents have been used. An American researcher could not be faulted for attributing reasons of efficient recycling as the motive for this purchase. This error in interpretation could mean a big blunder when it comes to positioning the product. In some cases, researchers find it easier to develop research instruments specific to one country and then coordinate and compare across countries. Here, both researchers who are familiar with the country and those who are not, examine the instruments and the data and draw conclusions. The second method of considering one country at a time and then comparing is preferable even though it is time consuming. This method also poses a number of intersection problems, as researchers from different cultural backgrounds have to be in constant touch with one another.

Relating Cross-cultural Research Insights to Cross-cultural Strategies

The success of any international research study is, how well the cross-cultural research insights translate into cross-cultural strategies that can used effectively in real time. Based on the emergence of globally shared meanings, (Alden, Steenkamp, & Batra, 1999) has designed a new brand positioning strategy designed to assist international managers who seek to strengthen their brand's equity in an increasingly competitive marketplace. The global consumer culture positioning (GCCP) strategy is defined as one that identifies the brand as a symbol of a given global culture. This is done by using meaning transfer (McCracken, 1993), an advertising process in which the brand is associated with other signs such as language, aesthetics and themes that reflect the cultural orientation. Examples of brands that have used such strategies include Sony ("My First Sony"), which positioned one of its products as appropriate for young people around the world; Philips ("Let's Make Things Better"), whose advertisements explicitly feature people from different countries; and Benetton ("The United Colors of Benetton"), whose slogan emphasizes the unity of humankind.

Another type of consumer culture positioning is the local consumer culture positioning (LCCP) strategy. This strategy is defined as one that associates the brand with local cultural meanings, reflects the local culture's norms and identities, is portrayed as consumed by local people in the national culture, and/or is depicted as locally produced for local people. Examples of brands that have utilized this strategy include, Chevy Trucks and Dr Pepper soft drinks. They have been positioned in U.S. as part of the "American" way of life.The third type of consumer culture positioning is the foreign consumer culture positioning (FCCP) strategy. It is defined as a strategy that positions the brand as symbolic of a specific foreign consumer culture; that is, a brand whose personality, use occasion, and/or user group are associated with a foreign culture. For instance, the use of "Singapore Girl" in Singapore Airline's global media advertising indicates the association of a brand with a foreign culture.

Scope of Consumer Culture Positioning

There are three central components to a cultural symbol set. They are language, aesthetic styles, and story themes. As the primary language of international business, the mass media, and now the Internet (*BusinessWeek*, 1996), English signals modernism and internationalism to many consumers. Hence, one way of effective GCCP communication is to use English words, written and/or spoken, in its communications. However, a brand manager incorporating LCCP would want to highlight the local language. And for using FCCP, a brand manager may use spoken and written words from the foreign culture in its advertising and/or brand name.The English language consists certain aesthetic styles that are becoming recognized as part of global consumer culture. For instance, while using spokespersons in advertising, it is possible that a separate set of characteristics would reflect GCCP and thereby, lend to the brand a mo re global image (e.g., Michael Jordan for Nike). While, an American businesswoman driving a Chevrolet in a U.S. television advertisement would reflect local culture, a German engineer spokesperson for Audi in a U.S. television advertisement would be reflecting a specific foreign culture. The alternative consumer culture positioning may also be indicated by the aesthetic construction and display of brand logos. For instance, certain logos may be tied less to specific cultures in terms of their appearance, such as AT&T (abstract globe), Nike (swoosh), Royal Dutch/Shell (shell), Mercedes-Benz (three pointed star) among others. Certain logos may be more symbolic of specific cultural traditions, such as Cathay Pacific, when they changed their logo to a white Chinese calligraphy stroke that suggests the wing of a bird to "give itself a more Asian air" (The Asian Wall Street Journal Weekly, 1994). It is also possible that most consumers would view the logo in its aesthetic entirety (including shape, color, texture, and overall design) and form associations to global, foreign, or local consumer culture.

Thus, identification of country, consumer segment, and product category factors that favor the use of GCCP, FCCP, or LCCP, is an important issue for mangers. While there are brands that use LCCP or FCCP, there is also the case of locally based marketers, who use GCCP, to fight global brands. For instance, local brands in Indian market such as Videocon (consumer durables), Amrutanjan (pain reliever), and Kenstar (appliances) show data on exports or visuals of foreign consumers consuming their products, to indicate that their product is of international quality. Thus, managers have to ascertain the country, consumer segment, and product category factors in order to come up with a suitable strategy that would convey their brand(s) effectively to the targeted audience. International Marketing Research thus links the organization with its future markets. It includes activities such as specification, gathering, analysis, and interpretation of information to help the management understand a particular market, identify the market specific problems and opportunities, and develop courses of marketing action. The research activity must recognize the country specific diversity in terms of culture, demographics, economy, etc. to yield a marketing strategy that will be both applicable and successful.

References

Aiken, L. S., & West, S. G. (1991). *Multiple regression: Testing and interpreting interactions*. Newbury Park, CA: Sage.

Alden, S., & and Batra, R. (1999). Brand positioning through advertising in Asia, North America and Europe: The Role of global consumer culture. *Journal of Marketing, 63*, 75–87.

The Asian Wall Street Journal Weekly. (1994). Cathay's new logo reflects Asian base. (September 5), 11.

Associated Press. (1997). Nike recalls shoes bearing log that Muslims found offensive. (June 25),.

Baumgartner, H., & Steenkamp, J.-B. E. M. (2001). Response styles in marketing research: a cross-national investigation. *Journal of Marketing Research, 38*, 143–156.

Bond, M. H. (1988). Finding universal dimensions of individual variation in multicultural studies of values: The Rokeach and Chinese values surveys. *Journal of Personality and Social Psychology*, *55*, 1009-1015.

BusinessWeek (1996). A World Wide Web for Tout le Monde. (April 1), 36.

Butcher, J. N., Lim, J., & Nezami, E. (1998). Objective study of abnormal personality in crosscultural settings: The Minnesota Multiphasic Personality Inventory (MMPI-2). *Journal of Cross-Cultural Psychology*, *29*, 189-211.

Byrne, B. M., & Campbell, T. L. (1999). Cross-cultural comparisons and the presumptions of equivalent measurement and theoretical structure: A look beneath the surface. *Journal of Cross-Cultural Psychology*, *30*, 555-574.

Cheung, G. W., & Rensvold, R. B. (2000). Assessing extreme and acquiescence response sets in cross-cultural research using structural equations modeling. *Journal of Cross-Cultural Psychology*, *31*, 160-186.

Demby. (1990). ESOMAR urges changes in reporting demographics, issues worldwide report. *Marketing News*, (January 8), 24-25

Devlin & Nicholas (2004). International research: Cross-culture calibration. *Quirk's Marketing Research Review*.

Douglas & Craig. (1983). *International marketing research* (pp. 196-198). Englewood Cliffs, NJ: Prentice Hall.

Fischer, R. (2004). Standardization to account for cross-cultural response bias. *Journal of Cross-Cultural Psychology*, *35*, 263-282.

Greenbaum (1996). Understanding focus group research abroad. *Marketing News*, (June 3), H14.

Hicks, L. E. (1970). Some properties of ipsative, normative and forced-choice normative measures. *Psychological Bulletin*, *74*, 167-184.

Hofstede, G. (1980). *Culture's consequences: International differences in work related values*. Beverly Hills, CA: Sage.

Honomichl, J. (2004). Honomichl's global top 25. *Marketing News,* (August 15), H4

Howell, D. C. (1997). *Statistical methods for psychology*. Belmont, CA: Duxbury Press.

Huang, C. D., Church, A. T., & Katigbak, M. S. (1997). Identifying cultural differences in items and traits: Differential item functioning in the NEO personality inventory. *Journal of Cross-Cultural Psychology, 28*, 192-218.

Jacobs, Keown, Worthley, & Ghymn. (1991). Cross-cultural comparisons: Global marketers beware. *International Marketing Review*, 21-30.

Kobayashi & Draper. (1990). Reviews of market research in Japan. *Journal of Advertising Research*, (April/May), 13-18.

Korzenny. The Evidence for Spanish Language Marketing and Market Research. http://www.cheskin.com/p/ar.asp?mlid=7&arid=5&art=1

Kumar, V. (2000). *International marketing research.* Upper Saddle River, NJ: Prentice Hall.

Leung, K., & Bond, M. H. (1989). On the empirical identification of dimensions for crosscultural comparisons. *Journal of Cross-Cultural Psychology*, *20*, 133-151.

Little, T. D. (1997). Mean and covariance structures (MACS) analysis of cross-cultural data: Practical and theoretical issues. *Multivariate Behavioral Research, 32*, 53-76.

——. (2000). On the comparability of constructs in cross-cultural research: A critique of Cheung and Rensvold. *Journal of Cross-Cultural Psychology*, *31*, 213-219.

McCracken, G. (1993). The value of the brand: An anthropological perspective. In D. A. Aaker & A. L. Bowl (Eds.), *Brand equity and advertising: Advertising role in building strong brands* (pp. 125-139). Hillsdale, NJ: Erlbaum.

Min-Han, Lee, & Ro. (1994). The choice of survey mode in country image studies. *Journal of Business Research*, (February), 151-162.

Monk. (1997). Marketing research in Canada. *European Research*, (November), 271-274.

Paulhus, D. L. (1991). *Measurement and control of response bias*. In J. P. Robinson, Ph. R.

Shaver, & L. S. Wright (Eds.), *Measures of personality and social psychological attitudes* (pp. 17-59).

San Diego, CA: Academic Press. Payne. Results of poor cross cultural awareness. Retrieved October 20, 2005, from http://www.kwintessential.co.uk/. Ricks, A. (1999). *Blunders in international business*, 3rd Ed. Oxford: Blackwell Publishing.

Sager. (1997). The stealth computer – Annual design awards. *BusinessWeek* (June 2), 103.

Sopariwala. (1987). India: Election polling in the world's largest democracy. *European Research* (August), 174-177

Stevens, & Davis. (1997). Battle of the brands. *Appliance*, (February), B21

Visionarymarketing, Lost in translation. Retrieved October 20, 2005, from http://www.visionarymarketing.com/articles/lostintranslation.

Wind, Douglas, & Perlmutter (1973). Guidelines for developing international marketing strategy. *Journal of Marketing*, 14-23.

Index

A

Ad Valorem Tariffs, 55
Administrative heritage, 285
Advanced countries, 83
Advantage of Bulk Buying, 76
Advertisement for washing powder, 226
Advertising models, 227
Advertising Specialities, 240
Aero Zambia, 169
Affiliate Programs, 265
Affinity specialists, 275
African and Caribbean countries, 28
African countries, 167, 185, 261
African countries radio, 181
African nations, 77
Agrexco office in Israel, 186
Agrexco subsidiary, 186
Agrexco terminal, 187
Agricultural machinery, 117
Agricultural systems, 214
Agriculture and Transport, 168
Airway bill, 198
Akzo Nobel, 283, 291
Albania, 105
Alternative duties, 190
American Dry Fruits, 242
American Football shorts, 26
American Management Association, 260
Amsterdam, 31, 169
Andorra, 90
Anglo American, 159
Angola, 169
Annual packaging budget, 188
Anti-dumping & Countervailing Measures, 69
Anti-dumping duties, 73
Antidumping duties, 190
Application Service Providers, 263
Arabic script, 318
Argentina, 114
Arrival of ex-ship, 197
Asian air, 331
Asian countries, 74, 125
Asian Development Bank, 74
Asian Pacific Rim countries, 79
Asian paints, 115
Asian Wall Street Journal Weekly, 331
Assessing market assess, 309
Assigning custody, 295
Association of South East Nations, 79
Australia, 114
Austria, 90, 205
Availability of company resources, 115
Average World Price, 164

B

Bamboo baskets, 72
Banks of Thailand, 76
Banks of Vietnam, 76
Barclays Bank, 27
Bargaining relationship between companies, 255
Bargaining View, 255
Barriers Related to Certification, 70
Barriers Related to Process Standards, 69
Barter trade, 105

Basic export documents, 198
Basic rules, 300
Beauty and dignity, 271
Belgium, 90, 91, 205
Ben Gurion, 187
Ben Gurion Airport, 186
Benefits of internet business, 263
Bill of exchange, 206
Bill of exchange accepted payable, 207
Bill of exchange drawn in sterling, 207
Bill of Lading, 193, 198, 205, 206
Bills of Exchange, 207
Blacklist Certificate, 202
Blackwell and Herta, 286
BMW automobiles, 268
Borrow foreign currency, 146
Borrowing capital, 129
Brand affinity, 270
Brand architecture, 285
Brand development index, 281
Brand domain, 269
Brand domain specialist, 270
Brand Environment, 271
Brand recognition, 270
Brand reputation, 270
Brazil, 114, 115
Breakup of Yugoslavia, 246
Bretton Woods, 80, 130
British Airways, 27
Brussels, 190
Brussels Nomenclature, 190, 191
Buenos Aires, 163
Build Long-Term Market Share, 238
Bulawayo, 177
Bulgaria, 90, 205
Bulk Drugs, 71
Business Environment Risk Index, 259
Businesses and management philosophy, 292
Buyer's currency, 146

C

Cadbury or Nestlé, 291
Cadbury's Milk Tray brand, 291
Campaign design, 183
Campaign scheduling, 185
Canada, 322
Canadian market, 329
Cargo, 170
Caribbean, 103
Caribbean Community and Common Market, 79
Carriage of Goods by Sea Act, 205
Cash Rebate Offers, 239
Cashel Valley Zimbabwe, 123
Category development index, 281
Causal research, 311
Central American Common Market, 79
Central office of information, 260
Central Statistical Office, 260
Centralized custody and brand manual, 293
Centralized research, 318
Chamber of Commerce Certificate of Origin, 202
Chambers of Commerce, 260
Charges on imports, 61, 65
China, 115
China and India, 13
Chinese culture, 274
Citrus Marketing Board, 112
Citrus Marketing Board of Israel, 99
Climatic Differences, 306
Clothes Shows, 234
Cluster Analysis, 316
Cluster analysis, 304
CNN news, 181
Coca Cola, 26, 108, 110
Coca-Cola, 278, 284, 318
Coke and Pepsi, 184
Cold Storage Company of Zimbabwe, 77

Colombia, 164
Combined invoice and Certificate of Origin, 202
Combined transport bill of lading, 204
Commercial newspapers, 260
Commercially important, 204
Common external tariff, 87
Common Foreign and Security Policy, 89
Common market, 88
Communication developments, 151
Communication systems, 224
Communist bloc, 77
Companies Act, 75
Company objectives, 115
Comparability of Tasks, 316
Comparative Analysis, 315
Comparative analysis, 304
Compensating import taxes, 190
Competitive bidding by the Indian importers, 76
Compliance audit, 295
Compound or mixed duties, 190
Conflict of law, 211
Consumer direct mail, 232
Consumer mobility, 290
Consumers and media, 273
Context suppliers, 265
Contracting countries, 205
Contracts Expressed, 196
Controlled atmosphere containers, 171
Convention Merchandises Routiers, 205
Copenhagen criteria, 89
Corporate dominant branding, 283
Corporate endorsement and brand extension, 290
Corporate Image, 234, 243
Cost Factors, 225
Cost Insurance Freight, 196
Council of Arab Economic Unity, 79
Country Bargaining Power, 256
Country grouping, 221
Country Image, 243
Creeping commitment, 102
Cross Cultural Response Bias, 320
Cultural Differences, 305
Cultural embeddedness, 288
Cultural Problems in International Negotiations, 254
Cultural setting, 328
Currency basket approach, 147
Customer relationship management, 256
Customs and Administrative Entry Procedures, 60
Customs Authorities, 202
Customs Cooperation Council, 190, 191
Customs Union, 87
Cyprus, 90
Czech Republic, 90
Czechoslovakia, 205

D

Dairy Milk, 291
Daniel Starch, 227
Dar es Salaam, 169
Data collection, 312
Data collection method, 301
Database Marketing, 257
David Ogilvy, 229
Dawson Partners, 211
De Beers, 282
Dealer mailings, 233
Dealer support, 233
Decentralized plans, 220
Decentralized Research, 318
Decision making unit, 234
Defining Advertising, 227
Delivery order, 207, 208
Demand Pattern Analysis, 314
Denmark, 90, 91, 205
Descriptive research, 311

Design Scales in Cross-National Research, 325
Designing international brand architecture, 293
Determinants of Bargaining Power, 255
Developing countries, 83
Development of International Branding Structures, 283
Differences in Actual and Potential Target Groups, 307
Different from Domestic Marketing, 305
Differing product classification, 66
Direct advertising, 231
Direct mail and direct marketing, 231
Documentary Credits, 206
Domain Specialists, 274
Domestic Company, 17
Domestic currency, 146
Domestic marketing, 12
Domestic practices, 224
Douwe Egbert, 291
Drafts covering exports, 208
Drivers of International Branding Strategy, 285
Dubai, 114
Dumping problems, 133
Dynamics of International Brand Architecture, 290

E

East Africa, 155
East African and South American, 27
East and West Germany, 246
East European countries, 107
East Germany, 77
Eastern countries, 103
Eastern Europe, 44, 80, 284, 291
Eastern European countries, 322
Economic and Monetary Union, 91
Economic and Political Union, 86
Economic Community of West African States, 79
Economic Differences, 306
Economic Environment, 41
Economic factors, 132
Economic Policies, 43
Economic status, 328
Economic Structural Adjustment Programmes, 77
Economic Times, 244
Economic Union, 86
Economics Risk, 114
Economist Intelligence Unit, 260
Effective management of international brand, 293
Egypt, 164
Electronic marketing, 262
Electronic media, 179, 262
Encourage Retailers, 238
Encourage Retailers to Advertise, 238
English judge, 211
Environmental Barriers, 73
Environmental differences, 224
Environmental stability, 224
Estimating market size, 309
Estonia, 90
Ethnocentric Approach, 118
Eurocurrency finance, 142
Europe, 113, 222
European car brands, 274
European Central Bank, 89, 91
European cities, 188
European Coal and Steel Community, 89
European Community, 88, 90
European countries, 72
European Development Bank, 29
European Economic Community, 90
European Monetary System, 91
European Single Act, 87
European System of Central Banks, 91
European Union, 28, 29, 60, 79, 89, 90
Evaluating performance, 223

Export documentation, 198
Export financing, 208
Export Import policy, 125
Export price of the product, 140
Export pricing zones (Mauritius), 79
Export processing zones, 108, 110
Export Subsidies and Domestic Support, 69
Export transaction, 192, 194
External Factors, 273

F

Factor infusing channel selection, 175
Federal German Republic, 205
Fertilizer manufacturers, 104
Final continental destination, 205
Financial and financing documents, 206
Financial Gazette, 184
Financial settlement, 105
Finland, 90, 91, 205
Firm-based drivers, 285
Fiscal Policy, 43
Florida tomato growers, 121
Follow-up mailings, 233
Food and Agriculture Organization, 23, 261
Ford Motor Company, 318
Foreign consumer culture positioning, 330
Foreign currency, 206
Foreign currency finance, 142
Foreign environment as a barrier to trade, 52
Foreign exchange controls, 66
Foreign exchange earnings, 242
Foreign exchange restrictions, 66
Foreign investment, 108
Foreign origin, 290
Formal control methods, 223
Framework for international marketing research, 311
France, 90, 91, 205, 316
Frankfurt, 31, 91, 145
Fraud in letter of credit transactions, 211
Free alongside ship, 195
Free on board, 195
Free on rail or free on truck, 194
Free Trade Agreement, 68
Free Trade Area, 87
Free Trade Arrangements, 68
Free trade zones, 108
Freight rates, 170
French red apples, 122
Fresh cut flowers, 31
Fuji, 114
Fundamental breach, 213

G

General Agreement on Tariffs and Trade, 28, 63, 67, 92
General Brand Strategies, 269
General Motors, 181, 318
Geneva, 169
Geocentric Approach, 118
Geographical proximity, 329
Gerber baby foods, 110
German, 170
German Democratic Republic, 205
Germany, 90, 91, 187, 222, 316
Germany television, 226
Gibraltar, 205
Global consumer culture positioning, 330
Global Electronic Supply chain, 265
Global environment, 32
Global marketing control, 222
Global marketing involvement, 30
Global Marketing Operations, 214
Global marketing organizations, 13
Global marketing planning, 219
Global media, 290
Global products, 117

Global programmes, 181
Government Food Agency of Japan, 75
Government of Vietnam, 71
Government Participation in Trade, 61, 65
Government procurement, 69
Grain Marketing Board in Zimbabwe, 103, 104
Great Britain, 90
Greater degree of integration, 220
Greece, 90, 91, 205
Gross Domestic Product, 82
Gross National Product, 82, 328
Guadalupe, 91
Gulf countries, 113
Gulf War, 80

H

Hague conventions, 213
Halal animal, 69
Halal certificate, 69
Halal logo, 72
Handling company crises, 235
Hanover Fair, 184
Harare, 26, 31
Harley Davidson, 276
Health, veterinary and sanitary certificates, 203
Hi-tech electronics, 244
Hierarchical View, 255
Historical Differences, 307
Holland, 170
Home country regulation, 225
Home Exhibitions, 234
Honda, 244
Honda City, 268
Hong Kong, 114
Horticultural Crops Development Authority, 103, 112
Horticultural development, 168
Horticultural exports, 172
Horticultural produce from Kenya, 189
Horticultural Promotion Councils, 184
House bill of lading, 204
Hungary, 90, 205
Hybrid branding strategies, 284

I

IBM and Macintosh, 26
Identifying sources of information, 310
Ignoring the message, 229
Impact of Non-Tariff barriers, 73
Impact on Brand Strategies, 273
Import Policy Barriers, 69
Import Quotas, 55
Imported French or South African wines, 23
Importing country, 202
Improved Efficiency, 263
Improvements in the quality, 232
Including overseas territories, 205
Income Elasticity Measurements, 303, 315
Increase Sales Force Support, 238
Increase Short-Term Sales, 238
Incremental Innovation, 252
Independent Multi-country Research, 320
Independent trade policy, 87
Indian exporters strategic, 114
Indian fresh vegetables, 112
Indian Jute Industries Research Association, 70
Indian meat, 70
Indian restaurants, 242
Indian women in beauty pageants, 246
Individual strategic brands, 295
Industrial growth patterns, 303
Industrial Products, 180
Industrialized countries, 83
Industry of Malawi, 121
Infant Industries, 53

Influences on marketing budgets, 223
Informal control method, 223
Information and communication technology, 274, 297
Inspection and sampling order, 207
Institute of Marketing, 260
Institutional sales, 180
Insurance certificates, 203
Insurance documents, 203
Insurance policy, 203
Interactive plans, 220
International Bank for Reconstruction and Development, 28, 80, 130
International Brand Architecture, 267, 277
International brand architecture audit, 295
International Branding Strategy, 281
International brands, 289, 290, 294
International Chamber of Commerce, 213
International Channel system, 154
International channels decisions, 160
International companies, 114
International Cotton Advisory Committee, 166
International currency, 192
International distribution system, 154
International division, 217
International Division structure, 216
International economic system, 28
International financial system, 80
International investment and financial flows, 51
International Involvement, 14
International Law rules, 213
International market, 118, 282
International Marketing, 9, 12, 154
International marketing communication, 225
International marketing hubs, 114
International Marketing Promotion, 177
International Marketing Research, 299, 331
International Marketing Strategy, 245
International Marketplace, 243
International markets, 116, 117
International markets, 115, 129, 148, 156, 267, 277, 294
International merchant, 160
International Monetary Fund, 28, 80, 130
International Monetary System, 80
International planning, 220
International pricing, 135
International product promotion, 267
International products, 117
International sale, 192
International Sale of Goods, 212, 213
International trade, 192
International Trade Centre, 261
International trade organization, 92
International trade regulation, 67
International trading system, 92
Internationalization of Business Operations, 317
Internationalization of Indian Firms, 36
Internet marketing, 262
Internet news sites, 235
Investor Relations, 236
Ireland, 90, 91
Irrevocable and confirmed letter of credit, 210
Issues with primary global research, 313
Issues with secondary research, 312
Italy, 90, 91, 205, 316
ITC training manual, 160

J

Japan, 113, 114, 243
Japan Monopoly Corporation, 75
Japanese products, 246
Joint venture, 175
Jute Bags, 73

K

Kennedy Round, 79
Kenya, 100, 110, 121, 159, 168
Kenyan fresh vegetable industry, 157
Kenyan horticultural produce, 103
Kilimanjaro, 169
Kimberley Clark, 286
Kirloskar Brothers, 246
Kleenex brand, 286
Knowledge of the market, 221
Knowledge of the marketing functions, 221
Knowledge of the product, 221
Kompass Register of companies, 260
Korea, 74
Kosher and Halal status, 69
Kosovo, 90, 91
Kronenbourg and Kanterbrau beers, 284
Kuala Lumpar, 26

L

Lack of access advertising media, 180
Language Differences, 307
Language factors, 225
Large mail shots, 232
Larger Customer Base, 264
Latin American Countries, 115, 323
Latin countries, 322
Latvia, 90
Lead market approach, 100
Lebkuchen Latte, 268
Less developed countries, 77, 83, 86
Letter of Credit, 76, 141, 192
Letter of credit arrangement, 209
Letter of insurance, 203
Level of Commitment, 115
Lex Focii, 212
Lex Loci Contracts, 212
Lex Locii Solutions, 212
Lex Situs, 212
Life Cycle Concept, 278
Life Cycle Concept and Brand, 280
Life cycle in various markets, 280
Limitation of secondary data, 310
Lithuania, 90
Liverpool Cotton Exchange, 166
Liverpool Index, 160, 165
Local consumer culture positioning, 330
Local Content Requirement, 55
Local products, 117
Logistics & value chain, 153
London, 26, 31, 131, 145, 169
London International Futures Exchange, 131
Long-term customer relationships, 239
Lord Summer, 211
Low brand loyalty, 180
Low promotional budgets, 180
Lower middle income, 84
Lower transfer price, 138
Lu and Jacob brands, 284
Luxembourg, 90, 91, 205

M

Maastricht Treaty, 89
Mail order, 231
Mail Surveys, 322
Malawi, 166
Malawi exporters, 142
Malaysia, 70
Mall Intercept Surveys, 322
Malta, 90
Management of international organisations, 25
Managerial Implications, 293
Managing international brand architecture, 294
Manufacturers analysis certificate, 201
Marine Insurance Policy, 193
Market dynamics, 289
Market Entry of Indian Firm, 241
Market Estimation by Analogy, 315

Market forces and development, 26
Market integration, 288
Market makers, 266
Market Research Society, 260
Market selection, 309
Market standardized products, 289
Marketing and Advertising, 264
Marketing and Non-marketing Public Relations, 235
Marketing Boards, 159
Marketing of international brands, 289
Marketing public relations, 235
Marketing research, 299
Martinique, 91
Mauritius, 169
Methanol complex, 105
Metric Equivalence, 327
Middle East, 70, 122, 169, 322
Middle East countries, 202
Middle Eastern markets, 269
Middle income economies, 84
Mineral and metals trading corporation, 105
Minimum country involvement, 220
Ministries of Finance, 168
Ministry of Agriculture and Rural Development, 71
Ministry of Health of Sri Lanka, 71
Minolta, 244
Mobile phone companies, 280
Modern technology, 84
Modern trademark law, 149
Money market, 145
Monitoring consistency of brand usage, 295
Montenegro, 90, 91
Moser Baer, 244
Moslem countries, 182
Motor Shows, 234
Multi-country Research, 319
Multi-Fiber Arrangement, 74
Multimedia presentations, 236
Multinational corporations, 47
Multinational products, 117
Multiple Factor Indices, 304
Multiple-Factor Indexes, 315

N

Named Port of Destination, 197
National boundaries, 277
National Differences, 305
National product brands, 284
National Security, 54
Native speakers of the languages, 323
Natural Resource Institute, 261
Nature of economic activity, 83
Nature of economy, 83
Necessary expenditures, 223
Negotiating with Regulators, 254
Netherlands, 90, 205
Netherlands, Austria, 91
New York, 131, 165, 211
New York Cotton Exchange, 166
New York Futures, 165
News papers, 179
Next-generation Technology Innovation, 252
Nissan, 244
Non-ethnic consumers, 242
Non-ethnic products, 242
Non-Market pricing, 137
Non-marketing public relations, 235
Non-monetarised trade, 105
Non-negotiable sea waybill, 206
Non-professional image, 243
Non-tariff barriers, 59, 60, 67, 88, 121
Non-tariff barriers, 51
Non-Tariff Barriers to Trade, 61
Non-tariff barriers to trade, 55
Non-tariff barriers to trade, 113

Non-tariff barriers today, 67
Non-Tariff Measures, 69
Norsk Hydro, 117
North American Free Trade Agreement, 29, 60, 80, 113
North American Union, 80
North-South trade, 78
Northern Europe, 186
Northern Ireland, 90, 205
Norway, 205

O

Office International des Epizooties, 70
Offices of the shipping company, 206
Official documents, 201
Olive brand, 274
Olivine industries, 109
Operational risks, 114
Organisation and control, 185

P

Packing credit guarantee, 141
Packing list and specification, 201
Pakistan, 114, 164
Paperless coupon systems, 239
Parallel Importing, 148
Paris, 169
Parker Pens, 319
Participating banks, 140
Patronage reward, 240
Pavord and Bogart, 101
Payment against another currency, 197
Payment and Logistic Specialist, 266
Pedigree house brand, 284
People's Republic of China, 326
Personalized trading networks, 157
Perspectives on International Branding, 282
Philippines, 70, 72
Planning and budgeting, 223
Point-of-Purchase, 240
Point-of-purchase promotion, 240
Poland, 90, 205
Political environment, 44
Political factors, 132
Political Risk, 114
Port of destination, 196
Portugal, 90, 91, 205
Post virtual coupons, 263
Postal service, 231
Potential customers, 265
Potential delegates in specific business, 233
Power Distance, 328
Power of knowledge, 271
Pre-shipment credit guarantee, 140
Pre-shipment inspection, 194
Preferential Trade Area, 79, 80
Preindustrial countries, 83
Prerequisites for Effective Negotiation, 254
Price-Based Consumer Promotion, 239
Primary Data Collection, 312, 325
Primary surveys, 301
Print Media, 179
Private International, 211
Private International Law, 211
Problems in International Marketing Communication, 224
Problems in international marketing research, 314
Problems of numerous markets, 314
Problems with data, 314
Process of International marketing Research, 307, 308
Product Categoris, 278
Product launch, 233
Product Life Cycle, 35
Product market structure, 288
Product Publicity, 236
Product trade cycle, 24

Product-dominant branding, 283
Product-dominant structures, 283
Product-level brand strategy, 287
Promissory note, 207
Promotion campaign, 183
Promotion Councils, 184
Promotional programs, 180
Proper labeling of products, 268
Protecting Consumers, 53
Protecting Domestic Employment, 53
Psychological factors, 132
Public Affairs, 236
Public relations, 234
Public Relations Campaign, 237
Public relations campaign, 237
Public Relations Objectives, 235
Public relations tools, 236
Purchase Agents, 266
Purchasing power, 148
Purchasing power parity, 131

Q

Qualitative Methods, 324
Quality control, 187
Questionnaire design, 301
Quotas and trade control, 191

R

Racial Differences, 306
Radical Innovation, 252
Rail consignment note, 205
Ranbaxy, 115
Rationale of State Trading, 75
Re-importing, 148
Recognition specialists, 276
Reduced Mailing Expenses, 263
Regression analysis, 304
Rejecting the message, 229
Relative Importance of the Project, 255
Religious Differences, 307
Republic of Macedonia, 89
Reputation specialists, 274, 275
Research design, 301
Research process, 300
Research techniques for analyzing international data, 314
Return on investment, 263
Return to the warehouse, 208
Revocable and unconfirmed letter of credit, 210
Richards Bay, 171
Road waybill, 205
Rolled forward, 220
Roman Empire, 90
Romania, 90, 205
Rosser Reeves, 228
Royal Agricultural Show, 184
Rules of origin, 87

S

Sale of Goods Act, 211, 213
Sales against cost advances, 209
Sales lead generation, 233
Sales of the drink, 268
Sales on a consignment basis, 209
Sales promotion, 232
Sales promotion objectives, 238
Sample size and selection, 302
San Marino, 91
San Pellegrino, 286
Saves Money on Office Supplies, 265
Scandinavian countries, 125
Scope of Consumer Culture Positioning, 330
Secondary data information sources, 311
Self service in retail system, 181
Self-funding obviates, 139
Self-Reference Criterion, 329
Seller's currency, 146
Sequential Multi-country Research, 320
Shipping documents, 209
Shipping lines, 206

Short form bills of lading, 205
Short-term increase, 234
Short-term sales, 239
Showroom or exhibition, 232
Simultaneous Multi-country Research, 320
Singapore, 114, 243
Singapore Airline's global media, 330
Singapore Girl, 330
Single-country Research, 319
Size of international operators, 224
Slovakia, 90
Slovenia, 90
Small Business Association, 263
Small Businesses, 264
Small Sample Size, 328
Small scale sector, 168
Society General de Surveillance, 201
South Africa, 46, 65, 80, 81, 169, 171
South African industry, 81
South African wines, 259
South Africans, 104
South America, 29
South American countries, 202
South Asian Association for Regional Co-operation, 68
South East Asia, 70, 81
South Korea, 243
Southern African Development Community, 79
Southern African Development Conference, 31, 80
Spain, 90, 91, 205, 316
Special Drawing Rights, 28, 130
Special trade terms in export sales, 194
Specific communications activities, 272
Specific Limitations on Trade, 60
Spot marketing trading, 147
Spring water, 105
Sri Lanka, 68
Sri Lanka Standards Institution, 72
Stages of market development, 83
Standardized plans, 220
State trading of India, 75
Strategic alliance partner, 137
Strategic audit, 296
Strategic Business Units, 218
Streamline business activities, 263
Structural Equation Modeling, 320
Subsidiary performance, 224
Sudan, 164
Sugar-free cola drink, 284
Supermarket culture, 181
Supermarket shelf dispensers, 239
Supply chain identifies, 265
Sweden, 90, 205
Switzerland, 205
Syria, 164

T

Taiwan, 243
Tanzania, 102, 166, 169
Tanzania export, 169
Target market, 288
Targeting the individual customer, 266
Tariff administration, 191
Tariff barriers, 52
Tariffs and Modern Trade, 58
Tariffs and Trade Barriers, 53
Tata Tea, 115
Technical barriers to trade, 67
Technological environment, 46
Telephone Interviews, 322
Temporary brand, 239
Temporary import surcharges, 190
Textile industry, 163
Thailand, 72
The doctrine of strict compliance, 211
Third party certificate of inspection, 201
Third World situation, 125

Time-series approach, 315
Tobacco companies, 27
Tokyo, 131
Tomato juice, 105
Tommy Hilfiger, 276
Toyota, 244
Trade Barriers, 51, 51, 113
Trade Fairs, 184
Trade promotion, 238
Trade promotion strategies, 238
Trade-Oriented Promotion, 241
Trademark owners, 150
Trading Environment, 51
Traditional postal mailing, 263
Transport documents, 204
Transportation costs, 133
Treaty of Rome, 91
True CIF Contracts, 196
Trust receipt, 207, 208
Turkey, 164
Types of air services, 170
Types of letters of credit, 210
Types of Non-Tariff Barriers, 62
Types of Tariffs and Trade Barriers, 54
Typical channel structure, 161
Typical value chain, 161

U

UN Statistical Yearbook, 260
Uncertainty Avoidance, 328
Under English Law, 203
Uniform Customs and Practice, 206
Uniform Law on International Sales Act, 213
United Bottlers, 108
United Kingdom, 90, 157, 205, 316, 326
United Nations, 261
United Nations Commission on International Trade, 213
United Nations Conference on Trade and Development, 67, 79
United Nations Convention, 213
United Nations International Comparison Project, 82
United States, 29, 121, 150, 316, 322, 327
United States Agency for International Development, 80
United States of America, 80
US Department of Agriculture, 121

V

Values of standardization, 224
Variable import charges, 190
Various chemical inputs, 71
Vatican, 91
Vertical coordination, 214
Veterinary Certificate, 202
Vivagel and Marie frozen foods, 284
Voluntary export restraint, 64, 55, 66

W

Warehouse receipt, 207, 208
Weak brand identity, 180
West Africa, 170
Western and Eastern Europe, 89
Western Europe, 78
Wilkinson Sword Blades, 47
World Bank, 28, 29, 80, 83, 92, 130, 257
World Bank - general statistics, 260
World Bank classification, 84
World brand, 117
World brand names, 117
World Economic Forum, 251
World Merchandise, 16
World trade, 77, 131
World Trade Organization, 13, 28, 58, 60, 91
World War II, 80, 89, 191

Y

Yugoslavia, 205

Z

Zambia, 102, 104, 107, 166, 169
Zambia and Tanzania, 304
Zambia and Zimbabwe, 29, 85
Zim dollars, 143
Zimbabwe, 99, 100, 107, 109, 110, 121, 132, 159, 164, 166, 169, 221, 222
Zimbabwe in, 171
Zimbabwe International Trade Fair, 177, 185
Zimbabwean dollar loan, 143
Zimbabwe's horticultural export, 171
Zimbabwe's trade with China, 78
Zimfreeze, 99
Zurich, 145